A History of Brazilian Economic Thought

This book provides a comprehensive analysis of the evolution of Brazilian economic thought ranging from colonial times through to the early 21st century. It explores the production of ideas on the Brazilian economy through various forms of publication and contemporary thoughts on economic contexts and development policies, all closely reflecting the evolution of economic history.

After an editorial introduction, it opens with a discussion of the issue of the historical limits to and circumstances of the production of pure economic theory by Brazilian economists. The proceeding chapters follow the classical periodization of Brazilian economic history, starting with the colonial economy (up until the early 19th century) and the transition into an economy independent from Portugal (1808 through the 1830s) when formal independence took place in 1822. The third part deals with the "coffee era" (1840s to 1930s). The last part covers the "developmentalist" and "globalization" eras (1930–2010).

This book is ideal for international and national scholars in social sciences, students in both undergraduate and graduate courses in economics, and any individuals interested in Brazilian economic and intellectual history.

Ricardo Bielschowsky is full professor of economics at Universidade Federal do Rio de Janeiro, Brazil.

Mauro Boianovsky is full professor of economics at Universidade de Brasília, Brazil.

Mauricio C. Coutinho is full professor of economics at Universidade de Campinas, Brazil.

The Routledge History of Economic Thought

History of Scottish Economic Thought
Edited by Alistair Dow and Sheila Dow

A History of Irish Economic Thought
Edited by Renee Prendergast, Tom Boylan and John Turner

A History of Ottoman Economic Thought
Developments before the 19th Century
Fatih Ermis

A History of Italian Economic Thought
Riccardo Faucci

A History of Australasian Economic Thought
Alex Millmow

A History of American Economic Thought
Mainstream and Crosscurrents
Samuel Barbour, James Cicarelli and J. E. King

A History of Czech Economic Thought
Antonie Doležalová

A History of Slovak Economic Thought
Julius Horváth

A History of Brazilian Economic Thought
From Colonial Times through the Early 21st Century
Edited by Ricardo Bielschowsky, Mauro Boianovsky and Mauricio C. Coutinho

For more information about this series, please visit: www.routledge.com/The-Routledge-History-of-Economic-Thought/book-series/SE0124

A History of Brazilian Economic Thought

From Colonial Times through the Early 21st Century

Edited by Ricardo Bielschowsky, Mauro Boianovsky and Mauricio C. Coutinho

Routledge
Taylor & Francis Group
LONDON AND NEW YORK

First published 2023
by Routledge
4 Park Square, Milton Park, Abingdon, Oxon OX14 4RN

and by Routledge
605 Third Avenue, New York, NY 10158

Routledge is an imprint of the Taylor & Francis Group, an informa business

British Library Cataloguing-in-Publication Data
A catalogue record for this book is available from the British Library

ISBN: 9781032029306 (hbk)
ISBN: 9781032029313 (pbk)
ISBN: 9781003185871 (ebk)

DOI: 10.4324/9781003185871

Typeset in Bembo
by Apex CoVantage, LLC

Contents

1 Editorial introduction

This book provides an account of the Brazilian history of economic thought ranging from colonial times through 2010. It documents the production of ideas on the Brazilian economy as published in books, articles, and government documents. It covers thoughts on economic contexts and policies as well as on economic development, all closely reflecting the evolution of Brazilian economic history. The book also deals with theoretical contributions by Brazilian economists from a broader perspective.

The book has been conceived to fill a void, namely the fact that the evolution of Brazilian economic thinking has never been covered from such a long-term perspective in the English language.[1, 2] It supplies an articulate set of chapters leading to a comprehensive understanding of the evolution of economic ideas throughout Brazilian economic history. Furthermore, it can be seen as a collection of self-contained chapters in which readers are able to access relevant elements concerning particular time periods and topics.

The book starts with a chapter on contributions by Brazilian economists to economic theory. The sequence of the other seven chapters, which follow consensual periodization of Brazilian economic history from the 17th century to current times, is divided into three parts.

The second part comprises two chapters, one on ideas on the colonial economy (basically written by Portuguese authors, and on sugar, slaves and gold in the 17th and 18th centuries) and one on the transition into an economy independent from Portugal, from the early 19th century to 1840 (formal independence took place in 1822).

The third part deals with the "coffee era" (1840s to 1930s). Its three chapters approach separately three major topics of political economy at the time, namely labor (slavery, up until 1888), economic stabilization versus growth policies, and early "industrialism".

The last part contains a chapter on the "developmentalist era" (1930–1980) centered on debates concerning economic transformation and industrialization, and another chapter showing how economic thinking evolved from 1980 to 2010, involving issues such as high inflation and slow growth in the 1980s and early 1990s, stabilization and neoliberalism in the 1990s and early 2000s, and the income redistribution record of President Lula's two terms (2003–2010).

DOI: 10.4324/9781003185871-1

Chapter 2, by Mauro Boianovsky, provides an overview of Brazilian economists' contributions to global economics since the mid-20th century, from the perspective of economics as transnational science. The contributions are organized into three sections, after a methodological and historiographical introduction: economic development and income distribution, inflation and indexation, and "pure theoretical economics" coming from both mainstream mathematical economists and heterodox (mainly post-Keynesian) authors. The chapter documents how Brazilian economists have become integrated into the international community and produced new ideas that have been absorbed, in larger or smaller measure, by their colleagues abroad. Whereas the other chapters discuss Brazilian economic debates and policies as the result of the mainly domestic economic issues of the time, Chapter 2 addresses how the Brazilian community of economists, after its formation and interaction with the international community since the 1950s/60s, has been able to put forward new concepts and approaches that may be regarded as part of economic science in general. That chapter highlights the pluralism that has characterized Brazilian economics in its different guises.

Chapter 3, by José Luis Cardoso, deals with ideas on the political and economic administration of the Portuguese empire, which had Brazil as its main colony. It points at the use of new forms of economic language as instruments of deciphering new economic problems and realities. Territory, natural resources, capital and investment, slave labour, goods, prices, currency, international competition, tax revenue, productive innovations, colonial pact: it is from the reflection on these themes that some fresh ideas are presented on the way in which production hubs and exchange circuits were established, within the context of the management of colonial empires. The author argues that at a time when economic discourse was yet to be a standardized conceptual language, it is from the description of everyday economic and financial practices that the emergence of a new way of capturing reality may be understood. Moreover, it is from political intervention purposes and projects, which affect economic and financial practices, that the scope of measures designed to contribute to the improvement of the relations between men and with the surrounding environment may be interpreted. In other words, Cardoso's chapter claims that to a large extent, the formation of economic ideas in colonial Brazil stemmed from the need to find explanations and solutions to improve the exploitation of productive resources and slave labour.

Chapter 4, by Mauricio C. Coutinho, covers the penetration of economic thinking in Brazil from the late colonial period until the early post-independence phase. The majority of the Brazilian economic thinkers followed the well-established traditions of the University of Coimbra, but they had to apply their knowledge to two central characteristics of the Brazilian economy: slavery – a long-lasting institution – and the commercial treaties and arrangements established from 1808 between Portugal and England, which impacted both the Portuguese and the Brazilian economies. These treaties and arrangements implied preferential commercial flows ("free trade") between Brazil and England, and growing pressures from England against the continuity of the slave traffic. The chapter also deals with other features of the economists' works, such as the analysis of regional problems, and describes the introduction of formal political economy teaching in Brazil, soon after the independence. An overview of some innovative appraisals of the economy, by eminent European mineralogists and botanicals that surveyed the Brazilian territory, complements the chapter.

Chapter 5, by Amaury Gremaud and Renato Marcondes, tackles ideas about Brazilian slavery in the 19th century, especially in its second half, and up until its abolition in 1888. It shows that the discussion of slavery involved a myriad of strands, ranging from moral, ethnic, educational, religious, political, cultural, and economic. The main authors surveyed in the chapter received several influences from foreign debates but adapted them to their reality and interests. The chapter reviews a selected group of thinkers and associations that debated labour in Brazil from an economic perspective, through newspapers, manifestos, speeches, books, etc. That survey of ideas shows that slavery and national free labour are mutually conditioned by the long period of coexistence since the beginning of colonization. The chapter undertakes the challenge of surveying the discussion on slavery during a time of major legal changes, from the prohibition of the slave trade to effective abolition of slavery. It reviews the intense debates around those laws, and about the continuity of slavery and its abolition.

Chapter 6, by André Villela, surveys the intellectual and policy debate on "money", which in view of Brazil's turbulent financial history naturally has been a highly contested topic. As Villela shows, that was pointedly the case in the decades spanning the mid-1850s to the early 1930s. Throughout this period, Brazil experimented with a variety of monetary and exchange-rate arrangements ranging from multiple private note-issuing banks to a state-run monopoly in the issue of gold-backed currency. The chapter charts monetary debates as they played out in three different sub-periods, namely, the 1850s, the turn of the 19th to the 20th centuries and, finally, the mid to late 1920s. The focus is on the views espoused by the main participants in the monetary controversies, their intellectual underpinning, and the occasional material interests lying behind their positions. The chapter concludes that, in the main, "orthodox" views aligned with the then-dominant gold standard dogma tended to prevail, although heterodox opinions and policies would occasionally gain the upper hand in the debates.

Chapter 7, by Flavio Versiani, examines Brazilian thinking on government policy toward local industry, circa 1840–1930. Contrary to a notion commonly found in the literature, it is shown that the period can hardly be described as an "age of liberalism" in Brazil. During the monarchy (1822–1889), most relevant policy-makers favoured protectionist policies, specifically in regard to import tariffs. Equally important, Versiani argues that the tariff policy was motivated not only by fiscal considerations, as frequently argued; protection of domestic industry via higher tariffs was forcefully defended by a rationale that foreshadowed pro-industrialization arguments later expounded, in the second half of the 20th century, by some Latin-American authors such as Raul Prebisch and Celso Furtado. Finally, the author discusses how the influence of pro-industry thinking on government policy gained force after the 1880s; and how in the Republican period after 1889, it was felt more strongly in the Parliament. According to Versiani, the 1920s may be seen as a turning point, as government decisions started to clearly reflect protectionist ideas.

Chapter 8, by Ricardo Bielschowsky and Carlos Mussi, deals with Brazilian economic thought in the 1930–1980 period as focused on "developmentalism", meaning the ideology of the transformation of the Brazilian society by means of State planning and support of industrialization. It reports economic arguments found in books, articles, and government documents on development ideas, and secondarily on macroeconomic issues. The authors elaborate the "movement of ideas" showing the formation and evolution of currents of economic thought, along what they name the "ideological cycle of developmentalism". This cycle started from the 1930s–1940s, reached its maturity in the 1956–1964 period, and its heyday from 1964 to 1980. Up until 1964, five currents of thought are identified, namely liberalism, three variants of developmentalism (authors in the private sector and, in the public sector, non-nationalist and nationalist authors), and socialism. The currents of thought in the 1964–1980 period are dealt with according to a slightly different composition as compared to the previous period, comprising only two developmentalist currents of ideas ("pro-government" and "opponents"), besides liberalism and socialism.

Chapter 9, by Carlos Pinkusfeld Bastos and Eduardo Bastian, discusses the 1980–2010 period. It initially describes a major shift in theoretical formulation and in ideas on policy making that occurred in the 1980s, away from the previous debate on development. It shows how in the new context of debt crisis of the Global South, the focus of the economic debate shifted to stabilizing the high inflation that had been plaguing the Brazilian economy since the late 1970s, and to cope with the balance of payments constraint. This motivation, plus the inability of traditional policies to bring inflation rates down, led to new ideas developed in new research centres that were fundamental in shaping the policies that successfully stabilized the economy in 1994. Next, the authors claim that, following the international trend, orthodox and neoliberal ideas became increasingly influential within the Brazilian economic debate, turning into the dominant approach in the early 1990s until the New Keynesian Consensus took hold in the 2000s. It finally deals with ideas generated in the context of disappointing social and economic outcomes, which eventually led in the 2010s to the resumption of academic and policy debate on new ideas under the labels "New Developmentalism" and "Social Developmentalism".

Since most of the economic ideas and debates reviewed in this book took place in specific historical political-economic settings, readers should benefit from some suggested background reading. *The Cambridge History of Latin America*, edited in several volumes by Leslie Bethell (1984–1995), contains several informative essays about Brazilian society, culture, political life, and economy from colonial times to 1990 (see especially volumes 1, 2, 3, 5, 6, 9 and 10). The 2018 *Oxford Handbook of the Brazilian Economy*, edited by Edmind Amann, Carlos Azzoni, and Werner Baer, includes several historical chapters from colonial times on. *Brazil in Transition*, by Alston, Melo, Mueller and Pereira (2016), covers the period 1964–2014.

Notes

1. Consentino and Gambi's (2019) volume partially overlaps with the current book in coverage, although the approaches are often distinct.
2. Ibid.

References

Alston, L.J., M. Melo, B. Mueller and C. Pereira (eds.). 2016. *Brazil in Transition: Beliefs, Leadership, and Institutional Change*. Princeton, NJ: Princeton University Press.

Amann, E., C. Azzoni and W. Baer (eds.). 2018. *Oxford Handbook of the Brazilian Economy*. New York: Oxford University Press.

Bethell, L. (ed.). 1984–1995. *The Cambridge History of Latin America*, 10 volumes. Cambridge: Cambridge University Press.

Consentino, D.V. and T. Gambi. (eds.). 2019. *História do Pensamento Econômico – Pensamento Econômico Brasileiro*. Niterói and S. Paulo: Eduff and Hucitec.

Part 1

Contributions to economic theory

2 Contributions to economics from the "periphery" in historical perspective

The case of Brazil after mid-20th century

Mauro Boianovsky

Abstract: This chapter provides an overview of Brazilian economists' contributions to global economics since mid-20th century, from the perspective of economics as transnational science. The contributions are organized into three sections, after a methodological and historiographical introduction: economic development and income distribution, inflation and indexation, and "pure theoretical economics" coming from mainstream mathematical economists and heterodox (mainly post-Keynesian) authors.

1. Transnational science, networks and the formation of the Brazilian economic scientific community

It was only between the mid-1960s and early 1970s that Brazilian economists started to form a scientific community that would become part of the transnational economic community. There was no proper scientific economic community in Brazil until the 1950s, although, of course, economic issues – particularly those related to economic policy-making in the monetary field – had attracted close attention since the 19th century (see chapters by Mauricio C. Coutinho, Flávio Versiani and André Villela in this book). This is in marked contrast with the history of most of the Brazilian scientific community, both in the natural and social sciences fields, which established itself in the 1930s, if not earlier (Schwartzman 1976, 1979; Ekerman 1989; Azevedo 1955; Haddad 1981).

As pointed out by Raul Ekerman (1989: 118; 126–129), a participant in that process, the emergence of scientific economic discourse in Brazil was determined by the formation of a group of "economic scientists" inserted into the broad international community. The intensification of formal and informal networks between Brazilian and foreign economists in the mid-1960s and early 1970s set the standards of economic research in the country and by that forged the beginning of an economic scientific community (see also Loureiro and Lima 1996). Unlike other fields, scientific immigration to Brazil was quite reduced in economics. The few economists who moved to Brazil during the great interwar scientific migration flow – the Austrian-born Richard

DOI: 10.4324/9781003185871-3

Lewinsohn, the Czech Alexandre Kafka and the Italian Giorgio Mortara – did have an impact. However, with the exception of Mortara's key role in the field of economic demography, that was not enough to warrant the formation of a national economic scientific community with strong ties with Europe and the United States (see Boianovsky 2021).

Historians and sociologists of science have recently become attracted to transnational perspectives, as witnessed by the September 2012 special issue of the *British Journal for the History of Science* and by Fourcade's (2006) study of the economics profession. As pointed out by Turchetti et al. (2012: 321–322) in their introduction to that issue, the current stress on "transnational" science as a cross-border activity should be distinguished from its traditional meaning as epistemic universalism in the sense of a truth-finding activity that is not affected by national, class or ethnic differences. The latter approach was challenged by the development of science studies in the 1970s and 1980s, which emphasized the social history of science as contingent on social, economic and political features. That was accompanied by thick-descriptions, micro-histories of laboratories and research institutions, and investigation of the history of science in local contexts.[1]

The transnationalization of science has accelerated in the 21st century and turned science into a global enterprise. Some aspects of that process are the increasing role of both international linkages and scientists' global geographical mobility, accompanied by changes in traditional concepts such as scientific peripheries and "Brain Drain", replaced by hierarchical networks and "Brain Circulation" (see The Royal Society 2011; Van Noorden 2012; for the Brazilian scientific "diaspora", see Carneiro et al. 2020).

Science studies' attempts to produce a sociologically framed history of science led to detailed narratives of its current and past paths, while its international dimension was only surmised. The analysis of transnational scientific networks has extended the science studies notion of the production of knowledge as a complex process – in which different actors negotiate the meaning and acceptance of new theories – to the discussion of "how locally produced knowledge becomes globally accepted". The establishment of such networks "confers the authority needed to strengthen locally sourced scientific ideas and propel them beyond borders – by means either of patronage, or wider circulation, or adherence to international standards" (Turchetti et al. 2012: 331).

Polycentric and hierarchical alternative networks, competing for power and knowledge, form the transnational system of science, featuring connections between individuals and groups rather than nations. By focusing on flows and circulation of peoples and artifacts, on "what is emerging, what is new in the interstices of encounter . . . on the fringes and 'peripheral' spaces", transnational science studies make it possible to contest the "unidirectional vision of the manufacture of the worlds" involved in the notion of colonial or peripheral science (Pestre 2012: 428–429). Gone is the center–periphery dichotomy in science, which cannot account for the emergence of "pockets of central science" on the periphery (see Medina and Carey 2020; and Rodriguez 2013 for a transnational approach to the history of Latin American social sciences).

The call for a transnational approach to the history of science has entailed a new emphasis on historical studies of the role of agencies and organizations in shaping the international flows of scientists and ideas, including large-scale scientific migrations such as forced exile in the 1930s and early 1940s. Transnational forms of patronage (especially the Carnegie, Rockefeller and Ford Foundations) have been instrumental in the reconfiguration or creation of scientific institutions, and in settling local research into international networks (see Turchetti et al. 2012: 327).

The funding of academic research by international institutions (called patronage) has been a major instrument in the transnationalization of science. That was the case in Brazil in the 1960s, when USAID and especially the Ford Foundation begun to fund the first graduate economics programs in the country, which eventually led to the creation of Anpec (Associação Nacional dos Centros de Pós-Graduação em Economia, the National Association of Graduate Centers in Economics) in 1973. As part of its broad program for social sciences in Brazil (with emphasis on economics) at the time, the Ford Foundation and USAID also became involved in encouraging and supporting American professors and researchers for medium-term visits to Brazilian economic departments, as well as providing fellowships for Brazilian economic students willing to pursue PhD programs in the US (see Haddad 1981; Ekerman 1989; Versiani 1997; Fernandez and Suprinyak 2018).

It would be a simplification, however, to assert that Ford, USAID or other patrons *created* the Brazilian scientific economic community. Rather, such funding institutions operated in a space developed from the 1930s to the 1950s, when incipient economic research carried out by Brazilian economists at universities, think thanks and government agencies established a demand for steady international ties with some of the main centers of production of economic knowledge.

The Ford Foundation's funding of Brazilian economics was part of its new overall strategy (adopted at the time by the Rockefeller Foundation as well) to fund large programs involving teams of economists instead of individuals. Around that period, Thomas Kuhn's (1962) *The Structure of Scientific Revolutions* argued that the scientific *community* was central to scientific activity and its history. That was not just a coincidence (see Weintraub 2007: 271). The new notion of science as a collective enterprise – whose quality standards, research agenda and criteria for resources allocation for science are decided by the scientific community itself – was one the features of Kuhn's concept of "normal science". In the words of Michael Polanyi's (1962) concomitant article, the scientific community worked (or rather should work) as a "Republic of Science", with its own rules for the production of knowledge.

Before the development of an economic scientific community in the 1960s–70s, the production of economic ideas in Brazil is better interpreted in terms of what Schumpeter (1954: 38–39) called "systems of political economy" and "economic thought", as distinct from "economic analysis" proper. Whereas the notion of "scientific progress" applies to the history of the latter, it was not, according to Schumpeter, a feature of the histories of systems of political economy – defined as a "set of economic policies", based on certain "unifying (normative) principles such as the principle of economic liberalism, of socialism and so on" – or of "economic thought" – understood as the sum of "all opinions and desires concerning economic subjects, especially concerning public policy bearing upon those subjects". From that perspective, economic policy mattered to the history of economics only to the extent that it was built on analytical work (Schumpeter 1954: 1145).

Schumpeter's distinction has been applied to historical studies in Brazil, carried out under the assumption of almost complete absence of proper analytical or theoretical work in Brazilian economic thought up to the 1950s – which has led to an emphasis on the history of "systems of political economy" as better suited to the Brazilian case (see e.g. the chapter by Bielschowsky and Mussi in this book). Although economic teaching in Brazil started as early as 1827 (as part of law and engineering schools, as in many other countries), usually featuring relatively up-to-date references to the international (European) economic literature, economic research did not become a practice until the mid-20th century (Hugon 1955; Love 1996).

One should distinguish, while working on the history of economic thought in Brazil, two or three phases, according to the turning point represented by the formation of an economic scientific community in the country in the mid-1960s. The first, long one goes from the early 19th century to the 1930s, when Brazilian economic thinkers essentially imported and adapted European and (later) American economic ideas to their own purposes (see e.g. Boianovsky 2013). The post–World War II period marks a transition stage, when the first research institutions were established – including Latin American ones with strong links with Brazil, such as the United Nations Economic Commission for Latin America (CEPAL), with headquarters in Chile – and the degree of originality of economic thought in Brazil started to increase, especially in the then-new field of development economics. Finally, since the mid-1960s and early 1970s, Brazilian economists have become part of the transnational economic community, connected through international hierarchical networks.

The model of "creative adaptation" as explanation of the international transmission of economic ideas to the "periphery" (see Mäki 1996; Cardoso 2003, 2017) assumes a very high degree of net imports of ideas from the "center", with virtually no exports or creation of original theories, hypotheses or analytical models on the periphery. It applies particularly to the first phase, even if "adaptation" continued to be a feature of the other phases.[2]

Basalla's (1967) seminal article provided a first analytical study of the international diffusion of modern science from Western Europe to the rest of the world, based on a three-stage model. Basalla's stadial model has been often compared to Rostow's (1960) modernization approach to growth through a succession of stages (see e.g. MacLeod 2000). Nevertheless, historians of economics have overlooked Basalla's model (Spengler's 1968 passing reference is an exception). In Basalla's stage 1, the new "non-scientific" society or nation provides a source for European science. Stage 2 corresponds to colonial (or dependent) science, when scientific activity is based upon institutions and traditions of nations with mature scientific culture. In stage 3, an independent national scientific tradition is established, so that scientists' major ties are within the boundary of the country where they work.

Basalla's center–periphery model was supposed to apply mostly to the successful historical experiences of the United States and Japan. However, it has been applied as well to particular or micro-historical episodes in other countries, as in Stepan's (1976) thesis that the Brazilian Oswaldo Cruz Institute – founded in the early 20th century as a research center for tropical diseases – developed as far as stage 3. After some initial success, Basalla's model was criticized for its association of science with nation, disregard for the transnational character of science, and the assumption of a linear and unidirectional trajectory that did not acknowledge the multiple characteristics of colonial science (see e.g. MacLeod 2000). Despite its drawbacks, Basalla's framework calls attention to some features of colonial science that may be applied to the transition phase towards the establishment of a fully developed scientific community. Colonial science provides the "proper milieu, through its contacts with established scientific cultures, for a small number of gifted individuals whose scientific researches may challenge or surpass" the work of scientists from the center (Basalla 1967: 614). As put by Basalla (1967: 614), "colonial scientists cannot share in the informal scientific organizations" of mature scientific cultures, in the sense that they "cannot become part of the 'Invisible College' in which the latest ideas and news of the advancing frontiers of science are exchanged".

The notion of the "Invisible College" is reminiscent of Kuhn's notion of "normal" – as opposed to "revolutionary" – science. Schwartzman (1979: 7–8) has argued for a history of science in Brazil aiming at "understanding science not in its most spectacular and visible aspects, but in its permanence and continuity". The goal of the history of transnational science as produced in the hierarchical periphery is to understand "efforts to establish a 'normal' science . . . and a capacity to participate effectively, even if not centrally, in the contemporary frontiers of knowledge" (ibid) – in other words, becoming members of the "Invisible College" formed by the international community. The following sections of the present chapter provide a narrative of some selected episodes of Brazilian economists' contributions to transnational economic knowledge, as illustrated by case studies from the fields of development economics, income distribution, inflation, mathematical economics, and heterodox economics.

2. Economic development and income distribution

Celso Furtado (b. 1920; d. 2004) was the only Brazilian economist included in all first three editions of M. Blaug's *Who's Who in Economics*, covering approximately the time span from the early 1970s to the mid-1990s. The *Who's Who* was based on citation counts collected from the Social Sciences Citation Index. The third (1999) edition, covering the period 1984–1996, included also another Brazilian economist, Edmar Lisboa Bacha (b. 1942). Like Furtado, Bacha is a development economist (see Bacha's [2018] autobiographical piece, published in a series of "recollections of eminent economists"). The fourth, last edition (Blaug and Vane 2003) of the *Who's Who* covered citations from articles published in the period 1990–2000. The mathematical economist José Alexandre Scheinkman (b. 1948) – who migrated to the United States in the 1970s but kept (mostly informal) links with Brazil – was the only Brazilian-born economist included in the fourth edition. Moreover, C. Furtado is featured in the *New Palgrave Dictionary of Economics*, together with the Brazilian macroeconomist and policy-maker Mário Henrique Simonsen (b. 1935; d. 1997) (see Boianovsky 2008a, 2008b).

Furtado was one of the participants in the well-known World Bank two-volume celebration of the "pioneers in development", who established the new field of development economics in the post-war period (see Furtado 1987a). He was the first Brazilian economist to obtain a doctor's degree abroad, at the Sorbonne in 1947. His main analytical contributions took shape in the 1950s, when he directed the development division of the United Nations Economic Commission for Latin America and the Caribbean (CEPAL), as recollected in his autobiography (Furtado 1985, 1987b).

Together with the Argentinean economist Raul Prebisch, CEPAL's Executive Secretary at the time, Furtado investigated how the economic structure of the "peripheral" Latin American countries differed from those of the industrialized "central" nations (see Boianovsky 2010). Latin American *structuralism*, of which Furtado was a main formulator, provides an illustration of Gerschenkron's (1952) famous hypothesis of "relative economic backwardness", which asserts that a country's degree of backwardness brings about a corresponding set of innovative ideas, policies and institutions for the reasons and attempted cure of the economic lag. Surely, Brazilian economic development had been a mater of concern since the 1800s (see the chapters by Coutinho and Versiani), but it was only in the 1950s that the new concept of *underdevelopment* became clear through Furtado's writings, collected in Furtado ([1961] 1964).

The 1954 translation of Furtado's 1952 article (Furtado [1952] 1954) established his international reputation as a development economist, especially after its reproduction in the first-ever collection of essays in the field, put together by Agarwala and Singh (1958). That was followed by Furtado's ([1959] 1963) historical account of the economic growth of Brazil since colonial times, with its methodological innovation of introducing (verbal) macroeconomic models into the analysis of each historical phase or structure of the Brazilian economy (see also Boianovsky 2010, 2015). Partly inspired by the Brazilian experience, Furtado ([1952] 1954) distinguished between the economic dynamics of industrialized mature economies, based on internal supply-side elements such as technical progress, and the development of tropical backward countries, induced from without by the exports of raw materials and determined by the demand side. The upshot is that underdevelopment is not a necessary stage in the process of formation of modern capitalist economies, but rather a special process caused by the penetration of modern imported technology into archaic structures beset by capital scarcity. The resulting socio-economic heterogeneity (sometimes called "dualism") tends to perpetuate itself in underdeveloped economic structures.[3]

Some of Furtado's analytical contributions would only be acknowledged much later. Furtado's ([1957] 2008) analysis of what would eventually be named the Dutch Disease (an aspect of the Natural Resource Curse) is a case in point. In his report about the Venezuelan economy – produced anonymously for CEPAL in 1957, but censored at the time and eventually published much later – Furtado discussed the perverse effects of oil production on the economic structure of that country. The oil boom had provoked an overvaluation of the Venezuelan currency, which raised the dollar value of money-wages and hurt the profitability of other exports and sectors of the economy, accompanied by higher imports. "The terms of the problem are simple enough," Furtado ([1957] 2008: 54) explained: "The average level of money-wages," calculated in dollars, "is above the average productivity level. Therefore, any tradable good comes with advantage into the Venezuelan market." Hence, although Venezuela was an exception to the balance of payments constraint faced by Brazil and other Latin American countries at the time, the absorption of a growing supply of foreign currency brought about problems of its own.

Furtado's 1950s approach to development naturally led in the 1970s to a theory of peripheral capitalism as "dependent" from the outside, involving domination and economic exploitation. Furtado (1987a) claimed that underdeveloped economies featured cultural dependence, as consumption patterns were transplanted from developed economies by the upper strata. Such a modernized component of consumption brought dependence into the technological realm by making it part of the production structure through import-substituting industrialization and investment by transnational corporations that control the access to modern technology.

The most influential formulation of dependency theory came from an essay produced in Santiago in 1969 by Brazilian sociologist Fernando Henrique Cardoso and Chilean historian Enzo Faletto at ILPES (Latin American Institute for Economic and Social Planning), a sociological complement to CEPAL (Cardoso and Faletto 1969, 1979). Cardoso emphasized the existence of internal and external subsystems – so that the international capitalist system was not the only determinant – together with the mutual interests among social classes across center–periphery. Unlike Furtado's stagnationist corner, Cardoso pointed out the possibilities of unequal growth in the stage of imperialism dominated by multinational corporations.

Although the influence of the Marxian framework is visible in Cardoso, its full application would be found in another branch of dependency analysis led by Theotonio dos Santos (1970) and Ruy Mauro Marini (1972) under the influence of the Chicago-trained German economist Andre Gunter Frank, who taught in Brazil in the early 1960s before the military coup d'état (see Love's [1996, chapter 12] detailed discussion; and the chapter in this book by Bielschowsky and Mussi). They all fled Brazil and moved (temporarily) to Chile after that. Frank, Santos and Marini took the position that Latin American capitalism was nonviable and that dependency could not be broken under a capitalist system. Significantly enough, Santos (1970) was apparently just the second publication by a Brazilian author in the highly prestigious *American Economic Review*.[4] It was part of a session on "Economic Imperialism", chaired by Paul Sweezy, together with other papers by R.D. Wolff and H. Magdoff, held at the December 1969 meetings of the American Economic Association (AEA). Radical economics was then on relative high demand in the US, which accounts for such a session as part of the AEA program. The "consumption" of Latin American (mostly Brazilian) dependency analysis in the US continued at high levels throughout the 1970s (Cardoso 1977). It deeply influenced the well-known historical model of world capitalism put forward at the time by Immanuel Wallerstein (1974, 1980 and 1989).

CEPAL's structuralist development research agenda would continue and attract international attention in another guise in a series of formal models produced by Bacha, some of them joint with the American economist Lance Taylor. Bacha and Taylor (1971) provided a method to estimate the shadow price of foreign exchange, a key variable in development planning and social cost–benefit analysis. They proposed a new formula to compute the "equilibrium" exchange rate that would equilibrate the foreign exchange market in the absence of tariffs and other distortions. A few years later, Bacha (1978) tackled the issue of the distribution of gains from trade between "central" and "peripheral" countries, which had attracted the attention of R. Prebisch, W. A. Lewis, H. Singer, A. Emmanuel and others. The model indicated absence of cross-country income convergence, since technical progress had asymmetrical effects in the periphery (unchanged wage-rates) and in the center (higher wages). Another influential model by Bacha (1990) built on the structuralist two-gap – the balance of payments and the saving constraints – approach to put forward a three-gap model incorporating as well the fiscal constraint under the assumption of complementarity between public and private investment.

After decades of economic growth based on import-substituting industrialization, Latin American countries (particularly Brazil) suffered from serious macroeconomic imbalances and economic recession in the 1980s and part of the 1990s. Under the impact of the experience of fast-growing Asian countries at the time, and as a reaction to the increasing influence of the "Washington Consensus" established in the early 1990s, "classical" structuralism was gradually replaced by neo-structuralism at CEPAL and by related "new-developmentalism" ("novo-desenvolvimentismo") theses advanced by a small group of Brazilian economists led by Luiz C. Bresser-Pereira (2010, 2020).

New-developmentalists share with neo-structuralists an emphasis on productivity and competitiveness in markets for traded goods as a main source of economic growth. New-developmentalists claim that firms in Brazil and other middle-income countries, due to both cyclical and chronic overvaluation of the exchange rate, are prevented from adopting the most efficient technologies in their investment decisions. Such overvaluation of the domestic currency is caused by cyclical balance of payment crises and by the permanent impact of Dutch Disease phenomena, further elaborated since Furtado's ([1957] 2008) original formulation. According to new-developmentalists, the severity of the impact of Dutch Disease on the Brazilian economy is indicated by the difference between the current exchange-rate equilibrium – which balances current account through time – and the exchange rate that brings about "industrial equilibrium" in the sense of competitiveness of the leading firms in the international market.

The links between natural resources and the Brazilian economy have been a persistent object of investigation by Brazilian economists from several perspectives. Those include sustainable economic development, land conflicts and deforestation in the Amazon, and the interplay between natural resources and institutions. Good illustrations of the former may be found in Reis and Margulis (1991) – as part of a conference volume about global warming – and in articles by Bernardo Mueller and his American co-authors (Alston et al. 2000, 2012). The inter-relations between institutional development and natural resources could be found already in Furtado's ([1959] 1963) account of the long-term trends of the Brazilian economy, particularly in connection with the persistence of the colonial heritage. Those links have been further investigated since the inception of neo-institutionalist economics in the 1970s and 1980s. Naritomi et al. (2012) have provided a quantitative examination of the determinants of local institutions and distribution of political power in Brazil, with emphasis on the long-term effects of the colonial sugar cane and gold booms.

By the early 1970s, as the first wave of Brazilian economists started to return from their PhDs abroad and the Brazilian economy was still experiencing high growth rates, an intense controversy took place – as new data showing a higher Gini coefficient of income distribution became available – about the causes of the unequal distribution of the fruits of economic progress. Those debates played a decisive role in establishing the Brazilian scientific economic community and its international links. The income distribution controversy engaged Brazilian policy-makers, foreign economists (particularly Fishlow 1972), international institutions (such as the World Bank and its president R. McNamara) as well as young Brazilian economic researchers.

That was the most important economic debate during the long period of military rule (1964–1985) in Brazil. It is apparently paradoxical that a relatively open economic debate that challenged the then-prevailing economic policy, amidst the restrictions imposed by political repression, could take place. But the puzzle is solved if the international character of the discussion is taken into account, as well as government policy-makers' belief that they had the best side of the argument in the attempted econometric demonstration (see Langoni 1975) that increasing inequality resulted from the market effects of economic growth under conditions of skilled labor scarcity (see Andrada and Boianovsky 2020; Ekerman 1989). Economists opposing the military regime believed increasing inequality resulted mainly from economic policies – particularly a minimum wage squeeze – implemented by the Brazilian military rule after the 1964 coup d'etat (see Bacha and Taylor 1978 for a survey).

That heavily contested econometric debate attracted worldwide attention and contributed decisively to turn economic inequality into a main theme of the development economics literature. The concern with economic justice, over and above economic growth, became pervasive (Hirschman 1981). One of the key issues was the so-called perverse "Brazilian model" of economic growth accompanied (or even stimulated) by increasing inequality, as outlined by Tavares and Serra (1973), among others, and formalized by Taylor and Bacha (1976).[5]

Brazilian income distribution issues came to the fore again after data indicated a continuous, unprecedented decline of the Gini coefficient between 2001 and 2014 (see Hoffmann 2018, who had participated in the 1970s debates as well). This led to the hypothesis of the formation of a new middle class in Brazil, advanced by Marcelo Neri (2015, 2021) as part of an international UNU Wider project (see Kopper 2020 for a historical account). The role of minimum wage legislation continued to attract attention (see e.g. Brito et al. 2017), although the long-term inequality trends shown by income concentration at the top seemed to persist (Souza 2018, whose research has kept links with T. Piketty's World Inequality Lab).

3. Inflation, indexation and stabilization

As discussed in Section 1 earlier, Schumpeter's (1954) distinction between "systems of political economy" and "economic thought" on one hand and "economic analysis" on the other has been sometimes applied to Brazil. From that perspective, economic policy matters to the history of economics as such only to the extent that it is built on analytical work, as Schumpeter (1954: 1145) acknowledged. That was the case of the successful 1994 "*Real* Plan" (*Plano Real*) of economic stabilization, which managed to curb the chronic accelerating inflation rate that had beset the Brazilian economy since the 1970s.[6] As put by Edmar Bacha, one of its architects, the *Real* Plan was based on a "homegrown monetary reform" conceived and implemented by members of the Department of Economics of the Catholic University of Rio de Janeiro (PUC-Rio) (Bacha 2003: 181). The development of the pure case of inertial inflation, and of its corollaries for economic stabilization in Brazil, may be seen as yet another manifestation of Gerschenkron's (1952) thesis about the influence of domestic economic problems on the creation of new ideas and policies at a national level.

Monetary economics, to a larger extent than other fields, has been influenced by historical events and institutions at both national and international levels (see e.g. Hicks 1967). South American monetary history is a case in point, as illustrated, for instance, by the pioneer detailed discussion of inconvertible paper money by Chilean economist Guillermo Subercaseaux (1912) in his *El Papel Moneda*. It attracted the attention of Knut Wicksell and other European monetary theorists at the time, in a rare case of transmission of economic ideas from the "periphery" to the "center" (see Alcouffe and Boianovsky 2013). Persistent inflationary conditions in the region would attract general attention again, when a large international conference on *Inflation and Growth in Latin America* was held in Rio in 1963. The 1964 conference volume, edited by Werner Baer and Isaac Kerstenetzky, has been regarded as the climax of a decade of intense debates between Latin American "structuralists" and "monetarists" – a term coined by Brazilian economist Roberto Campos in the late 1950s (see Boianovsky 2012, and the chapter later by Bielschowsky and Mussi).

Shortly after that, Brazilian policy-makers – in an attempt to avoid or minimize the negative impact of stabilization measures on employment and output, as well as the perverse effects of inflation on economic agents' decisions – introduced widespread indexation of economic contracts, the first of its kind in international monetary history. Again, that would not fail to draw the attention of American and European macroeconomists alike, especially after Milton Friedman approved of and supported the Brazilian indexation system upon visiting the country in December 1973, when Brazil was experiencing high economic growth accompanied by declining inflation rates. As Friedman pointed out, Alfred Marshall had advanced the theoretical argument for indexation back in the 1880s, but it was the first time it was put into practice. From Friedman's perspective, escalator clauses eliminated the effects of differences between actual and expected inflation, turning the short-run Phillips Curve into a vertical line (Friedman 1974; see also Boianovsky 2020 and references cited therein).

Between the mid-1960s and early 1990s, Brazil became the laboratory of indexation experience. Two international conferences on indexation were held in 1975 at the University of São Paulo (published 1977) and in 1981 at Getulio Vargas Foundation in Rio (published 1983), including papers about the Israeli indexation record (Nadiri and Pastore 1977; Dornbusch and Simonsen 1983). By then, models of wage indexation by Jo Anna Gray (1976) and Stanley Fischer (1977a) had become influential. Brazilian economist Mario H. Simonsen (1983) formally showed, in an extended version of the Gray-Fischer model, that, in the absence of supply shocks, *full* widespread indexation – as Friedman had suggested – relieves the output loss of anti-inflationary policies, as price expectations are eliminated from contracts. However, the type of indexed wage contract found in Brazil was based on a staggered rule, with money wages adjusted at time intervals according to previous inflation rates. As first modeled by Simonsen (op. cit.), *lagged* wage indexation, under the assumption of rational expectations, led to a Phillips relation analogous to the one with adaptive expectations. Simonsen's demonstration supported the policy-makers' contention that, in practice, wage indexation made disinflation more difficult.

The 1970s–80s international discussion about indexation and its effects was related to a broader debate about rational expectations, policy effectiveness and stabilization (see also Boianovsky 2022). It is in that context that the contributions of Brazilian economists to what became known as the theory of "inertial inflation" – and particularly to its original implications for the design of stabilization policy in Brazil – should be placed. As put by Tobin (1980a: 789, italics added), the "main practical controversy of the day is to what extent, if any, the ongoing inflation is *inertial* – i.e., reflects sluggishness in the adjustment of paths of nominal wages and prices – as well as expectational." Tobin (ibid; 1980b: 62–63) claimed that lagged prices and wages, resulting from institutional inertia and disequilibrium adjustment, challenged the new-classical policy-ineffectiveness proposition and vindicated the traditional Keynesian approach. Tobin did not provide a model of inflation inertia, but referred to the literature on contracts under rational expectations for analytical foundations (see e.g. Fischer 1977b; Taylor 1979).

In his suggested inflation taxonomy, Tobin (1981: 23) defined *inertial inflation* as "the self-replicating pattern of wage and price inflation", later called an "autoregressive process" in the sense that inflation depends essentially on its past values. Brazilian economists in the early 1980s identified staggered backward-looking wage indexation as a key feature of high chronic inflation that affected the country, as opposed to forward-looking rational expectations. From that perspective, backward-looking lagged indexation was the mechanism by which distributive conflicts between economic agents worked out in the Brazilian economy at the time (see e.g. Williamson 1994). This contrast – between the international emphasis on expectations and policy credibility issues on one hand and the role played by lagged indexation in Brazilian inflation on the other – became conspicuous among Brazilian economists from PUC-Rio (see e.g. Lopes 1984; Arida and Lara-Resende 1985; Bacha 1988). They pointed out that, in heavily indexed economies like Brazil, the main influence over the current inflation rate was not its future expected path but the past observed one, with crucial implications for the economic stabilization strategy.

Brazilian economists were, of course, aware of Taylor (1979) and other influential rational expectations articles featuring staggered wage contracts, which introduced price level inertia in the sense that the price level fully adjusts to a monetary shock only after a continued departure of employment from its natural level. Accordingly, it was often asserted in the international literature that Taylor's model accounted for inflation inertia as well. However, as shown by Simonsen (1986a), that model generated only price level inertia, not inflation inertia (see also Lopes 1983 for a similar criticism). Taylor's (1979) model inertia was *weak*, in the sense that a contractionary monetary rule was consistent with painless stabilization, contrary to the *strong* inertia proposition put forward by Brazilian economists (see also Andrade and Silva 1996: 441, n. 16). A similar point – that staggered price and wage changes à la Taylor do not account for the difficulty of reducing inflation through deflationary monetary and fiscal policy – would be made by Ball (1994), without referring, as one might expect, to the Brazilian literature (see also Romer 1996: 272–273).

Simonsen – a member of the Vargas Foundation in Rio, and a policy-maker and adviser from the mid-1960s to mid-1970s – put forward an early intuitive model of inflation inertia. The inertial element – then called "feedback component" ("coeficiente de realimentação" in Portuguese) – together with the "autonomous component" (supply shocks that change relative prices) and the "demand regulation component" (excess aggregate demand) – decide the rate of inflation according to a linear formula. Simonsen's model differed from the then-fashionable accelerationist Phillips curve by explaining inflation acceleration as a result not of revised expectations but of a reduction in the price and wage adjustment interval, captured by changes in the feedback coefficient.

Simonsen's (1970) model implied that even if inflation expectations fell to zero, the feedback inertial mechanism would keep working due to wage staggering in the indexation process. On the assumption of zero excess aggregate demand and a less than unity feedback coefficient, the lower limit to the current rate of inflation was given by the autonomous component divided by 1 minus the feedback coefficient. In particular, any attempt to reduce the inflation rate below its limit value would bring about a permanent reduction of the rate of growth. The limit value may be seen as the expression of purely "structural" inflation to distinguish it from price rises determined plainly by excess aggregate demand.[7]

With a few exceptions, Brazilian economists involved in the debates about inertial inflation and stabilization policies published relatively little abroad. Members of the department of economics at PUC-Rio formed a "closed" and "protected" community from the late 1970s to the mid-1980s that gave priority to debates among its own members – mainly Edmar L. Bacha, Francisco L. Lopes, André Lara-Resende, Eduardo Modiano and Persio Arida, later joined by Gustavo B. Franco – instead of extensive intellectual interactions with other groups either domestically or internationally. According to Arida (2022), that was behind the progressive research program à la Lakatos, on inertial inflation in indexed economies, carried out by that small set of economists. It predicted new facts and accounted for the empirical evidence by performing econometric tests, as revealed by going through the large number of Working Papers about inertial inflation produced at PUC Economics Department during that period. Although its members had studied economics and obtained PhDs at well-known universities abroad, the main goal of the group was not to achieve international academic recognition as such, but to influence domestic formulation and implementation of macroeconomic stabilization policies.

Faria's (2005) model of a trade-off between international (mostly American) and domestic publications by academic economists is useful in this connection. Faria argues that, under the assumption that productive scholars are reputation seekers in their own countries, they have an incentive to publish in journals in their home country and spend time outside academia. This is largely accounted for by the degree of government intervention in the economy, which induces academic economists to invest their human capital in specific knowledge of local economic problems and institutions, as was the case of Brazilian inflation. The argument implies that productive rankings, which value international top journals, are biased against economists outside the United States.

PUC-Rio economist Francisco Lopes (1999: 335) was clear about the "dilemma" between publishing abroad and domestically, that is, between gaining international academic recognition or trying to influence national economic debates and policies. Lopes (ibid) singled out his colleague Edmar Bacha as an author who managed to find balance between international and domestic publications. In his entry in the *Who's Who in Economics* – which lists his main publications and contributions – Bacha regarded the successful implementation of the "novel stabilization program" represented by the *Real* Plan his "most important contribution to economics" (Blaug 1999: 52; see also section 6 of Bacha's 2018 autobiographical piece).

Nevertheless, Brazilian economists did publish, on occasion, about Brazilian inertial inflation in international outlets, often because of connections with foreign economists who had an interest on the Brazilian economy and its chronic instability. John Williamson (from the Institute for International Economics, now the Peterson Institute for International Economics), Rudiger Dornbusch (from the Massachusetts Institute of Technology, known as MIT) and Lance Taylor (then at MIT, later at the New School for Social Research) played key roles in providing an international audience for some Brazilian economists' ideas about inertial inflation and stabilization, and by that turning those ideas into part of transnational economic networks.

British economist John Williamson moved to Rio in the late 1970s upon getting married to a Brazilian economist. For a couple of years, he taught at PUC-Rio, where he produced a joint paper about "The theory of consistent indexation" (Lopes and Williamson 1980). In the early 1980s, Williamson accepted an appointment at the Institute of International Economics in Washington, where he remained until retiring in 2012. He would become well known after advancing in the early 1990s the so-called "Washington Consensus" of economic policy guidelines for Latin America. In December 1984, Williamson put together an international conference on *Inflation and Indexation* (Williamson 1985), for which he invited Persio Arida and André Lara-Resende to present their new paper on "Inertial inflation and monetary reform" in Brazil (Arida and Lara-Resende 1985), which would eventually turn into one of the foundations of the 1994 *Real* Plan. Arida and Lara-Resende (1985) was the focal point of the conference.

Shortly after the implementation of that stabilization plan, Williamson participated at a conference held at Duke University about the "internationalization of economics" (see Coats 1996). Williamson (1996: 367) agreed that there was a general trend of internationalization or "Americanization" of economics, but pointed out that the "theory of inertial inflation in Brazil" was one of the instances illustrating that there was still an "important reverse flow of ideas" going on. As recalled by Williamson (2005),

> I agree that countries can sometimes benefit from heterodox proposals. We at the Institute for International Economics once sponsored a conference when the ideas that ultimately flowered into the Real Plan first took

> form, with the objective of trying to ensure that if Brazil did implement the plan it would not be sabotaged by the IMF's dinosaurs. To my mind the Real Plan was one of the most brilliant heterodox plans . . . and was totally country-specific. Its essence was not the use of the exchange rate as a nominal anchor, which was an unfortunate belated add-on, but the use of the indexation unit as the new monetary unit following monetary reform.
>
> (Williamson 2005: 50, n. 13)

R. Dornbusch, who discussed Arida and Lara-Resende's paper at the 1984 conference, called it the "Larida" proposal (Dornbusch 1985). Dornbusch, like Williamson, was an expert on the macroeconomics of exchange rates. He was familiar with the economic instability of Latin American economies (see the essays collected in Dornbusch 1993). Both Arida and Lara-Resende had been PhD students at MIT in the late 1970s and early 1980s. By that time, Dornbusch and some other MIT economists started to show interest on macroeconomic and stabilization problems in Brazil and other indexed economies (see e.g. Modigliani and Padoa-Schioppa 1978 on Italy). As recalled by Arida (2019: 16), Dornbusch was an important influence on his intellectual formation at MIT. Furthermore, a few days after the 1984 Washington indexation conference, Dornbusch set up a seminar at MIT about the Larida proposal, involving, besides Arida, Lawrence Summers, Franco Modigliani and Mario Simonsen (Arida 2019: 24).

In 1981, Dornbusch co-organized in Rio with M.H. Simonsen a large international conference on inflation and indexation that brought together some of the main experts in the field (Dornbusch and Simonsen 1983). That was the beginning of his collaboration with Simonsen, which would result in a couple of joint papers on the topic (see e.g. Dornbusch and Simonsen 1988) and in Simonsen's exposure to the international academic community (e.g. Simonsen 1988).[8] On the other hand, Dornbusch's interaction with Simonsen – together with the fact that he was married to the Brazilian macroeconomist Eliana Cardoso – stimulated the MIT economist's interest in the Brazilian indexation mechanisms and stabilization plans, both the failed *Cruzado* Plan of 1986 and the successful *Real* Plan of 1994 (Dornbusch and Simonsen 1988; Cardoso and Dornbusch 1987; Dorbusch 1997).

Lance Taylor, who cultivated long ties with the Brazilian neo-structuralist tradition of PUC-Rio, was then editor of the *Journal of Development Economics* and published a couple of influential articles about Brazilian inertial inflation at the time. Years later, Bacha (2003) would put out his detailed account of the *Real* Plan as a chapter contributed to L. Taylor's Festschrift. Lopes and Bacha (1983, section 2) formally established the relationship that, for a given initial real wage, the average real wage is lower the higher the inflation rate is for a given indexation lag from prices to wages. Moreover, the larger the number of readjustments in a given period, the more responsive wage increases become to the current inflation.

Lopes and Bacha (1983: 15–16) argued that full wage indexation would eliminate the recession bubble associated to economic stabilization, as well as the forced savings effect. Their conclusion – that a "distributionally neutral increase" in the intensity of wage indexation reduces the output loss of a deflationary monetary shock – was reminiscent of Milton Friedman's original proposition, as the authors observed. Furthermore, their policy conclusion adumbrated the notion of stabilization via an indexed currency, as later put forward by Arida and Lara-Resende (1985), further elaborated in Arida's (1986, section 9) *JDE* article and eventually implemented in the 1994 *Real* Plan.[9] Apart from Simonsen and economists at PUC-Rio, inertial inflation also caught the attention of Brazilian economists L.C. Bresser-Pereira and Y. Nakano in articles and a book published from 1983–87 (see the chapter by Bastos and Bastian later). Bresser-Pereira and Nakano's (1987) book was positively reviewed in the *Journal of Economic Literature* (Gapinsky 1988).

The Brazilian *Real* Plan involved a two-stage process of substitution of the old inflated currency by a new stable one, initially as a unit of value, and finally as a means of payment. It was based on the Larida proposal (Arida and Lara-Resende 1985) to curb chronic inflation in the Brazilian indexed economy through a monetary reform preceded by full indexation. In March 1994, the government introduced an inflation index (URV, meaning "unit of real value") to serve as an optional unit of account and to align the most important relative prices in the economy. Since the index had stable real value, economic agents adhered massively to the unit of account. In July 1994, the old money was extinguished, and the URV became the new currency, named "real", at a semi-fix par with the US dollar. The four-months URV period led to the elimination of backward-looking indexation without the need of ensuing price and wage freeze as in the failed 1986 "Cruzado Plan". The inflation rate fell abruptly from 45% a month in June to 6% in July 1994, and kept falling after that. Contrary to the interpretation prevailing among some foreign economists (see e.g. Fischer et al. 2002), the plan was much more than a mere foreign-exchange-based stabilization (see Bacha 2003).

The success of the *Real* Plan was striking, given its low credibility due to previous stabilization failures (see Almeida and Bonomo 2002). Thomas Sargent (1982) had stressed the credibility factor in an influential essay about the painless end of hyperinflation episodes following the introduction of fiscal reforms. According to Sargent, the sudden end of hyperinflations, especially in Germany and other European countries in the 1920s, was mainly due to expectational effects of regime changes brought about by fiscal reforms. Economists at PUC-Rio disputed that view and stressed instead the stabilizing effects of the 1923 German monetary reform represented by the introduction of the *retenmark*, and its similarities with the Brazilian indexed currency proposal (see Lopes 1984; Arida 1984; Arida and Lara-Resende 1985; and especially Franco 1987 and 1990). A main lesson from the end of German hyperinflation, from the point of view of Brazilian economists, was the shrinkage of the inflationary memory of the system as contracts were indexed for shorter periods of time.

Sargent – like M. Friedman (see Friedman and Friedman 1998, as quoted in Boianovsky 2020) – regarded the monetary reform introduced by the *Real* Plan as just a "cosmetic" measure, as much as the German *retenmark* (see Sargent 2013; Sargent et al. 2009). That betrayed Sargent's (and Friedman's) misunderstanding of the main features of the monetary reform carried out as part of the *Real* Plan. Sargent (2013: 242) – in a paper titled "Reasonable doubts about the Real Plan" originally written in 1995 and published at the time in the "Economic Letter" of a Brazilian investment bank – acknowledged the "technical skill and creativity of Brazilian monetary authorities", but charged that "the de-indexation of the economy accomplished by the Real Plan is a technical detail, a side-show that hasn't touched on the fundamental causes of inflation." The success of the stabilization plan, Sargent claimed, was due to the monetary and, especially, fiscal policies adopted. The first stage of the *Real* Plan was a balance budgeting constitutional mechanism, known as "social emergency fund" (see Bacha 2003). However, once that was taken care of, the monetary reform would tackle the main inertial component of Brazilian inflation.

Research about inertial inflation significantly diminished in Brazil after the 1980s–90s, as the indexation mechanism was largely removed from the economy and inflation stabilized at relatively low rates as part of the new "inflation targeting" policy. Contrary to some accounts (see e.g. Carvalho 2019), the "decline" of the inertial inflation hypothesis in Brazil and its absorption by New-Keynesian economics was a natural process that reflected the new historical circumstances and the working of international economic networks. Hence, as part of his New-Keynesian/neo-Wicksellian framework, Woodford (2003) worked out in his influential book the analytical consequences, for the theory of inflation targeting, of indexation to past inflation. Michael Bruno (1989), the main responsible for the successful Israeli stabilization in the 1980s and frequent interlocutor for some PUC-Rio economists before and during the implementation of the *Real* Plan, had argued, against Sargent and others, for the theoretical and policy relevance of the concept of inertial inflation. Referring to Arida and Lara-Resende (1985), the IMF acknowledged the theoretical status of that notion (see Chopra 1985), even if it did not endorse the 1994 *Real* Plan.

4. Contributions to theoretical economics by mainstream mathematical economists and by heterodox economists

Brazilian economists' contributions to purely theoretical economics – that is, economic models and ideas that are not immediately motivated by or applied to economic policy matters – over the last 60 years or so have increasingly reflected the "pluralism" of economics in the country. According to Dequech (2018), Brazil has been a conspicuous case of economic pluralism, as reflected by the institutional distribution of academic and political power and prestige, to such an extent that such terms as "mainstream" and "heterodox" economics must be applied with care to Brazil. Nevertheless, for the purposes of this chapter, that distinction shall be kept, as we are interested in how theoretical contributions by Brazilian economists have been connected to the international debates.

Heterodox research programs have been particularly strong in Brazil, going back to the structuralist approach put forward by Furtado and other CEPAL economists in the 1950s, as discussed in Section 2 earlier. Since the 1970s – when different sorts of heterodox economics took form and were institutionalized at the international level as reactions to dominant neoclassical theory (see Backhouse 2000) – a significant fraction of Brazilian economists has become integrated into distinct forms of international heterodoxies. This is well illustrated by the Brazilian prominent post-Keynesian economist Fernando Cardim de Carvalho (b. 1953; d. 2018). That is also true of Latin American neo-structuralism, which has adopted the modeling strategies of international heterodox streams (see Barcena and Prado 2015). Brazilian economists Cardim de Carvalho and David Dequech were the only Latin Americans interviewed by Mearman et al. (2019).

Brazilian mainstream economists' international contributions to economic theory have been particularly relevant in the field of mathematical economics. The extensive international spreading of mathematical economics from the 1950s on (see Weintraub 2002) found a fertile ground at IMPA (Instituto de Matemática Pura e Aplicada), the Institute of Pure and Applied Mathematics, established in Rio in 1952. From the beginning, IMPA attracted highly qualified mathematicians from Brazil and abroad. Prominent mathematical economics (e.g. C. Azariadis, E. Prescott, H. Sonnenschein, A. Mas-Colell, J. Heckman) visited the institute in the 1980s and 1990s. IMPA has played a key role in the development of the Brazilian community of mathematicians and mathematical economists as part of international networks (see Silva 2004, and especially Assaf 2022, chapter 3).

M.H. Simonsen's (1964) formal discussion of the cash-in-advance constraint, three years before Clower (1967) turned it into a main monetary model, provided a first instance of the impact of IMPA on economic analysis in Brazil. Simonsen (1964) explicitly introduced the cash-in-advance constraint as an inequality in a nonlinear programming problem featuring the Kuhn-Tucker mathematical approach. It represented an attempt to reinterpret the controversy over Don Patinkin's critical assessment of classical monetary theory (Boianovsky 2002; Walsh 2003: 100). Simonsen was trained as an engineer. That was shortly followed by mathematical studies at IMPA in 1955, where he also taught the first course in applied mathematics soon after.

Simonsen's (1964) article, as well as his general mathematical stance in economics displayed as professor of economics at the Vargas Foundation, grew out of his period at IMPA. This is clear in his 1994 book, which collected essays on the philosophy of science, history of mathematics and physics, and history of economics mathematically contemplated. In part because of Simonsen's initial influence, mathematical economics eventually became an important area of graduate teaching and research at IMPA in the 1970s, leading to its further internationalization and several contributions by Brazilian mathematical economists (sometimes based abroad) published in top journals ever since.[10] In the late 1980s, as part of the debates about inertial inflation, Simonsen (1986b, 1988) used game theory to model inertial inflation. He modeled inflation inertia as a consequence of a coordination failure between wage and price setters. Incomes policy can be used to resolve this coordination failure, in the sense of providing information to speed up the location of Nash equilibria by economic agents.

The leading figure concerning the teaching and research of mathematical economics at IMPA has been, since the 1980s, Aloisio Araujo, who, together with J.A. Scheinkman, had finished his master's degree at that institution in 1970. They both left to pursue PhD degrees in the US, and came back to IMPA in 1978 – for a brief period in the case of Scheinkman, who soon resumed his position as professor of economics at Chicago University and later at Princeton University, although he kept coming back for visits to IMPA. The main research topic of IMPA's mathematicians was dynamical systems, which proved to be instrumental when Scheinkman and Benveniste (1979) applied envelope theory to establish important new results for growth and macroeconomic dynamics. Sheinkman's background from IMPA also played a role in his pioneer study of chaotic non-linear systems in the capital market (Scheinkman and LeBaron 1989). Asked about his Brazilian roots, Scheinkman (1999: 285) replied that, although he had a permanent interest in the Brazilian economy, his academic output as an economist had no links with Brazilian issues. He regarded it a "signal of maturity" when "economists are able to do academic work that is not necessarily connected to the economic problems of their country" of origin (see also Blaug and Vane 2003: 739–740).

Araujo's main contributions to mathematical economics have focused on the working of capital and financial markets in general equilibrium, formed by influential papers, e.g., on the role of collateral constraints (Araujo et al. 2002), financial crises and bankruptcy (Araujo 2015), and the notion of homogenous expectations under complete markets (Araujo and Sandroni 1999). Alvaro Sandroni studied with Araujo at IMPA. That was also the case of Marilda Sotomayor and Sergio Werlang, among others. After her solution, with Alvin Roth, of the "Colleges admission problem" as a model of many-to-one matching in two-sided markets (Roth and Sotomayor 1989), Sotomayor joined forces with Roth again in their classic book about processes in which two disjoint groups of agents – e.g. in labor markets – meet and make bilateral transactions (matching) through cooperative games (Roth and Sotomayor 1990). Game theory was also the subject of a couple of well-known papers by Werlang. Dow and Werlang (1994) defined Nash equilibrium for two-person normal-form games in the presence of Knightian uncertainty. Tan and Werlang (1988) provided informational foundations of iteratively undominated strategies and rationalizable strategic behavior in non-cooperative games. Surely, Brazilian contributions to mathematical economics were not restricted to economists connected to IMPA. USP economist Juan Moldau's (1993) demonstration, that the existence of demand functions does not depend on the assumption of strict convexity of preferences, is a case in point.

Uncertainty was also the dominant topic in Cardim de Carvalho's post-Keynesian agenda, but from a distinct perspective altogether. As acknowledged by leading heterodox economists, Brazil has been since the 1980s a center of heterodox – particularly post-Keynesian – economics (see e.g. Chick 2004: 3). Cardim de Carvalho's first exposure to post-Keynesianism took place when he attended the first summer school in Trieste (Italy) in 1981. The year after that, he went to Rutgers University (US) to study with Paul Davidson. Cardim de Carvalho's main theoretical contributions to post-Keynesian economics include the study of the notion of a monetary production entrepreneurial economy, the analysis of decision-making and portfolio-choice under non-probabilistic uncertainty, liquidity preference theory (with attention to banking decisions) and the analysis of the finance-funding circuit (see Oreiro et al. 2020; and also Dymski 2020). Those are found in two books (Carvalho 1992, 2016) and in a number of articles published in the *Journal of Post Keynesian Economics* and the *Cambridge Journal of Economics*, among others. The study of how the economic system deals with uncertainty and expectations may be also found in contributions by other Brazilian economists to the international literature, particularly David Dequech, a former student of Geoff Harcourt in Cambridge. Dequech (1999, 2006, 2013) has approached those issues mainly from the institutionalist point of view.

As a by-product of his agenda, Cardim de Carvalho advanced the scholarship about Keynes (see e.g. Carvalho 2002–2003). Edward Amadeo is another Brazilian economist who contributed significantly to the reinterpretation of Keynes's ideas and their evolution. Amadeo (1989), which arose from his Harvard PhD dissertation, has been regarded by Harcourt (1990) as the definitive account of the transition from the *Treatise on Money* to *The General Theory*.

Mathematical modeling has attracted as well the attention of Brazilian economists off mainstream, who have put forward contributions to post-Keynesian Sraffian and neo-Schumpeterian economics involving formal modeling. The 1970s Brazilian debates on income distribution (see Section 2 earlier) led to the investigation of Piero Sraffa's Cambridge approach as an alternative to marginal productivity theory. Bacha et al. (1977) set out to tackle, through the use of the Sraffian framework, some analytical puzzles faced by David Ricardo and Karl Marx in their respective treatments of income distribution. Contributions to a related tradition established by Luigi Pasinetti may be also found, as illustrated by Teixeira's (1991) generalization of Pasinetti's model for an open economy with direct and indirect taxation and a fraction of the capital stock owned by profit-making public companies. The Pasinettian multi-sector macro-dynamic framework has been deployed to derive the equilibrium growth rate for economies constrained by the balance of payments (Araujo and Lima 2007). Multi-sectorial simulated models have been explored from a neo-Schumpeterian perspective in economies subject to structural change and shocks (Possas and Dweck 2004). The essentially pluralist character of Brazilian economics over the last 50 years or so is clear enough, even if Brazil has not featured in recent histories of "pluralist economics" (see e.g. Sinha and Thomas 2019).

Acknowledgments

I would like to thank Persio Arida, Matheus Assaf, Edmar Bacha, Keanu Telles, Bruna Ingrao, Gilberto Tadeu Lima, Joaquim Andrade, David Dequech, Ana M. Bianchi, John Davis, José Luís Cardoso, Roy Weintraub, Uskali Mäki, Mário Possas, Flávio Versiani, Aloisio Araujo, José Alexandre Scheinkman, Marcelo Neri, Joanilio Teixeira Roberto Silva, André Villela and Samuel Pessoa for helpful discussion of some of the points raised in this chapter. Research funding from CNPq (Brazilian Research Council) and bibliographical support from Guido Erreygers and Paulo R. Almeida are gratefully acknowledged.

Notes

1. See Weintraub 2020 for an account of how that has influenced the historiography of economics.
2. Cf. Cosentino et al.'s (2019) extension of the "creative adaptation" model to the Brazilian history of economic thought as a whole, regardless of the existence of an economic scientific community.
3. However, to his regret, Furtado was not able to put forward, before Lewis (1954), a full-fledged development model of dual economies. As he put it in a 1954 bitter letter to his CEPAL colleague Juan Noyola:

   > I am convinced that if we had not been discouraged to "theorize" at that stage, we would have been able to present two years ago the basic elements of a theory of development along the lines of this important contribution by Lewis. We are left with the fact that . . . we find ourselves today relatively behind and without anything of real significance to show for.
   >
   > (reproduced from Boianovsky 2010: 252)

4. Kafka (1968), also published in an *AER* "Papers and Proceedings" issue, was seemingly the first one. Like Santos (1970), it dealt with economic development issues, but from a distinct perspective altogether.
5. Maria Conceição Tavares (b. 1931) stands out as the most prominent female economist in the history of Latin American economics. Born in Portugal, she immigrated to Brazil in the 1950s and did graduate studies in economics at the CEPAL office in Rio in the early 1960s (see Boianovsky 2000). More recently, the Brazilian mathematical economist Marilda Sotomayor (b. 1944) should be mentioned as an important woman economist (see Section 4 later).
6. For background information about the Brazilian economy and economic policy in that period, see Baer 2008, especially chapter 8 on the *Real* Plan, and Andrade and Silva (1996).
7. The notion of inertial inflation can be found in incipient form in Furtado's (1954: 179; [1959] 1963: 252) concept of "neutral inflation", defined as inflation without any apparent real effects. Neutral inflation occurs if economic agents develop defense mechanisms to prevent the income redistribution required by the introduction of some disequilibrium in the system. As observed by Furtado, it would seem that it would not be difficult to stop a neutral inflation, "since none of the groups would have anything to lose as a result of stabilization." However, if one takes continuous time instead of discrete periods, the "difficulty in stopping the price rise in a neutral inflation process" becomes clear (see Boianovsky 2012).

8. Werner Baer had written a couple of papers with Simonsen about inflation and its effects in the mid-1960s (see Baer and Simonsen 1965; Baer et al. 1965), but that did not lead to a continuous flow of international publications by Simonsen.
9. Arida and Bacha (1987) – who worked out a disequilibrium fix-price model of balance of payments dynamics in order to sort out the historical debates between IMF- and CEPAL-based alternative stabilization frameworks – was another macroeconomic piece by Brazilian authors published in *JDE* in the 1980s.
10. For a list of the number of articles – published by IMPA graduates in *Econometrica, Journal of Economic Theory, Journal of Mathematical Economics, Review of Economic Studies* and *International Economic Review* – see Assaf 2022: 152.

References

Agarwala, A. and S. Singh (eds.). 1958. *The Economics of Underdevelopment*. London: Oxford University Press.

Alcouffe, A. and M. Boianovsky. 2013. Doing monetary economics in the south: Subercaseaux on paper money. *Journal of the History of Economic Thought*. 35: 423–47.

Almeida, H. and M. Bonomo. 2002. Optimal state-dependent rules, credibility, and inflation inertia. *Journal of Monetary Economics*. 49: 1317–36.

Alston, L.J., E. Harris and B. Mueller. 2012. The development of property rights on frontiers: Endowments, norms, and politics. *Journal of Economic History*. 72: 741–70.

Alston, L.J., G.D. Libecap and B. Mueller. 2000. Land reform policies, the sources of violent conflict, and implications for deforestation in the Brazilian Amazon. *Journal of Environmental Economics and Management*. 39: 162–88.

Amadeo, E. 1989. *Keynes's Principle of Effective Demand*. Aldershot: Elgar.

Andrada, A.F.S. and M. Boianovsky. 2020. The political economy of the income distribution controversy in 1970s Brazil: Debating models and data under military rule. *Research in the History of Economic Thought and Methodology*. 38B: 75–94.

Andrade, J. and M.L. Silva. 1996. Brazil's new currency: Origins, development and perspectives of the real. *Revista Brasileira de Economia*. 50: 427–67.

Araujo, A. 2015. General equilibrium, preferences and financial institutions after the crisis. *Economic Theory*. 58: 217–54.

Araujo, A., M. Páscoa and J. Torres-Martinez. 2002. Collateral avoids Ponzi schemes in incomplete markets. *Econometrica*. 70: 1613–38.

Araujo, A. and A. Sandroni. 1999. On the convergence to homogeneous expectations when markets are complete. *Econometrica*. 67: 663–72.

Araujo, R.A. and G.T. Lima. 2007. A structural economic dynamics approach to balance-of-payments constrained growth. *Cambridge Journal of Economics*. 31: 755–74.

Arida, P. 1984. Economic stabilization in Brazil. Working Paper # 149. Washington, DC: Wilson Center.

Arida, P. 1986. Macroeconomic issues for Latin America. *Journal of Development Economics*. 22: 171–208.

Arida, P. 2019. *Persio Arida. Colecão Historia Contada do Banco Central do Brasil*, v. 20. Brasilia: Banco Central do Brasil.

Arida, P. 2022. Money and indexation at the PUC-Rio school: The formative years. Unpublished typescript.

Arida, P. and E.L. Bacha. 1987. Balance of payments: A disequilibrium analysis for semi-industrialized economies. *Journal of Development Economics*. 23: 85–108.

Arida, P. and A. Lara-Resende. 1985. Inertial inflation and monetary reform: Brazil. In *Inflation and Indexation*, ed. by J. Williamson, pp. 27–45. Cambridge, MA: MIT Press for the Institute for International Economics.

Assaf, M. 2022. Tracing mathematical economics: Essays in the history of (Departments of) Economics. Unpublished doctorate dissertation. University of S. Paulo.

Azevedo, F. (ed.). 1955. *As Ciências No Brasil*, 2 vols. São Paulo: Melhoramentos.

Bacha, E.L. 1978. An interpretation of unequal exchange from Prebisch-Singer to Emmanuel. *Journal of Development Economics*. 5: 319–30.

Bacha, E.L. 1988. Moeda, inércia e conflito: Reflexões sobre políticas de estabilização no Brasil. *Pesquisa e Planejamento Econômico*. 18: 1–16.

Bacha, E.L. 1990. A three-gap model of foreign transfers and the GDP growth rate in developing countries. *Journal of Development Economics*. 32: 279–96.

Bacha, E.L. 2003. Brazil's *Plano Real*: A view from the inside. In *Development Economics and Structuralist Macroeconomics: Essays in Honor of Lance Taylor*, ed. by A.K. Dutt and J. Ros, pp. 181–205. Cheltenham: Elgar.

Bacha, E.L. 2018. On the economics of development: A view from Latin America. *PSL Quarterly Review*. 71: 327–49.

Bacha, E.L., D.D. Carneiro and L. Taylor. 1977. Sraffa and classical economics: Fundamental equilibrium relationships. *Metroeconomica*. 29: 39–53.

Bacha, E.L. and L. Taylor. 1971. Foreign exchange shadow prices: A critical evaluation of current theories. *Quarterly Journal of Economics*. 85: 197–224.

Bacha, E.L. and L. Taylor. 1978. Brazilian income distribution in the 1960s: Facts, model results and the controversy. *Journal of Development Studies*. 14: 271–97.

Backhouse, R.E. 2000. Progress in heterodox economics. *Journal of the History of Economic Thought*. 149–55.

Baer, W. 2008. *The Brazilian Economy: Growth and Development*, 6th ed. Boulder, CO: Lynne Rienner.

Baer, W. and I. Kerstenetzky (eds.). 1964. *Inflation and Growth in Latin America*. Homewood, IL: Richard D. Irwin.

Baer, W., I. Kerstenetzky and M.H. Simonsen. 1965. Transportation and inflation: A study of irrational policy making in Brazil. *Economic Development and Cultural Change*. 13: 188–202.

Baer, W. and M.H. Simonsen. 1965. Profit illusion and policy-making in inflationary Brazil. *Oxford Economic Papers*. 17: 279–90.

Ball, L. 1994. Credible disinflation with staggered price setting. *American Economic Review*. 84: 282–9.

Barcena, A. and A. Prado (eds.). 2015. *Neoestructuralismo y corrientes heterodoxas en América Latina y el Caribe a inicios del siglo XXI*. Santiago: CEPAL.

Basalla, G. 1967. The spread of Western science. *Science*. 156: 611–22.

Blaug, M. 1999. *Who's Who in Economics*, 3rd ed. Cheltenham: Elgar.

Blaug, M. and H. Vane. 2003. *Who's Who in Economics*, 4th ed. Cheltenham: Elgar.

Boianovsky, M. 2000. Maria da Conceição Tavares (b. 1931). In *A Biographical Dictionary of Women Economists*, ed. by R.W. Dimand, M.A. Dimand and E. Forget, pp. 415–22. Cheltenham: Elgar.

Boianovsky, M. 2002. Simonsen and the early history of the cash-in-advance constraint. *European Journal of the History of Economic Thought*. 9: 57–71.

Boianovsky, M. 2008a. Furtado, Celso (1920–2004). In *The New Palgrave Dictionary of Economics*, ed. by S.N. Durlauf and L.E. Blume, 2nd ed., pp. 2323–7. London: Palgrave Macmillan.

Boianovsky, M. 2008b. Simonsen, Mario Henrique (1935–1997). In *The New Palgrave Dictionary of Economics*, ed. by S.N. Durlauf and L.E. Blume, 2nd ed., pp. 5911–3. London: Palgrave Macmillan.

Boianovsky, M. 2010. A view from the tropics: Celso Furtado and the theory of economic development in the 1950s. *History of Political Economy*. 42: 221–66.

Boianovsky, M. 2012. Celso Furtado and the structuralist-monetarist debate on economic stabilization in Latin America. *History of Political Economy*. 44: 277–330.

Boianovsky, M. 2013. Friedrich list and the economic fate of tropical countries. *History of Political Economy*. 45: 647–91.

Boianovsky, M. 2015. Between Lévi-Strauss and Braudel: Furtado and the historical-structural method in Latin American political economy. *Journal of Economic Methodology*. 22: 413–38.

Boianovsky, M. 2020. The Brazilian connection in Milton Friedman's 1967 presidential address and 1976 nobel lecture. *History of Political Economy*. 52: 367–96.

Boianovsky, M. 2021. Economists, scientific communities and pandemics: An exploratory study of Brazil (1918–2020). *EconomiA*. 22: 1–18.

Boianovsky, M. 2022. Lucas' expectational equilibrium, price rigidity, and descriptive realism. *Journal of Economic Methodology*. 29: 66–85.

Bresser-Pereira, L.C. 2010. *Globalization and Competition: Why Some Emergent Countries Succeed While Others Fall Behind*. Cambridge: Cambridge University Press.

Bresser-Pereira, L.C. 2020. New developmentalism: Development macroeconomics for middle-income countries. *Cambridge Journal of Economics*. 44: 629–46.

Bresser-Pereira, L.C. and Y. Nakano. 1987. *The Theory of Inertial Inflation*, Tr. by C. Reeks. Boulder, CO: Linner Ryenner.

Brito, A., M. Fogel and C.L. Kerstenetzky. 2017. The contribution of minimum wage valorization policy to the decline in household income inequality in Brazil: A decomposition approach. *Journal of Post Keynesian Economics*. 40: 540–75.

Bruno, M. 1989. Theoretical developments in the light of macroeconomic policy and empirical research. *Scandinavian Journal of Economics*. 91: 307–33.

Cardoso, E. and R. Dornbusch. 1987. Brazil's tropical plan. *American Economic Review*. 77: 288–92.

Cardoso, F.H. 1977. The consumption of dependency theory in the United States. *Latin American Research Review*. 12: 7–24.

Cardoso, F.H. and E. Faletto. 1969. *Dependencia y desarrollo en América Latina: ensayo de interpretación sociológica*. Mexico City: Siglo Ventiuno.

Cardoso, F.H. and E. Faletto. 1979. *Dependency and Development in Latin America*, Tr. by M. Urquidi of Cardoso and Faletto 1969. Berkeley, CA: University of California Press.

Cardoso, J.L. 2003. The international diffusion of economic thought. In *A Companion to the History of Economic Thought*, ed. by W.J. Samuels, J.E. Biddle and J.B. Davis, pp. 622–33. Oxford: Blackwell.

Cardoso, J.L. 2017. Circulating economic ideas: Adaptation, appropriation, translation. In *The Political Economy of Latin American Independence*, ed. by A.M. Cunha and C.E. Suprinyak, pp. 32–40. London: Routledge.

Carneiro, A.M., et al. 2020. Diáspora brasileira de ciência, tecnologia e inovação: Panorama, iniciativas auto-organizadas e políticas de engajamento. *Idéias*. 11: 1–29.

Carvalho, A.R. 2019. A second-generation structuralist transformation problem: The rise of the inertial inflation hypothesis. *Journal of the History of Economic Thought*. 41: 47–75.

Carvalho, F.C. 1992. *Mr. Keynes and the Post Keynesians: Principles of Macroeconomics for a Monetary Production Economy*. Aldershot: Elgar.

Carvalho, F.C. 2002–2003. Decision-making under uncertainty as drama: Keynesian and Schaklean themes in three of Shakespeare's tragedies. *Journal of Post Keynesian Economics*. 25: 189–218.

Carvalho, F.C. 2016. *Liquidity Preference and Monetary Economics*. London: Routledge.

Chick, V. 2004. On open systems. *Brazilian Journal of Political Economy*. 24: 3–17.

Chopra, A. 1985. The speed of adjustment of the inflation rate in developing countries: A study of inertia. *IMF Staff Papers*. 32: 693–733.

Clower, R.W. 1967. A reconsideration of the microfoundations of monetary theory. *Western Economic Journal*. 6: 1–8.

Coats, A.W. (ed.). 1996. *The Post-1945 Internationalization of Economics. Annual Supplement to Vol. 28 of History of Political Economy*. Durham, NC: Duke University Press.

Consentino, D.V., R.P. Silva and T. Gambi. 2019. Existe um pensamento econômico brasileiro? In *História do Pensamento Econômico – Pensamento Econômico Brasileiro*, pp. 59–94. Niterói: Eduff; Sào Paulo: Hucitec.

Dequech, D. 1999. Expectations and confidence under uncertainty. *Journal of Post Keynesian Economics*. 21: 415–30.

Dequech, D. 2006. The new institutional economics and the theory of behavior under uncertainty. *Journal of Economic Behavior and Organization*. 59: 109–31.

Dequech, D. 2013. Economic institutions: Explanations for conformity and room for deviations. *Journal of Institutional Economics*. 9: 81–108.

Dequech, D. 2018. Applying the concept of mainstream economics outside the United States: General remarks and the case of Brazil as an example of the institutionalization of pluralism. *Journal of Economic Issues*. 52: 904–24.

Dornbusch, R. 1985. Comments. In ed. By J. Williamson, pp. 45–55. Cambridge, MA: MIT Press.

Dornbusch, R. 1993. *Stabilization, Debt and Reform: Policy Analysis for Developing Countries*. New York: Harvester Wheatsheaf.

Dornbusch, R. 1997. Brazil's incomplete stabilization and reform. *Brookings Papers on Economic Activity*. # 1: 367–404.

Dornbusch, R. and M.H. Simonsen (eds.). 1983. *Inflation, Debt, and Indexation*. Cambridge, MA: MIT Press.

Dornbusch, R. and M.H. Simonsen. 1988. Inflation stabilization: The role of income policies and monetization. In *Exchange Rates and Inflation*, ed. by R. Dornbusch. Cambridge, MA: MIT Press.

Dow, J. and S. Werlang. 1994. Nash equilibrium under Knightian uncertainty: Breaking down backward induction. *Journal of Economic Theory*. 64: 305–24.

Dymski, G. 2020. Mr. Carvalho and the post Keynesians: Scholar, theorist, writer. *Revista de Economia Contemporânea*. 24: 1–25.

Ekerman, R. 1989. A comunidade de economistas do Brasil: dos anos 50 aos dias de hoje. *Revista Brasileira de Economia*. 43: 113–38.

Faria, J.R. 2005. Is there a trade-off between domestic and international publications? *Journal of Socio-Economics*. 34: 269–80.

Fernandez, R.G. and C.E. Suprinyak. 2018. Creating academic economics in Brazil: The Ford Foundation and the beginnings of Anpec. *EconomiA*. 19: 314–29.

Fischer, S. 1977a. Wage indexation and macroeconomic stability. *Carnegie-Rochester Conference Series on Public Policy*. 5: 107–47.

Fischer, S. 1977b. Long-term contracts, rational expectations, and the optimal money supply rule. *Journal of Political Economy*. 85: 191–205.

Fischer, S., R. Sahay and C. Végh. 2002. Modern hyper – and high inflations. *Journal of Economic Literature*. 40: 837–80.
Fishlow, A. 1972. Brazilian size distribution of income. *American Economic Review*. 62: 391–402.
Fourcade, M. 2006. The construction of a global profession: The transnationalization of economics. *American Journal of Sociology*. 112: 145–94.
Franco, G.B. 1987. The retenmark miracle. *Rivista di Storia Economica*. 4: 96–117.
Franco, G.B. 1990. Fiscal reforms and stabilization: Four hyperinflation cases examined. *Economic Journal*. 100: 176–87.
Friedman, M. 1974. Monetary correction: A proposal for escalator clauses to reduce the costs of ending inflation. Institute of Economic Affairs Occasional Paper # 41.
Friedman, M. and R. Friedman. 1998. *Two Lucky People – Memoirs*. Chicago: University of Chicago Press.
Furtado, C. 1952. Formação de capital e desenvolvimento econômico. *Revista Brasileira de Economia*. 6(3): 7–46.
Furtado, C. [1952] 1954. Capital formation and economic development, Tr. by J. Cairncross of Furtado (1952). International Economic Papers. # 4, pp. 124–44 (Reprinted in A. Agarwala and S. Singh (eds) 1958, pp. 309–37).
Furtado, C. 1954. *A Economia Brasileira* (The Brazilian Economy). Rio: A Noite.
Furtado, C. 1959. *Formação Econômica do Brasil*. Rio: Fundo de Cultura.
Furtado, C. 1961. *Desenvolvimento e Subdesenvolvimento*. Rio: Fundo de Cultura.
Furtado, C. [1959] 1963. *The Economic Growth of Brazil – A Survey from Colonial to Modern Times*, Tr. by R. Aguiar and E. Drysdale of Furtado 1959. Berkeley, CA: University of California Press.
Furtado, C. [1961] 1964. *Development and Underdevelopment – A Structuralist View of the Problems of Developed & Underdeveloped Countries*, Tr. by R. Aguiar and E. Drysdale of chapters 1–5 of C. Furtado 1961. Berkeley, CA: University of California Press.
Furtado, C. 1985. *A Fantasia Organizada* (Organized Fantasy). Rio: Paz e Terra.
Furtado, C. 1987a. Underdevelopment: To Conform or to Reform. In *Pioneers in Development – Second Series*, ed. by G. Meier, pp. 205–27. New York: Oxford University Press for the World Bank.
Furtado, C. 1987b. *La Fantaisie Organisée*, Tr. by E. Bailby of C. Furtado 1985. Paris: Publisud.
Furtado, C. [1957] 2008. O desenvolvimento recente da economia venezuelana (exposição de alguns problemas). In *Ensaios sobre a Venezuela: subdesenvolvimento com abundância de divisas*. Rio: Contraponto and Centro Celso Furtado.
Gapinsky, J. 1988. Review of Bresser-Pereira and Nakano (1987). *Journal of Economic Literature*. 26: 1191–3.
Gerschenkron, A. 1952. Economic backwardness in historical perspective. In *The Progress of Underdeveloped Areas*, ed. by B. Hoselitz, pp. 3–29. Chicago, IL: Chicago University Press.
Gray, J.A. 1976. Wage indexation – A macroeconomic approach. *Journal of Monetary Economics*. 2: 221–35.
Haddad, P. 1981. Brazil: Economists in a bureaucratic-authoritarian system. *History of Political Economy*. 13: 656–80.
Harcourt, G.C. 1990. Review of Amadeo (1989). *Economic Journal*. 100: 295–7.
Hicks, J. 1967. Monetary theory and history – An attempt at perspective. In *Critical Essays in Monetary Theory*, pp. 155–73. Oxford: Clarendon Press.
Hirschman, A.O. 1981. The rise and decline of development economics. In *Essays in Trespassing*, pp. 1–24. Cambridge: Cambridge University Press.

Hoffmann, R. 2018. Changes in income distribution in Brazil. In *The Oxford Handbook of the Brazilian Economy*, ed. by E. Amann, C. Azzoni and W. Baer, chapter 22. Oxford: Oxford University Press.

Hugon, P. 1955. A economia política no Brasil. In *As Ciências No Brasil*, ed. by F. Azevedo, vol. 2, pp. 299–352. São Paulo: Melhoramentos.

Kafka, A. 1968. International liquidity: Its present relevance to the less developed countries. *American Economic Review*. 58: 596–603.

Kopper, M. 2020. Measuring the middle: Technopolitics and the making of Brazil's new middle class. *History of Political Economy*. 52: 561–87.

Kuhn, T. 1962. *The Structure of Scientific Revolutions*. Chicago, IL: The University of Chicago Press.

Langoni, C.G. 1975. Review of income distribution data: Brazil. Woodrow Wilson School, Princeton University. Discussion Paper # 60.

Lewis, W.A. 1954. Economic development with unlimited supplies of labor. *Manchester School*. 22: 139–91.

Lopes, F.L. 1983. Stabilization policy, rational expectations, and staggared real wage contracts. *Revista de Econometria*. 3: 43–62.

Lopes, F.L. 1984. Inflação inercial, hiperinflação e desinflação: notas e conjecturas. Working Paper # 77. Department of Economics, PUC-Rio.

Lopes, F.L. 1999. Francisco Lopes. In *Conversas com economistas brasileiros II*, ed. by G. Mantega and J.M. Rego, pp. 333–54. S. Paulo: Editora 34.

Lopes, F.L. and E.L. Bacha. 1983. Inflation, growth and wage policy: A Brazilian perspective. *Journal of Development Economics*. 13: 1–20.

Lopes, F.L. and J. Williamson. 1980. A teoria da indexação consistente. *Estudos Econômicos*. 10: 61–99.

Loureiro, M.R. and G.T. Lima. 1996. Searching for the modern times: The internationalization of economics in Brazil. *Research in the History of Economic Thought and Methodology*. 14: 69–89.

Love, J. 1996. *Crafting the Third World: Theorizing Underdevelopment in Rumania and Brazil*. Stanford, CA: Stanford University Press.

MacLeod, R. 2000. Introduction. *Osiris*. 15: 1–13.

Mäki, U. 1996. Economic thought on the outskirts: Toward a historiographical framework for studying intellectual peripheries. *Research in the History of Economic Thought and Economic Methodology*. 14: 307–23.

Marini, R.M. 1972. Brazilian sub-imperialism. *Monthly Review*. 23: 14–24.

Mearman, A., S. Berger and D. Guizzo. 2019. *What Is Heterodox Economics? Conversations with Leading Economists*. London: Routledge.

Medina, E. and M. Carey. 2020. Conclusion: New narratives of technology, expertise and environment in Latin America: The Cold War and beyond. In *Itineraries of Expertise: Science, Technology, and Environment in Latin America,* ed. by A. Chastain and T. Lorek. Pittsburgh: University of Pittsburgh Press.

Modigliani, F. and T. Padoa-Schioppa. 1978. The management of an open economy with "100% plus" wage indexation. Princeton University. *Essays in International Finance #* 130.

Moldau, J. 1993. A model of choice where choice is determined by an ordered set of irreducible criteria. *Journal of Economic Theory*. 60: 354–77.

Nadiri, M.I. and A.C. Pastore (eds.). 1977. Indexation: The Brazilian experience. *Explorations in Economic Research*. 4(1).

Naritomi, J., R. R. Soares and J.J. Assunção. 2012. Institutional development and colonial heritage within Brazil. *Journal of Economic History*. 72: 393–422.

Neri, M. 2015. Brazil's new middle classes: The bright side of the poor. In *Latin American Emerging Middle Classes*, ed. by J. Dayton, pp. 70–100. London: Palgrave Macmillan.

Neri, M. 2021. Brazil: What are the main drivers of income distribution changes in the new millennium? In *Inequality in the Developing World*, ed. by C. Gradín, M. Leibbrandt and F. Tarp, pp. 109–32. Oxford: Oxford University Press.

Oreiro, J.L., L. F. de Paula and J.P. Machado. 2020. Liquidity preference, capital accumulation and investment financing: Fernando Cardim de Carvalho's contributions to the post Keynesian paradigm. *Review of Political Economy*. 32: 121–39.

Pestre, D. 2012. Concluding remarks. Debates in transnational and science studies: A defense and illustration of the virtues of intellectual tolerance. *British Journal for the History of Science*. 45: 425–442.

Polanyi, M. 1962. The Republic of Science – Its Political and Economic Theory. *Minerva*. 1: 54–73.

Possas, M. and E. Dweck. 2004. A multisectoral micro-macrodynamic model. *EconomiA*. 5: 1–43.

Reis, E. and S. Margulis. 1991. Options for slowing Amazon jungle clearing. In *Global Warming: Economic Policy Responses*, ed. by R. Dornbusch and J. Poterba, pp. 335–74. Cambridge, MA: MIT Press.

Rodriguez, J. 2013. Beyond prejudice and pride – The human sciences in nineteenth– and twentieth-century Latin America. *Isis*. 104: 807–17.

Romer, D. 1996. *Advanced Macroeconomics*. New York: McGraw-Hill.

Rostow, W.W. 1960. *Stages of Economic Growth*. Cambridge: Cambridge University Press.

Roth, A. and M. Sotomayor. 1989. The college admissions problem revisited. *Econometrica*. 57: 559–70.

Roth, A. and M. Sotomayor. 1990. *Two-sided Matching: A Study in Game-theoretic Modeling and Analysis*. Cambridge: Cambridge University Press.

Santos, T. dos. 1970. The structure of dependence. *American Economic Review*. 60: 231–36.

Sargent, T. 1982. The end of four big inflations. In *Inflation: Causes and Effects*, ed. by R. E. Hall, pp. 41–98. Chicago, IL: University of Chicago Press for NBER.

Sargent, T. 2013. *Rational Expectations and Inflation*, 3rd ed. Princeton, NJ: Princeton University Press.

Sargent, T., N. Williams and T. Zha. 2009. The conquest of South American inflation. *Journal of Political Economy*. 117: 211–56.

Scheinkman, J.A. 1999. José A. Scheinkman. In *Conversas com economistas brasileiros II*, ed. by G. Mantega and J.M. Rego, pp. 281–303. S. Paulo: Editora 34.

Scheinkman, J.A. and L. Benveniste. 1979. On the differentiability of the value function in dynamic models of economics. *Econometrica*. 47: 727–32.

Scheinkman, J.A. and B. LeBaron. 1989. Nonlinear dynamics and stock returns. *Journal of Business*. 62: 311–37.

Schumpeter, J.A. 1954. *History of Economic Analysis*. New York: Oxford University Press.

Schwartzman, S. 1976. Struggling to be born: The scientific community in Brazil. *Minerva*. 16: 545–80.

Schwartzman, S. 1979. *Formação da comunidade científica no Brasil*. Rio: FINEP.

Silva, C.M. 2004. A construção de um instituto de pesquisas matemáticas nos trópicos: o IMPA. *Revista Brasileira de História da Matemática*. 4: 37–67.

Simonsen, M.H. 1964. A lei de Say e o efeito liquidez real. *Revista Brasileira de Economia*. 18: 41–66.

Simonsen, M.H. 1970. *Inflação: gradualismo versus tratamento de choque*. Rio: Apec.

Simonsen, M.H. 1983. Indexation: Current theory and the Brazilian experience. In *Inflation, Debt, and Indexation*, ed. by R. Dornbusch and M.H. Simonsen, pp. 99–132. Cambridge, MA: MIT Press

Simonsen, M.H. 1986a. Cinqüenta anos da *Teoria Geral do Emprego*. *Revista Brasileira de Economia*. 40: 301–34.

Simonsen, M.H. 1986b. Rational expectations, income policies and game theory. *Revista de Econometria*. 6: 7–46.

Simonsen, M.H. 1988. Rational expectations, game theory and inflation inertia. In *The Economy as an Evolving Complex System*, ed. by P.W. Anderson, K.J. Arrow and D. Pines, vol. 5. New York: Addison-Wesley.

Sinha, A. and A.M. Thomas (eds.). 2019. *Pluralist Economics and Its History*. London: Routledge.

Souza, P.H.F. 2018. A history of inequality: Top incomes in Brazil, 1926–2015. *Research in Social Stratification and Mobility*. 57: 33–45.

Spengler, J.J. 1968. Economics: its history, themes, approaches. *Journal of Economic Issues*. 2: 5–30.

Stepan, N. 1976. *Beginnings of Brazilian Science – Oswaldo Cruz, Medical Research and Policy, 1890–1920*. New York: Science History Publications.

Subercaseaux, G. 1912. *El Papel Moneda*. Santiago: Imprenta Cervantes.

Tan, T. and S. Werlang. 1988. The Bayesian foundations of solution concepts of games. *Journal of Economic Theory*. 45: 370–91.

Tavares, M.C. and J. Serra. 1973. Beyond stagnation: A discussion on the nature of recent developments in Brazil. In *Latin America: From Dependence to Revolution*, ed. by J. Petras. New York: Wiley & Sons.

Taylor, J.B. 1979. Estimation and control of a macroeconomic model with rational expectations. *Econometrica*. 47: 1267–86.

Taylor, L. and E. Bacha. 1976. The unequalizing spiral: A first growth model for Belindia. *Quarterly Journal of Economics*. 90: 197–218.

Teixeira, J.R. 1991. The Kaldor-Pasinetti process reconsidered. *Metroeconomica*. 42: 257–67.

The Royal Society. 2011. *Knowledge, Networks and Nations: Global Scientific Collaboration in the 21st Century*. London: The Royal Society.

Tobin, J. 1980a. Are new classical models plausible enough to guide policy? *Journal of Money, Credit and Banking*. 12: 788–99.

Tobin, J. 1980b. Stabilization policy ten years after after. *Brookings Papers on Economic Activity*. # 1: 19–71.

Tobin, J. 1981. Diagnosing inflation: A taxonomy. In *Development in an Inflationary World*, ed. by M.J. Flanders and A. Razin, pp. 19–30. New York: Academic Press.

Turchetti, S., N. Herran and S. Boudia. 2012. Introduction: Have we ever been 'transnational'? Towards a history of science across and beyond borders. *British Journal for the History of Science*. 45: 319–36.

Van Noorden, R. 2012. Science on the move. *Nature*. # 490: 326–29.

Versiani, F.R. 1997. A Anpec aos 25 anos: passado e futuro. *Revista Anpec*. 1: 219–59.

Wallerstein, I.M. 1974, 1980 and 1989. *The Modern World-system*, 3 vols. New York: Academic Press.

Walsh, C.E. 2003. *Monetary Theory and Policy*, 2nd ed. Cambridge, MA: MIT Press.

Weintraub, E.R. 2002. *How Economics Became a Mathematical Science*. Durham, NC: Duke University Press.

Weintraub, E.R. 2007. Economic science wars. *Journal of the History of Economic Thought*. 29: 267–82.

Weintraub, E.R. 2020. Science studies and economics: An informal history. SSRN Working Paper # 3575650.

Williamson, J. (ed.). 1985. *Inflation and Indexation – Argentina, Brazil, and Israel*. Cambridge, MA: MIT Press for the Institute for International Economics.

Williamson, J. 1994. The analysis of inflation stabilization. *Journal of International and Comparative Economics*. 3: 65–72.

Williamson, J. 1996. Comments. In *The Post-1945 Internationalization of Economics. Annual Supplement to Vol. 28 of History of Political Economy*, ed. by A.W. Coats, pp. 364–68. Durham, NC: Duke University Press.

Williamson, J. 2005. The Washington Consensus as policy prescription for development. In *Development Challenges in the 1990s*, ed. by T. Besley and R. Zagha, pp. 31–53. Washington, DC: World Bank and Oxford University Press.

Woodford, M. 2003. *Interest and Prices: Foundations of a Theory of Monetary Policy*. Princeton, NJ: Princeton University Press.

Part 2

Colonial and early post-colonial periods

3 Sugar, slaves and gold

The political economy of the Portuguese colonial empire in the 17th and 18th centuries*

José Luís Cardoso

Introduction

Throughout the two centuries of intense colonial exploitation analysed in this chapter, Brazil was arguably the jewel of the Portuguese empire.

It all started with navigator Pedro Álvares Cabral's exploratory voyage in 1500, which always raised doubts about the deliberate or accidental character of such a pronounced detour from the Cape of Good Hope route when he was sailing towards the riches of India. Whether by chance or with a programmed intention, there is no doubt that the approach to Porto Seguro proved to be providential. As they were located to the east of the meridian that set the boundaries for sharing the new worlds discovered by the Portuguese and the Spanish, defined by the famous 1494 Treaty of Tordesillas, the inhabited lands that the Portuguese found could be claimed for their sphere of influence.

The new territory was not readily appropriated in the early 16th century, except for the coastal exploitation of dyewood forests (Furtado 2001, 61–76). The Portuguese empire was too centred on the pepper and spice route in the East. All efforts to find and maintain safe routes were directed towards the Indian Ocean. However, the conquest and colonisation of the Brazilian territory and the exploitation of its productive resources – previously controlled by Indian tribes – intensified from 1580 onwards. Territorial expansion meant moving discontinuous borders in distant areas that extended to increasingly broader horizons, far beyond the limits established by the Treaty of Tordesillas.[1]

The expeditions in search of wealth could not hide the difficulties of adapting to a hostile environment of wetlands, forests and mountains that were difficult to overcome. Settlement was mostly effective in the immense coastal strip where urban centres that were relatively distant from each other were established (Belém, Recife, Salvador, Rio de Janeiro, Santos). The newly conquered lands were granted by the crown to *donatários* (i.e., the recipients of a territory portion), who could dispose of them under *sesmaria* (a system that regulated land distribution for agricultural purposes), thus creating favourable conditions for the settlement of Portuguese coming from the kingdom.

It was from the late 16th century that sugar, originally from Madeira, gradually became relevant as the main product of the Brazilian colonial export

DOI: 10.4324/9781003185871-5

economy, attracting a large number of settlers, especially in the northeast region, polarised by the cities of Recife and Salvador. Sugar production in Brazil was not a monoculture, as was the case in the French and Spanish colonies of the Antilles. In fact, tobacco and wood (for construction and furniture) production and cattle raising for leather production were a regular feature in the colonial market and in re-exports, even though they were never as strategically important as sugar.

Sugar cultivation and production in *engenhos* (mills) mobilised the use of indigenous slave labour and triggered a brutal extension of the slave trade from the West African coasts. Besides the technical requirements of agricultural work in sugar cane plantations, the technological requirements of the factories that guaranteed the final product, the capital available for investment in machinery and buildings and the ability to organise and manage *engenhos*, a massive labour force from the African slave trade was essential. There is no doubt that the economy of colonial Brazil would not have stood a chance without slave labour force. Between 1570 and 1670, about 400,000 African slaves were brought to Brazil by crown agents and private traffickers (Mauro 1983, 204).

In 1629, there was a total of 350 *engenhos* in all the captaincies in Brazil, which guaranteed a production between 15,000 and 22,000 tonnes per year (Schwartz 1998a, 216). Despite price variations, which were mainly due to changes in demand in the international market in the 1680s and 1690s, the early 17th century saw a relatively downward trend in the price of sugar and a fall in re-exports. The shift in the colonial economy due to the discovery of gold partly accounts for the phenomenon.

Brazil's riches were also disputed by other European nations (especially France and the Netherlands), which the Portuguese managed to divert, with greater or lesser difficulty. Nonetheless, for about 25 years, between 1630 and 1654, as a consequence of the conflicts between European powers and at a time when the Portuguese crown's own power was limited by the conditions of the Iberian Union and the Restoration wars, the region of Pernambuco and the Northeast was under Dutch domination and the powerful interests of the West India Company. Brazil's natural resources made it desirable to conquer a territory that supplied raw materials and colonial products for which there was increasing demand in the international market.

The discovery of gold in the late 17th century spelled the end of social stability and the predictability of slow changes in a colonial economy based on the exploitation of land and livestock, punctuated by sugar mills. It caused not only a change in the colonial production hub from the captaincies of Bahia, Recife and Pernambuco to the Minas Gerais region, but also a clear change in the nature of the economic relations between settlers, indigenous people, and slaves and in the flow of capital investments and tax revenues. The move of the capital of the Viceroyalty of Brazil from Salvador to Rio de Janeiro in 1763 was a clear sign of changes in an administrative framework that ensured greater proximity to the main source of wealth, whose port of departure was Rio de Janeiro itself.

The gold mining crisis that occurred during the period of the Marquis of Pombal's governance in the 1760s and 1770s naturally led to a change in colonial policy dynamics. Institutional procedures for capturing tax revenues were strengthened, and the organisation of market circuits that came under the leadership of monopoly trading companies, following a typical mercantilist blueprint, was improved. The greater rationality established by governance practices influenced by administration and police doctrines, which were largely dependent on cameral sciences, made it possible to find an antidote to the fall in income caused by the scarcity of gold (Cunha 2010).

In keeping with the enlightened mercantilism policies initiated by the Marquis of Pombal, the governmental actions of Martinho de Melo e Castro and Dom. Rodrigo de Sousa Coutinho (the ministers of the navy and overseas domains between 1770–1795 and 1796–1801, respectively) led to a new look on Brazil, no longer merely as a territory for extracting conventional wealth, but as a dynamic colonial space open to innovative scientific knowledge. The exhaustive survey of productive capacities and potentialities, encouraged by the promotion of philosophical voyages and the searching of new products designed to be used as raw materials for the kingdom's manufactures (namely in textiles and dyeing), effectively prolonged its status as the jewel of the crown, which seemed to have been compromised by the decrease in gold mining.

However, the effort to adapt Brazilian colonial products to a new market organisation and a different imperial rationality was no longer possible from 1808, when the seat of the Portuguese monarchy was transferred to Rio de Janeiro due to the invasion of the country by French troops. Portugal was then forced to allow the access of the powerful English merchant navy to Brazilian ports, thus putting an end to the colonial exclusive regime that had seen only a few short, irrelevant intermittences.

The historical framework that has been briefly presented here enables us to identify the issues that are at the background for the analysis carried out by protagonists whose perspective falls within the scope of the history of economic thought.[2]

Territory, natural resources, capital and investment, slave labour, goods, prices, currency, international competition, tax revenue, productive innovations, colonial pact: it is from the reflection on these themes that some ideas on the way in which production hubs and exchange circuits were established are presented. At a time when economic discourse was yet to be a standardised conceptual language, it is from the description of everyday economic and financial practices that the emergence of a new way of capturing reality may be understood. It is also from political intervention purposes and projects which affect economic and financial practices that the scope of measures designed to contribute to the improvement of the relations between men and with the surrounding environment may be understood. To a large extent, the formation of economic ideas in colonial Brazil stemmed from the need to find explanations and solutions to improve the exploitation of productive resources and slave labour.

In the next sections of this chapter, I shall analyse the contributions made by authors who were either born in Brazil or lived in Brazil for a long time, and for whom Brazil's economic issues were the main source of their intellectual and political concerns. Authors who did not dedicate special attention to reflecting on Brazil-related issues in the context of the Portuguese empire during the period under analysis will not be mentioned.[3]

António Vieira: preaching the benefits of trade

From the late 1640s, after the end of the Iberian Union, the restored Portuguese crown was able to gradually re-establish control of sugar production and exports and supplant the Dutch presence in the Pernambuco region. This was boosted by the establishment of the General Trade Company of Brazil in March 1649, which was based on a contract between the crown and Lisbon- and Porto-based merchants, who subsequently were granted the monopoly of wine, flour, olive oil and cod transport and commercialisation in Brazil, as well as exclusive rights to the commercialisation of Brazilian products in mainland Portugal, especially sugar, tobacco and dyewood. The crown thus obtained funding for the maritime defence of regular transport organised according to a fleet system at certain times of the year, and particularly important fiscal gains at a time when military expenditure in the Restoration wars required negotiating financing solutions with the merchant-bankers and businessmen who participated in the capital of the Company (Smith 1974).

The Company of Brazil included the participation of New Christian merchants, whose capital was used to boost commercial activities in the Portuguese Atlantic empire. They were partly drawn by the benefits resulting from the repeal of the legislation that allowed their assets to be confiscated by the Inquisition. Their expectation of the high profits obtained through the exclusive trade of products for which there was much demand on both sides of the Atlantic market was reason enough for their involvement in the Company, which greatly benefited from their skilful business practices.

New Christians were not the only capitalists interested in investing their capital in the Company. Lisbon- and Porto-based contractors and Old Christian businessmen joined in, lured by the profits provided by this new type of mercantile societies, which had proven a success in London and Amsterdam. The fearsome competition of the Dutch West India Company in Pernambuco was an additional incentive for the Company's raising of capital.

The doctrinal framework of the virtues of the Company of Brazil had the committed patronage of Jesuit Father António Vieira (1608–1697), one of the core figures of political, social and religious thought in the Portuguese empire in the second half of the 17th century. Vieira spent more than half of his long life in Brazil. The scope of his missionary action and his defence of the rights of indigenous peoples is widely recognised. He was a fierce fighter against the enslavement of Brazilian Indians, even though no such effort was made to defend the liberation of African slaves. One of his multiple facets was his contribution to a reflection on the economic issues of the kingdom and the empire through a consistent view on the mobilising virtues of trade.

The main motivation behind his economic writings was the social integration of New Christians and all those who, because of religious persecution, were prevented from living or enjoying basic civil rights in their country of origin. In his treatment of this delicate political problem, António Vieira ended up revealing his more general concerns with the factors and circumstances that would determine the economic restoration of the country, in the context of the re-establishment of the independence of the Portuguese monarchy in 1640, which had brought an end to 60 years of dynastic union with Spain.

The picture of the internal situation of the restored kingdom was painted in shades that were far too grey. The available financial resources, which had been amassed through the application of extraordinary fiscal measures, were not sufficient to meet the demands of a possible protracted war. Therefore, the country lacked the structures and means considered adequate for the defence of the territory.

The possibility of mobilising internal resources to counteract negative expectations about the future is another idea that was conceived in decidedly discouraging tones. The basic problem lay in the fact that, due to the shortage of revenue from production and trade activities, the various sources of taxation would inevitably be exhausted, which made the prospect of applying the corrective monetary policies that had been implemented in the past seem unappetising. In other words, the increase in the supply of metallic money or the decrease in its face value would cause inflationary effects that it would be hard for a population with low revenues to bear, particularly when productivity was low and there was no capacity to reverse the country's disadvantageous balance of trade. Furthermore, the crown could not meet the financial commitments arising from the creation of internal debt, which was further exacerbated by the need to channel material and human resources into the continued support of burdensome military campaigns.

In keeping with his diagnosis, in which the main emphasis is given to the scarcity or absence of the capital that is indispensable for financing production, trade and, above all, defence, António Vieira considers the circumstance that "throughout all the kingdoms and provinces of Europe are spread Portuguese merchants in great number, men of extremely great resources, who have in their hands much of the world's trade and wealth" (Vieira 1643, 8) and proposes that conditions and guarantees should be created to encourage these men to return to Portugal and set up business.

Vieira's insistent call for public recognition of the legitimacy and importance of the activities of New Christians must be seen within the much broader context of his concern for the social rehabilitation of mercantile activities. His benevolence towards Jews is also the result of a favourable attitude towards the ennoblement of merchants and businessmen in general and, even more importantly, the result of a premise by which trade in general, and especially colonial trade, are interpreted as unifying elements of economic activity as a whole.

Even though António Vieira does not undertake a particularly profound analysis of the advantages of a positive balance of trade, his writing nonetheless reveals an acceptance and a full awareness of the importance of such a requirement. In fact, the author considers that "Portugal cannot preserve itself without much money, and for there to be any, there is no more efficient means than that of trade" (*ibid*, 14). This amounts to saying that it would be necessary to guarantee the flow and accumulation of the money resulting from a profitable commercial activity. Further indication of his vision of the driving force of mercantile capital (or its representative sign) is to be found in his proposal for the creation of the aforementioned Trade Company of Brazil, which was conceived by Vieira as an instrument for both opposing the commercial predominance played by the Dutch West India Company and attracting the capital of the New Christian merchants.

Yet further proof of the importance that Vieira attributes to the mercantile capital brought into play by New Christians is to be found, on the one hand, in his allusions to an easier access to credit on the part of most Portuguese merchants and, on the other hand, in the concrete proposal which he makes for the creation of a bank

> similar to that of Amsterdam, of great public and private utility, and at the very least there will be a large quantity of money to be exchanged, of which Your Majesty will be able to avail himself in cases of need, without overburdening the people with too many taxes.
>
> (Vieira 1646, 67)

In the final part of this excerpt, we once again find ourselves faced with the original core of the author's economic meditations: the intensification of mercantile activity might be the essential element for the economic restoration of the kingdom, but, above all, it could provide a means of financial improvement and a way of strengthening the power of the State. Without the tax revenue from colonial trade and customs duties, the battles fought to ensure Restoration would be part of a lost war.

For António Vieira, the road to progress would be achieved through trade routes, featuring the Trade Company of Brazil as a major player. Therefore, Brazilian natural and economic resources were at the very heart of the elaborated perception that he gave of the merits of colonial trade in an emergent commercial society.[4]

The Company was extinguished in 1720 due to changes in colonial trade from the late 17th century, as a consequence of the discovery of gold in São Paulo and Minas Gerais region. This notwithstanding, the purposes of its creation would be rekindled with the establishment of companies by the Marquis of Pombal in the second half of the 1750s.

André Antonil and Brazil's newly found riches

The work of the Tuscan Jesuit André João Antonil (1649–1716), whose real name was João António Andreoni, is an exhaustive descriptive overview of the main colonial export products: sugar, tobacco, gold, cattle and leather. It also provides updated data on the annual export values of those products to Portugal and the associated tax revenues, as well as a variety of prices for food consumption goods, clothing, weapons, slaves, and beasts of burden. His primary aim was to show that

> Brazil has become the best and the most useful achievement, both for the royal treasury and for the public good, of all the others in the kingdom of Portugal, given the amount that each year leaves these ports, which are reliable and abundantly profitable mines.
>
> (Antonil 1711, 334)

Antonil met Father António Vieira in Rome in the early 1670s. He travelled with him to Brazil in January 1681, where he became a teacher and rector of the Jesuit College of Bahia and a visiting officer of the captaincy of Pernambuco. He lived in Bahia for 35 years and died in 1716. The information he collected on sugar *engenhos* in Bahia enabled him to record in his book the several complex technical operations related to sugar production, from the planting of sugar cane to the crystallisation and drying of sugar loaves. This is the most extensive and detailed part of his book, resulting from his direct knowledge of the routines of this productive process. Antonil noted the relevance of systematic collection of quantitative information for the construction of more accurate knowledge about the economic potential of sugar.

However, the section dedicated to gold mines was the one that attracted most attention – or rather the one that might have attracted it, as the Overseas Council (*Conselho Ultramarino*) ordered the book to be retained in the printing house and the copies in the press to be destroyed, claiming that it revealed sensitive information about the products of the Portuguese economy that were the target of foreign powers' greed. The royal decision explains why so few copies of the work – which was not circulated at the time it was written – have survived.[5] At a time when the discovery of gold mines was still very recent, but when the presence of people "who work on the mines and mine gold from streams" was already clear and intense (Antonil 1711, 242), the data published by Antonil regarding the main gold deposits and the paths and routes of access to the mines from São Paulo, Rio de Janeiro and Bahia were privileged information that the Portuguese crown preferred to remain undisclosed.

It is curious to note that the inclusion of this section on gold mines was motivated by a radically opposite reason. In other words, Antonil recorded the information about the gold findings, not to encourage its exploitation, but to demonstrate its nefarious character, both because it led to an increase in the price of other colonial products and of slave labour and because of production losses in the sugar, tobacco, wood and leather sectors, arising from the diversion of productive and market investments to the mining sector. Hence, Antonil's work was a landmark in the defence of the interests of *engenho* owners and sugar producers and traders, seeking to explain "for those who do not know what the sweetness of sugar costs to those who toil it, to be aware of it, and feel less as they give for it the price it is worth" (*ibid.*, 67).

Even though the fundamental interest of his book is the detailed description of the cultivation and manufacturing operations of the main colonial products – in line with the Antiquity classical works on agriculture – some passages reveal his interest in the framing and functioning of an economic system for which the emerging science of political arithmetic was beginning to make its early contributions. Antonil therefore goes beyond the mere scope of a treaty on agricultural and agronomic matters and reveals a special interest in capturing economic reality by means of numbers and data.

When he refers to the central role of the owners of *engenhos* as holders of an initial capital that sets in motion the several players involved in sugar production, Antonil highlights the organisational element of a business function without which investment would be at stake.

The merits and credit of *engenho* owners were therefore assessed by their ability to manage and command a complex web of relationships between multiple agents (tenants, cultivators, slaves, mechanical officers, traders), with emphasis on the attributes and obligations of an ethical nature indispensable for the creation of harmonious labour relations between such different social groups (Marquese 1999, 49–78).

Another aspect in which Antonil revealed his acumen in understanding elementary economic mechanisms is the way in which he discusses the validity of contractual practices in the purchase and sale of sugar in which the established price results from the expectation raised about its future value:

> Whoever buys or sells in advance for the price that sugar will be worth at the time of the fleet makes a fair contract, because both buyer and seller are equally at risk. And this is understood by the higher general price that sugar is then worth, and not by the specific price to which anyone settles, obliged by the need to sell it.
>
> (Antonil 1711, 104–105)

In other words, for Antonil, the market acts as a regulator of freely established purchase and sale intentions, and the previously agreed final price may correspond to benefits (which are not risk-free) for both parties – for the producer-seller, who has an advance sum that enables him to meet production costs, and for the buyer-trader, because he can negotiate a more advantageous price than the current price.

Also regarding the variations in the price of sugar, André Antonil discusses in his work the reasons for the surge in the 1610s, due to the increase in the price of capital goods, consumer goods and slave labour, as well as to the increase in monetary circulation, taking on the intuitive defence of an embryonic quantitative theory of money that supported a cause–effect relationship between money supply and price variation. It is precisely in this explanatory context that he regrets the discovery of gold mines "which were used to enrich the few and to destroy the many, as the best mines in Brazil are cane fields and the threshing grounds where tobacco is grown" (*ibid.*, 177).

Alexandre de Gusmão and the gold rush

The discovery of gold in Minas Gerais in the 1690s (and later in the Mato Grosso, Goiás and Bahia regions) led to a profound change in the Portuguese crown's attitude towards the colonial administration, given the need to guarantee the indispensable means to control the production of an asset of crucial strategic importance to the strength of the Portuguese empire. The discovery of diamonds in the 1720s, also in the captaincy of Minas Gerais, further strengthened the urgency of a more effective control, as the crown intended to exercise, avoiding solutions for decentralising the administration of the territory or creating institutions with delegated power.[6]

The gold rush caused a natural effervescence in a region that became attractive for the immediate enrichment of a multiplicity of private agents in search of a natural wealth over which the Portuguese crown wanted to exercise tight jurisdiction – and of course extract the inevitable highly coveted tax revenues.

During the 18th century, 865.5 tonnes of gold were mined in Brazil, representing between 53% and 61% (according to the several existing estimates) of world production (Pinto 1979). Thanks to Brazilian production, Portugal thus became the main country in gold reception and distribution in Europe. It may have absorbed around 45% of world production (Barrett 1990, cited by Costa et al. 2013, 50). The establishment of a tax regime that would allow the Portuguese crown to exercise rights over the mining and transport of this fantastic natural resource was obviously a matter that was readily considered a priority. The taxation of the *quinto* of the gold that was produced (a one-fifth tax on mining activities) and a 1% right on the gold carried to mainland Portugal were fundamental fiscal instruments designed for the Portuguese crown to obtain financial resources that allowed it to sustain a chronicle trade deficit and the typical demands of a baroque-era court.

However, the effectiveness of such a system was far from perfect. The importance of the gold mining revenues did not allow significant decreases in mining activities, the shipment of gold to mainland Portugal and tax collection for the benefit of the crown. After the euphoria of the early decades of the century, the tax levy based on the payment of *quinto* (i.e., the retention of 20% of the value of gold that was compulsorily smelted in facilities controlled by the royal administration in the Brazilian captaincies) began to show signs of inefficiency that were proper to an extractive tax system. The difficult task of administrative and tax control in very extensive, rugged territories, inevitable loss and smuggling, the venality and corruption of agents at the service of the crown who were also part of trade companies that carried gold to other European capitals were an invitation to a reform of the existing taxation model. Besides, increasingly urgent signs of local upheavals and insubordination created enormous instability in the capturing of this important source of income for the crown.

It was in this context that an innovative proposal to replace the *quinto* regime with a tax system based on a capitation tax (on the number of slaves) and a *maneio* tax (a kind of an income tax on the regular production and consumption activities) emerged in King João V's circle of main advisors. The proposal was presented by Alexandre de Gusmão, one of the king's main protégés.

Alexandre de Gusmão (1695–1753) was born in Santos, Brazil. He began his studies in Bahia, but moved to Lisbon, the capital of the kingdom, as young man, accompanying his brother Bartolomeu, the famous inventor of *passarola*, a birdlike gliding device. He graduated in law from the universities of Coimbra and Paris and performed diplomatic functions in Rome. From the early 1730s to the death of the king in 1750, he was King João V's personal secretary and a member of the Overseas Council, in charge of establishing the kingdom's policy guidelines regarding the Brazilian territory.[7]

Although he stayed in the court in Lisbon and left Brazil at a very young age (and therefore did not have the possibility of getting to know his native country in depth), Alexandre de Gusmão revealed a special ability to collect essential information for his proposals to change the gold exploitation tax regime. Hence, it should be highlighted the way he collected data and made calculations and estimates to justify the advantage of the measures he proposed. His knowledge based on facts and figures became a convincing instrument of persuasion, with a view to guaranteeing trust in the new political options and decisions.

The main reason against *quinto* were thefts and smuggling in gold delivery for smelting. There was a huge drop in revenue from the Royal Treasury and a clear benefit for the offenders, who sold it in Spanish possessions in exchange for silver, which was not subject to the same taxation process, or to the Dutch at a better price in Costa da Mina. For Gusmão, the commercial losses associated with this illegal gold business were due to fiscal options that questioned the assumptions on which colonial trade should be based: private agents should have greater freedom of action.

Besides increasing revenue and eliminating thefts and smuggling, Gusmão's main purpose was to establish a more equitable tax regime in which all economic agents were involved rather than just those who delivered gold to royal foundries. The mining tax would be replaced by a tax on property and income. Hence, he proposed the creation of a single direct tax on the number of slaves and freedmen who worked in the mines (capitation) as well as on shops and commercial establishments (*maneio*) that ensured the supply of essential goods for the development of economic activities.

The capitation tax would be 10 *oitavas* (1 *oitava* = 1520 *réis*) per slave, i.e., a net total of approximately 1,000 *contos* per year. In his project, Gusmão sets strict guidelines and rules for the compulsory registration of all slaves over 15 years old by their owners: non-compliance would mean heavy fines and the slaves being declared free (Gusmão 1733a, 67).

The *maneio* tax was levied on "the profits, which are estimated, that they make each year with their own work" (*ibid.*, 83), in the amount of 5% of those estimated profits. In addition to traders, sellers and manufacturers, all "lawyers, physicians, surgeons, apothecaries, and other people of similar professions [were] also included, even though they seem[ed] to exercise them for public convenience" (*ibid.*, 85).

The capitation and *maneio* tax would imply the elimination of *quinto* and all kinds of indirect tax charges (including tithes). The transport and circulation of gold would no longer be subject to the previous restrictions imposed by the crown, increasing the flow of precious metals between the captaincies of Brazil and Lisbon. Members of the administration and government and members of the clergy would be exempt from taxation.

Despite the enthusiastic support of the king, who was convinced of the increase in revenue that Gusmão had simulated, the new tax project met with understandable natural resistance from representatives of local interests (Gusmão 1733b). In effect, the statute that sought to establish the new fiscal policy guidelines, issued by the office of King João V on 30 October 1733, would only be effectively accepted and applied in January 1735, after more than a year of rejections and disputes (White 1977, 213–223). Still, it arguably introduced greater efficiency in tax administration and a substantial increase of gold coinage at the Lisbon and Rio de Janeiro mints and subsequently of the crown's tax revenues from Brazilian gold (Sousa 2006, 156–162). This was made possible thanks to the captaincy's governance and control capacity under Martinho de Mendonça, i.e., the political stability that enabled the census of the population on which the capitation tax was based and the regulation of economic activities that enabled the collection of the *maneio* tax.

Despite the undeniable success of the system outlined by Alexandre de Gusmão, local resistance channelled through the municipalities of Minas Gerais or demonstrated in public acts of riot and rebellion never ceased to be felt (Magalhães 2009).[8] Therefore, it was not surprising that the change of reign saw the return of the *quinto* tax on gold charged in smelting. The truth is that, as Alexandre de Gusmão had predicted in his contestation of the turning point that took place in 1750, gold shipments fell significantly, by around 50%, with the reintroduction of the *quinto* system by the Marquis of Pombal's administration (Sousa 2006, Table 19).

In a report in which he sought to contest the return to *quinto*, Gusmão insists on the losses caused by such a system, further increased by the impossibility of establishing a local control and surveillance system. "Is one to expect that there will be those who voluntarily deprive themselves of a fifth of their monies, if they are able to save it with little risk and work?" (Gusmão 1750, 240). He also highlights the social injustice resulting from the different ways to escape the payment of taxes due to the crown, considering that all the economic agents involved in gold mining and commercialisation (tenants, traders and manufacturers who exchange their products which are necessary for mine work for gold, and those who deal in slaves and beasts of burden for work on the mines) should be subject to taxes.

The drop in revenue was linked to the decrease in mining rather than to the tax regime in force. However, despite the subsequent collapse, it should be noted that the 1740s were the decade that saw a greater flow of gold shipments to the Lisbon Mint (Costa et al. 2013, 51–59), which may be partly attributed to fiscal innovations inspired by Alexandre de Gusmão's advice.

The gold taxation regime was not the only reason behind Alexandre de Gusmão's indisputable prominence in the formation of Brazilian economic and political thought in the mid-18th century. He also skilfully guided the negotiations on the Treaty of Madrid signed by Spain and Portugal in 1750, which guaranteed the establishment – in an official way and under international law – of the territorial sovereignty already exercised by each of the Iberian empires according to the naturally established geographic limits. In other words, according to the famous motto of Roman law that inspired the Treaty of Madrid: *uti possidetis, ita possideatis* – as you possess, so may you possess.

The technical superiority displayed in the accurate mapping of the territory enabled Portugal to impose its geographical reading of the natural borders, which would last (with small exceptions on the northern border of the Guyana region) until Brazil became independent in 1822. The outline of the Brazilian territory was defined by Alexandre de Gusmão in his supervision to the drawing of the Map of the Courts, presented as a cartographic-diplomatic asset for the negotiations of the Treaty of Madrid (Ferreira 2007). For Gusmão, the loss of Colonia de Sacramento to Spanish rule did not bring any political or economic damage to the Portuguese crown or commercial interests, as the smuggling that prevailed there prevented Portugal from having any prerogative of *de facto* jurisdiction. It was a strategic option for pacifying relations with Spain and its empire that contributed to alleviating existing tensions in multiple parts of Brazilian territory.

Alexandre Gusmão's possible projection in the sphere of European mercantilist economic literature was hampered by the fact that his text of greater doctrinal and analytical content (Gusmão 1749) remained unpublished until the early 19th century.

It is a programmatic document with a view to the possible definition of economic policy measures aimed at preventing the outflow of money from the kingdom, namely the issuance of legislation against the import of luxury items. By means of the usual mercantilist formulation, according to which "money is the blood of monarchies" (*ibid.*, 194), Gusmão regrets the decrease in gold mining for mintage purposes, which does not allow to restore the necessary outflow to pay the balance of trade deficit. His reasoning shows the author's adherence to the basic principle that establishes a relationship between the quantity of money in circulation and the price level:

> The circulation of money, and its abundance in our state of commerce, are the causes that give value to our goods; and for this reason, as the currency of our fund decreases, goods lose their value; and when it seems that they should increase it, it does not happen that way; because we give them in exchange for other goods, and for manufactures, and we are always indebted, because they do not reach the balance of trade, they lose their

value, because it is foreigners who set prices, which happens due to lack of money.

(*ibid*, 199)

Regardless of the validity of his abstract reasoning, it is important to note that Alexandre de Gusmão considered that all incoming gold would be used to settle the balance of trade deficit instead of being retained as currency, with positive implications for the whole of economic activity, as David Hume had analysed at the time.[9]

The Marquis of Pombal and Bishop Azeredo Coutinho: old and new colonial solutions

The crisis caused by the retraction in Brazilian gold production had economic consequences that have been deeply discussed by Portuguese and Brazilian historiography. The Marquis of Pombal's industrial development policy, mainly after the 1755 earthquake, was one of the responses to the breakdown of the gold flow to settle the balance of trade deficit. Colonial economic policy resumed the incentives for the exploitation of products already known and with a guaranteed place in the re-export market (mainly tobacco and sugar), also intensifying the exploitation of slave labour and slave capture in the areas of West Africa that were part of the Portuguese empire. Cocoa and cotton were the most valued products in the new imperial cycle – especially cotton, which was an essential raw material for the boost in manufacturing in the metropolis but was also re-exported to feed the more advanced British industry. The new Trade Companies of Grão-Pará and Maranhão (founded in 1755) and Pernambuco and Paraíba (founded in 1759) effectively fulfilled their role of mobilising capital invested in colonial traffic, both for the export of colonial agricultural products (namely rice and cotton) or the supply of slaves from the African coast, ensuring a stable partnership between the private sector and the crown (Schwartz 1998b).

Even though the Marquis of Pombal did not write any doctrinal texts that would enable the identification of the sources and foundations of his policy in relation to Brazil, his decisions and legislation made clear the main objective of fighting against situations of external dependence, especially regarding the balance of trade between Portugal and Great Britain. This had visible implications in the introduction of greater rationality in the fiscal and financial administration, under the influence of the sciences of government typical of the cameralist economic discourse (Cardoso and Cunha 2012). Quality control of exported products through inspection stations, the suppression of smuggling, the prohibition on the establishment of manufactures in Brazilian territory and the extinction of the fleet system towards a greater efficiency in the transport and commercialisation of Brazilian products were some of the signs of change and innovation of Pombal's legacy.

The eagerness for new colonial products and stable partnerships for their exploitation was at the origin of a process of renewal of the overseas policy after the death of King José I in 1777, in whose name the Marquis of Pombal's policy had been carried out. With the accession to the throne of Queen Maria I and the Prince Regent Dom João (who became King João VI from 1816), the actions of Martinho de Melo e Castro – and mostly Dom Rodrigo de Sousa Coutinho, in their capacity as ministers of the Navy and Overseas Domains – would be guided by the concern of deepening scientific knowledge of Brazil's natural resources.

The implementation of philosophical journeys, the exhaustive inventory of resources susceptible to economic use, the publication of natural history memories on the main Brazilian products, substantiated the presence of influences from the European enlightened thought and science (*Memórias Económicas*, 1789–1815). The Lisbon Academy of Sciences was a reference institution for the publication of a vast number of descriptive memories of Brazilian productive resources, especially the essays by Domingos Vandelli (Cardoso 1989).

The same institution promoted the publication of the main economic writings of José Joaquim da Cunha Azeredo Coutinho (1742–1821). Born in Campos de Goitacazes, in the captaincy of Rio de Janeiro, he was the son of an *engenho* owner but gave up the right to manage the family business. He graduated in Canonical Law from the University of Coimbra in 1780 and entered an ecclesiastical career that provided him with relevant positions, both in Brazil (between 1798 and 1802) and in mainland Portugal. He was rector of the Seminary of Olinda, bishop of Pernambuco (and interim governor of the local captaincy) and later bishop of Bragança and Miranda (he never actually served) and Elvas. In 1817, he abdicated his new investiture as bishop of the diocese of Beja and was Chief Inquisitor of the Portuguese Inquisition until its end after the Revolution of 1820. He was elected as an MP for Rio de Janeiro to the Constituent Assembly but died before taking office.

In the first of his economic writings, Azeredo Coutinho shows he knew well the problems associated with sugar production and trade, arguing in favour of not fixing its market price (Coutinho 1791). In his view, a fixed price would have negative consequences, both for producers (which Azeredo Coutinho explicitly represented), who would have no other way to compensate for the costs, and for traders who should be free to sell at the price that the market would determine to be the most appropriate. The high price that sugar had reached in the international market would act as an incentive to the continuity of its offer, at a time when the fall in the French Antilles acted as a stimulus to its production in Brazil.

Azeredo Coutinho is therefore in favour of the free play of economic interests in a competitive market that would not allow the rigidity of a fixed price: "One may forbid the monopoly, forbid fraud, but not the profits of a lawful trade that it is free to all" (*ibid.*, 276).

His adherence to enlightened ideas of freedom of trade is also defended, albeit in a cautious and mitigated way, in the economic essay that he dedicated to Portuguese colonial trade, with emphasis on the analysis of the Brazilian market (Coutinho 1794). The theme was of interest to a wide audience, which accounts for the several editions of the work in Portuguese and its translation into English, German and French. Even though he did not relinquish the exclusive relation between the colonies and the Portuguese metropolitan kingdom within the framework of the colonial pact, Azeredo Coutinho advocates a liberalisation of the colonial economic agency, as this opening could correspond to a better defence of individual interests. Hence, he expresses himself against the persistence of monopoly contracts and advocates the free exploitation of agricultural products and the creation of customs incentives that would allow a greater flow of trade between Brazil and the kingdom.[10] The maintenance of a ban on transactions between Brazil and other European powers and of restrictions on the establishment of manufactures ensured that any increase in freedom of trade would not lead to a rupture of the current colonial system. Also, maintaining the vitality of such a system presupposed an analysis of the balance of trade that dispensed with the need to explore gold mines (Coutinho 1804). In effect, for Azeredo Coutinho, the balance of trade would be the result of the countries' capacity to place on the international market products that they exported to pay off what they imported, with automatic adjustment processes between different countries in the long run.

The rejection of the importance of mining – at a time when the activity was showing signs of an enormous regression – stemmed from an anti-metallist stance expressed in almost all of his works, refusing to identify true wealth with its representative sign, i.e., denouncing "the blindness with which one ran after a representation, and a shadow of wealth, unaware that one was leaving behind the precious body that it represented; undoubtedly because the shadow often seems larger than the body" (Coutinho 1791, 279–280). That is why he insisted that "gold is only good for those who trade with it, as a representative sign of the value of things" (Coutinho 1804, 17), based on his reading of Adam Smith's *The Wealth of Nations*, which he quotes from the French translation, which enabled him to state that

> gold in itself is not wealth. It is a representation of wealth. All trade consists of permuting, or exchanging some things for others; Nature's produce, labour, industry, and all that can fit the enjoyment of men: those are the object of commerce, and of wealth.
>
> (*ibid.*, 27–28)

Azeredo Coutinho's enlightened mercantilist view was also influenced by the readings (not always made explicit) of the works of Montesquieu, Bielfeld and Forbonnais, as pointed out by the main interpreters of his economic thought (Holanda 1966; Pedreira 1992). However, the innovative tendency of some of his writings cannot mask his conservative attitude contrary to the spirit of the time, which he reveals in his essay on the defence of the legitimacy of the slave trade (Coutinho 1807).[11] In this apologetic commitment, Bishop Azeredo Coutinho does not resort to the common strategy of legitimising the slave trade due to the economic advantages associated with this violent form of recruiting labour.

His stance, animated by the desire to "unmask the insidious principles of the philosophical sect" (*ibid.*, IV), accentuates the virtues of the slave trade in the light of philosophical principles of reason and natural law, a reasoning that led to many critical remarks at the time (Neves 2001). For the bishop of Pernambuco and Elvas, a notion of absolute and abstract justice subject to the principles of the social contract was not permissible, and the application of the laws that regulate life in society "must weigh the circumstances and apply natural law to them, which orders them to do the greatest possible good of their nations in relation to the state in which each of them is" (Coutinho 1807, XII). In other words, in the case of the condemnation or approval of the slave trade, it would be a political decision of the sovereigns, who would act according to what they deemed as the most appropriate laws to the circumstances of the nations they governed. Applying this reasoning to the case of the Portuguese nation and its colonial territories, Azeredo Coutinho reveals the real problem that worried him in a straightforward, blunt way:

> Suppose that, in order to humour those who claim to be defenders of humanity, the word slave was banished from the midst of civilised nations, and the slave trade from the coast of Africa, and from any barbarian nation, was forever banned. What would become of agriculture in the colonies, and subsequently, of Portugal? How would Portugal ever survive without agriculture, without trade, and without money to pay those who defend it? (*ibid.*, 74)

Despite admitting the existence of abuses – "what trade is free from abuses?" (*ibid.*, 78) – and appealing for the necessary measures to avoid them to be taken, Azeredo Coutinho does not hesitate to pronounce the inevitable need to supply slave labour for agricultural and mining work in Brazil.

Dom Rodrigo de Sousa Coutinho and the political economy of the Enlightenment

In the same period that Bishop Azeredo Coutinho produced his political reflections and economic essays, another relevant figure became known for his decisive contributions to the affirmation of the enlightened political economy discourse in Portugal and Brazil: Dom Rodrigo de Sousa Coutinho (1755–1812). He was the Marquis of Pombal's godson, and his education and political training were designed to prepare him to hold government positions at the highest level. Sousa Coutinho began his career as a Portuguese ambassador in the Kingdom of Sardinia and Piedmont between 1779 and 1796. In Turin, he established cultural, scientific and political sociability networks that enabled him to deepen the reading of the works of the main authors who contributed to the study of political economy and public finance in Europe. The books that make up the remarkable library he built in those years are an undeniable testimony of his solid culture and his willingness to share the knowledge produced by the main figures of the European Enlightenment (Cardoso 2019).

After finishing his diplomatic mission in Turin, Sousa Coutinho successively served as Minister of the Navy and Overseas Domains (1796–1801), President of the Royal Treasury and Minister of Finance (1801–1803) and Minister of War and Foreign Affairs (1808–1812). He was awarded the title of Count of Linhares in 1808. His name is inextricably linked to all the political, economic, social and cultural events that took place in Portugal during the regency and reign of João VI, until his death in 1812. His participation in the reconfiguration of the empire after the opening of the ports of Brazil in 1808 and in the celebration of the Trade and Friendship Treaties between Portugal and Great Britain in 1810, under the aegis of principles of political economy that he held dear, are especially relevant.[12]

Of the essays Sousa Coutinho wrote in Turin, the only one that was printed during his lifetime was dedicated to the relevance of precious metal mines to the nations that owned them (Coutinho 1789). In this short – but relevant – essay, Dom Rodrigo de Sousa Coutinho seeks to demonstrate the incorrectness of the theses (namely Montesquieu's) that held that precious metals mines had an harmful effect on the economic development of the nations that owned them.[13] He admits that the existence of gold and silver mines and, consequently, access to goods that were used as numeraire or as general equivalent to facilitate exchange could negatively affect the creation of true productive wealth. However, these factors alone did not determine the state of ruin or decay of a kingdom that was forced to resort to precious metals to pay the balance of trade deficit. For Sousa Coutinho, the origin of the deficit were structural deficiencies that the existence of mines only helped to alleviate – "one cannot in all fairness blame mines for an effect that is independent of them" (Coutinho 1789, 180).

Sousa Coutinho's reflections are drawn from the situation of Brazilian gold mines and the debate on their profitability, as is also to be found in other writings of the time. However, that is not Dom Rodrigo's discursive script. Writing from an abstract perspective, it shows his acceptance of the ideas which were in vogue in some circles of economic discourse production, regarding the determination of the value of money and the influence of the monetary sphere in real economic life. The works of Locke, Hume and especially Galiani's famous *Della Moneta* were part of his personal library and were certainly an important source of inspiration.

The interest in issues relating to Brazilian colonial policy shown by Sousa Coutinho in this speech saw a significant development from 1796, when he took on a government position as Minister of the Navy and Overseas Domains. On that occasion, he wrote a founding text for a new political vision on the economic organisation of the empire (Coutinho 1797), which was a sort of programme and agenda for improvements that he proposed to carry out.[14]

Sousa Coutinho put forward a well-balanced programme of reforms which included the reduction of the tax burden that was associated with a wide range of economic activities taking place in Brazil. He was eager to accept a certain degree of economic autonomy in the colonies, knowing that the denial of that prerogative could inflame independent movements. As a reader of Abbé Raynal and other enlightened authors who presented critical reflections on the nature of colonial trade and the need for its reform, Sousa Coutinho knew that the old colonial system based on exclusive contracts and negotiated privileges could be propped up, but could not be kept alive forever. He was particularly attentive to the fiscal regime and to the policies instigated by the spirit of greed and rapacity in relation to colonial riches. As a reader of Adam Smith, he was well informed about the sound principles that governments should follow in the realm of fiscal policy, namely as regards the universal rules of certainty and convenience that should meet the needs and requests of taxpayers.

Among the fiscal reforms that Sousa Coutinho tried to implement during his mandate, between 1796 and 1800, one should mention the 50% reduction of the tax on gold mining, and a general reduction of (or even total exemption from) import duties for goods entering Brazilian ports from mainland Portugal, namely wine, olive oil, iron and manufactured consumption items. He was also particularly attentive to the need to improve the tax collection systems and the accounting techniques used in public finance administration.

Some of the proposals set out by the Minister Sousa Coutinho were not successfully implemented, even though his guiding principles were in keeping with a basic concern for providing Brazil with a modernised economic and financial structure that was adapted to the new needs of the whole empire. It is nevertheless quite clear that the achievement of the innovation and modernisation aims also implied the adoption of a number of measures that would endanger some of the basic privileges of a colonial regime of the mercantilist type. Such was the case with the proposals for the abolition of the monopoly contracts on salt and whale fishing and for the reduction or removal of tariffs on metropolitan products at Brazilian ports.

One of the main concerns revealed throughout Sousa Coutinho's enlightened colonial administration was the support given to a better knowledge of the Brazilian territory and its natural resources. The organisation of philosophical voyages, the collection of statistical data, the description of living conditions, and the new plans for the allocation of economic resources were all issues that gained increasing importance for the design of colonial policy, thus offering clear evidence of the trust placed in scientific knowledge as a sound basis for political decision-making. With that purpose in mind, Coutinho opened the printing house *Casa Literária do Arco do Cego*, intended for the publication of books and booklets on scientific subjects such as agronomy, botany, chemistry and mineralogy, applied to the better use and more efficient economic allocation of natural resources in Brazil, but also on social issues related to poverty, beggary and public health. They provided evidence on practical concerns with economic improvements in agriculture, cattle raising, manufacturing and commercial circuits. Many of them consisted of hands-on instructions aimed at making feasible new optimal ways of resource allocation.[15]

Casa Literária turned out to be an efficient network of Brazilian students and officials temporarily living on the mainland, but who continued to pay close attention to the immense potential of Brazilian resources. An informal system of scholarships was in place, which allowed for the payment of translations, with Coutinho masterfully managing this scholarly network.[16]

The undisputable leader of *Casa Literária* was Friar José Mariano da Conceição Veloso, a Franciscan priest born in Brazil who lived in Lisbon between 1790 and 1808. He was a reputed botanist and naturalist, self-formed in the knowledgeable tradition of the Franciscan colleges and of the literary and scientific associations in Rio de Janeiro and São Paulo. Sousa Coutinho acknowledged Veloso's scientific merits and made him the great supporter and guardian of his innovative enterprise: to create a printing house especially dedicated to the translation of scientific works and to the diffusion of useful knowledge in Brazil.

Most of Veloso's own contributions were to be gathered in his magnum opus *O Fazendeiro do Brasil*, a collection of translations and essays devoted to the economic use of plants originated from, or transplanted, to Brazilian soil, namely sugar, plants used for dyeing, coffee, cacao and spices (Veloso 1798).

The issues under scrutiny could be the arguments in favour of the transplantation of plants, or the amelioration of agronomic techniques, or a simple exposition of the uses of less-known botanic species. Diminishing costs and improvements in the productive power of the factors of production (land, labour and capital) were the usual claims justifying a new attitude towards the merits of scientific discoveries applied to economic life. Indeed, the progress in economic sectors was always conceived as being dependent upon the outcome of scientific progress.

Despite the inexistence of a coherent theoretical framework, some of the translators revealed awareness of a global contextualisation provided by political economy discourse. It is therefore apparent that the policy of improvements put into action by Sousa Coutinho, whether inspired by the language of political economy or not, greatly contributed to implement changes in Brazilian colonial life.[17]

Concluding remarks

Dom Rodrigo de Sousa Coutinho ended a cycle of reflection on Brazilian economic issues in the context of the Portuguese colonial empire. His attempt to reform colonial mining policies took place at a time when substantial changes in Brazil's role in the decomposing empire were becoming apparent. Sousa Coutinho himself witnessed it between 1808 and 1812, i.e., in the years that followed the settling of the Portuguese court in Rio de Janeiro following the invasion of the kingdom by Napoleon's troops.

Sousa Coutinho witnessed the beginning of a collapse process that he could no longer avoid, despite the enlightened reforms he tried to carry out. The colonial economy based on slave labour, gold mining and the intensive production of sugar and other items with guaranteed output in export markets had ceased to be viable through the usual recipes of the mercantilist colonial pact.

Still, while it lasted, this colonial economy gave rise to analyses and approaches that reveal the formation of embryonic principles of political economy, focusing on established issues such as value, prices and currency, and the definition of economic policy guidelines, namely regarding the capture of tax revenues and balance of trade control.

The authors revisited in this chapter, whose common feature was their interest in discussing the problems of the Brazilian economic reality, did not show enough eloquence or discursive relevance to be worthy of being included in a pantheon devoted to great figures in the history of universal economic thought. However, their importance in the Portuguese-Brazilian panorama is indisputable, as their analyses and political solutions are part of a framework of strategic reflection on the allocation of natural resources, the mobilisation of capital, the use of labour (indigenous and slave), the organisation of productive processes, the formation and distribution of wealth, the collection of tax revenues, the realisation of State expenses and the design of institutions which are essential to the functioning of the economy – in short, of the subjects on which political economy discourse is slowly constructed.

Notes

* Translated into English by José Manuel Godinho. This translation is supported by national funds through FCT – Fundação para a Ciência e a Tecnologia, I.P., in the context of strategic projects UIDB/50013/2020 and UIDP/50013/2020.

1. For a global perspective on the Portuguese imperial expansion, whose momentum occurred in the late 15th century, see Pedreira 2007 and Schwartz 2007. For a summary of the Brazilian case, see Magalhães 1998.
2. There is a vast bibliography available on the economy and society of colonial Brazil as part of the Portuguese empire until the independence process in 1822. English-speaking readers interested in an overview of the issues summarised in this introduction may see Russell-Wood 1975 and Bethel 1987.
3. Regarding the history of Portuguese economic thought at the time, see Almodovar and Cardoso 1998, 14–54. For an introductory approach to the political economy of colonial Brazil, see Aidar 2019.
4. For further details on this topic, see Boxer 1949.
5. Regarding this subject, see the detailed study by Andrée Mansuy Diniz-Silva, who is behind the definitive edition (in 2011) of his work (Antonil 1711, 15–55).
6. Only later, with the arrival of the Portuguese court in Rio de Janeiro in 1808, would the so-called "interiorisation of the metropolis" take place in Brazil, and the capital of the colony be provided with the institutions that were essential to the actual exercise of the attributes of a capital of the kingdom (Dias 1968).
7. Regarding Alexandre de Gusmão's life and work, including the edition of his most important writings and diverse documentation of the period, see the monumental study by Cortesão 1950–1960.
8. Some of the civil disobedience, insurrection and rebellion movements would become organised, albeit locally, suggesting the existence of purposes that came close to autonomous intentions to put an end to the Portuguese crown's political control. Regarding the subject, see Maxwell's pioneering study in Maxwell 1973a.
9. It should be noted that 72% of the gold coin issuances in the period between 1688–1797 were meant for payments abroad, with 18% being retained for domestic supply, whereas the remaining 10% was used for damage, wear and tear and recoining. Regarding the subject, see Sousa 2006, 245.

10. On Azeredo's Coutinho enlightened defence of Portuguese colonial regime, see Cantarino 2015.
11. The first edition dates from 1798. It was published in French and printed in London, following the Lisbon Academy of Sciences refusal to give it a publishing stamp.
12. This subject will be discussed in the next chapter of this book.
13. It should be reminded that the same opinion had been held by André João Antonil in 1711, and that it was later seconded by Bishop Azeredo Coutinho in 1804.
14. The subject was broached in Cardoso 2001. The approach in the following paragraphs closely follows the analysis included in Cardoso and Cunha 2012.
15. Regarding the publishing activities of the *Casa Literária do Arco do Cego*, see Campos et al. 1999, and Pataca and Luna 2019.
16. Among those who have contributed as authors or translators are Manuel Arruda da Câmara, José Feliciano Fernandes Pinheiro, António Carlos Ribeiro de Andrade, Hipólito José da Costa, Manuel Jacinto Nogueira da Gama, João Manso Pereira, José da Silva Lisboa, José Ferreira da Silva, José Francisco Cardoso de Morais, Vicente Coelho de Seabra Silva Teles and Vicente José Ferreira Cardoso da Costa. Some of these members of the Brazilian intellectual elite would later become important references of the reformist movement towards independence and to nation building after 1822. On this intellectual elite, see Maxwell 1973b.
17. For a global view on the scope and limitations of the enlightened reform policies in Brazil, see also Malerba 2020.

References

Aidar, Bruno, 2019. Pensar a riqueza do Brasil Colonial: das descrições à economia política. In Daniel Consentino and Thiago Gambi (eds.), *História do Pensamento Econômico. Pensamento Econômico Brasileiro*. Nitéroi and São Paulo: Eduff and Hucitec.

Almodovar, António and Cardoso, José Luís, 1998. *A History of Portuguese Economic Thought*. London and New York: Routledge.

Antonil, André João, 1711. *Cultura e Opulência do Brasil, por suas Drogas e Minas* (. . .). Lisboa: Oficina Real Deslandesiana (new edition, Lisboa: Comissão Nacional para a Comemoração dos Descobrimentos Portugueses, 2001, ed. Andrée Mansuy Diniz Silva).

Barrett, Ward, 1990. World bullion flows, 1450–1800. In James D. Tracy (ed.), *The Rise of Merchant Empire. Long Distance Trade in the Early Modern World, 1350–1750*. Cambridge and New York: Cambridge University Press, 224–254.

Bethel, Leslie (ed.), 1987. *Colonial Brazil*. Cambridge and New York: Cambridge University Press.

Boxer, Charles, 1949. Padre António Vieira, S.J., and the Institution of the Brazil Company in 1649. *Hispanic American Historical Review*, 29:4, 474–497.

Campos, Maria Fernanda, Leme, Margarida P., Faria, Miguel F., Cunha, Margarida, and Domingos, Manuela, 1999. *A Casa Literária do Arco do Cego. Bicentenário*. Lisboa: Biblioteca Nacional e INCM.

Cantarino, Nelson Mendes, 2015. *A Razão e a Ordem: o Bispo José Joaquim da Cunha de Azeredo Coutinho e a Defesa Ilustrada do Antigo Regime Português*. São Paulo: Alameda.

Cardoso, José Luís, 1989. *O Pensamento Económico em Portugal nos Finais do Século XVIII, 1780–1808*. Lisboa: Editorial Estampa.

Cardoso, José Luís, 2001. Nas malhas do império: A economia política e a política colonial de D. Rodrigo de Sousa Coutinho. In José Luís Cardoso (ed.), *A Economia Política e os Dilemas do Império Luso-Brasileiro (1790–1822)*. Lisboa: Comissão Nacional para as Comemorações do Descobrimentos Portugueses, 63–109.

Cardoso, José Luís, 2019. D. Rodrigo de Sousa Coutinho em Turim: Cultura económica e formação política de um diplomata ilustrado. In Isabel Ferreira da Mota and Carla Enrica

Spantigati (eds.), *Tanto Ella Assume Novitate al Fianco. Lisboa, Turim e o Intercâmbio Cultural das Luzes à Europa Pós-Napoleónica*. Coimbra: Imprensa da Universidade de Coimbra, 19–48.

Cardoso, José Luís and Cunha, Alexandre M., 2012. Enlightened reforms and economic discourse in the Portuguese-Brazilian Empire. *History of Political Economy*, 44:4, 618–641.

Cortesão, Jaime, 1950–1960. *Alexandre de Gusmão e o Tratado de Madrid*, 9 vols. Rio de Janeiro: Instituto Rio Branco.

Costa, Leonor Freire, Rocha, Maria Manuela, and Sousa, Rita Martins de, 2013. *O Ouro do Brasil*. Lisboa: Imprensa Nacional Casa da Moeda.

Coutinho, D. Rodrigo de Sousa, 1789. Discurso sobre a verdadeira influência das minas de metais preciosos na indústria das nações que a possuem, e especialmente da portuguesa. In José Luís Cardoso (ed.), *Memórias Económicas da Academia Real das Ciências de Lisboa*, Vol. I. Lisboa: Academia Real das Ciências de Lisboa (New edition, Lisboa: Banco de Portugal, 1991), 179–183.

Coutinho, D. Rodrigo de Sousa, 1797. Memória sobre o melhoramento dos domínios de Sua Majestade na América. In Andrée Mansuy Diniz-Silva (ed.), *Textos políticos, económicos e financeiros*, Vol. 2. Lisboa: Banco de Portugal, 1993, 47–66.

Coutinho, José Joaquim de Azeredo, 1791. Memória sobre o preço do açúcar. In José Luís Cardoso (ed.), *Memórias Económicas da Academia Real das Ciências de Lisboa*, Vol. III. Lisboa: Academia Real das Ciências de Lisboa (New edition, Lisboa: Banco de Portugal, 1991), 273–280.

Coutinho, José Joaquim de Azeredo, 1794. *Ensaio Económico sobre o Comércio de Portugal e suas Colónias* (ed. Jorge Miguel Pedreira). Lisboa: Academia Real das Ciências de Lisboa (New edition, Lisboa: Banco de Portugal, 1992).

Coutinho, José Joaquim de Azeredo, 1804. *Discurso sobre o Estado Atual das Minas do Brasil*. Lisboa: Impressão Régia.

Coutinho, José Joaquim de Azeredo, 1807. *Análise sobre a Justiça do Comércio do Resgate dos Escravos da Costa de África*. Lisboa: Oficina de João Rodrigues Neves.

Cunha, Alexandre Mendes, 2010. Police science and cameralism in Portuguese Enlightenment reformism. *E-journal of Portuguese History*, 8:1, 36–47.

Dias, Maria Odila da Silva, 1968. Aspetos da Ilustração no Brasil. *Revista do Instituto Histórico e Geográfico Brasileiro*, 278, 105–170.

Ferreira, Mário Clemente, 2007. O Mapa das Cortes e o Tratado de Madrid: A cartografia ao serviço da diplomacia. *Varia História, Belo Horizonte*, 23:37, 51–69.

Furtado, Celso, 2001. *Economia Colonial no Brasil nos Séculos XVI e XVII. Elementos de história econômica aplicados à análise de problemas econômicos e sociais* (1st ed., PhD dissertation, Sorbonne 1948). São Paulo: Editora Hucitec.

Gusmão, Alexandre de, 1733a. Projeto de capitação e maneio proposto a D. João V. In Jaime Cortesão (ed.), *Alexandre de Gusmão e o Tratado de Madrid*. Rio de Janeiro: Instituto Rio Branco (1950, Parte II, Tomo I – *Obras Várias de Alexandre de Gusmão*), 57–104.

Gusmão, Alexandre de, 1733b. Resposta a vários pareceres e dúvidas sobre o projeto de capitação, 1733. In Jaime Cortesão (ed.), *Alexandre de Gusmão e o Tratado de Madrid*. Rio de Janeiro: Instituto Rio Branco (1950, Parte II, Tomo I – *Obras Várias de Alexandre de Gusmão*), 110–127.

Gusmão, Alexandre de, 1749. Apontamentos discursivos sobre o dever impedir-se a extração da nossa moeda para fora, e reinos estrangeiros, por causa da ruína que daí se segue. In Jaime Cortesão (ed.), *Alexandre de Gusmão e o Tratado de Madrid*. Rio de Janeiro: Instituto Rio Branco (1950, Parte II, Tomo I – *Obras Várias de Alexandre de Gusmão*), 194–199.

Gusmão, Alexandre de, 1750. Reparos sobre a disposição da lei de 3 de Dezembro de 1750. In Jaime Cortesão (ed.), *Alexandre de Gusmão e o Tratado de Madrid*. Rio de Janeiro:

Instituto Rio Branco (1950, Parte II Tomo I – *Obras Várias de Alexandre de Gusmão*), 228–251.

Holanda, Sérgio Buarque, 1966. Apresentação. In Ruben Borba de Moraes (ed.), Coutinho, José Joaquim de Azeredo, 1794–1804. *Obras Económicas*. São Paulo: Companhia Nacional, 13–53.

Magalhães, Joaquim Romero, 1998. A construção do espaço brasileiro. In Francisco Bethencourt e Kirti Chaudhuri (eds.), *História da Expansão Portuguesa. Volume II, Do Índico ao Atlântico (1570–1697)*. Lisboa: Círculo de Leitores, 28–64.

Magalhães, Joaquim Romero, 2009. A cobrança do ouro do rei nas Minas Gerais: o fim da capitação, 1741–1750. *Tempo*, 14:27, 118–132.

Malerba, Jurandir, 2020. *Brasil em Projetos. História dos sucessos políticos e planos de melhoramento do reino. Da Ilustração portuguesa à independência do Brasil*. Rio de Janeiro: FGV Editora.

Marquese, Rafael de Bivar, 1999. *Administração e Escravidão. Ideias sobre a gestão da agricultura escravista brasileira*. São Paulo: Editora Hucitec.

Mauro, Frederic, 1983. *Le Portugal, le Brésil et L'Atlantiqie au XVIIe Siècle. Étude Économique*. Paris: Fondation Calouste Gulbenkian.

Maxwell, Kenneth, 1973a. *Conflicts and Conspiracies: Portugal and Brazil, 1750–1808*. Cambridge and New York: Cambridge University Press.

Maxwell, Kenneth, 1973b. The generation of the 1790's and the idea of the Luso-Brazilian Empire. In D. Allen (ed.), *The Colonial Roots of Modern Brazil*. Berkeley, CA: University of California Press, 107–144.

Memórias Económicas da Academia Real das Ciências de Lisboa, 1789–1815. Lisboa: Academia Real das Ciências de Lisboa, Tomos I a V (New edition, Lisboa: Banco de Portugal, 1990–1991 (ed. José Luís Cardoso)).

Neves, Guilherme Pereira das, 2001. Guardar mais silêncio do que falar: Azeredo Coutinho, Ribeiro dos Santos e a escravidão. In José Luís Cardoso (ed.), *A Economia Política e os Dilemas do Império Luso-Brasileiro (1790–1822)*. Lisboa: Comissão Nacional para as Comemorações do Descobrimentos Portugueses, 14–62.

Pataca, Ermelinda Moutinho, and e Luna, Fernando José (eds.), 2019. *Frei Veloso e a Tipografia do Arco do Cego*. São Paulo: EDUSP.

Pedreira, Jorge M., 1992. Introdução. In José Joaquim de Azeredo Coutinho (ed.), *Ensaio Económico sobre o Comércio de Portugal e suas Colónias*. Lisboa: Academia Real das Ciências de Lisboa, 1794 (New edition, Lisboa: Banco de Portugal, 1992), XI–XXXI.

Pedreira, Jorge M., 2007. Costs and financial trends in the Portuguese empire, 1415–1822. In Francisco Bethencourt and Diogo Ramada Curto (eds.), *Portuguese Oceanic Expansion, 1400–1800*. Cambridge and New York: Cambridge University Press, 49–87.

Pinto, Virgílio Noya, 1979. *O Ouro Brasileiro e o Comércio Anglo-Português (Uma contribuição aos estudos de economia atlântica no século XVIII)*. São Paulo: Companhia Editora Nacional.

Russell-Wood, A.J.R. (ed.), 1975. *From Colony to Nation: Essays on the Independence of Brazil*. Baltimore, MD: The Johns Hopkins University Press.

Schwartz, Stuart B., 1998a. A "Babilónia" colonial: A economia açucareira. In Francisco Bethencourt e Kirti Chaudhuri (eds.), *História da Expansão Portuguesa. Volume II, Do Índico ao Atlântico (1570–1697)*. Lisboa: Círculo de Leitores, 213–231.

Schwartz, Stuart B., 1998b. De ouro a algodão: A economia brasileira no século XVIII. In Francisco Bethencourt e Kirti Chaudhuri (eds.), *História da Expansão Portuguesa. Volume III, O Brasil na Balança do Império (1697–1808)*. Lisboa: Círculo de Leitores, 86–103.

Schwartz, Stuart B., 2007. The economy of the Portuguese empire. In: Francisco Bethencourt and Diogo Ramada Curto (eds.), *Portuguese Oceanic Expansion, 1400–1800*. Cambridge and New York: Cambridge University Press, 19–48.

Smith, David Grant, 1974. Old Christians and the foundation of the Brazil Company, 1649. *The Hispanic American Historical Review*, 54:2, 233–259.

Sousa, Rita Martins de, 2006. *Moeda e Metais Preciosos no Portugal Setecentista (1688–1797)*. Lisboa: Imprensa Nacional Casa da Moeda.

Veloso, Fr. José Mariano da Conceição, 1798. *O Fazendeiro do Brasil [cultivador] melhorado na economia rural dos géneros já cultivados e de outros, que se podem introduzir; e nas fábricas, que lhe são próprias, segundo o melhor que se tem escrito a este assunto*, Vol. I. Lisboa: Régia Oficina Tipográfica.

Vieira, P. António, 1643. Proposta feita a El-Rei D. João IV em que se lhe apresentava o miserável estado do reino e a necessidade que tinha de admitir os judeus mercadores que andavam por diversas partes da Europa. In *Obras Escolhidas*, Vol. IV. Lisboa: Clássicos Sá da Costa, 1951, 1–26.

Vieira, P. António, 1646. Razões apontadas a El-Rei D. João IV a favor dos cristãos-novos, para se lhes haver de perdoar a confiscação de seus bens que entrassem no comércio deste reino. In: *Obras Escolhidas*, Vol. IV. Lisboa: Clássicos Sá da Costa, 1951, 63–74.

White, Robert Allan, 1977. Fiscal policy and royal sovereignty in Minas Gerais: The capitation tax of 1735. *The Americas*, 34:2, 207–229.

4 The transition to a post-colonial economy

Mauricio C. Coutinho

Even though the Brazilian independence was declared in 1822, historians admit that the year 1808 marks the end of the Portuguese colonial rule. The transfer of the Portuguese Royal Court from Lisbon to Rio de Janeiro following the invasion of Portugal by Napoleon's troops was the reason for such a political and economic shift. D. João, the prince regent (from 1816, the king), only in 1821 returned to Portugal, meaning Rio de Janeiro remained as the seat of the Portuguese empire for thirteen years. Circumstances that emerged from this situation dismantled many colonial rules, most of all the exclusive trade agreements between the colony and the metropolis.

The Brazilian political independence was also atypical: it was declared by D. Pedro, D. João's eldest son and heir, who had not returned to Portugal with his family in 1821, staying in Rio de Janeiro as regent. D. Pedro then resigned his emperorship in 1831, going back to Portugal to engage in the fight against his brother, D. Miguel, in the Portuguese 'Liberal War.' Provisional governments – Regencies – ruled the new Brazilian empire from 1831 until 1840, when legal majority was conceded to the son of Pedro I, enthroned as Pedro II. D. Pedro II's long governorship, from 1840 until 1889, finally provided stability to the Brazilian political scene. The emergence of a new economic center of gravity – the export of coffee – indisputably contributed to stabilizing the political life, allowing the central government to shatter the regional strife and circumvent the major parliamentary disputes, typical of the 1821–1840 period.

Political economy emerged in Brazil in association with the new political and economic arrangements established in 1808, although its background was the Portuguese political and cultural tradition, especially those from the University of Coimbra. Until the independence, the Brazilian elite got its degrees in this university since no higher education institutions existed in the colony. Therefore, at the end of the eighteenth and beginning of the nineteenth century, Brazilian intellectuals shared the knowledge and the creeds of their Portuguese counterparts, deeply marked by the traditions of a university that, after the 1772 reform, adapted its methods to the new winds of the Portuguese Enlightenment (Maxwell, 1995; Araújo, 2013). Political economy penetrated Brazil from the teachings and intellectual ambience of Coimbra.

DOI: 10.4324/9781003185871-6

Rodrigo de Souza Coutinho (1755–1812) was one of the Coimbra-origin members of the Portuguese elite who strongly influenced a generation of Brazilian intellectuals and officials. Souza Coutinho was a great political figure, a reader of Adam Smith and well-read in political economy, having achieved international experience as a diplomat and Minister of the Navy and Overseas Domains; he also had financial expertise as president of the Royal Treasury.[1] Souza Coutinho was a strong defendant of the transference of the Royal Court to Brazil, becoming the Minister for Foreign Affairs and War – the central element in the Portuguese government – from 1808 until his death, in 1812. Three of the most prominent figures in the diffusion of political economy in post-colonial Brazil were connected to Souza Coutinho: José da Silva Lisboa (1756–1835), José Bonifácio de Andrada e Silva (1763–1838), Hipólito José da Costa (1774–1823). An account of their activities and of their involvement with political economy will situate the first efforts of diffusion and application of political economy in post-colonial Brazil.

Representatives of the spread of political economy in Brazil are also João Severiano Maciel da Costa (1769–1833), Miguel Calmon Du Pin e Almeida (1796–1865), João Rodrigues de Brito (1768–1835?), Pedro Autran da Matta Albuquerque (1805–1881) and Antonio José Gonçalves Chaves (1790–1837). Maciel da Costa's work on slavery (Maciel da Costa, 1821), and the precocious 'letters' on the economic and administrative problems of Bahia, by Rodrigues de Brito (1807), are openly referred to political economy. Although not appealing to the authority of political economists, Du Pin e Almeida's work on sugar (1834) shares a rigorous economic perspective. Matta Albuquerque's works, in turn, may situate how political economy was taught in Brazil around the 1840s, whereas Gonçalves Chaves' work (Gonçalves Chaves, 1817–1822) illustrates the spread of political economy and liberal principles throughout different regions.

Finally, a view of a few works by scientific travelers from Europe will allow us to explore economic thinking from another angle. The travelers who explored more than the natural resources and applied science to an ingenuous observation of the Brazilian social and economic background were John Mawe (1764–1829), Johann Baptiste von Spix (1871–1826), Carl Friedrich Phillipp von Martius (1794–1817), Wilhelm Ludwig von Eschwege (1777–1855). Although not openly appealing to political economy, their reports reveal a deep understanding of the economic scenario and, in the case of Eschwege, the influence of German cameralism.

The beginnings of political economy in Brazil: the University of Coimbra and Souza Coutinho

José da Silva Lisboa, the most important political economy writer in Brazil in the 1808–1830 period, was born in Salvador and got his degrees (Idioms and Law) in Coimbra, in 1779. Back in Brazil, he earned his living teaching, before being admitted into an important administrative position in Salvador, in 1797.[2]

Silva Lisboa published a well-accepted treatise on mercantile law in Lisbon in 1801–02; the projected last volume of this treatise was published in 1804 as an independent book, *Principios de Economia Politica* [Principles of Political Economy]. Overflowing in enthusiasm for Adam Smith, *Principios* is acknowledged as a pioneering work and, besides its importance in raising political economy debates in Portugal, is well representative of the particularities of Portuguese liberalism and of the controversy between 'Smithians' and 'physiocrats.'[3]

Silva Lisboa devised his 1804 book as a defense of liberalism and an attack on physiocracy and its Portuguese supporters, especially Joaquim José Rodrigues de Brito. In fact, Rodrigues de Brito, as the Portuguese physiocrats in general, was less concerned with the theoretical subtleties of Quesnay's system than with a staunch defense of agriculture. Silva Lisboa, in opposition, attacked the supposed priority of agriculture, defending the principles of the division of labor and of unrestricted mobility of labor. The division of labor was the major point of attachment of Silva Lisboa's arguments to *The Wealth of Nations* (hereafter, WN), but it is worth noting that his view of this issue, as of liberalism in general, can be taken most of all as representative of the Portuguese Enlightenment.[4]

Silva Lisboa situated the division of labor as a natural extension of the diversity of talents and endowments, both in individuals and in nature. Trade between individuals and nations was seen as an extension of the diversity of conditions and propensities established by God on earth. As a consequence, all measures devised to protect agriculture, as well as to block trade, would represent a blockage of the virtues of the division of labor; thus, an impediment to a natural order ordained by God.

The description of physiocracy found in *Principios* was not overtly based in Quesnay or in any other major physiocracy text, but on a French *Enciclopédie* entry on Agriculture (by Grivel), that mixed generalities with a sort of physiocratic common sense. Contrastingly, the quotations from WN were transposed from the original text; for instance, the description of the 'fundamental principles of Smith's system' consisted of a long transcription of the first paragraphs of WN's Introduction. It seems that Silva Lisboa effectively read the English edition, despite the eulogies to Garnier's French translation.

Yet, Silva Lisboa's praise for Smith was much less concerned with the theoretical innovations of WN than with general principles, such as the acknowledgment of labor as the origin of 'wealth.' Political economy, whose horizons are the 'system of natural order,' was seen as the science of the legislator, or of the 'public man.' The sovereign, in turn, was seen as the supreme driver of the 'system of social order.' To Silva Lisboa, the monarch was no more than the chief of a vast family, whose duty was to protect all subjects without distinction, as a father protects his dependents. For this reason, he rejected Rousseau's distinction between family's government and the state government. Stressing the similarities between these two bodies, Silva Lisboa held that this sort of monarchical paternal care necessarily repels the protection to special members of the State, be they monopolies or special branches of industry. In the end, the 'free employment of persons and capitals' was taken as a principle compatible with the defense of producers and civil liberty.

Principios de Economia Politica, like subsequent works, combines the defense of competition and private capitals with a monarchical view of government, associated with an organic approach to society; an idea far from Smith's perspectives, but very representative of the sort of 'Smithianism' prevalent in Brazil. In what refers to government and politics, it should be stressed that Silva Lisboa admired Burke, having edited a volume on his works (Lisboa, 1812).

The fact that Silva Lisboa converted the support to Smith's liberalism, well established in his 1804 work, into a theoretical basis for the defense of the policy measures put in action by D. João in Brazil is revealing. These measures reflected above all two factors: first, the disruption of the relations between the metropolis and its Brazilian colony, as a consequence of the invasion of Portugal; second, the privileged commercial and political relations between Portugal and England, which had to be adapted to the transference of the commercial flows into and from Europe to Brazil, which dispensed with the intermediation of Lisbon. Accordingly, in 1808 the Brazilian ports were opened to all 'friendly nations,' and, in 1810, a new agreement applied low custom duties to English products. These measures had a great impact on the economies of Portugal and Brazil.[5]

Having been integrated into the central staff of the prince regent, Silva Lisboa moved from Salvador to Rio de Janeiro and ascended in the high bureaucracy. A supporter of his ascension was Rodrigo de Souza Coutinho, with whom, around the turn of the century, Silva Lisboa had resumed contacts in Lisbon (Kirschner, 2009). It was certainly Souza Coutinho who sponsored Silva Lisboa's designation to the Royal Press – a strategic position for many reasons, mainly for opening him a channel to print his works. Among the works in defense of the new status quo, *Observações sobre o Comércio Franco no Brazil* [Observations on Free Trade in Brazil] (Lisboa, 1808–09) – symbolically, the first book to be printed by the Royal Press in Rio de Janeiro – *Observações sobre a Franqueza da Indústria e Estabelecimento de Fábricas no Brazil* [Observations on Free Manufacturing and the Establishment of Factories in Brazil] (Lisboa, 1810a); and *Observações sobre a prosperidade do Estado pelos liberais princípios da nova legislação do Brazil* [Observations on the prosperity of the State by the liberal principles of the new legislation of Brazil] (Lisboa, 1810b). These works defended the new policies, especially free trade, against the protest of many Portuguese merchants and manufacturers, who held that it would be impossible to face the British competition under a low external duties' regime. Although no full commercial reciprocity between Brazil and England was under way – for instance, Brazilian sugar was barred from the British territory – Silva Lisboa defended the new commercial treaties, adding to his defense of free trade precepts transposed from WN and from Malthus.[6] Among these precepts were specialization and comparative advantages; preference for employing capital in agriculture, rather than in manufactures; scarcity of capital and free labor in Brazil. Under these conditions, according to Silva Lisboa, Brazil should surely concentrate on agriculture, avoiding complex manufactures.

Silva Lisboa also wrote books envisaging the diffusion of political economy. Worthy of attention are *Estudos do Bem Comum e Economia Política* [Studies on Common Wealth and Political Economy] (Lisboa, 1819–20) and *Leituras de economia política, ou direito econômico* [Readings on Political Economy, or Economic Law] (Lisboa, 1827). *Estudos do Bem Comum*, conceived as Silva Lisboa's *magnum opus* in political economy, embraced references from Aristotle to physiocracy, Smith, Malthus, Say, Ricardo, not to mention Portuguese and other European authors (Germany, Italy, etc.). Despite summarizing several topics – money, value and prices, public revenue – the main efforts are directed at the development of the 'fundamental economic law,' according to which men are endowed by God with the capacity of comprehension, which allows them to escape misery. Human progress depends on 'industry.' Industriousness and other natural capacities, such as curiosity, desire of bettering one's condition, aversion to hard effort, drive men's efforts to avoid arduous work, ultimately conducing to wealth.

Silva Lisboa enthrones intelligence as the main human characteristic, distinguishing 'industry' from 'intelligence', the latter understood as compatible with free labor only, and not with slave labor. According to Silva Lisboa, economists put an excessive stress on 'industry,' forgetting that '*intelligence is the element which gives, raises, and well drives the General Industry*' (Lisboa, 1819: p. 188). In his view, even Smith had excessively extolled 'industry,' somehow underplaying 'intelligence,' even if the famous Smithian triad 'skill, dexterity, and judgment' can be subsumed into 'intelligence.' Of course, Silva Lisboa distinguished brutal labor, associated with slaves, from intelligent labor, practiced by free men.

Regarding the diffusion of political economy, a very important initiative by the Royal Press was the first printed translation of *The Wealth of Nations* into Portuguese, in 1811. Silva Lisboa, supported by Souza Coutinho, was behind this initiative. The work, *Compendio da Obra da Riqueza das Nações de Adam Smith* (Smith, 1811), translated by Bento Lisboa, Silva Lisboa's son, was an abridged version. The suppressions from the original text were guided, according to the editors, by the criterion of evading passages scarcely appealing to Portuguese language readers.[7] All in all, it must be admitted that Bento Lisboa's translation represents a valuable effort of presenting Smith's ideas to Portuguese-speaking readers.

Another member of Souza Coutinho's circle, José Bonifácio de Andrada e Silva, may be assumed as a representative of the general spirit of political economy, or at least as a proponent of 'natural law' principles in Portugal and Brazil. Born in the province of São Paulo and graduated in Coimbra in Philosophy (1787) and Law (1788), Andrada e Silva, after one year as an active member of the Lisbon Academy of Sciences, was sent, in 1790, to a ten-year formative tour in mineralogy across Europe. Back to Portugal, and under the sponsorship of Souza Coutinho, Andrada e Silva was designated to a leading position in the Portuguese mining and metallurgy sector and granted a professorship at the University of Coimbra. Contrarily to the majority of the Brazilian Coimbra graduates, Andrada e Silva stayed in Portugal until 1819. Back in Brazil, he got involved in political activities, becoming a representative in the emerging Portuguese Constitutional Assembly, an important consultant to the prince regent D. Pedro, followed by a position as a central agent in the process that led to Brazilian independence. His political career would proceed with ups and downs: minister to D. Pedro, participant of the Brazilian Constitutional Assembly, exiled in France by D. Pedro, back to Brazil and designated tutor of the son of Pedro (the future Pedro II) in 1831, then discharged of the tutorship.[8]

Although Andrada e Silva wrote no political economy books or pamphlets, his activities in Lisbon reflect the intellectual environment of the Portuguese Enlightenment and the fact that, since his European tour, he was perfectly acquainted with classical and modern literature: Plutarch, Cicero, Livy, Montesquieu, Bacon, Gibbon, Hume, Voltaire, etc. (Dolhnikoff, 1998). On the other hand, his political activities in Brazil reflect a scientific mind in action, envisaging solutions to the local problems based on a mix of illustrated reflections and a typically Portuguese centralist and Catholic view. Two texts are revealing of Andrada e Silva's thought and of a nuanced political economy background. *Memória sobre a pesca de baleias* [Memories on whale fishing] (Andrada e Silva, 1790), presented to the Lisbon Academy of Sciences, is representative of a sort of Smithian appraisal of competition. Andrada e Silva attributes the deplorable state of whale fishing in Brazil to the lack of competition. The activity was submitted to an ineffective public monopoly, and, in his view, opening it to private fishers would emulate competition, thus boosting production and the public revenue, because it is a 'political economy principle' that, under competition, the price of any commodity covers its cost, benefiting producers and everyone else. Referring to public revenues, in *Memória sobre a pesca de baleias* as in other texts, Andrada e Silva would circulate around principles of taxation, not alien to those exposed by Smith in WN's Book V.

However, it is in a very expressive text, *Representação sobre a Escravatura* [Representation on Slavery] (Andrada e Silva, 1825), that a unique aspect of Andrada e Silva's ethical principles, commitment to long-term perspectives and political economy insights, come to the surface. Andrada e Silva was indeed a courageous objector of slave labor in an ambience deeply entrenched in its defense: the Brazilian-Portuguese elite's milieu. *Representação sobre a Escravatura* is an indictment of slavery, based not only on diffuse ideas on the inferiority of slave labor as usually argued by Smith's readers, but on the strong opinion that a nation could only be erected upon the solid basis of free labor. Andrada e Silva goes further and proposes a mix of populations – European white, African and indigenous population – to solidify Brazil's labor force. He also adverts that the mere presence of slave labor turns white laborers lazy and averse to physical activities. Finally, Andrada e Silva was quite aware that the enormous concentration of land at the basis of occupation of the Brazilian territory was absurd. He was, as Smith, an admirer of diffused land tenure and of small properties. It is important to note that, contrarily to Silva Lisboa and other defendants of the immigration of free laborers, that in the end condescended to the slave labor regime, Andrada e Silva, more than scourging slave labor, proposed a timetable for the elimination of the slave traffic and alternatives on what to do with the already existent slave contingent. Despite being a conservative, Andrada e Silva held – maybe from his long European experience – a strong opinion on the political and economic miseries of slave labor and on the impossibility of erecting a nation upon it.

Hipólito José da Costa compounds the trio of Souza Coutinho's protégés involved in the diffusion of political economy. Hipólito da Costa's life experience was unique because, being a Brazilian born in Colônia do Sacramento, a Portuguese city on the La Plata river, he went in 1793 to Portugal, never to return to Brazil. Having graduated in law and philosophy in Coimbra, he was sent, in 1798, by Rodrigo de Souza Coutinho to the United States, in a journey dedicated to the prospection of building techniques and new agricultural products to be transplanted to Brazil. Back in Lisbon, in 1800, da Costa was sent to a professional journey in London in 1802, where he solidified a Freemasonry militancy that led him to jail in Portugal from 1802 to 1805. In 1805, he evaded prison and went to London, where he lived until death. In London, Hipólito da Costa founded and edited the *Correio Braziliense*, a monthly newspaper edited in Portuguese that remained in print from 1808 until 1822.[9]

Correio Braziliense presented an independent opinion on the European and American economic and political affairs directed at the Portuguese-speaking community in Brazil and in Portugal. In London, Hipólito da Costa was in contact with Portuguese merchants and travelers, being attentive to local and European political novelties, and to Portuguese-Brazilian economic policy details.

The openness of Brazilian trade after 1808 and 1810 received special attention in the periodical. Although in principle favorable to free trade, Hipólito da Costa promptly noticed that the lack of protection would damage the prospects of the Portuguese and Brazilian manufactures when faced by British competition. *Correio Braziliense* argued, on several occasions, that the 1810 commercial treaties signed by D. João presupposed leveled counterparts, which was not the case: Portugal and Brazil were not equals to England in terms of productive and financial capabilities. In fact, Hipólito da Costa held that the signature of the 1810 treaty could be only explained by the Portuguese dependence on English capitals. Going further, he suggested that even the Methuen Treaty, agreed by Portugal and England in 1703, had been detrimental to Portugal despite having been considered detrimental to England by Adam Smith. He commented that Smith was an excellent economist, but his authority was harmed by his partiality as a British in this case.

Comparisons with the United States – very frequent among economists – were cautiously undertaken. According to Hipólito da Costa, the North American prosperity should be attributed to this nation's freedom, and not to the liberty of trade. In Brazil, poverty, scarcity of capital and credit, not to mention unrestrained power, were the norm. In what refers to slave labor, *Correio Braziliense* frequently suggests its incompatibility with progress, being attentive to the British pressure towards the extinction of the Brazilian–African traffic.

However, Hipólito da Costa proposes a progressive and very cautious suppression of slave labor in Brazil, going as far as arguing against England's harsh interference in matters that were internal to other countries.

Since the early reports on his journey to the United States, Hipólito da Costa displayed his interest in economic themes and writers, especially financial matters. In Portugal, he had already translated and published a history of the Bank of England. In the *Correio Braziliense*'s section devoted to brief reviews of the scientific literature, there is a note, in the May 1817 edition, on Ricardo's *Principles of Political Economy*. Most importantly, the periodical published, from 1816 until 1820, an extensive translation of Simonde de Sismondi's *Political Economy*. Despite the lack of comments on Sismondi's work, the editorial effort is revealing of the interest in this author, who was very frequently cited by many Brazilian economists.

Influential Brazilian economists

Apart from Souza Coutinho's circle, João Severiano Maciel da Costa stands out as an important name in the Brazilian political economy circuit. Having graduated in Law and Canon Law in Coimbra in 1793, Maciel da Costa developed an expressive political career under D. João and D. Pedro I, and in 1821 published a short book – *Memoria sobre a necessidade de abolir a introdução de escravos africanos no Brasil* [Memoir on the need to abolish the introduction of African slaves in Brazil] – that defended the suspension of the slave traffic in a due term, and the development of manufactures in Brazil through protection by custom duties.

In Maciel da Costa's view, African slave labor had blocked the constitution of a free 'low people' class, inherent in the constitution of any dynamic society. Besides, slaves did not pertain to the common interests and traditions of the Brazilian society, which had Portuguese – and not African – origins.

Why defend 'industry' (meaning manufactures)? According to Maciel da Costa, because colonial agricultural products had already swollen up the European markets; as a consequence, their prices had plummeted. Industrial products, on the other hand, tended to escalate in prices.[10] Moreover, Brazil imported grains. Recurring to the authority of Malthus, Maciel da Costa insisted on the necessity of spreading the production of food.

The list of political economy texts and authors mentioned in *Memoria* is expressive. To begin with is Herrenschwand, who would have proposed the method of the science – an opinion in which Maciel da Costa appealed to Ganilh's and Arnould's authority.[11] In what refers to free trade and protection by custom duties, Ricardo and Say are included in the list of authors who would have propagated the 'errors' of Smith's doctrine, which consisted, first, in applying to inter-nation relations criteria only applicable to the relations among the internal provinces of a State; second, in caring exclusively about consumers, forgetting the interest of producers. Industry and wealth depend on producers, and Brazil stimulated the British producers, forgetting their Brazilian counterparts.

Maciel da Costa criticizes Malthus' *Essay on the Principle of Population* on the grounds that, despite its excellence in population, it did not evince a good understanding of wealth. Smith, on the other hand, was assumed as precise in what refers to wealth, despite making an untenable defense of free trade. Smith would have also underplayed producers in his inclination towards consumers. Say's abhorrence of taxes was also contested: since taxation can stimulate industry and provide public revenues, why not accept it?

On the relations between climate and population, the reference is Montesquieu. On the efficiency and profitability of slave labor, Maciel da Costa disagrees with a list of authors who would have taken on account moral principles only: Smith, Turgot, Steuart, Herrenschwand, Bentham, Bailleul. The right perspective on this topic, involving costs and revenue, had been held by Say. Ganilh – the best French political economist, according to Maciel da Costa – had also raised a suggestive point in devising no crucial differences between the net gains of the French colonial production vis-a-vis the metropolitan agricultural production.

Despite his critical opinion on slave labor, it is worth noting that the various mentions to the necessity of stimulating the slave's progeny suggest that Maciel da Costa combatted the African traffic, and not the Brazilian slave regime itself.

Another important contribution to the political economy of slavery is in Miguel Calmon Du Pin e Almeida's *Ensaio sobre o Fabrico do Açucar* [Essay on Sugar Manufacturing] (1834). Graduated in Law from Coimbra (1821), Du Pin e Almeida participated in the conflicts that marked the independence in his province, Bahia, in 1822 and 1823, and played an important role in Brazilian politics, as a parliamentary and finance minister during the Regency. *Ensaio sobre o Fabrico do Açucar*, dedicated to the analysis of the performance of the '*engenhos*,' Brazilian sugar mills, in its preliminary sections develops long considerations on the slave regime and on the possibilities of evolving towards free labor in Brazil. Without rejecting the African slave trade, Du Pin considers the difficulties of evolving towards free labor and, most of all, connects the labor regimes with the possible types of land tenancy, in what stands out as a true economic – and not only moral – appraisal of the Brazilian slavery.

Indeed, Du Pin scarcely mentions political economy texts and authors, excepted for Malthus. He mostly refers to several agricultural texts, from Roman classics – Columella – to North American and European updated magazines and handbooks. Du Pin's political economy references include no more than very general precepts, such as labor as the true and unique source of wealth. *Laissez-faire*, according to him, applies to developed economies – inducements by the government being necessary in economies where civilization and capital are scarce. Somehow rephrasing Silva Lisboa's formula, Du Pin insists that in non-advanced countries the sovereign is like a *pater familias*, who conducts and protects his sons, before emancipating them. Brazilian agriculture dispensed with governmental induction, since it was a long-developed activity; however, it was dependent on slave labor. Distinguishing free ('voluntary') labor from servitude, or forced labor, and subsistence provided by the lord from the simple payment of salaries, Du Pin affirms that in depopulated countries, where subsistence can be easily obtained, servitude applies; whereas under the prevalence of the opposite conditions, voluntary (or salaried) labor is the norm. Servants exist in Russia, Poland and Hungary; in the United States, Antilles, and Brazil, slaves. That is, Du Pin conditions the labor regime to the economic and geographical situation of the countries. From this background, Du Pin concludes that the transition to free labor would be difficult in Brazil, given the impossibility of transforming the indigenous population into free laborers. Given the negative birth rate of the slave population, the difficulties emerging from the abolition of the slave traffic would be hard to overcome.

Besides, Du Pin was entirely pessimistic about the possibilities of converting inhabitants of African descent, once free, into salaried laborers. In a sort of anticipation of Wakefield's approach,[12] he believed that former slaves would simply run towards the hinterland or establish themselves independently in the cities. It is important to note that, according to the treaties firmed up with England in 1826, Brazil would have to extinguish the African slave traffic in 1831. The traffic was not extinguished and persisted illegally.[13] Du Pin was quite aware of the illegality of the Brazilian formula – keeping on trafficking, under British pressure – and envisaged no economic solution to this dilemma.

João Rodrigues de Brito can be seen as a forerunner in the overt utilization of political economy as an instrument to address the Brazilian problems. His superb *Cartas Economico-Politicas sobre a Agricultura e Commercio da Bahia* [Economic and Political Letters on the Agriculture and Commerce of Bahia] (Rodrigues de Brito, 1807) attacks despotism and addresses several problems of a specific region, Bahia, aggravated by misconceived governmental practices. Such practices included inductions to the plantation of manioc, restrictions and controls over the free disposition of land in sugar cane, controls over tobacco production and trade, deficiencies in roads and waterways, commercial monopolies, inability to intervene on the commercialization of several products, interventions on the credit system.

As a general stand, Rodrigues de Brito supported free competition and abhorred any sort of protectionism. Among his cherished masters were Montesquieu, Adam Smith, Sismondi, Say, Condorcet – all of them repeatedly evoked – and Silva Lisboa. In many passages, Rodrigues de Brito either quotes Say, Smith or even Silva Lisboa, or indicates each author's chapters where the envisaged arguments can be found. An attentive reading of *Cartas Economico-Politicas* confirms that Smith's *Wealth of Nations* and Say's *Principles of Political Economy* were cautiously read, and that Rodrigues de Brito was not only aware of theoretical subtleties but showed inventiveness in applying the economists' lessons to the very specific problems found in Bahia.

Law schools were the loci of political economy teaching and the preferred institutions for the Brazilian elite to get their degrees. After independence, in 1823, law schools were established in Olinda and in São Paulo. In Olinda, Lourenço Trigo de Loureiro and Pedro Autran da Matta Albuquerque distinguished themselves by teaching and publishing on political economy.[14] Trigo de Loureiro's *Elementos de Economia Politica* [Elements of Political Economy] was published in 1854 and not as widely spread as Matta Albuquerque's many works. Both professors were long-standing rivals, and the first criticism of Trigo de Loureiro to his colleague was directed at Matta Albuquerque's translation of James Mill's *Elements of Political Economy*, published in Bahia in 1832. Political economy was a discipline offered in the last year of the law courses, meaning it would have been first taught around 1830. Olinda's students were likely presented to political economy by James Mill's book.

The first book written by Matta Albuquerque, *Elementos de Economia Politica* [Elements of Political Economy] (Matta Albuquerque, 1844), seems to be representative of how the discipline was taught in Olinda during the 1830s; at the very least, its inspiration in James Mill's *Elements*, at that time undergoing translation, is unequivocal. *Elementos* disputed the preference of Brazilian readers with Silva Lisboa's *Leituras de Economia Politica* (1827), and can be taken as an important benchmark in political economy classes in Brazil. One aspect to be remarked is that Matta Albuquerque, who was of French descent, got his Law degree in Aix, thus being immune to the then-dominant Coimbra tradition.

Elementos is divided into four parts: production, value and prices, distribution, consumption. The similarity with Mill's *Elements* – also divided into four parts: production, distribution, interchange, consumption – is evident. Matta Albuquerque, as Mill, defines political economy as the science of the laws that regulate the production, accumulation, distribution and consumption of objects that are useful and hold exchange value. Insisting on the difference between utility and exchange value, wealth is then restricted to objects that hold exchange value, which was also Say's formula. It seems that, by strictly distinguishing between wealth and free natural products, Matta Albuquerque envisaged the connection of wealth to appropriation, an effort that strengthened his final intent: the enthronement of property as a guiding principle, as an institution to be strictly preserved. Self-interest and individual property make up the framework of Matta Albuquerque's political economy, and a permanent concern with the safeguard of property pervades his entire body of work.

Part I encompasses issues such as the division of labor, capital and frugality, machinery and its non-oppositive relation to laborers, the self-regulating properties of money, credit and banks, different employments of capital, trade and external trade, population. Matta Albuquerque admits his adhesion to Malthus's thesis on population, and criticizes two hypotheses by Smith, one concerning the superior productivity of agricultural labor, the other, the preference for internal over external trade. In what refers to the benefits of competition and to the negative results of privileges and governmental protection, the author goes no further than Smith.

Part II, on 'Value and Prices,' associates 'real value' (or natural price) to costs, defining costs by the labor inputs of any reproducible commodity. A criticism of Torrens summarizes the defense of the labor theory of value. Money, a topic already handled in Part I by means of a soft approximation to the quantity theory of money, is restated in Part II in terms of cost or metallic content of the coins; that is, by the general rule on value. On the necessity of establishing a stable value relation between silver and gold, whenever one or both metals are legal tender, Matta Albuquerque recurs to Mill, whereas Smith and McCulloch are the references on circulation under a mixed circulation regime.

Part III discusses salary, rent, profit and interest. On salaries, Matta Albuquerque mixes Smith's arguments on wage differentials and Malthus' population principle. Yet, the chapter on land rent is quite Ricardian; or better, it in many aspects relies on Malthus' *An Inquiry into the Nature and Progress of Rent*. Curiously, the chapter on profits presents an explicit (and difficult to understand) denial of Ricardo's view of profits, arguing that Ricardo's perception that profits as the residue of salaries and the deduction of rent from the net product is erroneous – the Ricardian formula would not have taken into account that profits are necessarily related to capital, given a previously defined profit rate. According to Matta Albuquerque, Ricardo did not consider the possibility of a productivity increase; once considered, wages and profit can grow simultaneously, with no opposition. Matta Albuquerque admits he owed to James Mill on wages and profits, but it is indisputable that Mill's exposition is much more logical than his. Anyhow, Matta Albuquerque permanently upheld a sort of optimistic view of commercial society – in his opinion, a society open to the improvement of everyone's conditions, provided there is order and the safeguarding of property.

Part IV, on consumption, is not as relevant; however, an overall observation is that *Elementos* represents a long-range appraisal of political economy, less notable for its theoretical consistency than by the objective of displaying an all-encompassing proficiency in the science. The book is reasonably updated, or at least attuned to the novelties of political economy until the 1820s, and an exception in an ambience characterized by attempts to apply political economy to the Brazilian conditions.[15]

In parallel with Rodrigues de Brito's 'Letters', *Memorias Economo-Politicas sobre a Administração Publica do Brasil*, by Gonçalves Chaves, stands as an instance of the application of political economy to regional problems. Gonçalves Chaves' five memoirs, written from 1817, cover political and economic problems. The fifth Memoir – the most impressive and well documented – inspects the economy of the author's province, Rio Grande do Sul. The others touch on the government, political division of the territory, and, finally, slave labor and land tenure. In the first two memoirs, Gonçalves Chaves applies some lessons from political liberalism, whereas the other two are mostly based on political economy. The author, a Portuguese from Chaves, had amassed a great fortune in the production of jerked beef in the Brazilian extreme south, and as such was a great authority in slave labor: jerked beef, a typical slave food, was produced by huge masses of slaves.

In what concerns political economy, it is important to note that Gonçalves Chaves, besides constantly referring to Smith, collected large amounts of statistical information about his province. Gonçalves Chaves complained about the lack of more solid information and effectively tried to gather economic data, official or unofficial. Not only principles and doctrines, but data are the basis of his economic analysis.

Travelers

Post-colonial Brazil attracted the attention of many foreign visitors, not only merchants and government officials, but also artists, scientists, mineralogists and biologists. Among the adventurers and scientists who wrote books and reports on natural resources, and who, in travelling across the territory, advanced observations on the economy and on the social system in general, names to be mentioned are Auguste de Saint-Hilaire, who stayed in Brazil from 1816 to 1822 and left a large array of works on botany and on his travels across the diverse Brazilian regions; John Mawe, who stayed in Brazil during 1809 and 1810 and, back to London, published in 1812 the celebrated (and translated into many languages) *Travels in the Interior of Brazil*; Johann Baptiste von Spix and Carl Friedrich Phillipp von Martius, who stayed in Brazil from 1817 to 1820, and published many works on zoology, not to mention the important *Reise in Brasilien*, a three-volume collection published in 1823, 1828 and 1831; and Wilhelm Ludwig von Eschwege, who worked in Portugal from 1803 to 1809, in Brazil from 1809 to 1821, having written in his way back to Europe many travel reports and works on mineralogy, among them the famous *Pluto Brasiliensis*, published in Berlin in 1833.

Since a great number of these scientists and travelers' works were published in Europe – only some of them were translated into Portuguese and with a considerable delay – to frame them as contributions to the diffusion of political economy in Brazil would not be adequate. We would rather consider them European works driven by the Brazilian post-colonial scene. Under this restriction, one must admit that, in addition to their description of natural resources, Spix and Martius and Eschwege's works provide a penetrating view of the economy.

Spix and Martius' description of Rio de Janeiro, in the first volume of *Reise in Brasilien* (1823), presents an optimistic view of the city. After describing the landscape and the urban scenery, the food, and the most common diseases, the authors provide some considerations on the economic impacts of the transfer of the court to Rio de Janeiro. According to them, the Brazilian commerce, which had been harmed by the 'monopoly and jealousy' of the metropolis in the past, had finally been liberated, attracting the demand for native products and, as a consequence, enhancing the demand for African slaves. The text goes no further in describing the slave traffic, although in further passages there are descriptions of the overwhelming presence of slave labor and African-origin descendants in Brazil. However, it provides a detailed account of the imports from several countries of Europe, North America, and from East India, as well as a report of the most important exports to foreign countries and to other Brazilian provinces. Sugar, coffee and cotton are given major attention, including regional origins and the exported amounts.

Spix and Martius suggest that, since the overall exports exceed the imports, Brazil had become an attractor of metals; an inversion, considering the eighteenth-century situation, admitted as an only apparent paradox, given the country's richness. Part of the money attracted to Brazil was nonetheless diverted into the East trade, arousing criticisms on a paradoxical scarcity of money. One of the chapters concludes with a brief description of the activities of the bank founded in 1808 (Banco do Brasil) – sponsored by the crown and local capitalists – and an optimistic overview of the possibilities of spreading arts and offices in the city; detailed and extensive notes on taxation are also provided.

The other parts, chapters and volumes follow a similar pattern. We can say that the passages related to the countryside are dominated by descriptions of vegetation and terrain, even if the characteristics of the local population are also contemplated. In the description of cities, however, the social and economic scenery comes to the front: commercial activities, manufactures, taxation, data on production and population.

A comparison with the description of Rio de Janeiro essayed by John Mawe in 1812, in his book *Viagens ao interior do Brasil* (Mawe, 1978) is suggestive. Mawe, a traveler since his youth, specialized in visiting mines in England and Scotland at the end of the eighteenth century. After a long tour in South America, he arrived in Brazil, where he stayed between 1809 and 1810. Back in London, he became a merchant and became renowned as a specialist in precious stones.[16]

In his account of Rio de Janeiro, Mawe emphasizes the importance of the city as a commercial pole connected to large sections of the Brazilian hinterland and contextualizes the role of the city's port in international trade. Regarding trade, Mawe's main interest lies in the English–Brazilian trade, which, in his view, was open to English adventurers that flooded the city with imports in 1809 and 1810, shattering prices. Nevertheless, Mawe extolled the 1810 trade agreements, envisaging a promising future to the English–Brazilian trade.

Amid the large contingent of scientists who visited Brazil in the early nineteenth century, Wilhelm Ludwig von Eschwege can be considered the best example of a scientific mind in action. His academic training somehow explains his descriptions of Brazil. After elementary studies at home, in Eschwege, a small city in Hesse, he went to Eisenach and later to Göttingen, where he dedicated himself to the natural sciences, architecture and the set of disciplines that characterized cameralism. His studies were complemented in Marburg, where he added mineralogy and metallurgy to the cameralist disciplines. In 1802, Eschwege went to Portugal, where he got in contact with Andrada e Silva, on that occasion supervising mining and metallurgical activities in the country. In 1809, he embarked for Brazil, where he stayed until 1821.[17] Before glancing over the celebrated *Pluto Brasiliensis*, it is interesting to mention some passages from another book, *Brasil, Novo Mundo* [Brazil, New World] (1824), where Eschwege describes tours to Vila Rica and to lead mining regions, also touching on Arraial de Tijuco's diamond mining activities.

Some accounts are quite appealing. The description of the cotton-producing activities in the village of Formiga illuminates the characteristics of an economy where the main product – cotton – is money. According to Eschwege, commodities were paid in Formiga with raw cotton that was, in turn, used by Formiga's traders as means of payment to Rio de Janeiro's wholesale traders. Formiga's merchants profited simply from undervaluing the cotton delivered by the planters, in exchange for the commodities brought from Rio.

On a long account of a boat crossing in São Francisco River, Eschwege criticizes the duties charged by the boatmen, and examines the appropriation of the boat transport activity – leased by the Crown – by soldiers who offered protection to the boatmen and ended up sharing their earnings. An estimate of the costs and gains of the business, considering the several existing boat passages along the river, leads to the conclusion that the revenues of the crown were shattered, whereas the oppression over those who depended on boats to cross the river was huge. This is just one of the several episodes of abuse by officials and soldiers reported in the book.

Taxation is another frequent subject. Eschwege describes the internal (inter-province) duties system and the special taxation applied to diamonds. The description of the efforts to establish a reasonable taxation regime in the diamond mining activities is illustrative. The crown tried several methods, including a capitation on each mining slave, and special taxes (paid in gold) applied to any trader, not to mention the rental contracts established by the crown in the periods the mining activities were conceded to a unique and formidable agent. Since this rental arrangement was based on a capitation on each mining slave, it naturally led to an undercounting of slaves. Eschewe presents tables on diamond production in both quantities (carats) and values, adding accounts of the crown revenues under the several exclusive rental contracts (1740–1771) and in the period the mining activities were either open to all candidates, or managed by the crown (1772–1788). Tables on the royal administration's expenditures are also presented.

A special chapter on public revenues and expenditures presents a list of public revenue sources and types of public expenditure, complemented by accounts that detail the transfers between each province and the capital (Rio), and a list of the royalty's expenditures. Eschwege suggests that high officials were often involved in corruption, criticizing the Portuguese-Brazilian system of public administration, based on concessions, special favors, and privileged relations between high officials and the court.

Pluto Brasiliensis, a 'Memoir on the Brazilian richness in gold, diamonds, and other minerals,' can be taken as Eschwege's masterpiece. In the beginnings of the nineteenth century, the crown undertook many initiatives to improve the Brazilian ironworks, and attributed to Eschwege the inspection of mines and ironworks, as well as the writing of guidelines for their establishment in the province of Minas Gerais.

It must be mentioned that the lack of technical expertise and initiative of the people in agriculture and in mining activities was understood by many intellectuals as a drawback to the country's development. Eschwege shared this feeling and was an enthusiast of immigration. In his view, '*the growth of population is the principal basis of a state*' (PB, p. 196); on the other hand, the Brazilian '*race*' was '*physically and morally inferior, necessitating being purified with the blood and the effort of the Northerners*' (PB, p. 196).

Apart from the technical characteristics of the business, Eschwege was interested in the taxation of metals, especially gold. The general rule was the collection of 'one-fifth' – 20% of the mined gold – although on some occasions a smaller percentage was applied. Capitation based on the number of slaves was also tried – according to Eschwege, against the miners' will. Besides, Eschwege stresses that the mint value of gold, established by the authorities, oscillated, being the market value of gold in general above its mint price. To counteract the endemic evasion of gold, Eschwege suggested a 10% tax rate, instead of the usual 20%.

Eschwege's considerations on the mint taxes, such as the divergence between the mint and the market price of gold, resound the debates on scarcity of money and evasion of metals typical of pre-Smithian political economy. Moreover, despite the prohibitions, rough golden bars and gold powder circulated in remote regions as money. The local foundries authorized to receive the gold, certify the bars and tax the miners not only undervalued the gold, but were primitive and inefficient. The losses of metal and the high costs of the melting process, added to the loose controls against smuggling, incentivized the circulation of gold powder and primitive bars, thus evading certification and taxation. Eschwege adds that, as long as the minting process was not charged, all the costs and losses would be ultimately paid by the government.

In what refers to prices in general, Eschwege remarked that the inflow of gold raised prices in Portugal, harming the Portuguese manufactures and, in the end, producing an outflow of metal. What seems a usual recounting of the well-known story of the negative effects of the abundance of gold in Portugal, receives a special touch by Eschwege, who takes into consideration the particularities of the Brazilian mining process and the losses this process entailed. Ultimately, under consideration was the special character of the monetary economy in a region where gold and diamond were local products. Analyzing the issuing of paper money by Vila Rica's administration – paper money was allowed to circulate in the Diamond District only – Eschwege adds another angle, concluding that the huge devaluation of the paper notes – provoked by overissuing – smashed the public revenues, since the poor conditions of the mining activities and the smuggling of diamonds forced the authorities to accept the paper notes in the payment of taxes.

It is interesting to note that, against the accepted view that attributed the local (and national) miseries to the depletion of the gold mines, Eschwege concluded that 'complete observation' and 'accurate geological research' would show that the mines were not depleted. Instead, the legislation and the methods used in digging and exploring the mines were inadequate. Other legislation and other techniques were suggested, in a complex arrangement involving miners, the government, minting activities, and taxation.

In the analysis of the iron manufacturing, there are provocative considerations on the labor force regime. Souza Coutinho had delegated Eschwege the building of a small iron manufacture, and the major difficulties were on the labor force front. Eschwege advances that in the beginning he avoided making use of slaves, 'given my European mentality' (PB, p. 671); however, since the free laborers that were contracted ran away once trained, the solution was the acquisition of slaves. The same attitude – fleeing away – was also adopted by workers in coal production. Eschwege concluded that there were no means to comply with labor contracts in Brazil. The aversion of free laborers to work was extreme. Once pressed, everyone would argue that 'I am not a slave' (PB, p. 676).

The observations on the difficulties of getting contractual labor in a country where slave labor was the rule were complemented by a sharp observation on the character of capital the slaves assumed before their owners. According to Eschwege, every freeman, even of modest conditions, endeavored to buy a slave who would be their servant and means to make some money. A careful calculation of the lucrative character of a slave for any owner led Eschwege to ponder that the reason a free man rejects working for anyone is the possibility of getting his means out of a labor relation. Whenever access to some land to be plowed would open to anyone, contractual labor would be very difficultly enforced.

Eschwege's observations on the difficulties of finding contractual labor, or any kind of services, in a country dominated by slave labor were shared by many observers. The slave regime contaminated the methods and mentality of the freemen – a complaint usually heard from travelers and scientists. In the chapter on the impacts of the suppression of slave traffic on mining, Eschwege again stresses that the slaves – the universal labor force in the country – were the only capital of freemen, so that every freeman, even facing the most modest conditions, endeavored to buy a slave as a servant or means to make some money.

Eschwege's books point at two major specificities and challenges of Brazil's economy: the labor regime and the monetary regime. Slaves were the axis of the labor regime. Moreover, the availability of free land assured there were no major difficulties in getting access to subsistence. The monetary regime, on the other hand, was quite specific because gold and diamond mining, under a fallible administrative control, made it possible for gold to be either smuggled or illegally used as a means of payment. What distinguishes Eschwege's economic approach is, first of all, his attention to technical particularities, especially in mining, but also in agriculture and other activities. Second was his overall, but also detailed, interest in how governmental activities were developed. The first characteristic came from his training as a mineralogist and scientist; the second, certainly, from his training in cameralist sciences.

Conclusion

As we have seen, the most significant practitioners of political economy in post-colonial Brazil trod two major paths. One of them concerned the diffusion of the general principles of the science in text-books, aimed either at the general public or at students – most of all, law students. In the period under consideration, Silva Lisboa and Matta Albuquerque were the most important writers of books envisaging an exposition of the science as faithful to the state it had achieved in Europe as possible. One may argue that Matta Albuquerque's *Elementos de Economia Politica* was too close to James Mill's *Elements*, whereas Silva Lisboa's general political economy books essayed broad descriptions of the science, always laudatory of Smith and, in many aspects, influenced by Say's *Treatise of Political Economy*; originality did not exist.

The uses of political economy, or its application to the Brazilian reality, are the most interesting aspects. In this path, the problems to be faced were huge and required effort and imagination: slave trade and slave labor, above all, but also external trade under very special circumstances (British dominance), and quite peculiar fiscal and monetary problems. The taxes collected from the import of slaves and their internal traffic were not irrelevant; the fiscal relations between the several regions and Rio de Janeiro were tense; the control over mineral extraction was doubtful. Under these circumstances, what can be assumed is that the Brazilian writers and foreigner travelers who tried to apply political economy to the Brazilian situation were creative and skillful, to say the least. Silva Lisboa's efforts to directly apply Smith's lessons to the Brazilian external trade, or to persuade his readers in how correct it was to concentrate on agricultural production, are examples of the difficulties in transposing classical lessons to diverse contexts. On the other hand, Maciel da Costa's, Du Pin's and Eschwege's approaches to slave labor can be considered original and effectively representative of a contribution to the understanding of the crude reality of modern slave labor. Eschwege's attempts to apply well-known monetary lessons to the reality of a mining region permeated by smuggling are original, and his concern with the incentives that apply to diverse economic situations – crossing the river, employing free labor, bringing gold to the official mint – are innovative. The application of political economy to a very diverse reality proved to be a challenge successfully faced by many authors.

Notes

1. The previous chapter, by José Luís Cardoso, discusses the connections between Souza Coutinho and political economy.
2. Silva Lisboa became Secretary of the 'Table of Inspection,' a position that gave him awareness of the economic activities around Salvador, including agriculture, exports and slave trade. On Silva Lisboa, see Rocha (2001), Kirschner (2009), Novais e Arruda (1999), Paquette (2009).
3. On the Portuguese political economy, see Almodovar and Cardoso (1998).
4. On *Principios de Economia Politica* and other economic works by Silva Lisboa, see Almodovar (1993).
5. On the transfer of the Royal Court to Rio de Janeiro and the main economic policy measures, see Barman (1988), Schultz (2001), Arruda (2008).
6. On the Malthusian influences over Silva Lisboa's works, see Cardoso and Cunha (2020).
7. WN's book V was not included in the *Compendio*.

8. On Andrada e Silva's life, Costa (1972), Dolhnikoff (1998), Silva (2006).
9. Hipólito da Costa is considered a pioneer in Brazilian journalism, despite writing from London. On Hipólito da Costa's life and work, Paula (2001). Safier (2011), Almeida (2002).
10. Maciel da Costa's hypothesis was based on a sort of 'deterioration of the terms of trade' argument, proposed a century before it became diffused by Raúl Prebisch and by ECLA. On Prebisch's terms of trade, see Bielschowsky (2020).
11. A Portuguese version of Herrenschwand's *De l'economie politique moderne: Discours fondamental sur la population* (1786) was published in 1814 by the Royal Press (Rocha, 2001.
12. See Eschwege (1833).
13. On the abolition of Brazilian slavery, see Marquese (2004), Schultz (2005), Costa (1998).
14. In São Paulo, Say's *Traité d'Économie Politique* was the reference to political economy teaching (Gremaud, 2020).
15. Specific Brazilian conditions, especially slave labor, would be considered in other Matta Albuquerque's books.
16. A brief account of Mawe's life is found in Lessa (1978).
17. On Eschwege's life, Sommer (1952).

References

Alexandre, V. (1993). *Os sentidos do Imperio: questão nacional e questão colonial na crise do Antigo Regime Português*. Porto, Edições Afrontamento.

Almeida, P.R. (2002). O nascimento do pensamento econômico brasileiro. In: Dines, A e Lustosa (ed.) *I. Correio Braziliense ou Armazém Literário, Estudos*, vol. 30, t. 1. São Paulo, Imprensa Oficial.

Almodovar, P. (1993). Introdução. In: *José da Silva Lisboa – Escritos Económicos Escolhidos 1804–1820*, tomo I. Lisboa, Banco de Portugal, Coleção de Obras Clássicas do Pensamento Económico Português.

Almodovar, P. and Cardoso, J.L. (1998). *A History of Portuguese Economic Thought*. London, Routledge.

Andrada e Silva, J.B. (1790). Memória sobre a Pesca de Baleias. In: Falcão, E.C. (org.). *Obras científicas, políticas e sociais de José Bonifácio de Andrada e Silva*, Vol. I. Sao Paulo, Revista dos Tribunais, 1965.

Andrada e Silva, J.B. (1825). *Representação à Assembleia Geral Constituinte e Legislativa do Império do Brasil Sobre a Escravatura*. Paris, Firmin Didot.

Araújo, A.C. (2013). *A Cultura das Luzes em Portugal – Temas e Problemas*. Lisboa, Livros Horizonte.

Araújo, A.C., Costa, A.M.A., Costa, M.J.A., Fonseca, F.T., Figueiredo, R.M., Martins, D.R., Pimentel, A.F., Pita, J.R., and Prata, M.A.C. (2000). *O Marquês de Pombal e a Universidade*. Coimbra, Imprensa da Universidade de Coimbra.

Arruda, J.J.A. (2008). *Uma Colônia entre dois Impérios: a abertura dos portos brasileiros (1800–1808)*. Bauro, EDUSC.

Barman, R.J. (1988). *Brazil: The Forging of a Nation, 1798–1852*. Stanford, Stanford University Press.

Bielschowsky, R. (org.) (2020). *Cinquenta anos de pensamento na CEPAL*. Rio de Janeiro, Record.

Cantarino, N.M. and Oliveira, M.F. (2017). The treaties of 1810 and the crisis of the Luso-Brazilian Empire. In: Cunha, A. and Supryniak, C. (eds.) *The Political Economy of Latin American Independence*. London, Routledge.

Cardoso, J.L. and Cunha, A.M. (2020). The reception and appropriation of malthus in Portugal and Brazil. In: Faccarello, G., Izumo, M., and Morishita, H. (org.) *Malthus Across Nations: The Reception of Thomas Robert Malthus in Europe, America and Japan*. Chletenham, Edward Elgar.

Costa, E.V. (1972). José Bonifácio: homem e mito. In: Mota, C.G. (org.) *1822: Dimensões*. São Paulo, Perspectivas.

Costa, E.V. (1998). *Da senzala à colônia*. São Paulo, Editora UNESP.

Costa, H.J. (1800). *Memória sobre a viagem aos Estados Unidos*, v. 21. Rio de Janeiro, Revista do Instituto Histórico e Geográfido do Brasil, 1858.

Costa, H.J. *Correio Braziliense, ou Armazém literário*. Londres, ed. Fac-similar. Rio de Janeiro, Biblioteca Nacional. http://bndigital.bn.br/hemeroteca-digital.

Dolhnikoff, M. (org). (1998). *Projetos para o Brasil: José Bonifácio de Andrada e Silva*. São Paulo, Companhia das Letras.

Du Pin e Almeida, Miguel Calmon. (1834). *Ensaio sobre o Fabrico do Açúcar*. Salvador, Federação das Indústrias do Estado da Bahia, 2002.

Eschwege, W.L. (1824). *Brasil, Novo Mundo*. Brasil, Novo Mundo. Belo Horizonte, Fundação João Pinheiro, 1996.

Eschwege, W.L. (1833). *Pluto Brasiliensis*. Brasilia, Senado Federal, 2011.

Gonçalves Chaves, A.J. (1817–1822). *Memorias ecônomopoliticas sobre a administração pública do Brasil*. Porto Alegre, Erus.

Gremaud, A. (2001). São Paulo, Revista da Sociedade Brasileira de Economia Política, vol 8.

Gremaud, A. (2020). Ensino de economia. In: Aidar, B., Slemian, A. and Lopes, J.R.L. (orgs.) *Dicionário histórico de conceitos jurídico-econômicos (Brasil, séculos XVIII-XIX)*, vol. I. São Paulo, Alameda.

Kirschner, T.C. (2009). *José da Silva Lisboa, Visconde de Cairu – Itinerários de um Ilustrado Luso-Brasileiro*. S. Paulo, Alameda.

Lessa, C.R. (1978). Introdução. In: Mawe, J. (ed.) *Viagens ao Interior do Brasil*. São Paulo, USP/Itatiaia editora.

Lisboa, J.S. (1804). Princípios de Economia Política. In: Lisboa, J.S. (ed.) *Escritos Económicos Escolhidos. Vol. 1 Coleção de Obras Clássicas do Pensamento Econômico Português 5*. Lisboa, Banco de Portugal, 1993.

Lisboa, J.S. (1808–1809). Observações sobre o Comércio Franco do Brasil. In: Lisboa, J.S. (ed.) *Escritos Econômicos Escolhidos (1804–1821), vol 1. Coleção de Obras Clássicas do Pensamento Económico Português 5*. Lisboa, Banco de Portugal, 1993.

Lisboa, J.S. (1810a). Observações sobre a Franqueza da Indústria e Estabelecimento de Fábricas no Brasil. In: Lisboa, J.S. (ed.) *Escritos Econóomicos Escolhidos (1804–1821), vol 1. Coleção de Obras Clássicas do Pensamento Econômico Português 5*. Lisboa, Banco de Portugal, 1993.

Lisboa, J.S. (1810b). Observações sobre a prosperidade do estado pelos liberais princípios da nova legislação do Brasil. In: Lisboa, J.S. (ed.) *Escritos Económicos Escolhidos (1804–1821), vol. 1. Coleção e Obras Clássicas do Pensamento Econômico Português 5*. Lisboa, Banco de Portugal, 1993.

Lisboa, J.S. (1812). *Extractos das obras politicas e economicas de Edmund Burke*. Rio de Janeiro, Impressão Régia.

Lisboa, J.S. (1819). Estudos do Bem Comum e Economia Politica. In: *José da Silva Lisboa – Escritos Económicos Escolhidos 1804–1820*, tomo II. Lisboa, Banco de Portugal, Coleção de Obras Clássicas do Pensamento Económico Português.

Lisboa, J.S. (1827). *Leituras de economia politica ou direito economico*. Rio de Janeiro, Typographia Plancher-Seignot, 1827.

Lustosa, I. (2019). *O Jornalista que Imaginou o Brasil – tempo, vida e pensamento de Hipólito da Costa (1774–1823).* Campinas, Editora da Unicamp.

Maciel da Costa, J.S. (1821). *Memoria sobre a necessidade de abolir a introdução de escravos no Brasil.* Coimbra, Imprensa da Universidade.

Malerba, J. (2000). *A Corte no exílio: civilização e poder no Brasil às vésperas da Independência (1808–1821).* São Paulo, Companhia das Letras.

Marquese, R.B. (2004). *Feitores do corpo, missionários da mente: senhores, letrados e o controle dos escravos nas Américas (1660–1860).* São Paulo, Companhia das Letras.

Matta Albuquerque, P.A. (1844). *Elementos de Economia Politica.* Pernambuco, Typographia de Santos & Cia.

Mawe, J. (1978). *Viagens ao Interior do Brasil.* São Paulo, USP/Itatiaia editora, 1978.

Maxwell, K. (1995). *Pombal – Paradox of the Enlightenment.* Cambridge, Cambridge University Press.

Novais, F.A. and Arruda, J.J.A. (1999). Prometeus e Atlantes na forja da Nação. In: Lisboa, J.S. (ed.) *Observações sobre a franqueza da indústria, e estabelecimento de fábricas no Brasil.* Brasilia, Senado Federal, Coleção Biblioteca Básica Brasileira.

Paim, A. (1968). Vida e Escritos. In: *Cairu e o Liberalismo Econômico.* Rio de Janeiro, Secretaria de Educação e Cultura – Departamento de Cultura.

Paquette, G. (2009). José da Silva Lisboa and the Vicissitudes of enlightened reform in Brazil, 1798–1824. In: Paquette, G. (ed.) *Enlightened Reform in Southern Europe and Its Atlantic Colonies, c. 1750–1830.* Surrey, Routledge.

Paquette, G. (2014). *Imperial Portugal in the Age of Atlantic Revolutions: The Luso-Brazilian World, c. 1770–1850.* Cambridge, Cambridge University Press.

Paula, S.G. (ed.). (2001). *Hipólito José da Costa.* São Paulo, Editora 34.

Rocha, A.P. (1996). *A economia política na economia escravista.* São Paulo, Editora Hucitec.

Rocha, A.P. (2001). *José da Silva Lisboa, Visconde de Cairu.* São Paulo, Editorial 34.

Rodrigues de Brito, J. (1807). *Cartas Econômico-políticas sobre a Agricultura e Comércio da Bahia.* Salvador, FIEB.

Safier, N.A. (2011). Courier between empires. Hipólito da Costa and the Atlantic world. In: Bailyn, B. and Denault, P.L. (eds.). *Soundings in Atlantic History. Latent Structures and Intellectual Currents, 1500–1830.* Cambridge, Harvard University Press.

Schultz, K. (2001). *Tropical Versailles: Empire, Monarchy and the Portuguese court in Rio de Janeiro, 1808–1821.* New York, Routledge.

Schultz, K. (2005). *The Crisis of Empire and the Problem of Slavery. Portugal and Brazil, c. 1700–1820.* Durham, Duke University Press, Common Knowledge.

Silva, A.R.C. (2006). *Inventando a nação: Intelectuais ilustrados e estadistas luso-brasileiros na crise do Antigo Regime Português.* São Paulo, Hucitec/Fapesp.

Smith, A. (1811). *Compendio da obra da Riqueza das Nações de Adam Smith – traduzida do original inglez por Bento da Silva Lisboa.* Rio de Janeiro, Impressão Régia.

Sommer, F. (1952). *Guilherme Luís Barão de Eschwege.* São Paulo, Melhoramentos.

Spix, J.B. and Martius, C.F.P. (1823). *Viagem pelo Brasil 1817–1820,* vol. 1. Belo Horizonte, Itatiaia, 1981.

Part 3

The "coffee era"

5 Economic ideas about slavery and free labor in the 19th century[1]

Amaury Patrick Gremaud and Renato Leite Marcondes

Throughout the 19th century, issues relating to slavery and the replacement of captive labor force were intensely debated in Brazil. The debate grew mainly after the transfer of the Portuguese court to America in 1808, gaining momentum after independence in 1822. This question very likely became the most debated economic issue in the period. The centrality of the theme in the discussions in that period resulted, first, from the dimensions of Brazilian slavery. Brazil was the region of the globe where most slaves landed from Africa for more than three centuries, assuming particular vitality in the first half of the 19th century, just when slavery began to be more debated and the Atlantic slave trade became the object of restrictive laws.

Second, the longstanding debate lasted throughout the 19th century, also due to the very survival of slavery. Discussions in Brazil intensified, as well as throughout Latin America in the period of independence and the formation of new National States. Most Latin American countries extinguished the international slave trade in the 1820s and 1830s, and slavery itself was eradicated around the middle of the 19th century. However, Brazil was one of the last countries to stop the foreign trade in slaves in 1850, and the abolition of slavery only occurred in 1888.

The first discussions and legislation on the end of slavery in Brazil focused on the end of the international African slave trade. In this attempt, first, there were Anglo-Portuguese agreements in 1815 and in 1817 prohibiting trafficking to the North of the Equator, later the Brazilian treaty with England of 1826 and the law of 1831. This 1831 law represented an ineffective attempt in practice to suppress the traffic. The abolitionist Luiz Gama (1830–1882) affirmed the ineffectiveness of this legislation (A Província de São Paulo, December 18, 1880, p. 5). Despite an initial reduction after the 1831 law, the traffic intensified,[2] reaching tens of thousands of people landed and leading to increasing British pressure to comply with the agreements. Only 20 years later, a new legal framework was established to effectively end the influx of slaves from outside the country.

After another 20 years, the possibility of natural reproduction of slaves was suppressed with the law of the free womb of 1871. By emancipating all the children of slaves, the law still kept them under the protection of their masters

DOI: 10.4324/9781003185871-8

until they turned 21 years old. Again, a new 14-year interregnum to promulgate the Sexagenarian Law in 1885 emancipated slaves over 60 years of age and, finally, three years later, definitive abolition. Until the elimination of slavery in 1888, several laws restricted it in some way, ruling the debate at every moment.

The abolitionist laws in Brazil, especially the last ones, were in part the result of the movements of the slaves or freedmen themselves, along with the pressures of other actors. In Brazil, this discussion encompassed a wide range of people and institutions, from parliamentarians and the government itself to associations and private societies. Some of the latter were created specifically to influence the debate. Several issues were discussed, considering the moment (immediate or in the long term), the way (with or without reparation to the masters), for whom (all or part), effectiveness (applied or not), treatment, destination of the freed persons etc. The abolitionist movement of trafficking and, later, of slavery itself grew over time, increasingly encompassing a broader set of society. Throughout the period, there was always strong external pressure on Brazil. In the first half of the century, this pressure came in part from the diplomacy of some countries such as England, which had already suppressed the slave regime, including slavery in its colonies. Despite certain regional specificities and actions with local characteristics, the great international intellectual movements influenced Brazilian anti-slavery currents.[3]

Initial debates about slavery (1800–1850)

Independence produced the need to think about the country, defining new institutions that formed the Brazilian State. Among the various discussions, the debate around the issue of slavery stood out. At first, the issue of trading and the entry of new slaves was the essence of the debates. Several authors wrote supports for the extinction of slavery or the trade; we highlight Antônio José Gonçalves Chaves[4] (1781–1837), José Eloy Pessoa da Silva[5] (1792–1841), Frederico Burlamaque[6] (1803–1866) and José da Silva Lisboa[7] in the 1830s. Other two abolitionist defenses came from D. João VI's advisor, João Severiano Maciel da Costa and José Bonifácio de Andrada e Silva, who was a central figure of Independence. These political initiatives were defeated, and the first directed to D. João VI and the second to the Brazilian Constituent Assembly. Despite demands for an end to the slave trade and slavery itself in the first third of the 19th century, defenders of the slave regime managed to postpone the anti-slavery laws or their application.

We note in practically all abolitionist texts the presence of arguments connected to the question of the injustice of slavery or opposition to the slave condition, based on the Enlightenment conceptions of natural law, demonstrating the influence of the international abolitionist ideas. The economic issue is also pointed out in most abolitionist texts, highlighting the productive consequences of potential instability and the negative impact on security spending and the destruction and losses caused by insurrections and uprisings. On the other hand was the issue of the inefficiency of slave labor and the potential advantages of free labor, especially in terms of incentives, reducing waste and increasing productivity. They drew on arguments from authors of the political economy, such as Smith, Turgot, Bentham, which are also present in Brazilian abolitionist texts.

Some other economic arguments sometimes varied between authors. For Chaves ([1822] 1978), the negative economic effect of slavery was to prevent the growth of free labor available for agricultural work. For Costa (1821), slavery degraded the idea of work, creating an obstacle to a possible replacement of slave workers by free national ones. For this to occur, great power of persuasion and strong measures to limit the vagrancy of the free population would be necessary. Andrada e Silva (1825) also highlights the environmental degradation with economic consequences arising from the erroneous incentives arising from the use of slave labor.

The cited abolitionist texts are still concerned with the enormous inflow of slaves that was happening and the impact on the formation of the new country. There was a fear of founding the new nation on an unstable balance and in conditions of potential conflict, as an important part of the population did not maintain positive social ties with the country and the rest of the inhabitants. Instability could lead to permanent civil war and great difficulty in defending against external enemies. The Haitian revolt, like other ones at the time, often fomented the argument of insecurity and the possibility of conflicts and wars in slave societies, making it difficult to establish a stable government, especially at the beginning of the formation of new states. The end of slavery would be a fundamental element for the governability and homogenization of the nation, which could be achieved in a few generations. This seems to be the central argument against slavery among Brazilian abolitionists like Andrada e Silva (1825).

In some of the abolitionist texts, the recognition of some civilizational role for the trafficked Africans and slavery itself remains, such as in Costa (1821), as does a recognition of the importance of slavery in the Brazilian economy's development. As the vast majority of the slave and freed population was illiterate and had no voice in parliament or even through publications, most abolitionist projects had a moderate character that defended the end of slavery, but within a very spaced period, thus approaching the very slavery theses that the permanence of slavery as long as it was necessary. To alleviate the problems, this vision granted some reforms in the slave condition and in the management by the masters. Costa (1821) proposes better care and management of slaves, such as encouraging marriage and attention to children, from feeding them and not exposing them to unnecessary risks. Andrada e Silva (1825) observes similar elements, not only the moderation of the process through an emancipation in stages, gradually limiting the ways to become slaves and mitigating slavery itself, expanding the rights of slaves and reducing the possibility of free disposal of bodies by the slaveholders. Such changes aimed to reduce aspects of the inefficiency of slave labor and, on the other hand, the insurrectionary tendency of slaves with the gradual concession of improvements in their living conditions.

Later, the so-called farmers' manuals sought to rationalize the employment and treatment of slaves. Carlos Taunay (1791–1867) in 1837 [2001], even though he declared that slavery violated a natural right, argued that it was justified by the physical and intellectual inferiority of the Africans, who needed violence to subject them to work. The coffee farmer Francisco Lacerda Werneck[8] (1795–1861) also dealt with the food, clothing, housing, health, punishment and work of slaves. The latter defended greater concessions to captives, such as plots to cultivate and that the surpluses should be purchased by the masters at fair prices. Such discussion was not restricted to just a moral questioning, referring to the will of these men, but also economic.

The lawyer Caetano Soares was director of the *Instituto dos Advogados Brasileiros* (created in 1843) and member of *the Sociedade Auxiliadora da Indústria Nacional* (founded in 1827). He gave a lecture in 1845 on the first and in 1847 on the second on improving the lives of slaves, which was published in 1847. Soares (1845) proposed some improvements to the life of slaves, such as legislation to protect the earnings of the enslaved, which should be deposited in savings banks to earn interest. Another measure would be the provision by the government of the moral and religious instruction of the captives. These preparations proved necessary to avoid the inert idleness, the brutal degradation, the misery and the diseases of a hasty freedom. This criticism was not directed at slavery itself, but the mismanagement of the masters, and can also be seen in authors who defend slavery itself and who demand some reform in the rules. Several slavers used the development of England and its colonies as an example to question the necessity of slavery.

Therefore, if Brazil intends to progress economically, it needs slavery and a continuous supply of African labor, and it can even do as England did, which only after a certain level of development could do without trafficking and slavery itself.[9] In these sense, the deputy Raimundo Cunha Mattos[10] (1776–1839) delivered important speeches in the National Assembly in defense of trafficking. Matos supported the importance of slavery for the maintenance and progress of the Brazilian empire, and for this the different social groups had their functions, among which the African slaves. He was also based on traditional religious arguments that saw slavery as the fruit of sin and that trafficking and slavery were a form of ransom trying to free slaves from African savagery and their sinful conditions, providing them redemption and even progress.

The importance of slavery in economic development is the key element in defending the maintenance of slavery. Abolitionists themselves recognize this importance. Costa (1821) initially developed an economic argument against the idea of slavery. In addition to the superiority of free labor, slavery would not be suited to the growth of other economic sectors other than the production of products for export. For this author, the development of Brazil, by now independent, could not be based on the productive specialization of a few exportable primary products, criticizing parts of liberal authors such as Smith. According to Costa, Brazil should develop a more vigorous domestic market economy, investing on economic sectors aimed at domestic supply, both manufacturing and agricultural products aimed at local consumption. However, in this type of production, there prevails a way of producing that differs from the mills, a style of production based on smaller properties and with the setting of producers in the countryside. Cultures for the internal market were, like the production of manufactures, incompatible with slave labor. But Costa (1821) himself recognizes that development in the colonial period was based on the exploitation of labor and land to export some products. The transition to an internal market economy would be a lengthy process. Even if the end of slavery was defended, it should remain a reality in Brazil for some time, until it could be replaced by free labor, including Brazilian indigenous people and European immigrants. In order to allow the transition to take place in a non-abrupt way, it was important that the trafficking continued for some time, with the author predicting that the trafficking would remain in effect for at least 20 years. Thus, despite all the abolitionist arguments, Brazilian society depended heavily on slavery and trafficking, effectively moderating abolitionism.

This ambiguous position can be seen in the important politician and jurist Bernardo Pereira Vasconcelos. In a speech at the House in 1827, he defended the agreement with England to extinguish trafficking; in another speech in the Senate, in 1843 he defended the maintenance of the entry of slaves, reported realistically the importance of slaves in Brazilian development, used as an example the development of the USA and affirmed that Africa civilized Brazil (Vasconcelos, 1999, pp. 45–48; 268–269).

The importance of slave labor for the development of Brazil is normally due to two aspects: the continental dimensions of Brazil and an alleged lack of another source of workers. Caetano Soares argued that slavery was justified because of the circumstances of the Portuguesehaving to cultivate an almost limitless territory, and not having free labor force to do so for wages, either in the small, sparsely populated kingdom of Portugal, either in the same indigenous people, who, due to their nomadic, barbaric and savage state, were not suitable for this work.(1847, p. 15)

According to Soares, the justification of relative scarcity of arms in proportion to the availability of land for slavery was used to be "excusable" or tolerated, even if the slave was driven to work by violence. The growth of free arms would make slavery unnecessary, as happened in Europe. In this way, the circumstances that justified captivity would cease to exist. The author also called attention to the fact that the total abolition of slavery would generate the destruction of fortunes, since most of the farmers' wealth consisted of slaves.

The debates around slavery also took place in higher education institutions such as law schools. Many associations and newspapers, mostly abolitionist in nature, formed around these faculties, but the abolitionist view was neither homogeneous nor unanimous, since the students of these universities reflected the Brazilian elite itself, composed of many great farmers and slave owners. In these institutions, there were topics such as "political economy" and "natural law", and some professors like Mata Albuquerque and Avelar Brotero write compendiums. Brotero, a professor in São Paulo, wrote, in 1829, *Principles of*

Natural Law and, based on Gabriel de Mably, attacked slavery and stated that it "is the greatest of all evils" (Brotero, 1829, p. 87), which, however, did not prevent him from owning slaves and even leaving them as an inheritance.

We also observe Mata Albuquerque, who was the first professor of Political Economy at the Recife Faculty of Law. For Albuquerque (1860), slavery is a necessity in countries with a large territorial extension, where the demand for work is high relative to the lack of labor for work in agriculture. Despite accepting slavery as a necessary way of work given the conditions of supply in the labor market, Albuquerque considers the arguments in favor of the replacement of the slave; slave labor would be less productive than free labor. However, when there was a shortage of free labor and high wages absorbing the entire entrepreneur's profit and preventing the accumulation of capital, slaves were necessarily used. Thus, captive labor can be more profitable depending on the conditions of supply of free labor. Slavery ends up being a necessity in countries with great territorial extension, where the demand for work is great and there is a lack of arms. This tends to disappear if there is a growth in the number of free workers (or technological development).

The lack of alternative labor and the geographic dimensions in the country can also be observed in a wide use of arguments based on the open resources model, applicable to agrarian societies with private land ownership.[11] This discussion of the availability of production factors (too much land in proportion to workers) conditioned the existence of enslaved (or servile) labor, as exposed by Edward Wakefield (1796–1862) for English colonies (such as Australia and New Zealand) at the beginning of 19th century in newspapers and later in books (Wakefield, [1829] 2015, [1834] 1967 and [1849] 1969). The latter proposed the government charging for new areas of cultivation as a way of inducing a reduction in wages and the employment of salaried labor, even in a region with great availability of land relative to the working arms. For Brazil, the lawyer and president of the Pará province Bernardo de Souza Franco (1805–1875) had already proposed the adoption of the Wakefield system as a solution for the lack of salaried workers for the entrepreneurs in a region with large extensions of territory still to be occupied:

> sale of vacant lands . . . to replace colonization by itself, that is, with the same income, and to supply the market with a number of salaried labor force, which are sold at public auction, employing successively the proceeds from the sale of land in sending new settlers.[12]

A few years later, an article published in *Auxiliador da Indústria Nacional* (Sociedade Auxiliadora da Indústria Nacional, 1845, p. 26) also proposed the adoption of the Wakefield system. The sesmarias system was abolished in 1822, through which land was distributed in large dimensions to people who had the resources to occupy it throughout the colonial period. In the absence of this regulation, the takeover lasted until the mid-19th century, which generated conflicts in which the strongest one prevailed. In this way, the issue of access to and scarcity of land became crucial for the establishment of a free wage labor market, and the action of the State could "artificially" generate the scarcity of a fundamental productive factor in an agrarian society. The general and free distribution of land through land tenure or control through sale by the state and subsidizing immigration were measures widely discussed at that time. In the same year of trade abolition, the approval of the land law in 1850 constituted an attempt by the government to control access to land, taking over the administration of vacant lands, that is, not occupied land. However, this proposal proved to be ineffective in practice, maintaining the occupation logic at a time of great expansion of coffee cultivation in the Southeast into new productive areas, which became accessible with the railroads.

Debates after the end of the Atlantic slave trade

After a new law in 1850 and the government's efforts, the trade of African slaves to Brazil was ended. The end of the slave trade constituted the first step in the struggle for the end of slavery itself, assuming a progressive decline of the captive population in the absence of the arrival of new Africans and the difficulty for the vegetative growth of the enslaved.[13] Despite some improvement in the treatment of slaves and the constitution of slave families, the reproductive capacity of the captives proved not to be sufficient to meet the growing demand for labor power in the country.

The end of trafficking did not generate problems in Brazilian agricultural production; Sebastião Ferreira Soares (1820–1887) was public employee and member of the Instituto Histórico e Geográfico Brasileiro and published a very elaborate study of agricultural production, arguing that there was no shortage of foodstuffs due to the end of the influx of Africans (Soares, 1860). Although there was an increase in food prices, this fact resulted from the action of speculators in the big cities. In the same sense, Malheiro (1867) estimates that after 1850 there was an expansion of exports of the main Brazilian products, with the exception of those destined for Africa, such as cachaça. On the other hand, Malheiro stated that the elimination of African trafficking to Brazil had resulted in an improvement in the treatment of captives and their descendants and the reallocation of trafficking capital to more legitimate and honest activities.

Also, according to Malheiro, the shortage of slaves valued free work, whether by black people or not, which was once devalued. Interest in colonization through free workers and immigration grew after the end of the African slave trade. The *Sociedade contra o Tráfico de Africanos* (1852) was created shortly after the 1850 law. For the Society in 1852, the great dependence on the influx of Africans should be replaced by foreign colonization or the "civilization" of the indigenous people, expanding the supply of labor. Colonization would be divided between urban and rural areas. First, the replacement of slaves would take place in the more commercial maritime cities, through the importation of workers. In order to bear the cost of this immigration and not burden the public budget, the Society proposed the creation of companies, which should receive a guarantee of return from the government on their capital. The newly arrived free worker should lease his services to the company for a specified period. In rural areas, the government should create colonization companies, which would receive settlers and broker them to farmers. When it was not possible to create companies in a certain region, the government should do so at its expense.

Some immigration and colonization experiences had already taken place even before 1850; the company Vergueiro & Cia in Limeira (west of São Paulo Province) started with the Portuguese in the early 1840s and at the end of the same decade received an influx of settlers from Germany and Switzerland. The system was based on partnership contracts, with the colonists receiving advances on the costs of traveling from Europe to the farm and paying through the income from work in the coffee plantations. The experience brought the expansion of production, but it faced problems related especially to the living conditions and treatment of settlers, as well as the difficulty in paying off debts. The question was not only about the interest that was levied on the debts, but also about problems in weighing, in the price of coffee and in the settlers' debits with the farmers. The settlers' complaints led to conflicts in the region, and especially when the complaints reached Europe, there was a campaign against emigration to Brazil. Later, the Sociedade Democrática Constitucional Limeirense (1869), led by the farmer and great slave José Vergueiro (son of Senator Vergueiro), took a stand in favor of the owners' compensation and proposed a free womb only after 1880 and the end of slavery only in 1901.

After the end of the slave trade, the debate continued: how and when to achieve slave emancipation, which could be general and immediate or gradual. One of the main arguments for the freedom of slaves consisted in the greater productivity of free workers in relation to enslaved ones, defended by different authors. Malheiro publicly embraced abolitionism in the early 1860s, relying on Voltaire, Montesquieu and Bentham. Economists Smith, Say and Chevalier were evoked: "slavery profoundly impedes the development of industry, the production of public and private wealth" (Malheiro, 1867, pp. 135–136).[14] The author did not dispute that slave labor provides results. However, the free one has the advantage of being voluntary and intelligent, used in a natural and more fruitful way. The questioning of slavery stemmed from several arguments, including moral and religious ones. Although there was religious tolerance from the beginning of enslavement, the opposite position grew. In addition to the moral factors, Malheiro placed slavery as "an unspeakable iniquity; it is a very pernicious evil to society, the slave, and the master himself. Abolition is an act of complete justice, humanity, and the highest public convenience" (1867, 3rd part, p. XI).

Female voices participated in the slavery debate. The Afro-descendant Maria Firmina dos Reis (1822–1917), a daughter of a freedwoman was a teacher in Maranhão. She wrote the novel *Úrsula* ([1859] 2020), which told the sad condition of the slaves, shy and brutalized. She later published the abolitionist short story *A Escrava* (1887). The French Maria Josefina Durocher (1809–1893), based in Rio de Janeiro, midwife and member of the Brazilian Academy of Medicine, published a book.[15] In 1871, the Frenchwoman Maria Josefina Durocher (1809–1893), based in Rio de Janeiro, midwife and member of the Brazilian Academy of Medicine. The barbarity committed against slaves was the main justification for the abolition of slavery, comprising crimes of abusive punishment and on their families, especially women and children. However, freedom could be seen by the slave as an authorization for everything, without moral restriction. Thus, she proposed gradual abolition and improve the lot of slaves. In the latter case, a code of rights for slaves and their masters would be established, covering rations, clothing, hours and days of work, exit permits, well-defined punishments, religious practice, etc. Additionally, there would be a regiment of slave discipline and humanity. It suggested the creation of a philanthropic tax to raise funds for the freeing of slaves through a captive price list. Ultimately, legislative education would prepare them for life in freedom.

In addition to the moral issue, for the physician Adolfo Bezerra de Menezes (1831–1900), born in the state of Ceará, the principle of individual interest and the limited education of slaves made it difficult to make them more productive, as well as the "coarseness" resulting from violence suffered. There was little interest in investment in captives by their owners. The product of free labor is cheaper and of better quality than slave labor. An evidence of this reality was Ceará after the great drought of 1845, which resulted in the sale of a large part of its slaves. After the reduction of slavery in the province, there was greater growth in livestock and agriculture, with part of the production being exported. There was no shortage of workers; it only reduced their idleness.[16] Slave or free work differed between Brazilian regions, depending on the characteristics of the predominant economic activity, its own dynamism and availability of arms.[17]

The issue of idleness of free workers including freedmen was a controversial issue. The Pernambuco native Felix Peixoto de Brito (1807–1878) was in favor of slavery in 1870, because, despite not receiving a salary, the enslaved received food, clothing, housing and dressings from their owners, even if they were children or elderly. According to the author, "the master never abandons his slave because of his illness or old age", so, the slave does not starve (1870, p. 12). The number of working hours of the slave would be similar to that of the free, and the punishments to the slaves were limited due to the concern with the loss of value of a relevant property. Thus, slavery was a "beneficial guardianship" of the owner to his captive, not showing the ability to have a life without privations. Finally, the author casts doubt on the insertion of ex-slaves in the labor market, increasing poverty, idleness, in addition to public safety problems. He evidences such possibility through Jamaica's experience of post-abolition.

The novelist José de Alencar [1867/68] (2008) in his letters of 1867/68 pointed out the tendency of the freedman to become miserable and a beggar. Alencar highlights other problems of sudden abolition, such as the ruin of landowners and the bankruptcy of the country due to the destruction of the base of agrarian wealth, in addition to increasing the tendency for insurrections and social wars. Therefore, he recommended to the emperor prudence in the question of emancipation. His position was that no law was required for the establishment of slavery, so there should not be one for its extinction. The end of slavery would occur naturally as slavery itself was no longer necessary for Brazilian society, when the free population grew, expelling slavery. Alencar criticized new foreign theses and reaffirmed the idea of slavery as part of history and which re-emerged in Brazil due to the need to develop. Finally, Alencar affirmed the idea of beneficial or civilizational guardianship for slaves, as a duty of white men, flirting with racist theses that were once again being introduced in Brazil.

Peixoto de Brito (1870) defended another important issue in the debate, which would be the compensation of owners for the release of slaves due to abolition. The compensation or not of the slave owners for the loss of their patrimony was one of the crucial points of the debate, as the English and French experience of compensating the slavers proved to be quite costly. To make this possibility viable in Brazil, Benjamin Fontana (1865) proposed the creation of brotherhoods with voluntary contributions for the purchase of slaves who would work for the institution until the payment of the expense incurred, thus becoming freed.[18]

Lawyer José Penido also pointed out the immorality of slavery in the early 1880s, through the *Jornal dos Economistas* and later in a book.[19] Civilization would no longer include slavery, as well as morals and religion, consisting of an error that must be urgently and indispensable corrected.[20] The transformation of slave labor into free labor would produce a civilizing impulse for society. Salaried work should be the alternative, through spontaneous immigration. Financial expansion through a rural credit bank can mobilize idle land and immigrants. However, the rapid suppression of captivity would lead to the loss of capital and farm workers, contesting the property rights of slavers and extorting those of others.

According to José Penido, the compensation for the expropriation would have no reason to exist, since if the State allowed slavery, it would also be allowed it to suppress this concession. The author asks himself about the slaves themselves "who will compensate them for what they suffered and for what they still suffer in captivity" (1885, p. 25). As the slaves were the workers, the product of their labor should be their property, so they would also have the right to compensation. Previously, Silva Netto (1871) was already against liberation through compensation. The cost of compensating a contingent exceeding one million people at that time would be quickly unfeasible for the State. Later, especially during the passage of the law which freed the slaves older than 60 years old, in 1885, the abolitionist movement explicitly advocated immediate abolition without compensation.

A key issue for the debate represented the moment of emancipation. A widespread idea was that immediate abolition could disrupt agriculture, which is heavily dependent on captives. Caetano Soares (1847) suggests the gradual abolition, favoring the liberation of those who better serve at the initiative of the owners themselves. Referring to Bentham, the personal merit of good service and customs should be rewarded, especially when the owner passes away or in his will. Later, legislation could incorporate this principle, also to the children the slave women had had with their masters, and the mothers as well. He used the example of the English colonies of the failure of mass abolition to support the idea of progressive liberation. But there were critics of an excessively progressive liberation as in Silva Netto (1866). Malheiro (1867) observed that the establishment of a future moment for freedom could generate expectations in the slave; if too short, it could cause disorder and, if too long, discouragement and uprisings.

Many authors advocated a gradual way of emancipation from the 1860s onwards, starting with women to free the womb or provinces with smaller populations.[21] As stated by Bezerra de Menezes (1869), this option would allow for better assimilation into society, primarily by women and especially those born from the free womb. The latter constituted the simplest, easiest and most convenient means of all abolition options. Thus, he recommended educating slaves' children born free, through primary education and mechanical arts for boys and mother-of-a-kind duties for girls, accompanied by religious and moral principles. However, how to do it if the family was still in slavery? The author's suggestion was the creation of upbringing houses in municipalities and schools in capitals for education after the age of 6. After education, they would be taken to freed colonies. The author defended raising the resources to materialize this process of assimilation of the slaves' descendants, even if it was to the detriment of foreign immigration.

In addition to the release of female slaves and especially of those who would be born, another group of slaves deserved attention and legally fought for their freedom: the slaves who arrived in Brazil from 1831 onwards. There was a great discussion about the legality of the Atlantic trade from Africa to Brazil after the 1831 law that already prohibited trading. Those Africans who entered the country after the law would be free, as defended by the abolitionists, including in the courts. A significant portion of the existing slaves consisted of legally free Africans and their descendants who were supposed to be freed immediately, questioning slave property. Luiz Gama fought for these people. Gama was one of the forerunners of the conjunction of the most purist republican ideals jointly defending the abolition of slavery and the end of the Monarchy.[22] He was born free in Brazil, the son of a manumitted mother, but was illegally enslaved and, learning about this crime, he freed himself, starting to fight against the illegal slavery of Africans, being a member of the '*Sociedade Emancipadora Esperança*' and later another society with his own name.[23]

The debate intensified during the War of the Triple Alliance (1864–1870), due to the growing engagement in the cause of abolition. Not only did the military join the movement, but the emperor himself in the opening session of the Legislative Assembly in 1867 responding to external pressure. He called the attention of the Assembly to the issue that should be considered, but at the right time and respecting the property rights of the masters. Finally, the emperor stressed that it could not be an abrupt change, as it would shake the main economic activity in the country. After several bills in parliament, this debate would culminate in the approval of legislation that freed those born whose mother was enslaved in 1871, the so-called free womb law, which theoretically ended the second source of slaves, after the slave trade had been eradicated.[24]

From then on, theoretically, it was only a matter of time before slavery came to an end. However, the debates proved to be more complex, involving a series of rules regulating the free womb. After the 1871 law, the children of female slaves would be free, but they were subject to the "care" of the owners until they reached adulthood. Martinus Hoyer (1825–1881) stated that the latter found themselves in semi-slavery and criticized the law (1877, p. 242). Slavery would end slowly, which was widely criticized by abolitionists, and their institutions held a different position. The French senator Victor Schoelcher (1804–1893) criticized the Brazilian emperor, saying that he should feel humiliated for being the only sovereign of a civilized nation to have slaves as subjects. He still criticized the law of the free womb, in the same way as Hoyer and part of the Brazilian abolitionist movement, since in practice it kept a slave's child in this condition for at least 22 years, and he claimed, not without some exaggeration, that slavery would only be eradicated after two centuries.

The French scientist living in Brazil, Louis Couty (1854–1884),[25] responded to the French senator, defending the emperor, speaking of his concern with eradicating slavery, but of his care in not destroying Brazilian production. The non-radical nature of the free womb law provided precisely the time necessary for the Brazilian productive structure to adapt itself to a situation without slaves; gradual abolition would adjust the liberation of blacks to the arrival of immigrants to replace them. The deadline for restructuring was due to the lack of active free men, able for agricultural work and capable of regular activity. Couty (1884) criticizes the employment capacity of free people; the use of the free national worker would only occur in secondary functions or temporary works. Even in difficult jobs, they did not perform activities regularly and after a certain period left the post, as they were already satisfied with what they had achieved and preferred leisure. He also did not perceive the freed slaves and their descendants as being able to assume this role. For Couty, the solution to the labor issue in Brazil involved European immigration.

Regarding slavery, Couty (1884) also makes the usual criticisms of the slave regime, which leads to waste and makes it difficult to incorporate technological progress. The mechanization of production with the introduction of machines or the plow itself would only occur when the slave system was replaced and the instruments were entrusted to free, active and economic men. However, this work to be carried out by free men will not be the responsibility of future freedmen, as they would not continue in agricultural production; if blacks were not subjugated, they would not work. Liberation could in no way alter the mental and social defects of today's workers. Thus, from a critique of slavery, Couty turns to a racist one, saying that black people are not equal to white people and especially presenting the idea of the inferiority of black population. He is part of those who reintroduce in the debate during the second half of the nineteenth century, the thesis of differences between men, races, as opposed to the humanitarianism typical of the Enlightenment. Physician Nina Rodrigues (1862–1906) also defended the physical and mental inferiority of blacks and mestizos in several studies. Couty discarded the possibilities for blacks to evolve and adapt to the civilized way, it being a risk to use them as a constituent element of what the Brazilian people would be, as there was not enough time to wait for the improvement of blacks or mestizos. In his diagnosis, Brazil would only emerge from the crisis if it used immigration in its social structure, expanding the participation of white Europeans. He thus showed himself to be an ideologue of whitening.

The abolitionist movement that did not admit the idea of inferiority of slaves or blacks criticized segregationism. The author Joaquim Nabuco[26] (1849–1910) defends the black race as an integral part of the Brazilian people and that abolition has become a necessity, because so citizenship will be given to the former slave as that of any other Brazilian, allowing its complete insertion as an element of the people with all its rights and on which every development project must count. Abolition allows the generalization of citizenship and the complete formation of nationality, being founded entirely on equals. Together with Nabuco, the mulatto André Rebouças (1838–1898) was one of the main thinkers of the abolitionist movement. This engineer belonged to the "moderate" group, to which Nabuco also belonged, among others (JUCÁ, 2001). For them, abolition was part of a broader process of confronting the pillars of Brazilian society: slavery, latifundium and monoculture. Thus, they proposed to implement a kind of "Brazilian rural democracy". His ideas were published in the press in the 1870s and later reorganized in the 1883 book (Rebouças, 1988). In this book, there are different proposals for the revitalization of national agriculture, through land concessions, taxation of unproductive lands and enhancement of property rights in favor of producers at the expense of landlords. The concern encompassed free workers, ex-slaves and immigrants. Individual freedom is the essence of Rebouças' thought, being influenced by Smith and Stuart Mill and by French authors such as Gournay, Quesnay, Turgot, Chevalier and Say. The best social contract would combine a maximum of individual initiative and a minimum of government intervention, reducing regulation that favors small groups. The government maintained an obsolete and costly customs system for companies, benefiting smuggling and "facilitators", which interested few people.

Rebouças presented a view that the spirit of association was an important tool to increase the productivity of small farmers. For the author, the constitution of cooperation systems from public utility companies and the agricultural centralization in farms, plantations and central factories would allow small producers in lands that are often not very productive to obtain a return in the cultivation of sugarcane, cotton or coffee. The farms and central mills would buy agricultural goods for processing and marketing, complying with the principle of division of labor and providing better preparation for the products. They should train their apprentices, helping the Brazilian population to advance in education. Central companies could provide credit to farmers, possibly on better terms than rural banks. These companies would be a more advantageous option in relation to colonization by partnership, due to the division of the latifundium, the use of the intensive system, the improvement in productivity and the quicker return. The distribution of land to emancipated people, immigrants or settlers would meet their demands, but would also raise the production and productivity of the Brazilian economy.

For Rebouças, the slave was also underused, producing much less than if he were free. The routine work of the captives does not allow exploring the productive potential of this labor power and is not in keeping with the century of "steam and electricity". The lack of labor power resulted from the poor use of national workers, mainly the mestizos distributed in unproductive activities and far from the major means of communication. Although indigenous peoples were used to extract forest products, they lacked education and incorporation into other agricultural endeavors. The absence of agricultural and technology schools made their insertion difficult, in contrast to the existence of two law schools in the country. As stated in the constitution, Rebouças stated that it was essential to teach everyone to read and write, as well as a profession. The problem was not the lack of people in Brazil, but of capital, industry, work, education and morality. Thus, we will be able to improve the use of a large mass of individuals who "vegetated" in the hinterlands and even immigrants, who would be spontaneously attracted by the opportunities to become landowners, as in the USA.

A different view was presented at the time of the service leasing law of 1879. In this law, contracts for the provision of services and partnerships for free workers were established. The incorporation of free workers would take place through service lease contracts, to which they would be obligated, at the risk of including vagrancy judicial penalties, which was already foreseen for freed persons in the scope of the free womb law. The term of contracts was usually long with clauses that provided for penalties of imprisonment for absences and objection to work. The law also applied to employment and partnership contracts with immigrants, with specific clauses for such situation. The law was revoked in 1890 due to complaints from the immigration movement.

The issue of immigration also divided attention.[27] Couty (1886) advocated a series of reforms to make the Empire attractive to immigrants. If the settlers arrive in Brazil and are sent to virgin lands, "they will return discouraged; or, if they stay there, they will spend a lot and be of little use". It was therefore necessary that immigration had a direction, that of cultivated land. Its immigration project results from these findings. Couty opposed immigration aimed at clearing new lands in Brazil, but favored regions that were already considered productive. The second important point was that the immigrant received land to be exploited; the author thus associated immigration to small property, that is, receiving land even if not in large areas, but in arable areas. This in a way implied a review of the lands, as the arable lands were already somehow under possession. The *Sociedade Central de Imigração* incorporated this immigration proposal, mixed with colonization and small properties,[28] as it echoed the idea of democratization of national agriculture and the formation of a country with a strong middle class, composed of independent rural producers from European immigration. Immigrants in Brazil would become small agricultural producers, owners of their own lands, with full religious freedom and full civil rights. The *Sociedade Central* criticized the large farming that marked Brazilian agriculture, its connection with slavery and its technological backwardness.

However, not every immigration proposal took this direction. In São Paulo, the *Sociedade Promotora da Imigração* was founded in 1886, whose objective differed from the formation of independent producers with immigrants. Its goal was to bring European immigrant families, working on the coffee farms through contracts. This society was founded precisely by the great landowners of São Paulo, and was therefore more elitist than the *Sociedade Central*. Immigration was the solution to the problem of lack of labor power, as many of them were able to observe and even participate in previous experiences with immigration, such as the Souza Queiroz family, whose partner was Senator Vergueiro. The contracts were partially revised by the 1879 law and other contractual changes followed, guaranteeing some monetary remuneration to workers regardless of planting and harvesting conditions. An agreement with the state government of São Paulo solved the main obstacle in the contracts, which was the payment or reimbursement for the immigrants' travel expenses. Under the agreement, the state government became responsible for the payment of these expenses without any future obligation falling on the immigrants. These agreements allowed the promoting society to succeed in the immigration movement and resolved the labor issue especially for the coffee plantations in São Paulo, relieving the pressure on the issue.

In the decade of 1880, external and internal pressures for the definitive solution of abolition gained impetus. The aforementioned *Sociedade Brasileira Contra a Escravidão* (1880) maintained dialogues with European societies. José do Patrocínio was the son of a slave, a journalist with intense political activity and founder of the society. A few years later, the *Confederação Abolicionista do Rio de Janeiro* (1883) was founded, seeking to bring together the numerous abolitionist clubs that were created in the country. Patrocínio was, along with Rebouças and Aristides Lobo, the editor of the Confederation Manifesto. It defends an immediate abolition, affirming the need to found a nation on equality and on the right of all to freedom, and slavery to be morally unfair. Moreover, the Manifesto argues that Brazilian slavery is illegal from a legal point of view, since slaves are descendants of a period when the traffic of slaves was illegal (after 1831). The Manifesto reviews the history of Brazilian slavery and condemns the ongoing process that is considered excessively compliant with slavery itself. The Manifesto also condemns slavery on the economic plane, relating the problem of agriculture, not to a possible lack of labor power, but to its excessive specialization and problems of competition in the international market. Finally, it blames the large latifundium for the difficulties in developing the economy, not only a more productive, but also a more socially inclusive one.

Patrocínio and the confederation carried out different propaganda strategies and abolitionist actions, expanding their presence in the press, holding conferences and civic events throughout Brazil, seeking to popularize and nationalize the movement. On the other hand, they supported the confrontation at the national congress. In an attempt to increase the pressure on Congress to accelerate abolition, a reaction from the slave trades was also perceived. Once again, efforts were made to postpone abolition, granting freedom only to a group of slaves, the oldest ones. Thus, a project was discussed that provided for the release of older slaves, a project which, despite being concerned with a small and undervalued group of slaves, slavers continued to resist. The Sexagenarian Law was enacted in 1885, guaranteeing freedom to slaves over 60 years of age. However, it was up to the owners to be paid a compensation, which had to be paid by the slave, being obliged to provide services to the ex-master for another three years or until he/she reached 65 years of age. The Confederation also sought regional emancipation actions, together with provincial societies seeking to expand the manumission movement and mobilizing resources through emancipation funds. In places with less representation of slaves, it was possible to overcome the resistance of slaveholders and eradicate slavery.

At the congress, new emancipation projects were presented, new resistances and postponements were discussed. Abolitionists defended the injustice and illegality of slavery and slaveholders sought delay and especially compensation. The jurist and politician Rui Barbosa (1849–1923) already affirmed, in 1869, the illegality of slavery based on the 1831 law. In the 1880s, Barbosa (Senado Federal, 2012) vehemently repudiated any compensation to slave owners, which would be a recognition of the legitimacy of the crime of trafficking after 1831. The imperial government resisted, but social pressure made abolition unavoidable, just making it necessary to define the form and the time. At the same time, there was a growing movement in the slave quarters, sometimes stimulated and supported by abolitionist societies. The slaves themselves promoted negotiations seeking manumission, but to the extent that they did not obtain it, these movements became radicalized, leading to rebellions, with abandonment and mass flight. Part of the movement sought funding and logistical support to help these escapes.

Despite the entire emancipationist movement, in the mid-1880s a relatively large contingent of slaves was still held, many of them illegally, as the confederation pointed out. In the second half of that decade, the abolitionist movement gained popularity, legal manumissions gained greater dimension and the slaves themselves promoted rebellions and escapes, bringing enormous insecurity. On the slave side, in regions where crops expanded, there was an attempt to replace slave labor by European immigrants, as in São Paulo. Other slavers increased their pressure on the government to contain the rebellion that was promoted by the slaves and supported by the abolitionist movement. In this context, the definitive eradication of slavery was debated and was finally implemented in

1888, without compensation to owners and any compensation, promotion or facilitation of citizenship for former slaves.

Although finally abolished, a possible compensation to the former lords was still being discussed, to which Barbosa was intensely opposed, even after the proclamation of the Republic in 1889. For Barbosa, abolition consisted of a popular conquest, comprising a large social movement. As others mentioned earlier, this author was concerned with the fate of freed slaves, mainly in equipping them through elementary education, agronomic instruction and partial land ownership. Such goals should be achieved with government support, using resources earmarked for emancipation.

Conclusion

The eradication of slave labor in Brazil was a long and difficult process. The enslavers did not obtain the desired compensation, but they did manage to survive for a long time. Successive slaveholding generations managed to keep the institution functioning in Brazil, despite external pressures, internal movements and a whole series of arguments. The great defense of slavery has always been the idea of the difficulty in employing the national free worker and that the country would be impoverished without the captives.

In addition to the long permanence of slavery, immigration to the most dynamic areas relegated the national free worker (including former slaves) to fewer opportunities. Despite the discussions, few rules were intended for nationals, just attempts to avoid the supposed idleness or indolence. This population has always assumed important roles within Brazilian society, linked to the production process, security, incorporation and maintenance of land by national elites.

This free contingent in addition with ex-slaves undertook movements of escape and resistance, informally creating spaces in which they sought to develop their activities freely, but without any government support in order to gain access to land or other types of financial, educational or collaboration resources. They often ended up isolating themselves, suffering from two stigmas: slavery itself and a racial one, resulting from new eugenic theories, with pseudo-scientific foundations that spread in Brazil (and the world), rescuing more than a century later part of the ideas that justified slavery itself and were contested by the ideals of equality among human beings.

The end of slavery occurred at the same time that a process of European immigration to certain Brazilian regions was made possible. This option was defended based on ideas of whitening Brazilian society with two bases: i) allocation of immigrants to work in expanding agricultural areas; ii) the State assumed part of its costs as a kind of compensation for non-compensation. Thus, the expansion of the supply of workers constituted a powerful subsidy to the expansion of property, mainly of large ones, reducing the remuneration of labor relative to capital.

The much-debated possibility of changing Brazilian agriculture took place in conjunction with the issue of replacing slave labor, but it did not advance.

The constitution of a smaller property-based economy did not occur, which would also imply agricultural diversification. The distribution of land to the national free population, ex-slaves or even European immigrants was often suggested, but little prospered. The large export crops or even for the domestic market were made possible through immigrant or national labor, maintaining control of a large portion of the Brazilian territory.

Notes

1. Professors of the FEA-RP/USP.
2. Thus, there was a criticism of the illegal trade carried out after 1831. The judge of the Court of Appeal of Pernambuco Henrique Velloso de Oliveira (1804–1867) criticized this trade, not for moral or legal reasons, but for making it difficult to establish a new work system (Oliveira, 1845).
3. The basis of international revisionism of slavery was the criticism of the idea that there are differences between human beings and the affirmation of equality, in principle, between all men. The new jusnaturalist theses underlie practically all Enlightenment thought, including the conceptions of a new emerging science – Political Economy. Two basic sources form the body of this conception: Natural Law and the so-called "evangelical egalitarianism". Dorigny (2018) and Bosi (1988).
4. Chaves ([1822] 1978).
5. Silva (1826).
6. Burlamaque (1837).
7. Lisboa ([1851] 2001).
8. Werneck (1847).
9. Part of this argument can be seen in an publication by a influential English navy doctor in Brazil: Thomas Richard Heywood Thomson (1850).
10. Mattos (1827).
11. The modern discussion of the open resources model to slavery and the abolition process can be seen in Domar (1970) and applied to Brazil in Martins Filho and Martins (1983), Reis and Reis (1988) and Slenes (1983).
12. *Jornal do Comércio*, July 5, 1841, p. 1.
13. The jurist Agostinho Malheiro (1824–1881) stated that there would be no natural reproduction of slaves, due to the small proportion of women (1867, pp. 173–174).
14. Engineer Silva Netto (1866) relies on Adam Smith to defend the higher cost of slave labor relative to free labor.
15. Durocher (1871).
16. According to the 1883 Manifesto of the Abolitionist Confederation of Rio de Janeiro, the economic crisis in the Northeast of the country was not caused by the export of slaves to the Southeast, but due to the loss of competitiveness of its two main exported goods: sugar and cotton.
17. Versiani (1994) contributed by distinguishing between effort-intensive (sugar and coffee) and care-intensive (livestock, mining and urban) activities. These former activities had more positive incentives and less coercion and punishment.
18. It should be remembered that other countries compensated slave owners in their colonies, such as France and England.
19. Barreiros (2009).
20. Penido (1885, pp. 17–20).
21. Silva Netto (1866) and Cristiano Ottoni (1871).
22. Gama (2021).
23. The emancipatory society bearing his name was founded in July 1881, comprising 374 members, including 250 slaves (Cf. Rangel, 1881, p. 183).

24. These debates and the law of 1871 itself originates from propositions made by Jose Antônio Pimenta Bueno, Marques de São Vicente, who five years earlier began to write some propositions concerning the gradual extinction of slavery, including the idea of the free womb, the liberation of the nation's slaves and convents and the creation of rescue funds. These propositions were drafted at the request of the Emperor and originally presented to the Council of State (Bueno, 1868).
25. Couty worked at the Imperial Museum and was responsible for the chair of Industrial Biology at the Polytechnic School in Rio de Janeiro.
26. Nabuco (1883).
27. The preferred immigrants are European but could involve other immigrants, such the Chinese. Quintino Bocaiuva (1836–1912) was a republican and published a pamphlet in 1868, in which he defended the employment of Chinese immigrants as an alternative to slave for work in large plantations. Many abolitionists preferred European immigration to Chinese or free blacks from Africa (Malheiro, 1867).
28. On the board of the society, there were Rebouças, Rohan, Taunay etc.

References

Albuquerque, P. M. 1860. *Prelecções de Economia Política.* 2ª ed. Rio de Janeiro: Garnier.

Alencar, J. [1867/68] 2008. *Cartas a favor da escravidão.* São Paulo: Hedra.

Andrada e Silva, J. B. 1825. *Representação à Assembleia Geral Constituinte e Legislativa do Império do Brasil sobre a Escravatura.* Paris: Firmin Didot.

Barreiros, D. P. 2009. A intelectualidade urbana e a "questão servil": A proposta liberal para o fim do escravismo no Jornal dos Economistas (Brasil, década de 1880). *História & Economia.* v. 5, n. 1, pp. 49–65.

Bosi, A. 1988. Escravidão entre dois liberalismos. *Estudos Avançados.* v. 2, n. 3, pp. 4–39.

Brito, P. 1870. *Considerações gerais sobre a emancipação dos escravos no império do Brasil e indicação dos meios próprios para realiza-la.* Lisboa: Portuguesa.

Brotero, José Maria Avellar. 1829. *Princípios de direito natural.* Rio de Janeiro: Typografia Imperial e Nacional.

Bueno, J. A. S. 1868. *Trabalho sobre a extinção da escravatura no Brasil.* Rio de Janeiro: Typografia Nacional.

Burlamaque, F. L. C. 1837. *Memoria Analítica acerca do comercio de escravos e acerca dos males da escravidão doméstica.* Rio de Janeiro: Commercial Fluminense.

Chaves, A. J. G. 1978. *Memórias ecônomo-politicas sobre a administração pública do Brasil (1822).* Porto Alegre: Companhia União de Seguros Gerais.

Confederação Abolicionista do Rio de Janeiro. 1883. *Manifesto da Conferência Abolicionista do Rio de Janeiro.* Rio de Janeiro: "Gazeta da Tarde".

Costa, J. S M. 1821. *Memória sobre a necessidade de abolir a introdução dos escravos africanos no Brasil.* Coimbra: Imprensa da Universidade.

Couty, Louis. 1884. *Le Brésil en 1884.* Rio de Janeiro: Faro & Lino.

Domar, E. D. 1970. The causes of slavery or serfdom: A hypothesis. *The Journal of Economic History.* v. 30, n. 1, pp. 18–32.Dorigny, M. 2018. *Les abolitions de l'esclavage (1793–1888).* Paris: PUF.

Durocher, M. M. 1871. *Ideias por coordenar a respeito da emancipação.* Rio de Janeiro: Diário do Rio de Janeiro.

Fontana, B. 1865. *Ideias, lembranças e indicações para extinguir a escravidão no Brasil.* Santos: Comercial.

Gama, L. 2021. *Obras completas: liberdade (1880–1882).* São Paulo: Hedra.

Hoyer, M. 1877. *Estudos de economia política.* Maranhão: País.

Jucá, J. 2001. *André Rebouças: Reforma e utopia no contexto do Segundo Império*. Salvador: Odebrechet.

Lisboa, J. S. [1851] 2001. Da Liberdade do Trabalho. In: Rocha, A. P. (Org.) *Visconde de Cairu*. São Paulo: Ed 34.

Malheiro, A. M. P. 1867. *A escravidão no Brasil: Ensaio histórico-juridico-social*. Rio de Janeiro: Nacional.

Martins Filho, A. and Martins, R. B. 1983. Slavery in a nonexport economy: Nineteenth-century Minas Gerais revisited. *Hispanic American Historical Review*. v. 63, n. 3, pp. 537–567.

Mattos, R. 1827. *Sustentação dos votos dos deputados Raimundo José da Cunha Mattos e Luiz Augusto May sobre a convenção para a final extinção do comércio de escravos*. Rio de Janeiro: Plancher-Seignot.

Menezes, A. B. 1869. *A escravidão no Brasil e as medidas que convém tomar para extingui-la sem dano para a nação*. Rio de Janeiro: Progresso.

Nabuco, J. 1883. *O abolicionismo*. Londres: Abraham Kingdon.

Oliveira, H. V. 1845. *A substituição do trabalho dos escravos pelo livre no Brasil, por um meio suave e sem dificuldade*. Rio de Janeiro: Americana de I. P. da Costa.

Ottoni, C. B. 1871. *A emancipação dos escravos*. Rio de Janeiro: Perseverança.

Penido, J. 1885. *A abolição e o crédito*. Rio de Janeiro: Escola de Serafim José Alves.

Rangel, G. 1881. *Almanach paulista: Ano 1881*. São Paulo: Sem editora.

Rebouças, A. 1988. *Agricultura nacional: Estudos econômicos. Propaganda abolicionista e democrática, setembro de 1874 a setembro de 1883*. 2 ª ed. Recife: Fundação Joaquim Nabuco/Editora Massangana.

Reis, E. J. and Reis, E. P. 1988. As elites agrárias e a abolição da escravidão no Brasil. *Dados – Revista de Ciências Sociais*. v. 31, n. 3, pp. 309–341.

Reis, Maria Firmina dos. [1859] 2020. *Úrsula*. Jandira: Principis.

Senado Federal. 2012. *A abolição no parlamento: 65 anos de luta, (1823–1888)*. 2ª ed. Brasília: Senado Federal/Secretaria Especial de Editoração e Publicações.

Silva, J. E. P. 1826. *Memória sobre a escravatura e projeto de colonização de europeus e de pretos da África no Império do Brasil*. Rio de Janeiro: Plancher.

Silva Netto, A. 1866. *Estudos sobre a emancipação dos escravos no Brasil*. Rio de Janeiro: Perseverança.

Silva Netto, A. 1871. *A Coroa e a emancipação servil*. Rio de Janeiro: Universal de Laemmert.

Slenes, R. W. 1983. Comments on 'Slavery in a nonexport economy'. *Hispanic American Historical Review*. v. 63, n. 3, pp. 569–590.

Soares, C. A. 1847. *Memória para melhorar a sorte dos nossos escravos lida na sessão geral do Instituto dos Advogados Brasileiros no dia 7 de setembro de 1845*. Rio de Janeiro: Imparcial de Francisco de Paula Brito.

Soares, S. F. 1860. *Notas estatísticas sobre a produção agrícola e carestia de gêneros alimentícios no Império do Brasil*. Rio de Janeiro: Imp. e const. De J. Villeneuve e comp.

Sociedade Auxiliadora da Indústria Nacional. 1845. *O auxiliador da indústria nacional*, v. 13. Rio de Janeiro: Berthe e Haring.

Sociedade Brasileira Contra a Escravidão. 1880. *Manifesto*. Rio de Janeiro: G. Leuzinger.

Sociedade Contra o Tráfico de Africanos. 1852. *Sistema de medidas adotáveis para a progressiva e total extinção do tráfico e da escravidão no Brasil*. Rio de Janeiro: Philanthropo.

Sociedade Democrática Constitucional Limeirense. 1869. *Elemento servil*. São Paulo: Typ. do Correio Paulistano.

Taunay, C. A. and Marquese, R. B. (Org.). [1837] 2001. *Manual do agricultor brasileiro*. São Paulo: Companhia das Letras.

Thomson, T. R. H. 1850. *The Brazilian Slave Trade and Its Remedy, Shewing the Futility of Repressive Force Measures*. London: John Milrea and Marschall, Houlston and Stoneman.

Vasconcelos, B. P. 1999. *Bernardo Pereira de Vasconcelos*. São Paulo: Ed. 34.

Versiani, F. R. 1994. Brazilian slavery: Toward an economic analysis. *Revista Brasileira de Economia*. v. 48, n. 4, pp. 463–477.

Wakefield, E. G. [1834] 1967. *England and America. A Comparison of the Social and Political State of Both Nations*. New York: Harper and Brothers, rep.; New York: Augustus M. Kelley.

Wakefield, E. G. [1849] 1969. *A View of the Art of Colonization, with Present Reference to the British Empire*. London: John W. Parker, rep.; New York: Augustus M. Kelley.

Wakefield, E. G. [1829] 2015. *A Letter from Sydney, the Principal Town of Australasia. Edited by Robert Gouger. Together with an Outline of a System of Colonization*. London: Joseph Cross, Simpkin & Marshall e Effingham Wilson, rep. San Bernardino: Ulan Press.

Werneck, F. P. L. 1847. *Memória sobre a fundação de uma fazenda na província do Rio de Janeiro, sua administração e épocas em que se devem fazer as plantações suas colheitas etc*. Rio de Janeiro: Universal de Laemmert.

6 Debating money in Brazil, 1850s to 1930

André A. Villela[1]

Introduction

Between the mid-19th century and the Great Depression of the 20th century, Brazil experimented with several monetary and exchange rate regimes.[2] These ranged from a system consisting of a fiduciary currency issued by the Treasury under a floating exchange rate to periods where plurality of gold-backed notes issued by private banks prevailed. In the early 20th century, formal adherence to the gold standard was finally achieved, binding together not only monetary and exchange rate policy (with a fixed value of the milréis[3] to sterling) but, crucially, the all-important coffee "valorization" (price-support) schemes.

The combination of monetary and exchange rate regime, as expected, had major implications for all economic agents, as it affected, *inter alia*, government finances and the profitability of, among others, commodity exporters and, from the late 19th century onwards, the manufacturing sector. Material gains (and losses), thus, would have to be considered when setting financial policy. At the same time, intellectual considerations, world views, helped steer those policies in different directions. In light of these considerations – both material and intellectual – "money" was a hot topic of conversation in the press, in Parliament and among policymakers.

Two interrelated points dominated monetary controversies in the period under study here: issuing rights and convertibility. Issuing rights involved deciding on the implementation of either a monopoly or plurality of the right to issue notes,[4] and, if the former, if this monopoly should be exercised by the government or a private bank. A related concern – and which over time would gain increasing importance in the debates – was the desirability of setting up a bank entrusted with functions which would later be associated with a central bank, such as issuing notes, ensuring the stability of the monetary and foreign exchange markets and, in times of need, acting as a lender of last resort to distressed institutions.[5]

As for convertibility, gold-backed issues were deemed by almost all participants in the monetary debates as the default arrangement, echoing the internationally prevalent gold standard dogma of the day. However, alternative setups involving note issues backed by government (and, at times, private-sector) paper were sometimes discussed – and adopted. Unbacked note issues were

DOI: 10.4324/9781003185871-9

then considered anathema, but, as we shall see, this idea was entertained by a handful of contemporary heretics.

The reason issuing rights and convertibility were hotly disputed topics is that both had a direct bearing on the rate of exchange: *ceteris paribus*, an unchecked monetary expansion tended to cause the rate of exchange to depreciate, while convertibility would ensure that note issues maintained a fixed ratio to gold reserves and the rate of exchange remained fixed.

But why this fixation (no pun intended here) with the exchange rate? The fact is that the domestic value of foreign currency is, arguably, the most important price in the economy, its shifts resulting in gains and losses in income and wealth, depending on an individual's or group's position as a creditor or debtor in foreign currency. During the period under discussion here, the Brazilian government, for one, had material interests in seeking an appreciation of the milréis, as this implied a lesser burden (in domestic currency terms) when meeting its foreign-debt obligations. In this sense, exchange rate stability can be thought of as a public good, as it prevents the income/wealth shifts that would result from either an appreciating or depreciating domestic currency.[6]

The backdrop against which monetary debates took place involved Brazil's growing integration into an international division of labor as exporter of primary products and importer of manufactured goods, capital and, from the late 19th century onwards, European labor. Under these circumstances, the country's balance of payments was heavily dependent on its terms of trade and access to foreign capital. Should any of the two falter – and they tended to move in tandem – the rate of exchange bore the brunt of adjustment, setting in motion the shifts in income and wealth noted earlier.

From the second half of the 19th century through to the outbreak of the Great Depression of the 1930s, adherence to the gold standard was deemed *the* appropriate policy countries should follow in order to maintain a fixed rate of exchange while imposing discipline on monetary growth. One upshot of this was that contemporary demands on the part of exporters, industrialists, and the productive sector in general for monetary and credit expansion were met with stiff opposition from "hard money" advocates, who insisted on the merits of a fixed (and, preferably, appreciated) rate of exchange.

This chapter seeks to chart the evolving nature of monetary debates in Brazil from the 1850s until 1930, that is, from the heyday of the Empire through to the end of the First Republic. In the process, I shall draw attention to the intellectual origins of the debates, their theoretical strengths and weaknesses, and, when appropriate, the material underpinnings involved, thus allowing for an interpretation of their concrete manifestations as expressions of particular political-economic preferences.

A convenient starting point for this discussion is a long-term series of the nominal exchange rate between the milréis and sterling.[7] Not only are the data readily available but, more importantly, the behavior of the rate of exchange itself was keenly monitored by contemporaries and constituted the foremost yardstick by which monetary (and economic policy as a whole) policy was

Figure 6.1 Monthly average rate of exchange (pence/milréis)

gauged. Other things being equal, a slipping (that is, depreciating) rate of exchange was considered by many as proof of financial mismanagement on the part of the government and, more specifically, of monetary "excesses". The reverse, of course, was held to be true, that is, for most contemporary observers an appreciating milréis constituted confirmation that the government of the day was conducting financial policy in a properly "sound" fashion.

Over the course of almost a century, three subperiods stand out as witnessing an intensification of monetary controversies: the mid-19th century; from the 1890s to the early 20th century; and the 1920s.[8] The chapter will discuss the views entertained by some of the most prominent participants in the monetary controversies in these three subperiods, their coherence, intellectual foundations, and the practical concerns of the individuals who professed different opinions.

Monetary debates in mid-19th-century Brazil: 1850s–1860s

The first significant outburst of monetary debates in Brazil took place in the mid-19th century and stemmed from major institutional shifts that took place in 1850. That year witnessed the passing of three pieces of legislation which sought to organize the markets for capital (by means of a Commercial Code), labor (via Law No. 581, which made the importation of slaves from Africa illegal), and land (through the Land Law) in Brazil.

While the Commercial Code barely delved into the business of banking (having dedicated a mere two short articles to the matter – out of more than 900) it is probable that the end of the transatlantic slave trade brought about by Law No. 581 helped release significant amounts of capital that, in part, found their way into new business ventures. As funds hitherto employed in the traffic sought alternative destinations, the demand for currency in the economy would most likely have increased.

In the occasion, two parallel movements were set in train. On the government's side, Minister of Finance Joaquim José Rodrigues Torres (from December 1854 onwards, Visconde de Itaboraí) put before the Senate, on February 4, 1850, a bill aimed at "provincializing" the circulating medium.[9] By means of this bill, the minister sought to gradually replace what he perceived as a haphazard collection of notes and all sorts of scrip in circulation with new paper issued by the government and endowed with legal tender status. Crucially, article 3 of the bill established that "under no circumstance and pretext shall the amount of circulating paper (money) in the Empire increase, even if temporarily."[10]

Itaboraí's concern with maintaining the money supply under control (preferably, backed by gold reserves) – and, hence, averting a depreciation of the milréis – would guide his ideas and, crucially, his actions as Brazil's most influential policymaker in the financial arena from the late 1840s, when his second stint as Minister of Finance began, until his death in 1872.[11]

A few months after the Itaboraí bill passed in Parliament, a group of investors in Rio de Janeiro, led by Irineu Evangelista de Souza (Barão and, from 1874 onwards, Visconde de Mauá), founded the (second) Bank of Brazil. Its aim, as stated by Mauá in his memoirs, was to "amass capital suddenly set free from the illicit [slave] trade and have it converge towards a center where it could nourish the country's productive forces".[12]

The broad terms in which monetary controversies in Brazil would be couched were thus established: control over the money supply vs. provision of credit to the productive sector. Deep down, all attendant clashes – opposing, *inter alia*, proponents of a monopoly of note issues and those in favor of plurality, gold-backed paper versus a purely fiduciary circulation, an appreciating rate of exchange against a depreciating milréis – harked back to this initial conundrum. In a nutshell, how could these two objectives best be reconciled, the maintenance of monetary and exchange rate stability and the provision of money in sufficient amounts as to accommodate/stimulate transactions in the economy.

Disputes between the so-called *metalistas* and *papelistas* in Brazil (roughly equivalent to Currency School and Banking School advocates, respectively, in England) have been the subject of an extensive literature.[13] Authors appear to agree that the ideas espoused by Itaboraí and Mauá on monetary matters serve as benchmarks for the positions entertained by participants in opposite camps of the controversies that played out in Brazil in the middle of the 19th century and beyond.

Defense of a gold-backed currency was a key feature of *metalista* discourse. While debating his 1850 bill in the Senate, for instance, Itaboraí remarked that

> if our circulating medium, instead of being [made of] paper, were metallic and if there were a situation in which its amount became superabundant,

> it would follow that part of this currency would be exported overseas and that [part] which remained in circulation, by keeping the proper relationship with [current] needs for transactions, would not depreciate and, as a consequence, no alteration would be produced either in contracts or in private fortunes.

Hume's price-specie-flow mechanism clearly underlies Itaboraí's stance in favor of convertibility. Moreover, this passage illustrates his keen perception of the disruptive consequences of exchange rate movements on wealth holders and economic agents at large. Bearing in mind that at the time he was the Minister of Finance and that the central government was the single most important holder of sterling-denominated liabilities, his defense of exchange rate stability through adoption of convertibility becomes self-explanatory.

Itaboraí, of course, was not alone in his advocacy of gold standard orthodoxy. Indeed, most contemporaries involved in the monetary disputes of the day shared the view that, ideally, the milréis should be convertible into gold and, preferably, at the 27d parity instituted by Law 401 in 1846. Francisco Salles Torres Homem (from 1872, Visconde de Inhomirim) was, arguably, the fieriest champion of monetary and financial orthodoxy at the time. His brief tenure at the helm of the Ministry of Finance from December 1858 to August 1859 would be indelibly marked by the bill presented in Parliament and which would serve as the template for the infamous 1860 banking and corporate "Law of Impediments" (*Lei dos Entraves*), which curtailed banking and corporate activity in general.

Torres Homem's views on what he considered the advantages of convertibility over a system consisting of fiat money were abundantly clear in the following passage from the annual report of the Minister of Finance presented to the Assembly:

> the essential condition which industry everywhere needs in order to grow and prosper is the stability of the value of the instrument used in the circulation of its products. This condition is met by a metallic currency, which, on account of the precious material from which it is made, is the universal equivalent, the uniform and almost invariable unit of all other values, the basic product to which they are reduced, as into a common denominator. Bank paper – a mere promise to pay – cannot replace it in circulation unless under the condition of it being converted into this real object.[14]

Itaboraí's nemesis and, arguably, the foremost champion of the *papelista* cause, was Bernardo de Souza Franco. Author of one of the best contemporary works dealing with monetary and banking policy, Souza Franco's ideas on convertibility were thus summarized:

> Of itself . . . metallic circulation, or [circulation] under a metallic base and bank paper redeemable on demand, is preferable to non-redeemable

> Treasury notes. . . . And the main reason for this is that precious metals are for general use and, being independent of the credit of public or private establishments, the circulating medium is not subject to repeated oscillations in value, which is totally lost as a result of fortuitous and unforeseen events. The same can be said of the notes of well-organized banks of issue, for they will always retain in reserve metal and bonds representing good debt in order to ensure convertibility [of their notes] into metal upon request.[15]

Just like his Banking School counterparts in Britain, Souza Franco too was in favor of convertibility of note issues. His main concern then – as with *papelistas* and the Banking School – was to ensure a proper money supply to accommodate the demands of the real economy. To *papelistas* such as Souza Franco, convertibility could be suspended under extreme circumstances (such as during banking panics) and the ratio of specie in reserve to notes outstanding might be relaxed temporarily. But, again, convertibility of note issues into gold was considered by most *papelistas* the default arrangement, just as for their *metalista* opponents.

Still, within the *papelista* family a few voices entertained opinions that challenged the dominant *metalista* credo more forcefully. Two mainstream views in particular were critiqued: the claim that the exchange rate was determined by the money supply alone and, consequently, the requirement that excessive monetary growth be constrained by instituting (gold-backed) convertibility.

Sebastião Ferreira Soares, a contemporary civil servant based in the Treasury and author of a number of books on Brazil's commercial statistics, was one of those who understood that the rate of exchange was not influenced by the money supply only, but also depended on the balance of international payments of the country. In his own words,

> Everything that has been said in the chambers and outside about the metallic circulating medium are nice theories, which fail completely in practice, for no state will succeed in retaining gold and silver coins in circulation unless the value of production and exports is greater than imports and consumption. . . . Brazil will not achieve a stable circulating medium in gold and silver as desired unless its exports exceed its imports.[16]

While Soares' views on the determinants of the exchange rate went against the grain of most expert opinion of the time, it was not as heretical as the position maintained by Mauá, the leading business tycoon of the Empire. In a series of articles that appeared in 1878 in Brazil's major financial newspaper, *Jornal do Commercio* – and subsequently published as "O Meio Circulante do Brasil" – Mauá expounded what amounts to a rare defense of fiat money, although with the proviso that this should be seen as a temporary arrangement:

> If metallic currency and banknotes convertible on demand constitute the engine par excellence of the monetary transactions of most countries, on

> account of their not being just orders on the capital of the country but [of their] having the advantage of being accepted . . . by the value convened by their mint price . . ., it does not follow that these superlative conditions of an excellent circulating medium . . . could not be replaced at a gain, at a substantial gain even, by temporary, non-convertible paper from banks . . . which may be led by special circumstances . . . to keep in their portfolios not gold, but private and State paper of good credit representing their notes in circulation.[17]

If the question of convertibility involved opinions ranging from a defense of purely fiduciary circulation (as exemplified by Mauá's remarks previously) to proposals in favor of instituting a gold-backed currency, such as desired, among others, by Itaboraí and Torres Homem, when it came to whose liabilities should be allowed to circulate as money (issuing rights), conflicting views also emerged. For *papelistas* in general, plurality of issue appeared to be the logical means to ensure not only that every corner of a continental territory like Brazil's would be served by an adequate supply of circulating medium but that banks could be used to foster economic activity at large.[18]

Once again, Itaboraí would lead the attack on this tenet of *papelista* discourse. To him, the downside to allowing plurality of note issue (as opposed to granting a monopoly to a single institution) seemed obvious. When debating in the Chamber of Deputies the creation of the (third) Bank of Brazil, he averred:

> Competition among banks, gentlemen, has been the main cause of virtually every commercial crisis. It is the dispute in which everyone seeks to do more business, lure more customers, offer more dividends to their shareholders, which usually leads them to discount bills without the necessary guarantees; which forces interest rates down too much; which excites firms randomly; which leads real capital to vanish from the market, and replaces it with fictional, imaginary, capital; it is the rivalry among banks which contributes greatly to produce failures, ruin, and despair in thousands of families, when the day comes in which this illusion fades away.[19]

By the mid-1860s, the demands of the Paraguayan War on the Treasury rendered these controversies of little practical importance. Under those circumstances, a gold-backed note circulation was out of the question. Monopoly of (an unconvertible) note issue was once more in the hands of the government, and a long truce in the monetary debates would ensue.

Money in the transition from empire to republic: 1880s–early 20th century

Monetary controversies in Brazil would be rekindled during debates held in Parliament in connection with a bill presented in 1887 by Senators Lafayette Pereira, Teixeira Jr. and Afonso Celso (the future Visconde de Ouro Preto) authorizing a number of banks to issue notes backed by government bonds (*apólices*). Avowedly inspired by the experience of the national banking system in the United States, the bill's proponents sought to address a pressing demand of the business sector for a money supply that would be sufficiently "elastic" to accommodate changes in the demand for currency.

In the end, the proposed system of national (regional) banks in Brazil was dropped, being replaced by the arrangement promoted by the last imperial cabinet (headed by Ouro Preto) consisting of a dominant bank – Banco Nacional do Brasil – and smaller players authorized to issue gold-backed notes at the rate of 27d/1$000 that had been reached recently. This latter scheme was itself overrun by the monetary and banking acts passed by the incoming republican government in 1890.

In spite of several crucial details setting this new legislation apart from the measures previously put forth by the Ouro Preto cabinet – the most important of which being the substitution of note issues backed by government securities for gold-based convertibility – their *motivation* was essentially the same. Both Ouro Preto and the new Minister of Finance, Rui Barbosa, sought ways to meet the growing demand for money and credit in a country that had recently abolished slavery and was welcoming hundreds of thousands of immigrants from Europe amid a boom in exports of both coffee and wild rubber.

In spite of his relatively short tenure as Minister of Finance (for just over one year), Rui Barbosa's banking reforms and their consequences – both real and purported – would exercise enormous influence over monetary debate and policy in Brazil. Part of the reason for this lies in Barbosa's controversial figure as one of Brazil's most notable statesmen, but also on account of the boom-and-bust cycle – the so-called Encilhamento – that accompanied (was caused by, according to Barbosa's detractors) his policies and the massive exchange rate collapse that would be indelibly associated with the economic history of the early years of the Brazilian republic.[20]

When it comes to the many participants in monetary controversies in Brazil, one would be hard-pressed to find an author as erudite, untiring, and meticulous as Rui Barbosa. These traits are abundantly clear in what is perhaps his most celebrated speech in the Senate dealing with monetary matters, delivered on November 3, 1891, months after he had stepped down from the Finance portfolio.[21] Over more than four hours, transcribed in 40-plus double-columned pages of the Senate Papers, Barbosa emphatically stood by his policies and attacked those of both Ouro Preto, the last minister of the Monarchy, and of his successors.

Many of the major themes in the Brazilian monetary controversies were visited in Barbosa's speech, which stands as one of the most eloquent defenses of the *papelista* position in the debate.

On the matter of what was the main determinant of the foreign value of the milréis, for instance, Barbosa ruled out the possibility of excessive monetary circulation. After presenting a number of tables containing data for Brazil and foreign countries, he was confident to conclude that "there is no necessary correlation between exchange rate variations and the amount of issues."[22]

Even ascertaining the "proper" amount of money required by the economy was a task fraught with difficulties, he realized. A large country like Brazil, with a scattered population, insufficient means of communication and a fledgling banking system – and, therefore, where hoarding was commonplace – required a greater amount of currency per capita than the more mature economies of Europe and the United States. Looked at from a different angle, the velocity of money was not a given.

Concerning the rate of exchange, Barbosa was in no doubt that it was the balance of international payments – and not the money supply – that ultimately governed its movements.

> The mutability of the exchange rate, its habitual depreciation, reveals the insufficiency of the country's ordinary resources when settling its accounts with markets overseas. It shall not be, therefore, metallic circulation that will secure an appreciated rate of exchange; on the contrary, it is the exchange rate at par . . . that shall allow us [to have] a convertible currency.[23]

As for the choice between a monopoly or plurality of note issue, Barbosa appears more agnostic. According to him, the policies of the last imperial cabinet showed both arrangements to be feasible. His ultimate decision siding with plurality had been imposed, he claimed, by the circumstances of a federalist revolution in which the states would interpret the establishment of a sole issuer of money (controlled by the federal government) as a provocation.[24]

The prolonged depreciation of the milréis over the course of the 1890s – with the attendant negative impact on public finances – would ultimately force the Brazilian government into signing in 1898 a Funding Loan with the Rothschilds and agreeing to a set of severely deflationary policies.[25] This was in keeping with foreign creditors' staunch defense of macroeconomic orthodoxy, at the time understood as the pursuit of balanced budgets and adherence to monetary restraint – preferably under the gold standard. Under the stewardship of Minister of Finance Joaquim Murtinho, taxes were raised, government expenditures significantly slashed, and the monetary supply reduced via the incineration of notes, plunging the Brazilian economy into, arguably, the deepest recession in its history.

In contrast to Rui Barbosa's eloquent defense of his policies and, more generally, of *papelista* doctrine, such as it was, all Murtinho could offer in support of his draconian measures were muddled incarnations of the *metalista* orthodoxy grounded on the quantity theory of money and support for the gold standard. For instance, in the introduction to the 1898 report of the Ministry of Finance he asserted that

> Issues of paper money are not always . . . an evil; on the contrary, they may act as a great agent of progress and prosperity for nations. It all depends, as is the case with all matters of credit, on the moderation, prudence, and judgment with which the issue is made and on the productive employment thereof. . . .

> Of the two types of issue that can be made: of notes convertible on demand and of legal tender [fiduciary] currency, only the former meets the conditions indicated above for the successful outcome of the operation.[26]

As for the ultimate driver of the exchange rate collapse in late-19th-century Brazil, he maintained that "expansion of legal tender paper money led to the growing depreciation of the said paper, (an appreciation) of sterling and depreciation of the rate of exchange."[27] No reference to balance of payments deficits here.

In spite of the superior quality – both in form and substance – of Rui Barbosa's arguments over Murtinho's, the opinion of participants in the monetary debates in subsequent decades would be overwhelmingly critical of the former, whose policies would be blamed for the foundering of the exchange rate in the late 19th century and, as a consequence, the government's fiscal woes.

A contemporary expert, Joseph Wileman, kept a careful distance in the controversy. Writing in 1896 – and, thus, before the 1898 Funding Loan and Murtinho's austerity measures took their toll on the Brazilian economy – he ascribed the depreciation of the milréis to the policies of both the Empire and the Republic, but especially the former.[28]

Subsequent authors were not as even-handed. Pandiá Calógeras laid squarely on Rui Barbosa the blame for the "flood of paper money that almost drowned the country during the disasters leading to the 1898 moratorium".[29] Ramalho Ortigão, in turn, when comparing the policies of both Ministers of Finance, ascribed to Rui Barbosa the "demoralization of the circulating medium";[30] Murtinho's deflationary policies, in contrast, were considered "a series of correct and timely measures . . . that had become necessary . . . in order to salvage Brazil's credit and honor".[31] In a similar vein, Antonio Carlos R. de Andrada agrees with Murtinho's reference to a "mirage of paper [*miragem do papelismo* in the original]" entertained by Barbosa and endorses the former minister's extreme policies, including the incineration of paper notes withdrawn from circulation as successive tranches of the 1898 Funding Loan were disbursed.[32]

One of the few contrarian opinions overheard amid the *metalista* chorus was that of Luiz R. Vieira Souto. Professor of Political Economy at the Polytechnic School in Rio de Janeiro, he penned a series of articles in the local press in November and December 1901, brought together in book form in the following year.[33] In these articles, Vieira Souto mounted a scathing assault not only on Murtinho's deflationary policies but also on the minister's competence for the office, which he deemed lacking. As for his own ideas on monetary matters, these were expounded in detailed form just over a decade later.[34] Among other things, Vieira Souto inveighed against the dominant adherence to the quantity theory of money and its predecessor, the currency principle.[35] Authors who subscribed to the these ideas, he reckoned, failed to consider that both the supply and demand for money mattered when ascertaining whether a given amount of currency in circulation should be deemed excessive or not. As regards the cause of the variations in the exchange rate, he sided with his *papelista* predecessors, ascribing it to the country's "balance of accounts" (payments).[36]

Be it as it may, by the early 1900s, as the milréis started to regain some of the ground previously lost – and, thus, seeming to vindicate Murtinho's deflationary policies – alarm bells rang among coffee planters already at pains to deal with depressed prices for the commodity in the international markets. In the fateful year of 1906, direct intervention in the coffee market was agreed to in the Taubaté Convention. Thereafter, price support schemes by means of the withdrawal of excessive supplies would become routine. As a complement to this measure, in December the federal government set up a Conversion Office (*Caixa de Conversão*) responsible for the issue of gold-backed notes at the rate of 15d/1$000.[37] In practice, this suggested that, after decades in which the 1846 gold parity of 27d/1$000 had been pursued almost as a "Holy Grail", contemporaries had given in to reality and accepted a new, depreciated, ratio of the milréis to sterling as the basis for the issue of notes by the Caixa.

Months earlier, on December 30, 1905, a new Bank of Brazil arose from the ashes of the Banco da República (under receivership since 1900), with the federal government as its major shareholder. Apart from operating as a deposit bank for the private sector, the Bank of Brazil would act as banker to the Treasury and be expected to play a major part in the foreign exchange market, acting as a countervailing force to the dominance hitherto exercised by foreign banks.[38] In the words of Calógeras, (the bank) was expected to be of "major importance for the solution of the monetary problem, [serving as] a sort of regulator of the exchange rate, destined to become the core of a bank of issue entrusted with a monopoly".[39] Creation of a central bank – and the attendant monopoly of note issues this entailed – would gradually come to dominate monetary debates in Brazil.

The 1920s

In its early years as an institution partly owned by the State,[40] the Bank of Brazil would act forcefully in the foreign exchange market, assisting in the Conversion Office's maintenance of the parity of the milréis until the Caixa's reserves were exhausted in 1914. During the Great War, the Bank's functions would be extended to include rediscounting operations with funds provided by the Treasury.

As the economy underwent the boom-and-bust cycle of the post-War years, in November 1920 the Epitácio Pessoa administration gave permission to the Bank to open an Issuance and Rediscount Office (Carteira de Emissão e Redesconto – CARED). With an issuing limit of 100,000 contos[41] (subsequently increased by the government) in legal tender notes, CARED was to assist not only banks in difficulty (that is, via rediscounting proper) but, also, in discounting commercial paper in general, including coffee bills.

Creation of the new facility within the Bank of Brazil was greeted with a measure of optimism in some quarters of the financial press. In its annual Review of 1920, at a time when the world economy was suffering from a major slump, CARED was welcomed by the *Retrospecto Commercial do Jornal do*

Commercio as a provider of desperately needed rediscounting operations for the banking system.[42] For the editors of the *Retrospecto*, though, there was a prior concern to be addressed by the government, one of a structural nature. Echoing complaints heard over the decades involving seasonal drains of currency from coastal cities to the interior during harvest months, they insisted on the need to create an "issuing and rediscount bank", with metallic reserves to back up its notes, as a means to "permanently regulate the money market".[43]

These *desiderata* were not uttered casually by Brazil's foremost financial newspaper. They actually encapsulated the zeitgeist of the post-War years amid the monetary and exchange rate disarray spreading to all corners of the globe. In an attempt to redress this state of affairs, conferences convened by the League of Nations in Brussels in 1920 and in Genoa in 1922 brought together representatives from dozens of countries and heard some of the most distinguished financial experts of the day. Among the resolutions adopted on both gatherings, one called for banks of issue (central banks) to be "freed from political pressure" while the other maintained that countries' currencies should be backed by gold.[44]

In mature economies with working central banks, this would serve as the clarion call for the haphazard efforts at resumption that would ensue. For peripheral economies, the resolutions emanating from both conferences opened the way for repeated visits from European and American money doctors intent on dispensing the then dominant financial gospel comprising the creation of "independent" central banks entrusted with the issue of gold-backed notes.[45]

For many contemporary observers, however, CARED was, definitely, *not* a step in this direction. Antonio C. R. de Andrada, for one, asserted that "the Carteira, as anticipated by its critics, did not take long in becoming . . . a mechanism for the disorderly production of paper money."[46] Carlos Inglez de Souza, an active participant in the monetary controversies of the time, blamed the precipitous decline in the exchange rate – from an average of 14 15/32 pence/1$000 in 1920 to 7 5/32 in 1922 (see Figure 6.1) – to the increased money supply resulting from CARED's issuing activities.[47] Some of the harshest criticisms of the Rediscount Office and its operations were meted out by Waldemar Falcão, professor of political economy at the University of Ceará. In an influential book published in 1931, he refers to the "rising tide of monetary 'paperism' (*papelismo monetário* in the original) starting in 1920".[48] The Treasury's reliance on CARED to plug its recurrent deficits was met with equal reproach by the author.[49]

In 1923 – and after two years of CARED operations leading to issues amounting to approximately 400,000 contos (a 25% increase over 1921 in the stock of money) – the incoming administration felt the time had come to move ahead with the idea of creating a proper central bank of issue. In what, at first glance, appeared to be a move in the direction of the recommendations coming out of the financial conferences sponsored by the League of Nations, President-elect Arthur Bernardes vowed to "endow the national economy with a complete banking framework (consisting of) a central issuing bank and the organization of mortgage, rural and urban credit".[50] Accordingly, on January 8, 1923 a government decree conferred on the Bank of Brazil the monopoly of note issues for ten years.[51] Bank of Brazil notes would forthwith enjoy legal tender status and be convertible into gold on demand at the rate of 12d/1$000 – provided this rate had been in place for the previous three years (at the time of the Decree it stood at 6d). Profits from its commercial operations would have to be partly directed to the withdrawal of the stock of unconvertible Treasury notes in circulation. Furthermore, the Bank's President would be freely appointed and could be sacked by the President of the Republic and would enjoy veto powers over decisions of the board of directors.

In practice, therefore, notes issued by the Bank would *not* be convertible and, moreover, the institution would *not* enjoy political freedom as recommended by the monetary conferences.[52]

Reactions in the press to the new arrangement were mixed. Having carried out two interviews with the mastermind behind the banking reform, Cincinato Braga, appointed by Bernardes President of the Bank of Brazil, the *Jornal do Commercio* sounded moderately optimistic. Just over one month after it started to operate as a bank of issue, the Bank of Brazil was commended by the newspaper for not having issued a single note! The publishing of its monthly statement and the explicit demonstration therein of credits advanced to the Treasury in anticipation of revenues constituted, in the newspaper's view, "most auspicious circumstances".[53]

Wileman's Brazilian Review, in contrast, was opposed to the new arrangement from the very start. Shortly after the first interview with Cincinato Braga was published by its rival, the paper asserted it was not convinced of the plan's utility. Somewhat prophetically, it went on to add that "theoretically, Dr. Cincinato's Project is not feasible, and in practice will prove disastrous to the currency and therefore exchange."[54] In the same vein, Waldemar Falcão pointed out the depreciation of the milréis in 1923–4 (with a low of just under 4.22 pence on November 7, 1923) in tandem with increasing note issues by the Bank of Brazil as unequivocal evidence of the "disastrous results" of Cincinato Braga's plan.[55]

In view of the negative impact of the exchange rate depreciation upon its finances and given the government's failure to secure a foreign loan in London in 1924, the Bernardes administration was led to performing an about-face in its monetary and banking policy. Cincinato Braga was replaced at the head of the Bank of Brazil, and new guidelines required that the institution "take a step back in its issues, which had advanced excessively, . . . and deflate the circulating medium up to the point allowing for a reasonable increase in the value of our currency".[56] The ensuing monetary contraction and recession, coupled with an improvement in Brazil's balance of payments position, put pressure on the exchange rate, which, having averaged just over 6d/1$000 in 1924 and 1925, reached the 7.8d mark in June 1926 (see Figure 6.1).

All the while, Washington Luis, elected in March 1926 to succeed Bernardes as President of Brazil, had been advocating an "immediate stabilization of the exchange rate", without further appreciation of the currency.[57] The desired return to gold, he argued, would require stabilizing the milréis at a low level, thus improving the trade balance, which, coupled with expected increases in inflows of foreign capital, should allow for the build-up of sufficient reserves to ensure full convertibility within a few years.[58]

Accordingly, soon after taking office in November, Washington Luis presented to Congress a bill proposing a monetary reform. Passed with little opposition in both Houses, it would become Decree 5108 on 18 December 1926. Among other things, the new legislation did away with the Bank of Brazil's issuing rights, the notes it had placed in circulation since 1924 being taken over by the Treasury. New issues of legal tender paper would henceforth be entrusted to a Stabilization Office (*Caixa de Estabilização*), whose notes would be convertible on demand at a rate of 5.9d/1$000, the average rate prevailing in the previous five years.

When presenting his annual Message to Congress in May 1927, Washington Luis emphasized the gradual nature of the monetary reform, consisting of three successive phases. The first one involved stabilization of the exchange rate at the new legal parity (thus breaking with the 1846 rate of 27d/milréis) and the operation of the Stabilization Office. Once a sufficient amount of gold had been amassed, through a combination of trade and capital account surpluses (phase 2), the government would announce a period for the setting up of full convertibility of all outstanding note issues (including previous issues of fiduciary paper still in circulation). The third step in the reform would follow with the introduction of a new monetary standard (the Cruzeiro in lieu of the milréis), and the minting of coins under this new standard, to be issued by a proper central bank of issue (the Bank of Brazil).[59]

The *Retrospecto Commercial* voiced its disapproval of the reform. Instead of "stabilization", it argued, the government should have sought "revaluation" (*valorização* in the original) of the milréis, persisting on the deflationary policies which the Bernardes government had been pursuing since 1924. Such revaluation, it went on, should be carried out up to the point when "the country reached a 'natural' rate (of exchange), one not so vile, so humiliating and against civilization."[60]

The Caixa would start its operations in April 1927, and for the next several months it helped sustain an export-led boom while maintaining a stable rate of exchange. However, a reversal in foreign capital flows as monetary conditions were tightened in the USA, combined with a stringent credit policy on the part of the Bank of Brazil from August 1928 onwards as it began preparations to take over central banking functions, set Brazil on a deflationary course which preceded the world slump of the 1930s.

Undeterred, in early May 1930, the President's annual message to Congress still maintained an optimistic outlook. To Washington Luis,

> Brazil's readjustment to its new economic situation is already under way; possibly this year we shall accomplish the reorganization of the Bank of Brazil, transforming it into a central bank of issue and rediscount on a metallic foundation.[61]

By then, the Caixa de Estabilização had lost some 40% of its gold reserves, entailing an equivalent reduction in the outstanding stock of its notes in circulation.[62] Later in the month, Washington Luis travelled to New York and then to London in attempt to obtain foreign assistance to sustain his policies, to no avail. After a brief lull, gold losses would resume, resulting in additional monetary stringency and plunging Brazil further into recession. Reserves would be finally exhausted by November, and the task of terminating the Caixa would fall on the incoming revolutionary government led by Getulio Vargas.

In regard to the two main points of contention in the monetary controversies, by the end of 1930 convertibility was permanently put to rest in Brazil and, as the decade progressed, elsewhere as well. As for issuing powers in the hands of a monopolist central bank, this would prove an elusive goal in Brazil, consuming the energies of another two-three generations until a proper institution under that name would perform, somewhat independently of the government, the tasks expected from a monetary authority.[63]

Concluding remarks

Brazil's integration into the international division of labor during the so-called classical globalization placed the exchange rate at the center not only of policymakers' concerns but also of a varied array of economic interests. As a result, the ultimate determinants – prominent among which monetary policy – of the price of the milréis against sterling were the object of permanent controversy that played out in Parliament, in the press and within government circles.

Contrasting views on monetary matters in Brazil can be conveniently grouped into two groups, *metalistas* and *papelistas*. The former, which counted among its many adherents Itaboraí and Torres Homem during the Empire, had in Joaquim Murtinho and Antonio C. R. de Andrada some of its most ardent representatives during the First Republic. Their main tenets were similar to those entertained by Currency School advocates and involved, *inter alia*, the belief that exchange rate movements were caused exclusively by the money supply; the validity of the price-specie-flow mechanism as a description of the frictionless adjustment of a country's balance of payments; and that interest rates were independent of the money supply. Issuing rights should ideally be entrusted to a monopolist entity, maintained most *metalistas*. In practical terms, they were firmly bound to the 27d/1$000 parity established in 1846, which acted as the "target" rate of exchange for the economy throughout subsequent decades.

Papelistas, in turn, included among their group illustrious participants in the monetary controversies, among which the names of Bernardo de Souza Franco, Mauá, Sebastião Ferreira Soares, Rui Barbosa and Vieira Souto stand out. The planter class, as one would expect, tended to favor the soft money policies associated with this "school". This was made explicit in the course of a number of speeches made during the Agricultural Congress convened in Rio de Janeiro in July 1878. In the occasion, representatives from the coffee-growing region overwhelmingly supported the creation of banks entrusted with the right to issue unbacked notes as a means to provide more (and cheaper) credit to agriculture.[64]

Convertibility of notes into gold was espoused by most *papelistas*, although practical considerations (insufficiency of gold in Brazil, for instance) sometimes led some authors to advocate the "unimaginable" – a fiat currency. The exchange rate, in their view, was mainly caused by real factors linked to the balance of international payments. Plurality of note issue was considered preferable to monopoly and issuing banks should have as their main goal the support of business activity. Overissue, in their opinion, was constrained by the "real bills doctrine".[65]

Metalista thought prevailed for most of the c. 1850–1930 period, without a doubt. Notable exceptions occurred during the brief interval in 1857–8 when Souza Franco authorized new banks of issue to operate; at the time of Rui Barbosa's banking reforms in 1890; and in the early 1920s, as CARED and then the Bank of Brazil issued large amounts of unconvertible legal tender notes. Apart from these occasions, proponents of easy money were mostly on the defensive.

Ascribing a reason for the prevalence of hard money views and policies in the period is not a straightforward task. Furtado famously attributed the dominance of financial orthodoxy during the 19th century and up to the 1930 crisis to "mimicry" of mainstream thought in Europe on the part of Brazilian policymakers and participants in the monetary debates in general.[66] This assessment does not seem entirely compelling. To be sure, at the time the Brazilian elite – to which participants in the monetary controversies, ultimately, belonged – was, unquestionably, enthralled to the intellectual (and material) fashions emanating from Europe and, increasingly, the United States. However, this did not entail an acritical acceptance of mainstream doctrine by all of those involved in the monetary debates, as suggested by Furtado. So much so that heterodox approaches to monetary matters were present throughout and, at times, converged into effective policy decisions.

Moreover, what Furtado fails to appreciate is that as most participants in the debates were themselves policymakers, members of the State apparatus, their hard money views and policies often translated the concrete preference of governments overly indebted in foreign currency and hence reliant on foreign capital and on the opinions of its creditors. Under these circumstances, the degrees of liberty for deviating from received wisdom as regards both monetary doctrine and "proper" financial policy were much diminished.

Needless to say, these external constraints on economic policy[67] did not entail an immobile approach to monetary matters, on the contrary. Adherence to financial orthodoxy notwithstanding, the Brazilian government did not hesitate in pursuing – often indirectly, though the Bank of Brazil – expansionist (and countercyclical) monetary policies in the aftermath of the 1857 and 1864 crises and, again, in the early 1920s. By the same token, suspension of convertibility was decided with no meaningful opposition from *metalistas* as the conflict with Paraguay unfolded in the mid-1860s.

The point here is that these decisions were made by men who were attuned to the latest developments in monetary thought and policy overseas and tried to apply the relevant lessons to Brazil's peculiar context consisting, among other things, of a large territory with poor communications, an underdeveloped banking system, extreme reliance on the exports of a few commodities, and visceral dependence on foreign capital flows. This was the concrete context in which monetary controversies played out, and the evidence surveyed in this chapter indicates that contemporaries attempted to adapt ideas borrowed from abroad to Brazilian reality.

Another feature of the monetary debates was the existence of gradual learning on the part of participants. For instance, the exchange rate collapse of the 1890s and its association with Rui Barbosa's banking reforms would cast a long shadow on monetary debates, imparting, perhaps, a more cautious approach to monetary policy in the early decades of the 20th century. Likewise, Murtinho's deflationary overkill at the turn of the century – in spite of its many subsequent admirers – would also render extreme *metalista* views less acceptable to future generations.

More than any other period, the post-WWI years display how learning from past experience, combined with close observation of both debates and policy decisions overseas, allowed for a measure of convergence between opposing schools in Brazilian monetary controversies. Creation of a central bank of issue, along the lines recommended by the 1920 and 1922 financial conferences, would figure in the platforms of all three presidents in the decade (Epitácio Pessoa, Arthur Bernardes and Washington Luis) and was endorsed by most *papelistas* and *metalistas*. The other major point of contention in the controversies – convertibility – was a different matter, with defense of the gold standard dominant in Brazil (and across the world) to the very end, that is, 1930.

Yet, as regards the *level* at which the exchange rate would be fixed, the debate had definitely moved on. This started in 1906 with the adoption of the 15d–16d/1$000 rate for the exchange of Conversion Office notes into gold. Even more shockingly from the point of view of diehard *metalistas* was the decision taken, as the Stabilization Office was set up in 1926, to break with the mythical 27d legal parity instituted in 1846. Learning and willingness to adapt to changing circumstances, therefore, were hallmarks of monetary debates and policy in the 1920s.

To conclude, in spite of the wealth of evidence left by monetary debates in Brazil between c. 1850–1930, it would be otiose to claim the existence of anything indicating a specifically "Brazilian" school of thought on these matters. That said, contemporaries were, for sure, attuned to and influenced by the latest doctrine produced overseas but, nonetheless, capable of adapting foreign ideas – be they mainstream or of a more heterodox bent – to Brazilian reality. One area in which this was plainly clear was the understanding, by the likes of Mauá and Rui Barbosa, of the asymmetrical working of the gold standard in countries, such as Brazil, heavily dependent on foreign capital flows and where the latter's instability would often plunge these economies into severe balance of payments crises and recession.[68] In the end, however, these dissenting voices – and one could add those of Souza Franco, Sebastião F. Soares, and Vieira Souto – would be drowned by the orthodoxy espoused by *metalistas*, which would prevail until 1930.

Notes

1. EPGE Escola Brasileira de Economia e Finanças – FGV EPGE. Comments from an anonymous referee on a preliminary version of the chapter are gratefully acknowledged.
2. For an overview of the Brazilian economy in the period spanning, roughly, the mid-19th century till 1930, Villela (2018).
3. From colonial times until 1942, the Brazilian currency was the milréis (expressed as 1$000). One thousand milréis corresponded to a conto de réis (or conto, for short), expressed as 1:000$.
4. Occasionally, the issue of other types of paper acting as "money" as well.
5. For the evolution of central banking functions in history, Ugolini (2017).
6. For an elaboration of the political economy of the rate of exchange in 19th-century Brazil, Villela (2020).
7. Figures refer to monthly averages of rates on 90-day bills on London traded in Rio de Janeiro. The dashed line at the 27d mark in Figure 6.1 indicates the "legal" parity of the milréis relative to sterling, in force between 1846 and 1926.
8. These subperiods are highlighted in Figure 6.1.
9. In practice, this would have entailed the issue of Treasury notes which would circulate within the boundaries of a given province alone. See Gambi (2012).
10. See Brasil, Senado, *Anais do Senado do Império* (henceforth, *ASI*), 1850, vol. I, p. 146. The bill would eventually pass into law, although "provincialization" of note circulation would never be implemented.
11. Apart from serving as Minister of Finance on three occasions and for a combined duration of just over seven years, Itaboraí would twice hold the office of President of the Bank of Brazil. Moreover – and in his capacity as a lifetime Councilor of State – he would exercise considerable influence on the debates held at the Finance Standing Committee of that Council, where he often acted as *rapporteur* in the consultations brought to the members' attention.
12. Mauá (1878, p. 20). This and all subsequent translations from the Portuguese originals are my own.
13. A sample of this literature would include Saes (1986), Andrade (1987), Gremaud (1997), Villela (2001), and Gambi (2013).
14. *Proposta e Relatorio Apresentados á Assembléa-Geral Legislativa Pelo Ministro e Secretario d'Estado dos Negócios da Fazenda* (henceforth, *RMF*) – 1858, p. 2, cited in Villela (2001, p. 87). This and subsequent paragraphs draw heavily on the latter.
15. Franco (1984, p. 87).
16. Soares [1860] (1977, p. 312).
17. Ganns [1878] (1942, p. 316).
18. For this point as applied to the views of Souza Franco, Schulz (2013). There are clear echoes here of the disputes pitting the advocates of free banking in the United States in the mid-19th century and proponents of greater federal oversight of bank chartering and note issuing activities. For a discussion, Rockoff (1991) and Dwyer (1996).
19. Session of 20 June 1853. Brasil, Câmara dos Deputados, *Annaes da Camara dos Deputados* (henceforth, *ACD*), 1853, vol. II, p. 260.
20. The Encilhamento refers to the period in the in the late 1880s–early 1890s, coinciding with the transition from monarchy to republic, in which a combination of expansionist monetary policy, balance of payments surpluses and a relaxation of corporate law set the stage for a speculative mania in the Rio stock exchange, followed by the usual crash. For

a detailed discussion of both the Ouro Preto and Rui Barbosa banking reforms leading up to the Encilhamento, Franco (1983) and Schulz (2008).

21. See Barbosa [1891] (2005).
22. *ASI* 1888, Tome II, p. 227. Moreover – and in proper *papelista* (and Banking School) fashion – he asserted that "the barometer of the exaggerations of the circulating medium is not the rate of exchange. . ., it is the rate of interest." Ibid., p. 248.
23. Ibid., p. 219. In a sense, Barbosa was hinting at the inherent instability of peripheral countries' balance of payments, where – unlike the pattern noted in most industrialized economies – capital imports and terms of trade tended to be positively correlated. Under such circumstances, increased current account deficits coupled with capital flight had to be countered by a combination of massive exchange rate devaluations and recession. For an elaboration, Franco (1991), Chapter 2.
24. Ibid., p. 221.
25. For details, Fritsch (1988), Chapter 1. On the Brazilian funding loans, Abreu (2002).
26. *RMF* 1898, p. vi.
27. Ibid., pp. x–xi.
28. Wileman (1896, p. 258). Wileman, who in 1900 would be appointed by Murtinho to head the statistics bureau of the Rio de Janeiro customs house, published one of the best contemporary investigations of the determinants of the exchange rate in Brazil. After detailed analysis of Brazil's monetary and exchange rate history over the preceding decades, he felt confident to conclude that the rate of exchange was caused by both monetary factors ("the ratio between the demand and supply of the circulating medium") and "the equilibrium of international payments". Ibid., p. 231.
29. Calógeras (1910, p. 232).
30. Ortigão (1914, p. 101).
31. Ibid., p. 117.
32. See Andrada (1923, pp. 368 and 387). Antonio Carlos R. de Andrada was a politician from the powerful state of Minas Gerais. A bulwark of financial orthodoxy, his 1923 book is a classic monetary and banking history of Brazil.
33. Vieira Souto (1902).
34. Vieira Souto (1925). The articles compiled in this collection had been originally published in the *O Paiz* newspaper in 1914.
35. Ibid., pp. 4–7.
36. Ibid., p. 22.
37. In December 1910, the parity would be changed to 16d/1$000 and the Caixa's note issue limit increased to 900,000 contos. Fritsch (1988, p. 24).
38. See Topik (1987), chapter 2.
39. Calógeras (1910, p. 409).
40. The Brazilian government would become its major shareholder in 1923.
41. Franco (2017, pp. 309–12). This amount corresponded to roughly 10% of the money supply (M1) in 1915.
42. *Retrospecto Commercial do Jornal do Commercio* 1920, pp. 5–6. A similar assessment would be made one year later, when the Review maintained that "the Carteira (CARED) was operating successfully. . .; its purpose not being to spill money (into) but rather to regulate the market." *Retrospecto Commercial* 1921, p. 46.
43. *Retrospecto Commercial* 1920, p. 5.
44. *Brussels Financial Conference 1920*, pp. 225–6; and *Papers Relating to International Economic Conference, Genoa*, p. 60.
45. On the influence of the monetary conferences in Brazil, Franco (2017, pp. 305–9). For the money doctors' more limited impact in the country, Abreu and Souza (2011).
46. Andrada (1923, p. 405).
47. Souza (1925, pp. 21–2).
48. Falcão (1931, p. 20).
49. Ibid., pp. 37–9.

50. *Mensagem Apresentada ao Congresso Nacional* . . . 1923, p. 21.
51. Decree 4635-A. For the Bank of Brazil's long history as a proto central bank, Villela (2017).
52. This departure – albeit not radical – from monetary orthodoxy may have been facilitated by the progressive waning, in the 1920s, of the influence of Brazil's British bankers as London's preeminence in world capital markets was progressively diminished in favor of New York.
53. *Jornal do Commercio*, 16 June 1923, p. 2.
54. *Wileman's Brazilian Review*, 10 January 1923, p. 9.
55. Falcão (1931, pp. 56–7). For monetary and banking policy in the second half of the 1920s, Triner (2000, pp. 53–9).
56. President Arthur Bernardes, in *Mensagem Apresentada ao Congresso Nacional* . . . 1925, p. 18.
57. Fritsch (1988, p. 121).
58. Ibid.
59. *Mensagem Apresentada ao Congresso Nacional* . . . 1927, p. 19.
60. *Retrospecto Commercial do Jornal do Commercio* 1926, pp. 54–5. Similar criticisms were levelled against the reform by Waldemar Falcão, who questioned why the rate of exchange used for convertibility of Caixa notes should be an average of the past five years (5.9d) instead of the 1914–25 period (approx. 10.5d/1$000).
61. *Mensagem Apresentada ao Congresso Nacional* . . . 1930, p. 38.
62. *Retrospecto Commercial do Jornal do Commercio* 1930, pp. 13–5.
63. For an elaboration of this point, Franco (2017), chapters 5 and 6; and Villela (2017).
64. See *Anais do Congresso* (1988). At the time the Congress was held the exchange rate stood at the relatively appreciated 23d/1$000 mark, which would have been detrimental to exporters' interests. International coffee prices at 14 cents/lb., however, partially compensated for this. An internal rate of return of 15% p.a. on an "investment" in slaves by *fazendeiros* in the Paraíba Valley coffee zone in 1876–8 indicates the sector's buoyancy at the time. Mello (1978).
65. For example, Art. 50 of Law 4230 of 31 December 1920 explicitly restricted CARED's rediscounting operations to paper "not resulting from mere speculative businesses", that is, paper derived from "legitimate transactions in agriculture, industry and commerce".
66. Furtado [1959] (1970), p. 160.
67. To borrow the title of Fritsch's classic account of economic policymaking during the First Republic, and which broadly applies to the imperial period as well. See Fritsch (1988). For the imperial period, Villela (2020).
68. This asymmetry is elegantly discussed in Furtado [1959] (1970), chapter 27.

References

Abreu, Marcelo de P. 2002. "Os *Funding Loans* Brasileiros – 1898–1931". *Pesquisa e Planejamento Econômico* 32 (3): 515–540.

Abreu, Marcelo de P. and Pedro C. Loureiro de Souza. 2011. "Palatable Foreign Control: British Money Doctors and Central Banking in South America, 1924–1935". *Textos para Discussão*. PUC-Rio, No. 597, October. Working paper, Department of Economics of the Catholic University of Rio de Janeiro.

Anais do Congresso Agrícola do Rio de Janeiro. [1878] 1988. Rio de Janeiro: Fundação Casa de Rui Barbosa.

Andrada, Antonio C. R. de. 1923. *Bancos de Emissão no Brasil*. Rio de Janeiro: Livraria Leite Ribeiro.

Andrade, Ana Maria R. 1987. "1864: conflito entre metalistas e pluralistas." Unpublished MSc dissertation, Universidade Federal do Rio de Janeiro.

Barbosa, Rui. [1891] 2005. *O Papel e a Baixa do Câmbio: um discurso histórico*. Rio de Janeiro: Reler.

Brasil, Câmara dos Deputados. *Annaes da Camara dos Deputados*. Various years.

Brasil, Senado. *Annaes do Senado do Império do Brasil*. Various years.

Brussels Financial Conference 1920 – The Recommendations and Their Application (A Review After Two Years). 1922. Geneva: League of Nations.

Calógeras, João P. 1910. *La Politique Monetaire du Brésil*. Rio de Janeiro: Imprensa Nacional.

Dwyer Jr., Gerald P. 1996. "Wildcat Banking, Banking Panics, and Free Banking in the United States". *Federal Reserve Bank of Atlanta Economic Review* (81): 1–20.

Falcão, Waldemar. 1931. *O Empirismo Monetário no Brasil*. São Paulo: Cia. Editora Nacional.

Franco, Bernardo de S. [1848] 1984. *Os Bancos do Brasil*. Brasília: Editora da Universidade de Brasília.

Franco, Gustavo H. B. 1983. *Reforma Monetária e Instabilidade Financeira Durante a Transição Republicana*. Rio de Janeiro: BNDES.

Franco, Gustavo H. B. 1991. *A Década Republicana: o Brasil e a economia internacional – 1880/1900*. Rio de Janeiro: Ipea.

Franco, Gustavo H. B. 2017. *A Moeda e a Lei: uma história monetária brasileira, 1933–2013*. Rio de Janeiro: Zahar.

Fritsch, Winston. 1988. *External Constraints on Economic Policy in Brazil, 1889–1930*. London: Macmillan.

Furtado, Celso. [1959] 1970. *Formação Econômica do Brasil*. São Paulo: Companhia Editora Nacional.

Gambi, Thiago F. R. 2012. "Centralização Política e Desenvolvimento Financeiro no Brasil Império (1853–66)". *Varia Historia* 28 (48): 805–832.

Gambi, Thiago F. R. 2013. *O Banco da Ordem: política e finanças no Império brasileiro (1853–1866)*. São Paulo: Alameda.

Ganns, Claudio (ed.). [1878] 1942. *Visconde de Mauá, Autobiografia (Exposição aos Credores e ao Público) seguida de O Meio Circulante no Brasil*. Rio de Janeiro: Zélio Valverde.

Gremaud, Amaury P. 1997. "Das Controvérsias Teóricas à Política Econômica: Pensamento Econômico e Economia Brasileira no Segundo Império e na Primeira República (1840–1930)". Unpublished PhD thesis, Universidade de São Paulo.

Jornal do Commercio. Rio de Janeiro. Various issues.

Mauá, Visconde de. 1878. *Exposição do Visconde de Mauá aos Credores de Mauá & C e ao Público*. Rio de Janeiro: J Villeneuve & C.

Mello, P. C. de. 1978. "Aspectos econômicos da organização do trabalho na economia cafeeira do Rio de Janeiro, 1850–1888". *Revista Brasileira de Economia* 32 (1): 19–67.

Mensagem Apresentada ao Congresso Nacional na Abertura da Primeira Sessão da Décima Terceira Legislatura pelo Presidente da República Washington Luis P. de Sousa. 1927. Rio de Janeiro: Imprensa Nacional.

Mensagem Apresentada ao Congresso Nacional na Abertura da Primeira Sessão da Décima Quarta Legislatura pelo Presidente da República Washington Luis P. de Sousa. 1930. Rio de Janeiro: Imprensa Nacional.

Mensagem Apresentada ao Congresso Nacional na Abertura da Segunda Sessão da Décima Segunda Legislatura pelo Presidente da República Arthur da Silva Bernardes. 1925. Rio de Janeiro: Imprensa Nacional.

Mensagem Apresentada ao Congresso Nacional na Abertura da Terceira Sessão da Décima Primeira Legislatura pelo Presidente da República Arthur da Silva Bernardes. 1923. Rio de Janeiro: Imprensa Nacional.

Ortigão, Ramalho. 1914. *A Moeda Circulante do Brazil*. Rio de Janeiro: Typographia do Jornal do Commercio.

Papers Relating to International Economic Conference, Genoa, April-May, 1922. 1922. London: His Majesty's Stationery Office.

Proposta e Relatorio Apresentados á Assembléa-Geral Legislativa Pelo Ministro e Secretario d'Estado dos Negócios da Fazenda. Various years.

Retrospecto Commercial do Jornal do Commercio. Rio de Janeiro. Various issues.

Rockoff, Hugh. 1991. "Lessons from the American Experience with Free Banking". In: F. Capie and G. E. Wood (eds.) *Unregulated Banking: Chaos or Order?* London: Macmillan.

Saes, Flavio M. de. 1986. *Crédito e Bancos no Desenvolvimento da Economia Paulista, 1850–1930*. São Paulo: IPE/USP.

Schulz, John. 2008. *The Financial Crisis of Abolition*. New Haven, CT: Yale University Press.

Schulz, John. 2013. "Souza Franco and Banks of Issue as Engines of Growth". *História e Economia Revista Interdisciplinar* 11 (1): 15–38.

Soares, Sebastião F. [1860] 1977. *Notas Estatísticas Sobre a Produção Agrícola e Carestia dos Gêneros Alimentícios no Império do Brasil*. Rio de Janeiro: IPEA/INPES.

Souza, Carlos I. de. 1925. *A Solução da Crise Econômica Brasileira*. São Paulo: A Renascença.

Topik, Steven. 1987. *The Political Economy of the Brazilian State, 1889–1930*. Austin, TX: University of Texas Press.

Triner, Gail D. 2000. *Banking and Economic Development: Brazil, 1889–1930*. New York: Palgrave.

Ugolini, Stefano. 2017. *The Evolution of Central Banking: Theory and History*. London: Palgrave.

Vieira Souto, Luiz R. 1902. *O Último Relatório da Fazenda*. Rio de Janeiro: L. Malafaia Junior.

Vieira Souto, Luiz R. 1925. *O Papel Moeda e o Câmbio*. Paris: Imprimerie de Vaugirard.

Villela, André A. 2001. "The Quest for Gold: Monetary Debates in Nineteenth-Century Brazil". *Revista de Economia Política* 21 (4): 79–92.

Villela, André A. 2017. "Las Funciones de Banca Central antes del Banco Central: el caso del Banco de Brasil". In: Daniel D. Fuentes, D. H. Aparicio, and Carlos M. Salinas (eds.) *Orígenes de la globalización bancaria: experiencias de España y América Latina*. Santander: Genueve.

Villela, André A. 2018. "The Nineteenth and Early Twentieth Centuries". In: Edmund Amman, Carlos Azzoni, and Werner Baer (eds.) *The Oxford Handbook of the Brazilian Economy*. New York: Oxford University Press.

Villela, André A. 2020. *The Political Economy of Money and Banking in Imperial Brazil, 1850–1889*. London: Palgrave Macmillan.

Wileman, Joseph P. 1896. *Brazilian Exchange: The Study of an Inconvertible Currency*. Buenos Aires: Gali Brothers.

Wileman's Brazilian Review. Rio de Janeiro. Various issues.

7 Industrial development and government protection

Issues and controversies, *circa* 1840–1930

Flávio Rabelo Versiani

The possibility and perspectives of industrial development, in a country with clear comparative advantage on agricultural exports, originated, in the Brazil of the nineteenth century and beginnings of the twentieth, opposing views as to the orientation of government policy: should it lean towards free trade, or should it be protective to local industrial endeavours? The central point of contention was usually the fixation of tariffs on imported manufactures. Tariffs were, and would remain until the 1940s, the chief source of governmental revenue. Accordingly, the debate was mainly focused on practical questions of tariff policy – whether they should be purely a fiscal instrument, or should they protect local production – rather than on the doctrine of international trade relations.

To recognize the predominant views and opinions that influenced governmental actions in the period, it is convenient, therefore, to examine directly the decisions taken by the main political actors of the time, and, when present, justifications of those decisions, as expressed by the relevant actors. This is all the more necessary as a conventional view, in the literature, ascribes a liberal orientation to government actions, in the nineteenth century, not only in Brazil but also in Latin America; consequently, tariff policy would have been exclusively determined by fiscal considerations.[1] The influential Brazilian historian Caio Prado Jr. labelled the first half of the nineteenth century in Brazil "the age of liberalism". Heitor Lima, a historian of Brazilian economic thought, goes further: liberalism would have dominated the whole nineteenth century.[2]

The idea of a dominant liberal outlook may have been influenced by two factors. First, by what could be called the intellectual climate of the period. Writings on the doctrine of international trade by Brazilian authors were rare, in the period, but their influence is recognizable. More important would be the influence of classical economists, whose ideas were taught (even though superficially) in Law schools; the large majority of statesmen in the period were lawyers.

A second point is the objective fact that no consistent and durable government policy in favour of industry can be identified, at least up to the first decades of the twentieth century. This was probably taken by many as a clear sign

DOI: 10.4324/9781003185871-10

of a decided preference for free trade, in governmental circles. It is arguable, however, as seen later in this chapter, that lack of protectionist policies, rather than revealing a preference of policy makers for liberalism, should be attributed to other factors, as the political activity of merchants against government support to local industry. There are reasons to suppose that lobbying of merchant interest groups, in particular commercial associations, was very effective in this respect. In other words, results were liberal, especially in the first part of the period under consideration; but the prevalent views and opinions, in particular those of the relevant policy makers, were not necessarily liberal.

The intellectual climate

Writings of José da Silva Lisboa, in 1810, and Aureliano Tavares Bastos, later in the century, were significant part of the intellectual climate of the time, and frequently quoted in support of liberal arguments.

Lisboa, Viscount of Cairu (1756–1835), an avowed disciple of Adam Smith, wrote extensively on various subjects, and was also an influential journalist and government official. In a book published in 1810, he argued forcefully against governmental support for industrial enterprises in Brazil. He was not unfavourable to government intervention in the economy; but he thought that protection should be given to all economic activities, without distinction: "The government acts wisely protecting, by equal and impartial laws, the general industry of the population, not this or that industry in particular, unless this should be indispensable to the safety of the country".[3]

He accepted the idea of restricting manufacture imports competing with national production, in order to support infant industries: "Even if [the products of those industries] are at first more expensive and imperfect, they will in time get better and cheaper". But this was only operative in advanced economies; that policy could not be applied in Brazil. The problem would be the smallness of the market, not allowing a sufficient scale of production: "It is improbable that mechanized industries can be introduced in a country with no large demand for their manufactures". Big machines, large factories "where a vast population does not exist, are a chimera". Only with the increase in population and capital accumulation "will we able to have, little by little, gradually, in due time, many local factories".[4]

Tavares Bastos (1839–1875) was, in the few years of his active political life, a powerful voice in defence of liberal ideas. In his writings, he criticized the excessive centralization of the Brazilian political system, to him a legacy of colonial times and old Portuguese institutions. Influenced by Tocqueville and the example of the United States, he favoured a federative system, and a limited interference of the State in economic life; accordingly, he was a fierce critic of protective tariffs. Quoting Bastiat, he insisted that the government should aim to protect the interests of consumers, not of this or that local producer. His ideas on economic liberalism were influential in the Chamber of Deputies, of which he was a member for seven years.[5]

The influence of Law Schools was emphasized by Celso Furtado:

> European economic science in Brazil was filtered through law schools and tended to become transformed into a body of doctrine which was accepted independent from any endeavor to compare it with reality. . . . The Brazilian statesman with some background in economics was a prey to a series of doctrinaire prejudices.[6]

Brazilian political elites showed, in the nineteenth century, a remarkable homogeneity as to educational background: during the monarchy (1822–1889), fully 73% of all Ministers had Law degrees; of those, more than three over four had studied in the Law Schools established in São Paulo and Pernambuco provinces in 1828 (the remaining ones had studied in the University of Coimbra). In the Senate, the proportion of lawyers was even higher.[7] As shown by Lima, Economics teaching in both São Paulo and Pernambuco Law schools was based on the classical works of Smith, Malthus, Ricardo, Say, Stuart Mill.[8]

The acritical acceptance of the ideas of those economists, mentioned by Furtado, was probably influenced by the fact that law students took a single course in Economics, so their knowledge to the subject could not be very profound.[9] And it is possible, as mentioned by Carvalho, that quotations of foreign authors, very common in writings and parliamentary speeches at the time, rather than supporting a conceptual reasoning, were actually a rhetorical strategy in defence of preconceived ideas, or economic interests.[10] Especially, we may suppose, in what concerned tariff policies, where the interests of importers and local producers were squarely opposed.

Commercial associations and their influence

The influence of commercial associations in the determination of tariff policies has been convincingly argued by Ridings, in his detailed study of the activities of those institutions, in the nineteenth century. The principal commercial associations were established in the 1830s, in Rio de Janeiro (1834), Pernambuco (1839) and Bahia (1840). Their members and directors were mostly foreign merchants in the overseas trade. Created with the "central purpose of . . . influencing government", their actions in this direction were inconspicuous, to avoid nationalistic resentments, but no doubt strong. Indeed, their power would have been "underestimated in both past and present, because their leaders wished it so".[11]

The most influential Commercial Association, that of Rio de Janeiro, had very close associations with the government. When it was formally founded, the largest contribution for its installation was made in the name of the nine-year-old Emperor, who attended the festivities, in 1834, installed on a specially prepared throne.[12]

As it was to be expected, a central concern of members of commercial associations, as to government decisions, was related to taxation and, specifically, the fixation of tariffs. In this respect, they were in an especially favourable position, in two ways. First, as experts on trade, in which capacity they were frequently consulted by the government officials, who commonly had little expertise on matters related to trade (in fact, "the 'technocrat' had yet to make an appearance on the government stage".) This was particularly true in relation to the intricacies of merchandise classification, needed to design a tariff schedule. Second, by their close contact with customs officials, who "usually gave way to importers". Actually, as mentioned in an 1853 report on tariffs, ill-paid customs employees often depended on merchants for personal loans. One way in which importers could bring down tariff collection was by fixing the official prices of imported goods (on which percentage rates were applied) well below the market value.[13]

Tariff debates: 1840–1865

In examining the disputes and debates on protection and tariff policy, it is convenient to consider separately the periods before and after 1865, for reasons that will be made clear later.

The issue of tariff fixing was raised forcefully in the early 1840s, with the expiration of an 1827 treaty with England, in which a maximum rate of 15% had been established for tariffs on English goods – a limit soon extended to imports from all countries. The treaty, very advantageous to England, replicated one signed by the Portuguese government in 1810, the last on a long series of treaties, starting in the seventeenth century, in which Portugal granted economic concessions to England in exchange for political support.[14] The 1827 treaty was part of the price paid for recognition of Brazilian independence from Portugal, in 1822. In the early 1840s, its termination was eagerly anticipated with a view to an increase in tariff rates, as a way to augment government revenues. Balancing the government budget had been a problem, in the years since Independence. The treaty expired in 1844.[15]

The end of the treaty would also bring about, for the first time, the possibility of establishing protective tariffs. The budget law for 1842–43 already foresaw, as one means to cover the estimated deficit, the establishment of a new tariff schedule, "as soon as the present Treaties expire". Accordingly, the Minister of Finance appointed, in 1842, a Commission to elaborate the new tariff.[16]

The next Minister, Joaquim Francisco Viana, gave the commission strongly protectionist instructions: imported articles that caused Brazilian producers to "suffer the competition of imports" should be identified, and heavily taxed, at rates from 50% to 60%. Those rates should also be applied to articles that could be easily come to be produced in the country, due to ample availability of the necessary raw materials. In the particular case of coarser cotton textiles, the rate should be 60%; machinery to produce them locally should enter free of duties. Food articles and other commodities of general consumption should be levied at 20%; lower rates than that, only on a few small goods of high value, to avoid smuggling.[17]

The commission members, who were customs officials, chose, however, to ignore those instructions: in the new Tariff, few items were taxed at 60% or

50%; no special mention was made of cotton textiles, included in the residual rate of 30%. This clearly displeased Alves Branco, the Finance Minister who put in effect the Tariff, in 1844. The reason why a commission could prevail over a minister was probably the fact that its president was an important personage, Saturnino Oliveira, who would later be minister; his freedom of action was probably reinforced by a powerful backing: his brother Aureliano, Viscount of Sepetiba, had a very strong influence on the young Emperor.[18]

Be that as it may, in his report to the Legislature, Alves Branco confessed that the protectionist effect of the new Tariff was not satisfactory, "not because he lacked the will" to fulfil this purpose; and he urged the legislators "not to let our future in the hands of merely fiscal Tariffs, as the one that happily expired last year" – an implicit admission of incapacity to do it himself. With the expired Tariff, "which protected nothing, many attempted manufactures failed, and it was impossible to employ free and intelligent labour, so we had to depend entirely on slave labour". It was necessary to protect the interests and rights of the country: "let us move in pursuit of industry in large scale". This could be accomplished by improvements in the tariff, year by year (that is, on the initiative of the Legislature). But he warned that obstacles would certainly oppose this course of action: "the doctrines that dominate our schools, and above all the interests of those who come to Brazil not as a new homeland, but in search of rapid gains".[19]

It is noteworthy that he mentioned – as Celso Furtado would do – the influence of free-trade doctrines taught in Law schools; and his final reference points, no doubt, to the interference of merchants involved in the import business, the great majority of them were foreigners. Foreign businessmen "usually refused to become Brazilian citizens when naturalization was convenient and easy".[20]

Branco made explicit, in his report, the reasons why he thought protection to industry was necessary. His ideas bring to mind some arguments developed, one century later, by authors from ECLA, the UN Economic Commission for Latin America. He thought, as would be elaborated by Prebisch, Furtado and others, that specialization in the production of agricultural food products and raw materials was not a good strategy for economic development, in Brazil, as international demand for those goods is unstable; some raw materials may become obsolete, when substitutes are developed. Sustained growth should be based on the internal market:

> No nation should base their hopes only on agriculture, on production of raw materials, on foreign markets. A country in those circumstances is always at the mercy of any eventuality, as wars, production in any part of the world of the articles it produces, or development of new substances that substitute those articles. A country without manufactures is always dependent on other countries [and cannot] advance a single step on the way to its wealth. Any country's Internal factory industry is the first, safer, and abundant market for its agriculture; its agriculture is the first, safer, and abundant market for its industry.[21]

The protectionist Alves Branco, later Marquis of Caravelas, hold various important positions in the monarchy: Prime Minister, Minister of Finance in four Cabinets, Senator from 1837 on, Member of the Council of State from 1842 on.

The Legislative was receptive to the appeal of Alves Branco in favour of protection to national industries. In the following years, significant incentives to local producers were voted. The first was a stimulus specific for industries of cotton textiles, for a period of ten years: no taxation on machinery importation, interprovincial sales, or exports; and exemption of military service for part of their employees.[22] The purpose was probably to induce the establishment of new factories; there were at the time only six cotton textile mills in the country, three in Bahia and three in Rio de Janeiro.[23] In 1847, a substantial governmental loan to the owner of one of the Rio textile mills was approved, and, in the next year, a still larger loan favouring an ironworks and shipyard establishment in Rio de Janeiro (owned by Irineu Evangelista de Sousa, Baron of Mauá, famous for his multiple investment initiatives).[24]

The first loan was the cause of a heated debate in the Senate, after it had been approved in the General Assembly (Chamber of Deputies). Alves Branco, again Minister of Finance (also Prime Minister), worried about the effect of the loan on government finances, all the more so as quite probably other requests would follow, argued against the concession. But he faced the opposition of Bernardo de Vasconcelos, one of the most influential politicians of the period, known for his pugnacious oratory. Vasconcelos had the upper hand, and the loan was approved by the senators – confirming the protectionist tendencies of the Legislature, at the time.[25]

Exemptions for industrial raw materials

Protectionist measures in fact antedated the 1840s. One way to favour national industries, circumventing the 15% limit, was to exempt industrial raw materials from tariffs. This expedient had been adopted since before Independence, in 1809;[26] the exemptions were maintained after Independence. When the 1844 tariff was enacted, the question was raised: should the exemptions be maintained? The matter was submitted to the Council of State.

The Council of State was a consulting body to assist the Emperor in his decisions. The importance of the Council derives from the fact that D. Pedro II, who reigned from 1841 to 1889, far from being a ceremonial head of state, had a decisive role in many crucial decisions, during his long period as monarch; in fact, accusations of a "personal power" on his part were not infrequent.[27] The Emperor generally accepted the predominant opinions expressed in the Council sessions, and important pieces of legislation originated there. Therefore, debates in the Council, though not deciding, were relevant elements of many political decisions taken in the period. And they are also useful as a means to examine the points of view and intellectual tendencies of its members, nearly all of them important political personages of the monarchy. "The political vision of the main leaders of the two great parties of the monarchy [Conservative and Liberal], and some of the principal public servants with no party affiliation, was concentrated [in the Council]".[28] Chosen by the Emperor and appointed for life, the Councillors could express themselves all the more freely, in the Council sessions, as debates were not published.

The discussion on exemptions to raw materials took place in February, 1847.[29] Alves Branco reported the opinion of the Council's Financial Section: exemptions should be maintained. A question had been raised in the Section: the existing rules stated that exemptions would be given to inputs of "national factories": should it be understood that factory owners had to be Brazilian? In a written vote, Araújo Lima, who was not present, concurred with the maintenance of exemptions, but added that factories owned by foreigners should be included. All Councillors but one approved the opinion of the Financial Section, and the majority followed Araújo Lima's vote on the definition of national as located in the country.[30]

Councillor Carneiro Leão, other important figure of the monarchy, concurred that the 1844 Tariff "was not sufficient" to protect local industries; it had favoured some branches of industry, but other branches might develop in the future.[31] His vote reaffirmed his position in a previous Council meeting, when a treaty with the German Zollverein was discussed. He had then opposed the concession of differential tariffs on imports of coarser cotton fabrics from the German states, "because we could expect to promote their production in Brazil". (Curiously, as shown by Mauro Boianovsky, Friedrich List took a personal interest in the approval of such treaty, which finally was not signed).[32]

Bernardo de Vasconcelos, mentioned earlier, also agreed with the position of the Financial Section: the 1844 Tariff was not sufficient for the protection of national industry. The purpose of the exempting legislation had been "to nationalize industry; as such nationalization depends on the help of government favours, that legislation subsists, it has not been revoked".[33]

The opinion of the Financial Section was approved: seven votes to one. The only dissenter was Lopes Gama, Viscount of Maranguape, a free trader; he thought that all raw materials should be exempted.

In the next year, however, the Minister of Finance, Limpo de Abreu, expressed misgivings about the exemptions: some materials were also goods of general consumption, which opened the way to abuses; and it was impossible to verify whether the amounts imported were compatible with the needs of local producers. But he was no free trader; he only thought that this type of exemption was not the best way to protect local industries. That goal should rather be attained by "a well-planed adjustment of the tariff schedule", ensuring that foreign manufactures "would not supplant" local production.[34]

Rodrigues Torres, the next Finance Minister (after a series of short-lived cabinets), also criticized, in his 1850 Report to the Legislature, the raw material exemptions established by the Council of State. But, at the same time, he expressed forcefully his convictions on protection. "I do not adhere to the principles of unlimited freedom of commerce and industry as applied to our country", he wrote. His arguments were close to those of Alves Branco:

> [N]o country can be truly independent, and make great progress, when it is limited, as we are, to produce almost exclusively raw materials or agricultural products that are only consumed in foreign markets. An external war, changes in commerce flows, cultivation of products similar to ours in countries where lands are equally or more fertile, and where labour is cheaper and capitals more abundant, any of those circumstances can easily reduce our country to a state of decadence and penury.

The means to overcome the inferiority in productivity, in relation to other countries, was industrialization:

> It is necessary, thus, to excite new productive forces, so that part of the population start producing some of the articles we receive from abroad. We will thus create in our country markets for a greater amount of all our products, bringing more movement and activity to internal commerce, more variety of occupations to which our countrymen may apply themselves, and develop their natural talents.

Bu protection should be temporary:

> No branch of manufacture should, in my view, be protected, at least for now, if its raw materials are not produced in Brazil, or can be easily produced here; none that does not promise benefits, if not immediate, not too distant in time, and that could not, in a more or less brief period of time, attain a certain point of robustness that allows it to exist and grow on its own force, and provide higher benefits than the sacrifices it costs.[35]

Some years later, now a member of the Council of State, Rodrigues Torres reasoned that increases in productivity were more to be found in industry than in agriculture:

> Production among manufacturing nations has infinite elasticity, and is almost unlimited: products that were made, years ago, in many days and for a high price can now be made in a much shorter time and with much reduced expense. Agricultural products are not susceptible to such progress: they are subject to the inflexible law of seasons; no invention of mechanisms would make coffee or sugarcane to produce more than once per year; this is the reason why no exclusively agricultural nation can grow and prosper as the manufacturing nations.[36]

It could perhaps be said that Torres was, as Alves Branco, a forerunner of Latin American developmentalist thinking. For, in the previous quotation, he was, in a way, outlining a notion that would be later developed, in the 1950s and 1960s, as part of a conceptual basis for import-substituting industrialization: industry would be the only source of productivity gains then available to Latin American countries.[37]

As Alves Branco, Rodrigues Torres, Viscount of Itaboraí, was an important personality in nineteenth-century politics. He was twice Prime Minister, four times Minister of Finance (the longest occupant of this Ministry during the monarchy), Senator from 1844 on, Member of the Council of State from 1854 on. Contrary to Alves Branco and Limpo de Abreu, members of the Liberal Party, he represented the Conservative Party: protectionist views crossed party lines.

What was said earlier suggests that the defence of an industrial development by Rodrigues Torres, Alves Branco and others had the rudiments of an intellectual foundation. It seems unjust to suppose that "the interventionists of the Council [of State] did not see clearly how to make industry develop from the agrarian basis of the country".[38]

The 1853 tariff report

In his 1850 Report to the Legislature, Rodrigues Torres, quoting Alves Branco, complained that the 1844 Tariff had failed to give adequate protection to national industries; he intended, then, to propose a new Tariff, revoking the exemption for imported inputs, but at the same time introducing the necessary changes, so that the manufacturing industry should "be reasonably protected". To this effect, he had asked the Financial Section of the Council of State to prepare a proposal.

In his next Report, however, he mentioned that, as the elaboration of such proposal was quite complex a task, he had decided to charge it to a commission specially formed for that purpose. He gave the commission precise instructions: determine which existing manufacture producers in Brazil could succeed, if reasonably protected; impose on competing imports a sufficient tax to allow those producers to prosper; find out what are the raw materials used by such factories, and tax those materials at rates from 2% to 15%, according to the lesser or greater possibility of their local production; decrease the duties applied on materials needed in the construction and equipment of ships (certainly, a reference to the shipyard benefited by a government loan in the previous decade, the only one in existence at the time); finally, apply low rates on necessaries consumed by persons of lower income, as long as this provision does not impair the previous ones.[39]

The list of members of the Commission appointed by Rodrigues Torres brings to mind Ridings' arguments concerning the influence of Commercial Associations on tariffs, as well as the reason why merchants were commonly consulted on the matter: they were considered the authorities on commercial practices. As Torres wrote in the Report: he had chosen for the commission "men in contact with those who can provide information [as needed], and knowledgeable about the facts that support such information". The chosen members were "the Inspector of the Customs, employees of the Rio de Janeiro Customhouse, and some merchants".[40]

The Commission took a long time to prepare their Report, made available in 1853: a very extensive and heterogenous document, with rather confusing passages but containing, with a companion volume of trade statistics, much valuable information. A central argument is a strong but badly argued criticism of the 1844 Tariff and, more specifically, of Alves Branco's 1845 Report; the leitmotif is the notion that "the true orientation and purpose of a Tariff is to provide the State with the means to cover its expenses". Cairu is quoted repeatedly, and there are passing references to Smith, Say, Carey and Senior; "the celebrated List" is mentioned to call attention to the fact that his defence of a protectionist policy did not apply to a country as Brazil.[41] The commission prepared also the project of a whole new tariff, aligned to their free-trade orientation.

The consequences of the Report were misjudged by some authors. Richard Graham wrote that "the recommendations of the [1853] commission were adopted", which would have caused the country to begin to feel the "influx of free-trade theories". Nícia Luz recognized in the Report a "strengthening of liberal tendencies" in government, probably enforced by "the pressure of agricultural interests". Stanley Stein stated that "the views of the 1853 tariff commission continued for many years to enjoy official sanction and wide dissemination".[42]

But, as stressed by Carvalho, this is a mistake.[43] In fact, the Report, which the Emperor sent to the Council of State for analysis, was almost unanimously rejected there: eight votes to one. The Report's tariff proposal was never adopted.

The opinion of the Finance Section of the Council, reported by Councillor Montezuma, was very critical of the 1853 Commission Report: it would be wrong to base government decisions on abstract principles of economic science, overlooking the specific circumstances of the present stage of development of the country's economy; the 1844 Tariff had been greatly beneficial, stimulating national industry. The Section proposed, as originally recommended by Rodrigues Torres, only reductions on food articles and tariffs on raw materials for existing factories, eliminating the criticized system of concessions for specific factories.[44]

Rejection of the Commission's proposal, and acceptance of the Section's opinion, was general; the Council was, no doubt, aligned with the views of Alves Branco and Rodrigues Torres. The votes in agreement with the Section included those of Calmon du Pin, Marquis of Abrantes; Cavalcanti de Albuquerque, Viscount of Albuquerque; Araújo Viana, Viscount of Sapucaí; and Costa Carvalho, Marquis of Monte Alegre. The only dissenting vote was that of Lopes Gama, who had also been the isolated dissenting vote eight years before.[45] The new Tariff, adopted in March of 1857, followed the instructions originally fixed by Rodrigues Torres in his 1851 Report.

The focus of Finance Ministers' attention, as far as tariffs were concerned, would be, of course, their effect on government revenues. The 1857 Tariff, in spite of rate reductions in "necessaries consumed by persons of lower income" (per instructions), had not brought a reduction in tariff proceeds, in the following years; the latter had in fact increased. Encouraged by that, Sousa Franco, Minister in 1857–1858, decided to make further reductions, using previous authorizations of the Legislative. He favoured a small government: when a Councillor of State, in a discussion over new taxes, he insisted that

> it is necessary to habilitate tax payers to pay for those taxes, by giving an impulse to productive forces, for which little more is needed than cutting the fetters that the government has imposed on private initiative and freedom of labour.[46]

But even free traders would ask for tariff increases, when pressed by budgetary worries. Indeed, Silva Ferraz, who had presided the ultra-liberal 1853 Commission, so critical of Alves Branco, was forced to do so, when Minister of Finance, in 1859–61. Government revenues had decreased, in the fiscal year 1858–59, and would apparently decrease even more, which Ferraz blamed in part on the reductions made by Franco; it was necessary to review the Tariff, increasing rates. In his 1860 Report, he wrote: "I regret deeply that different causes had created [this situation], but a remedy is necessary, to avoid greater sacrifices in the future".[47] The new Tariff, the last one up to 1865, was decreed in November, 1861.

Summing up the years 1840 to 1865, it is clearly seen that an examination of the ideas and positions of personages in the higher levels of government, in the period, shows that the notion of an "age of liberalism", as applied to the first half of the nineteenth century, is untenable – at least in what concerns trade policy. Indeed, most of the time such policy was conducted by Ministers of Finance that expressed, in one way or another, their preference for protectionism. During those twenty-five years, Joaquim Viana, Alves Branco, Rodrigues Torres, Calmon du Pin, Cavalcanti de Albuquerque and Carneiro Leão, all of them avowed protectionists, headed the Ministry for two thirds of the time.[48]

The fact that the intellectual position of finance ministers did not result in a coherent protectionist policy was probably influenced by contrary pressures from the importers' lobby. But, in all probability, tariff protection would not have been sufficient to promote significant industrialization, at the time, as objective conditions were very unfavourable: the market for industrial goods was still small and fragmented, due to a limited internal transport network; capital for industrial endeavours was scarce, and joint-stock companies hindered by an outdated commercial legislation.[49]

The period after 1865

Various elements had a positive effect on local manufacturing industry, in this period. The dividing line, 1865, takes as a point of reference the beginning of the Paraguayan War (December 1864 to March 1870). The war brought about a large increase in government expenses, which were, in the fiscal years 1865/66 to 1869/70, close to 230% of what they had been, on average, in the previous five-year period. The large governmental deficits of the period were in part covered by monetary expansion: money supply (M1) more than doubled, from 1864 to 1870, with a possible stimulating effect on demand.[50] Another stimulus would come from the great increase in coffee exports, starting in the 1870s.[51] Celso Furtado famously argued that the increase of wage labour in coffee plantations, in the 1880s, was instrumental in the development of an internal market for manufactures.[52]

The effect of the war on tariff policy was significant. Various ad-hoc increases were adopted, in the second part of the Sixties. In 1869, the Finance Minister argued that the situation "required new sacrifices by taxpayers": a new Tariff was introduced, with a general increase of 30% to 40% on all rates.[53] The 1869 Tariff has been seen as a turning point in tariff policy, in the monarchy period: in round numbers, the average tariff rate (value of tariff collection over value of imports) went from 27% in 1845–69 up to 37% in 1869–89.[54]

In the all-important case of textiles, it has been shown that, from 1870 to the eve of World War I, the combination of import tariffs and exchange devaluations provided a steady level of protection, largely shielding local producers from periods of falling external prices.[55]

As to supply of capital, an important trend has been noted, starting in the 1880s: investments of import merchants in local industries, especially in textile production – in part compensating for the fact that "many entrepreneurs had been long on ideas and short on working capital".[56] Warren Dean has stressed that the importing business was "clearly the progenitor of an industrial sector" in São Paulo.[57] Those investments seem to have been, at least in part, a hedge against unexpected decreases in the external value of the Brazilian currency (*mil-réis*, at the time), which could cause losses, even bankruptcies, to importing firms; exchange rate oscillations were then frequent, and generally ill understood.[58] They were later shown to be associated to cycles in the price of coffee.[59]

Another favourable factor, it has been argued, was the railway network built in São Paulo province from the 1870s, on the initiative of coffee producers and traders, which opened markets in the interior of the province to industries installed in São Paulo city.[60]

Under those positive influences, investment in local production of textiles was significant, in the 1870s and 1880s, as indicated by the large number of textile mills founded in those decades, and also by an increase in machinery imports.[61] Import substitution reached a relevant level in some areas: British consular reports mentioned a sharp decline, in the 1880s, of imports from Britain of domestics, a coarse type of cotton cloth. In 1889, it was reported that "the unbleached cotton trade has been killed by local factories".[62]

The advances in industrial production had a counterpart in efforts to congregate industrialists in trade associations. The *Associação Industrial do Rio de Janeiro* was founded in 1880; even though short-lived, it divulged in the occasion a vigorous manifesto attacking free trade and defending protection to national industry. An Industrial Bulletin soon started to circulate; members of the Association (especially the president, Antônio Felício dos Santos) frequently published articles in Rio newspapers in defence of industry. Their avowed purpose was to raise support from the public opinion for their cause. As soon as 1881, the Association edited a 350-page volume collecting those texts.[63]

As expected, the articles had various nationalistic appeals. Echoing Alves Branco, "the noxious education provided by the academies" is criticized; also criticized is the composition of commissions charged to prepare tariff schedules, where only customs officials were present. But there are more solid arguments; it is argued, cogently, that frequent changes in tariffs, common at the time, gave confusing and contradictory signals to investors. And it is supposed that competition in local markets would provide an incentive for productivity gains and a gradual lowering of prices to the level of imports – protection would be temporary.[64]

The Legislature was increasingly the scene where debates on industrial policy and the defence of industrial interests took place, in this period. Elected to the General Assembly, Felício dos Santos, himself a successful industrialist, defended those ideas as a lawmaker. He was there, for a time, "the leader of industry".[65]

Another influent pro-industry deputy was Amaro Cavalcanti. His approach was more analytical (he authored various books on Brazilian public finances): worried about the frequent insufficiency of exports to cover necessary imports, and the "rapid and ruinous fluctuations of the exchange rate", he thought that industrialization was needed to decrease demand for imports.

In a curious passage, Cavalcanti seems to have touched on the idea of decreasing terms of trade for Brazil – a well-known argument of Prebisch's writings, in the 1950s and 1960s: "The acquisitive power of [agricultural] wealth decreases with the increase in economic transactions, for . . . manufactured goods imported from industrialized regions become more and more expensive".[66]

The influence of Commercial Associations was still felt in tariff policy, in the 1870s and early 1880s. In 1879, a new tariff was generally favourable to industrial interests. Protests of the Rio Commercial Association were rapid and strong, causing the 1879 Tariff to be reviewed only two years later.[67] By the late 1880s, however, the climate had changed. The budget laws of 1886 and 1887 authorized changes in tariffs in order to protect national producers of paper and textiles. A full tariff reform was to be adopted, but the Republic came first; still, a change introduced in the last months of the monarchy – a sliding scale of tariff rates, increasing with the increase in the external value of the *mil-réis* – was seen as "the first openly protectionist measure of any Brazilian tariff".[68]

Republic 1889–1930

Historians have stressed that in the republican regime, installed in November 1889, the provinces, now called states, gained more power, at the expense of the central government. Consequently, "as the dominant classes in each state became more articulate . . . there occurred a greater convergence between the dominant class and the political and administrative elite".[69] The political influence of landowners increased, and with it the relevance of the more important agricultural states, São Paulo and Minas Gerais, in the national political scene. Therefore, the central government, after the first years of military rule, tended to become more averse to industrial protectionism. But in the Legislative, as in the last years of the monarchy, the presence of industrial interests was increasingly significant.

The first Minister of Finance of the Republic, Ruy Barbosa, viewed the industrial sector from a political viewpoint: the new regime needed the support of emerging forces.[70] A new Tariff was enacted; but the larger effect of Barbosa's policies was the extraordinary increase in credit supply, which had been scarce, in the 1880s: there was a fivefold increase in deposits of commercial banks, between the fourth quarters of 1889 and 1991. The ensuing devaluation of the mil-réis (affected also by unfavourable movements in the balance of payment's capital account), increasing import prices, strongly protected local industries: the average value of the pound sterling in mil-réis was, in round numbers, 10 in 1889–90, 20 in 1892–93, and 30 in 1899–1900.[71] Increased protection stimulated investment in local factories, as witnessed by the substantial volume of machinery imports, in the early Nineties. This has led some authors, as Fishlow, to put the beginning of the process of import substitution in Brazil in those years; but there are indications that, at least in the case of textiles, investment in this period was made mainly by firms founded in 1870s and 1880s.[72]

In the first five years of the republican regime, the two presidents were military, intensely nationalistic. Floriano Peixoto, who was in office from 1891 to 1894, made this clear by the forceful way in which he conducted the question of government help to national industries. Some factory owners who had imported machinery in the early Nineties were unable to pay for them, with the intense exchange devaluation that followed, and asked for governmental help. In spite of opposition from the Legislature, Floriano authorized the government-controlled Banco da República to issue bonds to be lent to industrialists, to be paid in twenty years with a low interest rate. The enormous amount of bonus issued in 1893–95 was equivalent to approximately 30% of the average tax revenues of the federal government in those years.[73]

The civilian presidents, after 1894, tended to be noninterventionists, in what concerned industrial activities, as mentioned earlier. On the other hand, an increasing protectionist tendency could be noted, in the Legislature, possibly a reflex of the growing presence of industrial units in and around the larger cities. Serzedello Correa, a military who had a prominent participation in the republican movement, was a typical and influent defender of industry and protectionism in the Chamber of Deputies, of which he was a member on various occasions, from 1895 to 1912.[74] A decided nationalist, he maintained that Brazil was still in a colonial condition, from the viewpoint of economic interests. In his frequent articles in the press, he stressed that in a country, as Brazil, where private initiative was still weak, it was the task of the government to promote productive activities, stimulating local industries. Tariffs are the instrument that modern countries use to support national production and labour; it is necessary to increase rates on manufactures, and lower those on raw materials.[75]

Divergent tendencies of the executive and legislative branches of government, as to support to industry, were a mark of this period. The Budget Laws from 1892 onwards increased tariffs for various articles produced locally, and decreased rates for their inputs; but the ministers of finance resisted, and introduced contrary dispositions.[76] In 1895, the Chamber of Deputies (not the Ministry of Finance, contrary to the established norm) appointed a commission to review the existing tariff. Their report was openly protectionist; they had met various industrialists "to learn the needs of each branch of industry"; accordingly, they proposed protective measures for inclusion in the next budget law. The Chamber of Deputies concurred. Minister Rodrigues Alves could only lament such "protectionism without reservations" and the fall in revenues caused by reduced rates on inputs.[77]

But local industry was a reality increasingly present, and politically difficult to ignore. This was made clear when Joaquim Murtinho, Minister of Finance in 1898–1902, sent to the Legislature his proposal of a new tariff (which, for the first time, was prepared with no representation of Commercial Associations). Murtinho, who conducted in those four years an extremely rigorous program of reduction of government expenses, was, as a social Darwinian, an avowed adversary of protectionism; for him, "existing [Brazilian] industries do not provide any benefit to compensate for the burdens of the protectionist system, loss of revenue and high prices for consumers". However, he stressed, in his tariff proposal, that as to imports of cotton textiles, "the national product is guaranteed"; only imports of articles "with no similar production in the country" would be allowed.[78]

Murtinho adopted also two measures with results contrary to his beliefs. The service of external debt weighted significantly in government expenses, at the time; the great exchange devaluation of the 1890s had caused a serious fiscal crisis. In order to shield government revenues from devaluations, his tariff reform made part of the duties (which were fixed in mil-réis) to be paid in gold. This, of course, also helped to avoid sudden falls in the protective effect of tariffs, in case of devaluations; the 1900 tariff was, consequently, well received by the industrial sector. The second measure was a rise in taxation of local industrial production, in order to decrease the dependence of government revenues on tariffs (which accounted for more than 50% of total revenues, at the time). This had the indirect effect of giving a boost to the power of industrialists to influence government policies, as they were, increasingly, substantial tax payers: from the first to the third decade of the twentieth century, taxes on industries increased nearly eightfold, while tariff revenue less than tripled.[79]

The 1900 Tariff stirred up protests from commercial interests; industrialists were accused of profiting at the expense of consumers.[80] In the succeeding years, various attempts were made to change this situation. The story of those attempts illustrates well the opposing positions of the Executive and the Legislature on the matter, and the increasing force of the interests of industry. Successive ministers of finance sponsored, from 1909 to 1922, a project to lower tariffs, which had, after World War I, the explicit support of President Epitácio Pessoa (1919–22). The project was never approved; significantly, the deputies representing São Paulo state voted unanimously against it, when it was discussed in a parliamentary committee, in 1919. In the coffee state, industrial interests were now quite strong.[81]

The 1920s

The 1914–1918 war was advantageous to industry, stimulating demand for local production; increased profits were a stimulus and a source of finance to a marked increase in industrial investment, in the early Twenties.[82] Industrial production advanced vigorously, in the post-war decade: an average growth rate close to 8% per year, in 1918–28. A boom in coffee exports, starting in 1924, was probably a factor stimulating demand.[83]

The decade witnessed also a significant change in the attitudes of government in relation to industry. This can be illustrated by the about-face of President Arthur Bernardes (1922–26) in relation to industrial policy. In the beginning of his period, he defended, as his predecessor Pessoa had done, a reduction of import tariffs. But in his final Message to the Legislative, he confessed that he had changed his mind, in the name of *realpolitik:* "Since the State has sponsored and stimulated the establishment of certain industries, even if they do not represent the more convenient employment of national activities, its duty is to defend their existence".[84]

This was not only a formal statement. Even though some governmental measures had been taken before to stimulate local manufactures, especially under the impression of supply scarcities during the War, they had been isolated episodes. In Bernardes' period, a substantial change occurred: a pattern of incentives to industry was established. Various decrees were enacted, following the same model, with the purpose of stimulating local production of cotton and silk textiles, cement, iron products, fertilizers, coal, rubber. Not much came out of those projects, but they indicate a new attitude: stimulating industrial enterprises was now seen as a normal function of government.[85]

In 1928, São Paulo state industrialists created a new association to defend their interests. In an inaugural speech, Roberto Simonsen, the vice-president, made a forceful defence of industrialization. Industry was the only way to economic independence, a condition for political independence; nations economically weak tended to suffer unfavourable terms of trade (prefiguring a famous ECLA argument). Industry also brings about increases in productivity, a necessary prerequisite for increases in income.[86] Simonsen was a mix of industrialist, historian and politician, who would be the driving force behind various initiatives favouring the sector, in later years. It can be argued, with Schmitter, that "the industrial class had found a new and dynamic leader and the creator of a persuasive ideology of national independence through industrialization".[87]

Conclusion

A view commonly found among historians is that a free-trade orientation was prevalent in Brazil, in the 1800s, especially in the first half of the century; and this would have influenced, or even determined, economic policy. Bethell and Carvalho, for instance, mentioned, among the reasons why there was no significant industrial development in Brazil until the 1870s, "the prevalence of *laissez-faire* ideas amongst both Brazilian landowners and the merchants of the coastal cities; and the failure of the government in any way to encourage the growth of industry".[88] According to this view, tariffs may have favoured local industry, but this would have been a fortuitous side effect. As put by Dean, "High tariffs. . . were largely the inadvertent result of the government's impecuniousness".[89]

Colin Lewis argued that the idea that *laissez-faire* dominated the nineteenth century, in Latin America, is simplistic. "Whether due to the strength of inherited Iberian mercantilist traditions, or pressing immediate fiscal and political considerations, government policy was pragmatic and interventionist".[90]

But those ideas do not seem to square with the Brazilian case. The period up to the 1870s was not an age of liberalism, as seen earlier. And politicians as Alves Branco and Rodrigues Torres tried hard, as ministers, to balance the government budget; but their defence of protectionist policies was not derived only from fiscal worries: they had, to some extent, a conceptual basis for it. It is possible that the same can be said about other official personages of the period.

Some authors have supposed that free trade thinking was dominant among agricultural producers, who would oppose tariff increases.[91] An assumption perhaps suggested by the well-known opposition to protectionist policies on the part of Southern agricultural producers, in the nineteenth-century United States. But, in fact, tariffs were generally viewed, by sugar and coffee producers, as an acceptable form of taxation ("imposed on all classes of society", not on "a single class, that of farmers"[92]) – especially in comparison with undesirable alternatives sometimes proposed at the time (but never adopted), as taxation on rural landed property, or an income tax. Export taxes faced strong protests from Northeastern sugar producers, but not much from Southern coffee planters – probably because the former faced strong competition in the international market, while Brazilian coffee dominated world supply.[93] Proceedings of two large meetings of agricultural producers, held in 1878 in Recife and Rio de Janeiro, clearly show the divergent positions of sugar and coffee planters as to export taxation, but no worries about tariffs.[94]

In the period after 1870, increasing industrial production increased also the capacity of industrialists to influence policy decisions, particularly through the Legislature. The lobby of importers, many of them turned into industrial producers, gradually lost force. The ideas of Amaro Cavalcanti, Serzedello Correa,

Roberto Simonsen and others, sometimes anticipating later *desenvolvimentismo*, gained growing acceptance.

What was the origin of this "proto-developmentalism"? Influence of nineteenth-century writers favouring protection for infant industries, such as List, is sometimes argued; but evidence on this is extremely limited.[95] Reference to foreign authors, in texts defending protectionist policies, are sometimes found, but suggesting a very superficial comprehension of their ideas – most probably, a mere rhetorical practice. Much more common is an appeal to the example of other countries, especially the United States. Nationalism is probably an element. Right after Independence, as Gilberto Freyre noted, nativistic sentiments were widespread (many even discarded their Portuguese family names); later, anti-British feelings predominated, as argued by Bethell and Carvalho, "as Britain stepped up its international crusade to suppress the slave trade".[96] Pro-industry writings had frequently a marked nationalistic tone. But the question of the roots of a protectionist thought, in Brazil, is certainly a matter for further research.

Notes

1. Lewis 1986: 298, 321.
2. Prado Júnior 1959: 123ff; Lima 1975: 91ff.
3. Lisboa 1999[1810]: 59. Here and in subsequent texts in Portuguese, translation is mine.
4. Lisboa *ibid.*: 97, 101. On Lisboa's economic ideas, Paim 1968. It is usual to refer to Brazilian personages of the nineteenth century by their titles, as it was customary at the time. Lisboa is generally mentioned in the literature as Cairu.
5. Bastos 1863: Appendice 1, 361–70. For his activity and influence in Parliament, see Luz 1961: 26, 39, 65; Nabuco 1975[1897–99]: passim.
6. Furtado 1968: 116.
7. Carvalho 1996: 55–82. Percentages from pp 71–74.
8. Lima 1976: 106–107.
9. *Ibid.*: 105.
10. Carvalho 1996: 330.
11. Ridings 2004: 2, 329, 335.
12. *Ibid.*: 25.
13. *Ibid,*: 3, 212; Commissão . . . 1853a: 97. With every new tariff schedule, a new list of official prices (supposedly representing market prices) was established. The possible influence of foreign merchants on tariff policy was noted by Luz 1961: 56–57.
14. See, for instance, Manchester 1972[1933].
15. For the history of the 1827 treaty, and the failed attempts of British diplomacy to renew it in the 1840s, Manchester *op.cit.*: chaps. 8, 11. Attempts were renewed in the 1860s: Graham 1968: 107–108.
16. Câmara dos Deputados 2021. Law 243, Nov. 30, 1841; Decree (Executive) 205, June 28, 1842.
17. Câmara dos Deputados 2021. Decree (Exec.) 294, July 5, 1843. Viana was Minister of Finance in 1843–44 and would be Senator from 1853 on. Senators were chosen (for life) by the Emperor from a list of three names sent by the provinces.
18. Nabuco 1975[1897–99]: 80, 96n.
19. Ministério da Fazenda. 1845: 35–39. Hereinafter, reports of the Minister or Finance will be referred to as RMF.
20. Ridings 2004: 35.

21. RMF 1845: 38. On ECLA (later ECLAC) thinking, see Bielschowsky 2016.
22. Câmara dos Deputados 2021. Decree (Legislative) 386, Aug. 8, 1846.
23. Commissão . . . 1853a: 337–342.
24. Câmara dos Deputados 2021. Decrees (Legisl.) 491, Sept. 28, 1847; 510, Oct. 2, 1848.
25. Senado Federal 2021a. Anais . . . : Sept. 10, 1847.
26. Câmara dos Deputados 2021. Alvará, Apr. 28, 1809.
27. On this point, see Holanda 1997: part I, chap. 1; part II, chap. 1.
28. Carvalho 1996: 327.
29. Senado Federal 2021b. Atas do Conselho de Estado . . . : Feb. 11, 1847.
30. Araújo Lima, later Marquis of Olinda, had been Regent of the monarchy in 1838–40 and would be four times Prime Minister, and Minister in various other cabinets. He was Senator since 1837 and member of the Council of State since 1842.
31. Carneiro Leão, later Marquis of Paraná, had been Minister in three cabinets and would be Prime Minister and simultaneously Minister of Finance in 1853–56. Senator and member of the Council of State from 1842.
32. Senado Federal 2021b. *Atas* . . . : Sept. 9, 1845; Boianovsky 2013.
33. Vasconcelos was Senator since 1837, and member of the Council of State since 1842.
34. RMF 1848: 28. Limpo de Abreu, later Viscount of Abaeté, occupied various political positions, from 1833 to 1859: Prime Minister in 1858–59, Minister of Finance in two cabinets, head of other Ministries in ten different cabinets, Senator from 1847, member of the Council of State from 1848.
35. RMF 1850: 32–34.
36. Senado Federal 2021b. *Atas . . . , Apr. 26, 1867.*
37. As Celso Furtado (1985: 62) wrote in his memories, recalling 1950s discussions around the writings of Raúl Prebisch: "To escape the constraints of the existing international order, countries in the periphery had to adopt the way of industrialization, the essential path to access the fruits of technical progress".
38. Carvalho 1996: 382.
39. RMF 1851: 30–31.
40. *Ibid.*: 30.
41. Commissão . . . 1853a: 87, 295; Commissão . . . 1853b.
42. Graham 1968: 107; Luz 1961: 22; Stein 1957: 12.
43. Carvalho 1996: 355n19.
44. Senado Federal 2021b., *Atas . . . , Nov. 22, 1855.* Members of the Finance Section, other than Montezuma, were Alves Branco (not present in that session) and Rodrigues Torres, now a member of the Council. Francisco Montezuma, Viscount of Jequitinhonha, had been twice Minister, was Member of the Council of State since 1850, and Senator since 1851.
45. Abrantes was four times Minister of Finance, twice Minister of Foreign Affairs, Senator from 1840, Member of the Council from 1843; Albuquerque, five times Minister of Finance, four times head of other ministries, Senator from 1838, Councillor from 1850; Sapucaí was also Minister of Finance, twice head of other ministries, Senator from 1840, Councillor from 1842; Monte Alegre had been Regent during the minority of D. Pedro II, Prime Minister in 1849–1852, Senator from 1839, Councillor from 1843. Finally, Maranguape, the dissenter, was twice Minister of Justice and twice Minister of Foreign Affairs, Senator from 1839 and Councillor since 1842.
46. Senado Federal 2021b., *Atas* . . . , Apr. 26, 1867. Bernardo de Souza Franco, Viscount of Souza Franco, was president of various provinces, Senator since 1859, and Member of the Council of State since 1859.
47. RMF 1860: 13–20. Ângelo da Silva Ferraz, later Baron of Uruguaiana, had been Inspector of the Customs in the early Fifties, and was both Prime Minister and Minister of Finance in 1859–61. Senator since 1855, Member of the Council of State since 1853.
48. Those six Ministers of Finance were in office for 202 out of 300 months: 67.3 per cent of the time.

49. Bethell and Carvalho 1985: 723–24.
50. IBGE 1990: 616, 534.
51. Due to a combination of rises in price and quantity exported, the average pound value of coffee exports rose about 70%, from 1860–69 to 1870–89.
52. Furtado 1968: ch. 26.
53. RMF 1869: 17–19.
54. Villela 2005.
55. Versiani 1980. It is noteworthy that this evidence runs counter previous assertions that tariffs would not have had a protectionist effect in the nineteenth century, as in Fishlow 1972: 312, Baer and Villela 1973: 221. The relative importance of textile production is attested by the fact that both in an industrial census in 1907, and in the general 1920 census, close to 40% of industrial workers, and 30% of the value of industrial production, were accounted for by the textile sector. Directoria Geral de Estatística 1927: Introduction.
56. Stein 1957: 71; also 72, 77; Ridings 2004: 221.
57. Dean 1969: 20.
58. Versiani and Versiani 1978: 126–128; Wileman 1969[1896]: ch. 1.
59. Delfim Netto 1979[1959].
60. Saes 1981.
61. Suzigan 1986: app1, 3. Machinery imports more than doubled in the 1870s, and quintupled in the 1880s, in relation to the 1860s.
62. Rickets 1888: 1; Gough 1889: 20.
63. Bibliotheca da Associação Industrial 1881.
64. *Ibid.*: passim.
65. Luz 1961: 51, 61–63.
66. Cavalcanti 1983[1893]: 26; Luz 1961: 67.
67. Câmara dos Deputados 2021. Decrees 7552, Nov. 1879; and 8360, Dec. 1881; RMF 1882: 33, 49.
68. Ridings 2004: 221.
69. Fausto 1986: 788.
70. RMF 1891: 294.
71. IBGE 1990: 535, 569–70.
72. Suzigan 1986: app1; Fishlow 1972; Versiani 1980.
73. Topik 1987: chap. 5.
74. Luz 1961: 73ff.
75. Corrrea 1903: *passim*.
76. Versiani 2012.
77. Commissão Mixta de Revisão das Tarifas Aduaneiras 1895: 3; RMF 1896: 199.
78. RMF 1899: 39–40; RMF 1901: 26. On Murtinho ideas, Luz 1980.
79. IBGE 1990: 618.
80. Luz, 196 1: 131ff.
81. Luz 1961: 137–152; Versiani 1987: chap 5.
82. Fishlow 1972: 320–22.
83. Versiani 1987: 28.
84. Quoted in Versiani 1987: 75.
85. Versiani *ibid.*: 86–96.
86. Simonsen 1973: 53–65.
87. Schmitter 1971: 147.
88. Bethell and Carvalho 1985: 724.
89. Dean 1986: 717.
90. Lewis 1986: 321.
91. For instance, Bethell and Carvalho 1985; Graham 1998: 320.
92. Luz 1961: 26, quoting from a parliamentary report of 1869, when a tax increase was being discussed.

93. Devesa 1995; Canabrava 1995: 128–9, 1996: 245ff; Ridings 2004: 189ff. The fact that the burden of an export tax could be transferred to buyers, given the dominance of coffee in Brazilian exports and the inelasticity of demand for coffee, was perceived at the time: "[the increase caried out in the export tax] will not fall . . . on the exporter, but rather on the foreign consumer". RMF 1872: 75.
94. In the Recife Congress, attended mostly by sugar mill owners, protests against export taxes were universal; tariffs were not mentioned. In the Rio Congress, with participants from all coffee-producing regions, the focus was on two main points: demand for credit availability, and worries about labor supply, considering the impending abolition of slavery; taxation was not an issue. Sociedade Auxiliadora da Agricultura de Pernambuco 1978[1878]; Congresso Agrícola 1988[1878].
95. On the hypothesis of List's influences, Boianovsky 2013.
96. Freyre 1986[1933]: 458; Bethell and Carvalho 1985: 746.

References

Baer, W. and A.V. Villela. 1973. Industrial Growth and Industrialization: Revisions in the Stages of Brazil's Economic Development. *Journal of Developing Areas* 7: 217–234.

Bastos, A.C. Tavares. 1863. *Cartas do Solitário*, 2nd ed. Rio de Janeiro: Typographia da Actualidade.

Bethell, L. and J.M. Carvalho. 1985. Brazil from Independence to the Middle of the Nineteenth Century. In L. Bethell (ed.) *The Cambridge History of Latin America*, vol. III. Cambridge: Cambridge University Press.

Bibliotheca da Associação Industrial. 1881. *O Trabalho Nacional e seus Adversários*. Rio de Janeiro: Leuzinger.

Bielschowsky, Ricardo (org). 2016. *ECLAC Thinking; Selected Texts (1948–1998)*. New York: United Nations, Economic Commission for Latin America and the Caribbean.

Boianovsky, Mauro. 2013. Friedrich List and the Economic Fate of Tropical Countries. *History of Political Economy* 26(4).

Canabrava, Alice. 1995. A Grande Lavoura. In: O Brasil Monárquico: Declínio e Queda do Império. Vol. 6 of S. B. Holanda (ed.) *História Geral da Civilização Brasileira*, 5th ed. Rio de Janeiro: Bertrand Brasil.

Carvalho, José Murilo de. 1996. *A Construção da Ordem; A Elite Política Imperial. Teatro de Sombras; A Política Imperial*, 2nd ed. Rio de Janeiro: Editora UFRJ.

Cavalcanti, Amaro. 1983 [1893]. *O Meio Circulante Nacional*. Brasília: Editora Universidade de Brasília.

Câmara dos Deputados. 2021. *Coleção de Leis do Império do Brasil*. Available at: https://www2.camara.leg.br/atividade-legislativa/legislacao/colecao-anual-de-leis. Accessed June 21, 2021.

Commissão Encarregada da Revisão da Tarifa em Vigor. 1853a. *Relatorio*. Rio de Janeiro: Paula Brito, Impressor da Casa Imperial.

Commissão Encarregada da Revisão da Tarifa em Vigor. 1853b. *Documentos Estatisticos sobre o Commercio do Imperio do Brasil nos Annos de 1845 a 1849*. Rio de Janeiro: Typographia Nacional.

Commissão Mixta de Revisão das Tarifas Aduaneiras. 1895. *Relatorio*. Rio de Janeiro: Imprensa Nacional.

Congresso Agrícola 1988 [1878]. *Collecção de Documentos*. Rio de Janeiro: Fundação Casa de Ruy Barbosa.

Correa, I. Serzedello. 1903. *O Problema Economico no Brazil*. Rio de Janeiro: Imprensa Nacional.

Dean, Warren. 1969. *The Industrialization of São Paulo, 1880-1945*. Austin, TX: University of Texas Press.

Dean, Warren. 1986. The Brazilian Economy, 1870–1930. In L. Bethell (ed.) *The Cambridge History of Latin America*, vol. V. Cambridge: Cambridge University Press.

Delfim Netto, A. 1979 [1959]. *O Problema do Café no Brasil*. Rio de Janeiro: Editora da Fundação Getúlio Vargas.

Devesa, Guilherme. 1995. Política Tributária no Período Imperial. In O Brasil Monárquico: Declínio e Queda do Império. Vol. 6 of S.B. Holanda (ed.) *História Geral da Civilização Brasileira*, 5th ed. Rio de Janeiro: Bertrand Brasil.

Directoria Geral de Estatística. 1927. *Recensamento do Brazil – 1920*, vol. 1, 1ª pt. Rio de Janeiro: Typographia da Estatística.

Fausto, Boris. 1986. Brazil: The Social and Political Structure of 2the First Republic, 1889–1930. In: L. Bethell (ed.) *The Cambridge History of Latin America*, vol. V. Cambridge: Cambridge University Press.

Fishlow, Albert. 1972. Origins and Consequences of Import Substitution in Brazil. In: L. E. Di Marco (ed.) *International Economics and Development; Essays in Honor of Raúl Prebisch*. New York: Academic Press.

Freyre, Gilberto. 1986 [1933]. *The Masters and the Slaves*. Trans. S. Putnam. Berkeley, CA: University of California Press.

Furtado, Celso. 1968. *The Economic Growth of Brazil; A Survey from Colonial to Modern Times*. Trans. R.W. Aguiar and E.C. Drysdale. Berkeley, CA: University of California Press.

Furtado, Celso. 1985. *A Fantasia Organizada*. Rio de Janeiro: Paz e Terra.

Gough. 1889. *Report for the years 1887–88 on the Finances, Commerce, and Agriculture of the Empire of Brazil. AS no. 504, C5618–57. British Parliamentary Papers 1889*, LXXVIII (Accounts ana Papers, 32).

Graham, Richard. 1968. *Britain and the Onset of Modernization in Brazil, 1850–1914*. Cambridge: Cambridge University Press.

Holanda, Sérgio Buarque de. 1997. *O Brasil Monárquico: do Império à República*. Vol. 7 of S. B. Holanda (ed.) *História Geral da Civilização Brasileira*, 5th ed. Rio de Janeiro: Bertrand Brasil.

IBGE, Instituto Brasileiro de Geografia e Estatística. 1990. *Estatísticas Históricas do Brasil; Séries Econômicas, Demográficas e Sociais de 1550 a 1988*, 2nd ed. Rio de Janeiro: IBGE.

Lewis, Colin. 1986. Industry in Latin America before 1930. In: L. Bethell (ed.) *The Cambridge History of Latin America*, vol. IV. Cambridge: Cambridge University Press.

Lima, Heitor Ferreira. 1976. *História do Pensamento Econômico no Brasil*. São Paulo: Editora Nacional.

Lisboa, José da Silva (Visconde de Cairu). 1999 [1810]. *Observações sobre a Franqueza da Indústria e Estabelecimento de Fábricas no Brasil*. Brasília: Senado Federal.

Luz, Nícia Vilela. 1961. *A Luta pela Industrialização no Brasil (1808 a 1930)*. São Paulo: Difusão Européia do Livro.

Luz, Nícia Vilela. (org). 1980. *Idéias Econômicas de Joaquim Murtinho*. Brasília: Senado Federal.

Manchester, A. K. 1972 [1933]. *British Preeëminence in Brazil Its Rise and Decline*. New York: Octagon Books.

Ministério da Fazenda. 1845. *Proposta e Relatorio*. Rio de Janeiro: Typographia Nacional.

Nabuco, Joaquim. 1975 [1897–99]. *Um Estadista do Império*. Rio de Janeiro: Nova Aguilar.

Paim, Antônio. 1968. *Cairu e o Liberalismo Econômico*. Rio de Janeiro: Tempo Brasileiro.

Prado Júnior, Caio. 1959. *História Econômica do Brasil*, 5th ed. São Paulo: Brasiliense.

Rickets. 1888. *Report for the year 1887 on the Commerce and Trade of Rio de Janeiro. AS no. 865. C-5252–42. British Parliamentary Papers* 1888, C.

Ridings, Eugene. 2004. Business Interests Groups *in Nineteenth-Century Brazil*. Cambridge: Cambridge University Press.

RMF. 1845. Ministério da Fazenda 1845. *Proposta e Relatorio*. Rio de Janeiro: Typographia Nacional.

RMF. 1848. Ministério da Fazenda 1848. *Proposta e Relatorio*. Rio de Janeiro: Typographia Nacional.

RMF. 1850. Ministério da Fazenda 1850. *Proposta e Relatorio*. Rio de Janeiro: Typographia Nacional.

RMF. 1851. Ministério da Fazenda 1851. *Proposta e Relatorio*. Rio de Janeiro: Typographia Nacional.

RMF. 1860. Ministério da Fazenda 1860. *Proposta e Relatorio*. Rio de Janeiro: Typographia Nacional.

RMF. 1869. Ministério da Fazenda 1869. *Proposta e Relatorio*. Rio de Janeiro: Typographia Nacional.

RMF. 1872. Ministério da Fazenda 1872. *Proposta e Relatorio*. Rio de Janeiro: Typographia Nacional.

RMF. 1882. Ministério da Fazenda 1872. *Proposta e Relatorio*. Rio de Janeiro: Typographia Nacional.

RMF. 1891. Ministério da Fazenda 1891. Relatorio. Rio de Janeiro: Imprensa Nacional.

RMF. 1896. Ministério da Fazenda 1896. *Relatorio*. Rio de Janeiro: Imprensa Nacional.

RMF. 1899. Ministério da Fazenda 1899. *Relatorio*. Rio de Janeiro: Imprensa Nacional.

RMF. 1901. Ministério da Fazenda 1901. *Relatorio*. Rio de Janeiro: Imprensa Nacional.

Saes, Flávio A.M. 1981. *As Ferrovias de São Paulo 1870–1940*. São Paulo: Hucitec.

Schmitter, Philippe. 1971. *Interest Conflict and Political Change in Brazil*. Stanford, CA: Stanford University Press.

Senado Federal. 2021a. *Anais do Império*. Available at: www.senado.leg.br/publicacoes/anais/asp/IP_AnaisImperio.asp. Accessed June 21, 2021.

Senado Federal. 2021b. *Atas do Conselho de Estado*. Available at: www.senado.leg.br/publicacoes/anais/asp/AT_AtasDoConselhoDeEstado.asp. Accessed June 21, 2021.

Simonsen, Roberto C. 1973. *Evolução Industrial do Brasil e Outros Estudos*. São Paulo: Editora Nacional.

Sociedade Auxiliadora da Agricultura de Pernambuco. 1978 [1878]. *Trabalhos do Congresso Agrícola do Recife*. Recife: Fundação Estadual de Planejamento Agrícola.

Stein, Stanley. 1957. *The Brazilian Cotton Manufacture*. Cambridge, MA: Harvard University Press.

Suzigan, Wilson. 1986. *Indústria Brasileira; Origem e Desenvolvimento*. São Paulo: Brasiliense.

Topik, Steven. 1987. *The Political Economy of the Brazilian State, 1889–1930*. Austin, TX: University of Texas Press.

Versiani, Flávio Rabelo. 1980. Industrial Development in an 'Export' Economy: The Brazilian Experience Before 1914. *Journal of Development Economics* 7: 307–329.

Versiani, Flávio Rabelo. 1987. *A Década de 20 na Industrialização Brasileira*. Rio de Janeiro: IPEAS/INPES.

Versiani, Flávio Rabelo. 2012. As Longas Raízes do Protecionismo: 1930 e as Relações entre Indústria e Governo. *Revista Economia* 13: 867–895.

Versiani, Flávio Rabelo and Maria Teresa R.O. Versiani. 1978. A Industrialização Brasileira antes de 1930: uma Contribuição. In F.R. Versiani and J.R. Mendonça de Barros (orgs.) *Formação Econômica do Brasil; a Experiência da Industrialização*. São Paulo: Saraiva.

Villela, André. 2005. Política Tarifária no II Reinado: Evolução e Impactos, 1850–1889. *Nova Economia* 15: 35–68.

Wileman, J.P. 1969 [1896]. *Brazilian Exchange; the Study of an Inconvertible Currency*. New York: Greenwood Press.

Part 4

The "developmentalist" and the "globalization" eras

8 Brazilian economic thought in the "developmentalist era": 1930–1980

Ricardo Bielschowsky and Carlos Mussi[1]

1. Introduction: movement of ideas, currents of thought

This chapter presents a survey of the evolution of ideas on Brazilian economy as published during the country's industrialization process, from 1930 through 1980.

The period has attracted many historians who explored the main aspects of the economic, political and social formation of Brazil. Its fast GDP growth, with a yearly average of 6.5% (8.0% in the manufacturing sector), and quite continuous expansionist policies supported by what has been named a convention of guaranteed growth (Castro, 1993) conveyed to intellectuals, entrepreneurs and politicians a perception of irreversible historical change.[2] In most of that period, pro-growth and structural change policies were the Brazilian "chapter" of worldwide ideological and historical processes in capitalist economies, i.e. Keynesianism and state support for the infrastructure and for technical progress.

One of the parts of the chapter, on the 1930–1964 period, is largely based on Bielschowsky ([1985] 2022 and 1991).[3] The chapter as a whole also benefits from a growing literature on Brazilian economic thought in the developmentalist era.

Knowledge about the views expressed by economists and other intellectuals on Brazilian economy during the developmentalist era is indeed supplied by a considerable number of studies. Besides the three texts previously mentioned, books and articles with comprehensive approaches include, for instance, Lima (1975), Magalhães (1964), Mantega (1984, 1997), Love (1996) and Bresser-Pereira (1997). The volumes organized by Biderman et al. (1996) and by Mantega and Rego (1999) contain interviews with 25 leading Brazilian economists. Loureiro (1997), Szmrecsányi and Coelho (2007), Malta (2011a) and Cosentino and Gambi (2019) are relevant collections of essays covering varied aspects of the Brazilian history of economic thought during the developmentalist era and other periods. The historiography of Brazilian economic thought concerning the period 1930–1980 has been progressing steadily through works related to authors,[4] currents of thought,[5] specific subjects,[6] and specific periods of time.[7]

The chapter covers an extensive economic literature, as published in books, specialized periodicals and government documents produced during the period

DOI: 10.4324/9781003185871-12

under consideration. It includes macroeconomic issues but is centred on development ideas. The key concept that both organizes it and gives it unity is "developmentalism", meaning the ideology of Brazilian society's transformation by means of state planning and support for full industrialization. It can be defined as an economic project based on the following postulates:

i) Integral industrialization is the way to overcome poverty and underdevelopment in Brazil.
ii) There is no possibility of achieving an efficient and rational industrialization of the country through the spontaneous play of market forces, and it must therefore be planned by the state.
iii) Planning must define the desired expansion of economic sectors and the instruments for promoting such expansion.
iv) The state must also guide investment by procuring and managing financial resources and by making direct investments in those sectors where private enterprise is insufficient.

Two features distinguish this chapter from the bulk of the existing bibliography on Brazilian economic thinking. First, it defines different currents of thought taking into consideration their views on developmentalism as defined previously. Second, it describes the evolution of an ideological cycle of developmentalism over the period 1930–1980, i.e., the movement of ideas. The methodological approach consists in taking ideas as a close reflection of Brazilian economic and political evolution.

Besides this Introduction (Section 1) and the Conclusion (Section 5), the chapter is divided into three parts. Section 2 describes the movement of ideas.

Section 3 analyses the basic features of the five main currents of economic thought that existed in the period 1930–1964, namely liberalism, socialism and three variants of developmentalism (one in the private sector, two in the public sector – nationalist and non-nationalist).

Section 4 deals with the currents of thought prevailing in 1964–1980, which were years of a military regime. The currents of thought are presented with a slightly different composition, as compared to the previous period, comprising only two developmentalist currents of ideas, namely "pro-government" and "opponents" (the latter comprising those who were against the authoritarian regime and in favour of progressive income distribution), besides liberalism and socialism.

Before we move on, a word of warning is in order. We are not concerned here with the theoretical contribution made by Brazilians, which is dealt with in Chapter 2 of the book; the history of economic thought told in this chapter is a survey of ideas and controversies belonging to developmentalism, which is understood as a particular "system of political economy" in the sense used by Schumpeter (1954, p. 38), which differentiates such the evolution of ideas form a history of economic analysis. Accordingly, the use of developmentalism as the central concept organizing the currents of thought means that the authors whose ideas are surveyed are not classified primarily in terms of the economic theory they used – neoclassical, Keynesian, Marxist, etc. – but rather in terms of the views they held on strategies and policies intended to implant industrial capitalism in Brazil.[8]

2. The movement of ideas: the "ideological cycle" of developmentalism (1930–1980)

2.1. Introduction

This section summarizes the movement of developmentalist thought in the period 1930–1980.[9] The key concept used is the "ideological cycle of developmentalism", consisting of its birth (1930–1943), its maturing period (1944–1955), its maturity (1956–1964) and its heyday (1964–1980).

2.2. The birth of developmentalism: 1930–1943

Among the studies on the history of ideas on Brazilian industrialization, several show that some awareness of the need for industrialization existed since the 19th century (for instance, Luz, 1961; Dean, 1969; Lima, 1975; Carone, 1976; Leme, 1978; Fonseca, 2004; and, in the present book, Chapter 7, by Versiani).

Three basic elements in the views expressed by supporters of industrialization prior to 1930 were present in the ideological framework of the transitional period of the 1930s and early 1940s: i) the attack on liberalism associated with the defence of protectionism; ii) the attack on liberalism associated with other forms of support for the industrial sector, such as credit and tax and tariff exemptions, and iii) the association between manufacturing and "prosperity" or "progress".

This ideology of Brazilian industrialization prior to 1930 was nonetheless marginal to the country's life, just as was industry itself. Though Fonseca (2004) is correct in arguing that a good number of texts on the potentiality of industrialization as the main development avenue for Brazil had been put forward before 1930, conditions for the continuous, uninterrupted creation of developmentalism as an ideology embedded in historical circumstances were only in place after 1930.

The decade of 1930 and the years of World War II were the starting point for profound changes. Many historical and ideological processes coincided in time to form an ideal context for the beginning of what was to become a long-term developmentalist course in economic thinking in Brazil. First, the crisis in coffee and other food exports in the early 1930s and the currency devaluation that followed resulted in accelerated growth in the production of manufactured goods. Second, following the inauguration of nationalism as a relevant ideology in cultural and political terms in the 1920s, economic nationalism came to be important in the 1930s in both the left and right wings of the political spectrum. Third, and mainly during Vargas' 1937–1945 authoritarian regime, corporatism was adopted by a number of intellectuals, politicians and industrialists, as was positivism.[10]

All of this paved the way to a whole range of new ideas which appeared more or less simultaneously and were of central importance for the developmentalist project. They were superimposed on and went beyond the limits of the previous industrialization ideas. State support for private enterprise ceased to be an isolated proposal made by a few industrialists and gradually gained some legitimacy among the entrepreneurial and technocratic elites of the country, as did planning and state investment in transport, mining, energy and heavy manufacturing sectors.

This, however, was still the period of the "origins" of the ideological cycle of developmentalism. The 1930 Revolution led by Vargas had no clear connection with industrialization, its main political significance being the breakdown of the political hegemony of regional oligarchies, thus opening some space for new actors to enter the limited cast of the country's ruling elites. At best, it might be said – as asserted by Ianni (1971) – that suitable conditions were created for the development of a bourgeois state.

Developmentalism, as the ideology of overcoming underdevelopment based on a strategy of industrialization, was only to mature and occupy its leading position in the second half of the 1950s. In the 1930s and early 1940s, there was a first, limited awareness of the project by a small elite of entrepreneurs (for instance, the Federation of Industry of the State of São Paulo [FIESP], created in 1931, and the National Confederation of Industry [CNI], created in 1938) and by a small group of civil and military government technicians who formed the technical cadres of the new institutions set up by the centralized state under Vargas. The nationwide issues that these technicians tackled in their offices led them to think about the long-term problems of the economy and hence about the possibility of the historical solution of industrialization.

2.3. The maturing period of developmentalism: 1944–1955

Several ideological episodes lead to choosing the year 1944 as a turning point to a phase of continuous maturing of developmentalism; some examples were the First Brazilian Economic Congress, in November/December 1943, and the First Brazilian Congress of the Manufacturing Sector, in December 1944.

The idea of progress towards maturity is used here in two senses: that of progress in the spread of developmentalist ideas in economic literature, and that of progress in the analytical content of the proposals put forward.

There were three markedly different stages in this process.

First, the process of democratic transition in the post-war years – the early signs of which appeared in 1944, after seven years of Vargas' authoritarian regime – brought with it an intensive political and institutional mobilization in the country, which naturally influenced Brazil's intellectual life. The establishment of political parties, the presidential election and that of members of the Constituent Assembly, the writing of a new Constitution, and the organization of new institutions in civil society were all aspects that helped create an atmosphere of controversy that the country had not previously known.

It was a "doctrinaire" period *par excellence*, one in which economic liberalism, feeding on expectations of the normalization of international trade, confronted the young developmentalist ideology in a dispute over the ideological orientation that should prevail in the new 1946 Constitution of the Brazilian "economic order" – in which after all there were no clear victors in those immediate postwar years.

Perhaps a case in point was the influential controversy between liberalist Eugênio Gudin and the pioneer of developmentalism, Roberto Simonsen, a dispute that took place already in 1944 (IPEA, 1977). In the debate, the first, who a few years later published a textbook on principles of monetary economy (Gudin, [1947]1970) was better prepared analytically, as to concepts and methods of economic theory; whereas the latter, who a few years before published a book on Brazilian economic history (Simonsen, [1937]2005), was better prepared to discuss history and anticipate the future. Simonsen made the first basically complete and organized statement of the developmentalist position, thus paving the way for maturing its ideas.

The second stage of the maturing period of developmentalism occurred between 1947 and 1952. In 1947 there was a sharp reversal of the expectations that international trade would soon be normalized (regarding dollar scarcity, non-convertibility of the pound sterling, proliferation of bilateral treaties, etc.), and that became clear when Brazil faced an unexpected balance of payments crisis. At that point, Brazilian external trade policy once again underwent heavy state intervention, frustrating liberalization.

Another important element in the maturing of developmentalism in those years was concern over the *reaparelhamento econômico* [economic refitting], an expression abundantly used since the end of the war meaning the need to renew the fixed capital stock in Brazilian economy, especially in the economic infrastructure. This naturally led to reflections on economic planning and the needs of the ongoing industrialization process.

Frustrated expectations of using foreign exchange reserves accumulated during the war to import capital goods for the industry and infrastructure, and criticisms that the Marshall Plan was excluding Latin America from USA's priorities were important to reinforce the maturing of the developmentalist stance. A step towards maturation came up during successful negotiations in 1949–1950 with the United States on special treatment for Brazil, in exchange for unrestricted political alignment in the context of the Cold War and the Korean conflict. An agreement on *reaparelhamento* [refitting] culminated in the establishment of two developmentalist institutions, namely the Brazil–United States Joint Commission, for designing major infrastructure projects, in 1951, and the Development Bank (BNDE) in 1952, as well as in massive imports of capital goods in 1951 and 1952.

That was also a period of intense nationalism, centred on the campaign for nationalization of the petroleum industry. The decision on this issue was made by Parliament in 1952 with the creation of PETROBRAS. To a certain extent, the conscious developmentalism of the second Vargas administration

(1951–1954) was a direct result of the frustrations caused by previous Dutra's government (1946–1950) on those who advocated a policy of industrialization for the country.

In that favourable climate for debate, economic literature gradually began to reflect the relative strengthening of the developmentalist view. To its right, liberals witnessed an evolution of events that ran counter to their principles: they tried to argue that the international system tended toward the recovery of equilibrium and concentrated their attention on the problems of fiscal imbalances and monetary instability. To the left of developmentalists, socialists divorced themselves from the national context under the impulse of a radicalization of the Communist Party's political tactics in view of the repression they suffered – starting with the revocation of their members' political rights and the elimination of those members' mandates in the Brazilian Parliament in 1947. The participation of socialists in the period's intellectual life was almost entirely restricted to campaigning for nationalization of the petroleum industry, the debates on which they followed closely, especially through their military sympathizers and the *Revista do Clube Militar*.

During that period, developmentalist ideas gained wide currency in economic literature. For example, in 1946 the CNI created an economics department headed by nationalist Rômulo de Almeida, and began in 1950 to publish *Estudos Econômicos*, a periodical with a clearly developmentalist orientation. This was shown in March 1950 with the publication of a paper on planning by Almeida (1950) and of two of Prebisch's inaugural texts in the UN's Economic Commission for Latin America (ECLAC, henceforward referred to in its Spanish acronym CEPAL, i.e. Comisión Económica para América Latina): a summary of CEPAL's *Economic Survey of Latin America 1949* (ECLAC, 1951), published in September 1950, and again, in September 1951 a preliminary version of Prebisch's *Theoretical and Practical Problems of Economic Growth* (ECLAC, 1952).

In 1947, the Getúlio Vargas Foundation [Fundação Getúlio Vargas (FGV)] started publishing their periodical *Conjuntura Econômica*, initially headed by a team of nationalist developmentalist economists, and as from the early 1950s by a team of liberals headed by Eugênio Gudin and Octávio Gouveia de Bulhões Gudin. The same team had just inaugurated the *Revista Brasileira de Economia, RBE*, in 1950. Despite its liberal leanings, it included articles by developmentalists – for instance, in their Vol. 3 (3), Prebisch's ([1949] 1962) inaugural text at CEPAL, concerning deterioration of the terms of trade; in Vol. 4 (1), 1950, Hans Singer's (1950) version of the same thesis; and in Vol. 5 (1), 1951, Prebisch's Introduction to the *Economic Survey of Latin America 1949*, published by CEPAL (ECLAC, 1951).

The publication of Prebisch's and CEPAL's inaugural texts both by CNI and FGV supported the diffusion and legitimacy of the developmentalist ideology, as they were no less than signed declarations by a United Nations body asserting that a vigorous process of industrialization was under way in the continent and considering it a new stage in the history of mankind. The texts also gave the advocates of state planning and support for industrialization a whole new set of arguments built on analytical bases and far superior to those used hitherto. We shall come back to this point in the next section.

The third and last stage of the "maturing period of developmentalism" (1953–1955) consisted of both a resurgence of liberal economic ideas and a reassertion of developmentalism. Those were years of marked political instability. From 1953 onwards, there was increasing opposition to Vargas from various sectors of the Brazilian civil and military elite. The crisis culminated in the President's suicide in August 1954, but instability continued, jeopardizing and nearly preventing the assumption of office by developmentalist president Juscelino Kubitschek, elected at the end of 1955.

The 1953–1955 context gave way to a liberal counterattack on developmentalist ideas. Developmentalists reacted with a reassertion of their fundamental principles. Perhaps the most important feature in this interesting dispute in the field of ideas was that it brought out the fact that the formulation and acceptance of the industrialization strategy had matured considerably in the country.

In contrast with previous periods, what was under discussion then was not the validity of an economic policy of support for industrialization, but the intensity of state intervention and the speed at which urban-industrial development should be carried out. This debate split up between discussions on the permissible degree of tolerance of monetary and exchange imbalances generated by the process under way and, on the other hand, discussions on the relationship between state intervention, the correction of imbalances and the continuity of development.

Eugênio Gudin's views, for example, were still strong when this liberal leader spoke of reducing state intervention or achieving monetary stabilization, but they began to sound outdated when he insisted in questioning the very possibility of heavy industrialization. This line of argument seems to have represented an ever-smaller threat to the developmentalist project and was refuted in a manner often strengthened by CEPAL's analytical arguments.

In that advanced stage of developmentalist maturing, the range of institutions engaged in intellectual production was renovated and expanded. The five currents of thought referred to in the introduction to this article – liberalism, the three developmentalist currents, and socialism – were very clearly located in their respective institutions.

FGV liberal economists Eugênio Gudin and Octavio Gouveia de Bulhões, leaders of RBE, had just gained complete control over the institution's other main instrument for disseminating ideas, *Conjuntura Econômica*, following the departure by 1952 of developmentalists Richard Lewinsohn and Américo Barbosa de Oliveira, who left its editorial board; they also controlled the periodicals published by the National Economic Council [Conselho Nacional de Economia, CNE] and the National Confederation of Trade [Confederação Nacional do Comércio, CNC].[11]

Non-nationalist developmentalists – less numerous but maintaining an active intellectual participation – made up the Brazil–United States Joint Commission and were also influential in BNDE.

Nationalist developmentalists set up two important institutions: the Higher Institute of Brazilian Studies [Instituto Superior de Estudos Brasileiros (ISEB)] and the Economists' Club [Clube dos Economistas], the latter being initially formed on the basis of a nucleus from BNDE under the leadership of Celso Furtado, who had moved from Santiago, Chile, to Rio de Janeiro in order to work with the CEPAL-BNDE Joint Commission on a project of economic planning in Brazil. Private sector developmentalists continued to publish *Estudos Econômicos* at the CNI; the journal was discontinued in 1954 but was restored in 1956 under the name of *Desenvolvimento e Conjuntura.*

As for socialists, grouped together in the Brazilian Communist Party, they once again stepped up their participation in the country's intellectual life after Vargas' death. Their important periodical *Revista Brasiliense*, for example, was first launched in 1955.

2.4. Maturity (1956–1964)

In his presidential campaign in 1955, Kubitschek had announced that mandate would achieve 50 years of progress in five. His administration (1956–1961) combined relative political stability with rapid economic and industrial growth under a developmentalist strategy. In the early days of his government, he created the Conselho de Desenvolvimento [Development Council], which formulated and followed up on the implementation of what is considered to have been the most important planning instrument in Brazilian history, namely, the Plano de Metas (Target Plan). By 1956, the state of perplexity and indecision over the economic courses to be followed, which had affected the country in previous years as a result of the political crisis, had already been overcome. The developmentalist ideology was now incorporated into the official policy statements of the government.

The country's economic literature very clearly expressed the perception of these changes by intellectual elites. Developmentalist economic thinking, which had matured in the previous ten years, now reached its maturity.

The planned industrialization project was widely disseminated in economic literature and also gained the upper hand over the liberal school of thought. Although the latter did try to attack, it had been weakened by historical circumstances and was now on the defensive. The current of thought that would gradually move to the offensive was socialism. During that period, this helped to disseminate issues of nationalism and income distribution that were to be of great importance later on in the ideological turmoil of the first half of the 1960s.

The central ideological reference during Kubitschek's administration was the proposal to intensify the industrialization process by planning it, expanding the infrastructure of goods and services, guaranteeing the necessary imports of capital goods and basic inputs, and avoiding contractionary anti-inflation policies. At the same time, the acceleration of inflation in the last years of the 1950s gave way to a renewed debate on its causes and on policies to confront it. After the frustrated attempt of the 1958 Stabilization Plan, conceived for Kubitschek by Lucas Lopes and Roberto Campos, then respectively the finance minister and the president of BNDE, a heated debate known as structuralism vs. monetarism arose. We will come back to it in Section 3.

The period between 1961 and the 1964 military coup comprised years of great political instability, unprecedented mobilization in favour of social reforms, growing inflation and serious fiscal and foreign exchange difficulties, and as of 1962, but above all in 1963, a pronounced decline in the growth rates of income and employment.

The industrialization project, which until a few years before had been increasingly guiding the thinking of Brazilian economists, ceased for some years to act as the ideological backbone of economic proposals and analyses. Economic thinking was subordinated primarily to three aspects: inflation and balance of payments problems, nationalism – as a reaction to large inflows of transnational corporations – and "basic reforms" (agrarian, fiscal, educational). Social reforms – especially in agrarian matters – first became a basic element in the economic debate, as part of an appraisal of previous experience and of the economy's future development possibilities.

There was thus an interesting combination between the emphasis on short-term problems, typical of a current crisis, and the emphasis on basic changes in the growth pattern, typical of a structural crisis. The latter feature was further heightened by economic nationalism. By stimulating the debate on the nation's economic and political assertion, nationalism also helped stimulate discussion of the changes in the course followed by Brazilian economy up to that point.

The debate now was on a new style of developmentalism, one that was less optimistic and wrapped up in "reform" campaigns. It contained a rather widespread notion that continuity of development was difficult, if not impossible, within the existing institutional settings. Several aspects contributed to this.

First, it was felt that the country lacked a financial equation that might permit growth without serious fiscal and monetary imbalances, and this would call for far-reaching fiscal and financial reforms; indeed, there was even a reasonable degree of consensus that the Brazilian state was not financially prepared to cope with the demands that economic and social development was imposing upon it.

Second, it was asserted that unless there were reforms in the agrarian structure and a change in income distribution, industrial development would not be able to solve the problems of unemployment and poverty of the majority of the population and of extensive regions in the country, such as its Northeast; the 1963 recession further accentuated this pessimism and helped undermine the traditional developmentalist outlook.

Third, the country was beginning to take into account a newly arrived theory in Latin America that stated that institutional reforms in income distribution were not only necessary as a matter of social justice but might also be essential to recover growth in the region's economies.

In other words, the problem arisen in the early 1960s was no longer that of defending or attacking the strategy of creating an industrial economy, since the irreversible nature of that was perceived by all. What was now involved was the need to define macroeconomic policies, social goals, and the nationalist content of the Brazilian industrial economy. Faced with this thematic redefinition, economists regrouped in accordance with political and ideological considerations that had not existed in the past. The now mature developmentalism showed within its ranks a clearer division between conservative and progressive economists.

At the "right" of the political spectrum, liberals and non-nationalist developmentalists, as well as developmentalists in the private sector, began to work together, sometimes getting involved in a political movement to attack president João Goulart – the centre-left vice-president of Jânio Quadros who had taken the latter's place after he resigned in 1961. Two cases in point were the Brazilian Institute of Democratic Action [Instituto Brasileiro de Ação Democrática (IBAD)] and the Social Research and Studies Institute [Instituto de Pesquisas e Estudos Sociais (IPES)], which with entrepreneurial financial support attacked progressive reforms under Goulart's government – labelling it a "communist" one and aiming at its political destabilization – and published a good number of books, articles and pamphlets. But perhaps the best example of that fusion was the later "partnership" between Bulhões and Campos, respectively Finance and Planning ministers in the first military government (1964–1967), while the best example of separation was perhaps that of the split-up of the Brazilian left, which spread out over a multitude of tendencies and organizations.

2.5. Heyday under the military regime (1964–1980)

The climax of the ideological cycle of developmentalism occurred during the military regime. It started with the regime's reassurance of developmentalism, in 1964, in line with the Brazilian armed forces' historical leaning toward the advocacy of industrialization (Fiori, 2014), and ended in 1980, after the second oil shock and the huge increase in international interest rates.

Developmentalist hegemony was guaranteed by three simultaneous and complementary processes. First, by the fact that economic policy from 1964 on was radically developmentalist up to 1980, in the sense of granting government support for the creation of a complex industrial structure. Second, it so happened that in the field of economic thought developmentalism – i.e. industrialization with strong state participation – was adhered to by both government supporters and a large number of economists who were critical of military administrations. As we shall see, divergences among government supporters and critics were of a different nature and involved above all the advocacy of or opposition to the "development model" then adopted by military administrations with regard to income distribution – alongside, of course, the profound political divergence concerning lack of democratic liberties.

Third, as formerly mentioned, during a large part of the industrialization process initiated in the 1950s there prevailed among Brazilian elites a belief that the economy was bound to grow, that is, some sort of "convention of guaranteed growth" (Castro, 1993). Given the need to gain legitimacy before the people, the military regime consolidated that convention through reforms and economic policies that privileged investment and growth.

Brazilian reflection on the two basic thematic fields examined in this chapter – macroeconomic situation/inflation and especially characteristics and limits of growth and development – was intensified after 1964. Starting in the mid-1960s, there emerged a form of academic life with previously uncommon characteristics, which caused a large increase in the number of intellectuals, promoted a far-wider dissemination of economic ideas than in former years, and brought a whole new analytical refinement into Brazilian economic thought.[12]

The first postgraduate course in economics was created at FVG in 1964 – with an essentially orthodox orientation in the field of macroeconomics and a neoclassical and liberal one in that of resource allocation. It was soon followed in 1965 by a course offered at the Sao Paulo University (IPE/USP), with an initially plural orientation that became gradually orthodox. From the teaching staff of those two think tanks, there came important economists who would serve the military administrations, among them Delfim Netto, himself a heterodox, and Mario Henrique Simonsen, Carlos Langoni and Afonso Celso Pastore.

Many other postgraduate centres were created shortly afterwards, during the 1970s, some of them following a generally heterodox or plural theoretical orientation, as in federal universities in the states of Minas Gerais (CEDEPLAR/UFMG), Rio Grande do Sul (FCE/UFRGS), and in the late 1970s in Rio de Janeiro (IE-UFRJ), as well as in São Paulo state university of Campinas (UNICAMP) and in the major Brazilian private university, PUC, located in Rio; others were more inclined to neoclassical theory, as in the federal universities of Pernambuco (PIMES/UFPE) and Ceará (CAEN/UFC). Together they formed an unprecedented forum of debate on the characteristics and destinies of the country's economy. At the same time, countless economists obtained their doctoral degrees at prestigious foreign universities, and many of them went on to integrate academic staffs and government bodies in Brazil.

Equally relevant to bring analytical maturity into the debate on Brazilian economy was the creation, in 1973, of the National Association of Postgraduation in Economics [Associação Nacional de Pós-Graduação em Economia (ANPEC)] (Loureiro, 1997). It established a long-lasting acceptance of pluralism in the Brazilian academy on economics, under the initial decisive support of the Ford Foundation and its representative in Brazil, Professor Werner Baer,[13] as well as the initial decisive leadership of its first Executive Secretary, CEDEPLAR's Professor Paulo Haddad (Fernandez and Supriniak, 2015, 2019).

Furthermore, and somewhat compensating for the 1964 coup's elimination of some centres of progressive thinking, such as the Economist's Club and ISEB, there appeared a whole new constellation of non-governmental organizations, like the Brazilian Centre of Analysis and Planning [Centro Brasileiro de Análise e Planejamento (CEBRAP), sponsored by the Ford Foundation and the McArthur Foundation. No less important was the 1964 creation, in the Planning Ministry, of the Institute of Applied Economic Research [Instituto de

Pesquisa Econômica Aplicada, IPEA], where ministers Roberto Campos and Reis Velloso created an atmosphere of plural economic thinking in spite of the dictatorship (Loureiro, 1997).

The oppositional reaction caused by Brazilian dictatorship in the society's progressive and democratic currents – hence in a large number of intellectuals – found ways to circulate their criticism regarding the government and economic policies. Despite repressing unionists, progressive politicians and several intellectuals, the military regime did not prevent the emergence of a vigorous production of ideas on Brazilian economy from a critical perspective. Unlike other dictatorial regimes in Latin America and except for the years when repression was tightened (especially in the late 1960s and first half of the 1970s), the Brazilian military dictatorship not only did not oppose the emergence of new institutions dedicated to research and critical thinking, but did actually finance them as of the mid-1970s, through the Ministry of Education (CAPES/MEC) and the National Fund for Scientific and Technological Development [Fundo Nacional de Desenvolvimento Científico e Tecnológico (FNDCT)], the latter headed by progressive democrat José Pelucio Ferreira and under the patronage of minister Reis Velloso, who also supported Isaac Kerstenestky as a progressive president of the influential Brazilian Institute for Geography and Statistics, IBGE.

All that process of institutional formation resulted not only in a large increase of intellectual production concerning Brazilian economy but also in a stronger commitment to academic rigorousness in published books and articles. Alongside the pre-existent *Revista Brasileira de Economia* and *Conjuntura Econômica* (IBRE/FGV), there appeared, for instance, periodicals like *Estudos Econômicos* (FIPE-USP), *Pesquisa e Planejamento Econômico* (IPEA) and *Cadernos CEBRAP*, as well as an entire set of discussion papers in university departments of economics and an intensified publication of books on Brazilian economy.

As formerly noted, developmentalism – whether "pro-government" or "critical" – was hegemonic throughout the period in question, both following and supporting the reinforcement of the state to favour the industrialization project. The socialist current had a more meaningful presence only in the 1960s, while the liberal current would re-emerge with some strength only as of the mid-1970s.

In the late 1970s, some entirely new political stirrings in Brazilian society gave way to a battery of criticism against government policies. Workers, as in their several strikes in 1979 and in creating the Workers' Party [Partido dos Trabalhadores (PT)], advocated democracy as well as better wages and working conditions. Among entrepreneurs, there were, as in the "group of the eight"[14] (Oliveira, 2020, p. 98), those who demanded greater participation in decision-making concerning economic policy and those who, in a more radical stance, put pressure against growing state ownership of the economy and thus inaugurated the resurgence of liberalism after approximately two decades of relative withdrawal. The major conservative newspaper in São Paulo, *O Estadão*, would come to lead a full campaign against State intervention. Nevertheless, those were still years of developmentalist hegemony.

3. The five currents of thought in the 1930–1964 period

3.1. Liberalism

Liberal economists played a prominent part in the economic debate, giving rise to economic policies that were criticized by developmentalists and in turn criticizing the latter's proposals.

To some extent, Brazilian economic ideology from the early nineteenth century until the 1930s was liberal by tradition, despite the advocacy of state intervention in favour of agrarian interests. The 1930–1932 crisis, however, and the political, economic and social changes that followed weakened its real support base. From that time onwards, other conceptions of Brazilian economic development arose. In response to that, liberal ideology had to undergo some changes in order to be able to face the new realities, and Brazilian liberalism in the 1930–1980 period was the result of this process.

Liberal economists favoured a reduction of state intervention. Some of them, as Eugênio Gudin and Daniel de Carvalho, adhered to the principle of the classic international division of labour. Others, as Octavio Gouveia de Bulhões, Dênio Nogueira and Alexandre Kafka, had a much clearer perception of the force and irreversibility of the industrialization process then under way, but were moved by the achievement of monetary stability rather than by growth policies. None of them proposed policies in support of industrialization and more often than not were critical of them.

However, in spite of strongly opposing the growing state intervention in Brazilian economy, they made some concessions as compared to what a pure liberal economist might be willing to make. Thus, for example, they accepted the idea that the government should have some influence on the country's foreign trade in order to tackle problems resulting from the characteristics of international supply and demand of commodities. They also accepted the idea of government support for activities connected with health, education and technical assistance to agriculture, as well as some credit support for infrastructure activities (though arguing that they should preferably be carried out by the private sector, including foreign corporations, and not by state enterprises).

Eugênio Gudin was the leading advocate of liberalism.[15] His importance in Brazilian economic thinking, however, went beyond the bounds of his long and influential period of conservative leadership: he was also a pioneer in the teaching of economic theory and in the legitimation of the profession of economics in Brazil. He dealt with all the main aspects of Brazilian economic affairs with easy assurance and framed his questions in a lively and coherent manner. He not only attracted the attention of conservative economists and politicians looking for arguments to back up their proposals, but also that of developmentalist intellectuals who were compelled to counter Gudin's analyses given their practical importance and the consistency of his arguments. In view of the way he propagated liberal views, it is easy to understand why the anti-liberal interpretations inspired by Prebisch-CEPAL's arguments were so important to developmentalists.

With regard to foreign trade, Gudin recognized that there were special features in the way the crisis of the 1930s affected "reflex economies" – an expression coined by him in 1940 – and he continued to admit it during the many years of dollar shortage which followed World War II. He acknowledged the problems deriving from the world's low price and income elasticities for commodities as well as the fragility of "reflex" economies like Brazil vis-à-vis the cyclical oscillations of developed economies.

Unlike developmentalists, however, Gudin was not led by this type of acknowledgment to advocate industrialization. According to him, the solution lay in using a number of preventive measures essentially designed to influence prices and production level. His concessions with regard to the maximum permissible state intervention in external trade went no further than that. In his opinion, the Brazilian economy was simply not ready for industrialization – except perhaps for "light industrialization" where international comparative advantage might allow it – and the proof was that market forces themselves did not promote it.

Regarding inflation, Gudin systematically referred to the idea of the existence of full employment in Brazilian economy – "hyperemployment and hypoproductivity", as he used to say – as though he acknowledged, in a Keynesian way, the importance of taking into account the capacity of supply to respond to demand pressures. In this sense, using the term "monetarist" to describe Gudin is open to challenge, though it is not so in two other senses: first, from the point of view of the structuralist interpretation – referred to later on in this chapter – to which Gudin was strongly opposed, and second, from the perspective of Keynesian-type criticisms, according to which the economic policy proposed by Gudin was of a monetarist nature, both because it stated that the idea of the existence of full employment was a fallacy, and because it did not take into account the depressive effects of stabilization policies.

3.2. The developmentalist currents

Three currents of developmentalism may be distinguished in the period 1930–1964: one consisting of people associated with private sector institutions and another two made up of people in the public sector. They all shared the aim of establishing modern industrial capitalism in the country and the conviction that, in order to achieve that goal, it was necessary to plan the economy and practice various forms of government intervention.

Developmentalists who worked in the private sector naturally defended business interests in a manner not always shared by those who worked in the public sector, given the commitments the latter had to make by virtue of their office.

In the public sector, there were two basic developmentalist positions regarding state intervention. Non-nationalists proposed maximizing private solutions for industrial and infrastructural projects, using foreign or national capital, but were willing to accept state intervention when private capital showed neither interest nor entrepreneurial capacity. Nationalists, on the contrary, called for nationalization of the mining, transport and energy sectors, as well as of public services in general and some branches of heavy manufacturing industries. Among private sector developmentalists, there was no uniform position on the subject.

The three currents adopted different stances regarding inflation control: the non-nationalist current leaned towards stabilization programs that were somewhat more orthodox than the other two, which stressed concerns about the effects of those programs on economic activity. In the private sector, the great concern was to avoid credit reduction, and nationalists in the late 1950s took a structuralist view of the matter, as shall be discussed later on in this section.

Two pillars of developmentalism were simultaneously created in the early stages of developmentalism. First, in the private sector, bodies representing business interests, such as FIESP and CNI, broadened their range of demands as of the 1930s and elaborated and publicized an industrialization strategy involving planning and heavy state intervention.

Second, and especially during the period known as "Estado Novo" (1937–1945), various agencies were established in the public sector for the purpose of tackling problems of national scope. Naturally, their civil and military technicians were forced to reflect on the problems of national economic development in a broad and integrated manner, and this helped giving rise to the developmentalist ideology.

The developmentalist current in the private sector was based on the first of those pillars. Public sector developmentalist currents – especially the nationalist one – were based on the second of those pillars, but were greatly influenced by and received much support from private entrepreneur Roberto Simonsen. In the second half of the 1940s, for example, when the liberalism that had prevailed in the early part of President Dutra's administration managed to partially immobilize the economic agencies founded by Vargas, Simonsen set up a Department of Economics at CNI and appointed Rômulo de Almeida to head it. After Simonsen's death in 1948, Almeida was to be the main developmentalist economist in Brazil until the mid-1950s, when leadership passed on to Celso Furtado (among nationalists) and Roberto Campos (among non-nationalists).

The year of Simonsen's death coincided with that of the establishment of UN's Economic Commission for Latin America, CEPAL. This historical coincidence is a landmark in the evolution of developmentalism, because CEPAL came to offer a set of anti-liberal analytical instruments (summarized later on in this section) which was to be partly incorporated in the 1950s by some private sector developmentalists and, to a larger extent, by nationalist developmentalists.

a) Developmentalism in the private sector

The historical events that succeeded the 1930 Revolution opened up a new prospect for a small group of industrialists organized in trade associations, i.e., a prospect that the manufacturing sector might have a central role in the future of the national economy. This entrepreneurial elite – Roberto Simonsen, Puppo Nogueira, Euvaldo Lodi, Jorge Street, Morvan Figueiredo, etc. – conducted what might be called a pioneering exercise in planning, in several public sector institutions that were set up at the time. Thus, there was a fertile crossing of ideologies between them and the developmentalist ideas and concepts that emerged in new public sector bodies, where discussions were held and decisions were made on issues like foreign trade, energy, transport, the iron and steel industry, and many other national-scale concerns. This amalgam of ideas corresponds to a by-product of "corporatism" in its Brazilian version.

As far as economic ideology is concerned, Simonsen's work contains most of the basic elements of the developmentalist repertoire of the currents of thought which favoured the establishment of industrial capitalism in the country: the understanding of the fact that a process of profound restructuring of production patterns was taking place in Latin American economies and that this offered a historical possibility of overcoming underdevelopment and poverty; the idea that the success of the industrialization project would depend on strong government support (with planning and protectionism); and the proposal that the state should make direct investments in the sectors where the part played by private enterprise was insufficient. Simonsen can thus be considered the founder of developmentalism.

The economics department of CNI, set up in 1946 by Roberto Simonsen, was to become the main source of the formulation of economic ideas by private sector developmentalism in the following years and in the 1950s. Those ideas reflected a dual concern: to advocate a project for planned industrialization and to protect short- and long-term interests of private industrial capital. In other words, private sector developmentalists could both further economic policy proposals, in line with all developmentalists, and focus their attention on proposals designed to defend specific and sometimes immediate interests of the entrepreneurial class.

In spite of its diminishing importance after Simonsen's death in 1948 as a current of thought, the private sector retained some relevance in the diffusion of development ideas, as can be seen, for instance, in the publication by CNI of the periodicals *Estudos economicos* (1950–54) and *Desenvolvimento e Conjuntura*, launched in 1956 under the leadership of João P.A. Magalhães. From the early 1960s onwards, this current of thought merged with public sector "non-nationalist developmentalism", in the support of military government's interventionism in favour of industrialization.

b) Non-nationalist public sector developmentalism

The non-nationalist developmentalist current in the public sector – not quite as large as the nationalist current, but rather active and influential in the governmental sphere – was made up of economists who believed that foreign capital could make a large contribution to the industrialization process.

From its origins in the 1930s, developmentalism was an economic ideology with strong links to nationalism. Among those who believed that industrialization was the way to leave poverty behind, the majority felt that it was not possible to expect large contributions from foreign capital for this purpose. The most radical of them saw foreign capital as a monolithic group of imperialist interests, basically antagonistic to the developmentalist project. Among the more moderate nationalists, most felt that, at least in sectors that were vital to the industrialization process, such as energy, transport, mining and heavy manufacturing, the state should ensure that there was national control over decisions.

Though non-nationalist developmentalism already existed in the 1930s and 1940s, it gained momentum in the early 1950s in connection with the task force implemented during the second term of the Vargas administration – the Brazil–United States Joint Commission (1950–1954) – which came up with 41 infrastructural investment projects, as well as the project for creating the National Economic Development Bank (BNDE), founded in 1952.

The initiatives were in line with nationalist concerns and ideas, but essentially included most of the main figures in non-nationalist developmentalism, such as Horácio Lafer, Valentim Bouças, Ary Torres, Glycon de Paiva and, in a process of ideological preparation for a subsequent realignment, the then-nationalist Roberto Campos, the leading economist in this current.[16]

Campos had a good theoretical grounding in economics and a powerful critical capacity, aside from being a penetrating and skilled polemicist who was able to confound even his most intelligent adversaries. In the light of the real historical process experienced by Brazil, Campos appears against the background of the 1950s as a thinker who foresaw the future of the Brazilian manufacturing sector. He wagered on industrialization through the internationalization of capital and through state support, and he won his bet.

In the Brazilian political scene of the period under exam, Campos represented the "right" of the developmentalist stance. On the one hand, he worked for the country's industrialization project, for example, as the main formulator of President Kubitschek's Target Plan and also as its main executor, in his capacity as executive secretary and subsequently president of National Development Bank (BNDE) between 1956 and 1959. Campos's argument behind the sectorial planning that governed the Target Plan – which would be theoretically elaborated by Hirschman (1958) at a later date – was this: the ideal government intervention strategy should be to concentrate on the "bottlenecks" of the industrial system, such as transport and energy, so that these would become points of burgeoning growth, since they would automatically generate backward and forward linkages and market stimuli for the private sector in the remaining economic activities. This was clearly a "winner". Celso Furtado's work in a BNDE-CEPAL Joint Group in 1954–1955 to influence the use of CEPAL's planning technique, based on a Harrod-Domar macroeconomic formula, may be considered no more than a complementary subsidy to the Target Plan.[17]

At the same time, Campos defended the idea of attracting foreign capital even into the mining and energy sectors, and attacked a state solution in cases where a private solution seemed possible. Furthermore, as will be mentioned later in this chapter, he disagreed with the structuralist interpretation of inflation. Although in his writings of that period he did not share the strictly monetarist position and differentiated himself from the IMF's ideas on it, the importance he attached to the adoption of anti-inflation policies that could be understood as recessive caused many of his opponents to identify him with the orthodox view on monetary issues.

c) Nationalist developmentalism in the public sector (and the structuralist analysis)

Power centralization under Getúlio Vargas in the 1930s gave rise to a set of planning bodies (such as the Public Service Administrative Department, the Federal Council for External Trade, the National Petroleum Council, etc.) within which the first teams of civil and military technicians concerned with the problem of Brazilian industrial development were formed. Men like Horta Barbosa and Macedo Soares formed the embryo of the nationalist developmentalist current which, together with the liberal current, was to be the most important line of thinking in Brazil in the 1950s.

In the immediate postwar period, the nationalist developmentalist current survived the liberalism of Dutra's administration through the inauguration of some centres of resistance, such as the Department of Economics of CNI, already referred to, and the FGV (where Gudin and Bulhões' group was to occupy the leading position only from 1952 onwards). The second Vargas term (1951–1954) gave nationalists fresh opportunities to organize themselves through the establishment of institutions such as the President's Economic Advisory Group, formed by nationalists like Rômulo de Almeida, Jesus Soares Pereira, Ignácio Rangel and, very close to them, Ewaldo Correia Lima, Cleantho de Paiva Leite and Lucio Meira. The great meeting of nationalist developmentalists took place after Vargas's death, in the mid-1950s, when Celso Furtado and Américo Barbosa de Oliveira set up the Economists' Club, a body grouping together several dozen technicians from the federal government and some developmentalists from the private sector, all of whom expressed their views mainly through its *Revista Econômica Brasileira*, issued from 1955 until the 1964 military *coup d'État*.[18]

Three elements distinguished their views from the non-nationalist current of thought. First, they considered that investment in infrastructure, oil, iron, steel and part of the chemical sectors should not be made under the initiative and decisions of foreign capital, but instead needed the creation of mechanisms for substantial financing as well guidance and control by national capital, which meant direct investments by the public sector, since the weakness of private national capital ruled out private solutions. In the other manufacturing sectors, however, foreign capital was welcomed by nationalist developmentalists. This point is not always grasped by those interested in the history of Brazilian industrialization. It explains, for example, why nationalist Lucio Meira was the major promoter of the Target Plan with regard to bringing foreign automotive industry into the country. As to the rest of the manufacturing sector, nationalist developmentalists were basically concerned with controlling the remittance of profits abroad and with the need to build the presence of national entrepreneurs in input sectors such as that of auto parts.

Second, nationalists tended to express concern with unemployment, poverty and bad income distribution. The influence of those issues on their thinking before the late Fifties should not be overstated, however. In the 1940s and 1950s, the basic message conveyed by their texts was that by itself industrialization was a process of change capable of doing away with backwardness and making it feasible to overcome poverty. Furtado's creation of the Superintendency for Development of the Northeast (SUDENE)[19] can be seen as a first significant move towards social policies, inaugurating an agenda of "basic reforms" (on land, taxes, education, etc.). Not surprisingly, Furtado became an important reference for social democrats.

The third divergence with non-nationalist developmentalists concerned inflation issues. Nationalists claimed that monetary policy should not have priority over growth and development policies, and that policy makers should confront IMF pressures. In this respect they allied with private sector economists, but differed from them by adopting, with Celso Furtado, the structuralist interpretation of inflation, and by not adopting the private sector's leaning toward fighting it with wage cuts.

By the mid-Fifties, Celso Furtado became the most important national development intellectual. That leadership was due to the analytical power of his ideas.[20] He was the main disseminator in Brazil of Prebisch's and CEPAL's structuralist theory of peripheral development, to which he added a number of analytical contributions that deeply influenced Brazilian developmentalist thought.

The Prebisch/CEPAL structuralist analytical system contained the following central elements:[21] i) Identification of underdevelopment as a condition of the periphery (the "centre–periphery" concept); ii) Identification of the process of spontaneous industrialization that had been taking place since the 1930s and acknowledgment of its historical significance for the continent's underdeveloped economies; iii) The argument that industrialization was taking place in the typically underdeveloped structures of the periphery and should therefore be seen as an unprecedented and uncertain pattern of development, due to "a low degree of production and diversification", "structural dualism/heterogeneity" and "institutional backwardness"; iv) The argument that such characteristics give rise to perverse tendencies toward deterioration of the terms of trade, external imbalances, inflation and the persistence of underemployment); v) The need for planning and strong state intervention, presented as a corollary of the diagnosis of structural imbalances typical of the spontaneous industrialization process in peripheral economies; vi) Industrialization seen as a process of import substitution; vii) The interpretation of inflation as a phenomenon that may not originate in public deficits and monetary causes, but rather in structural causes, among which are external constraints and severe shocks on the exchange rates, hence on inflation.[22]

Furtado made several contributions to the structuralist theory of development, of which three are mentioned in what follows.

First, in his classical *History of Economic Growth in Brazil*, Furtado ([1959] 1963) included a historical dimension in the structuralist approach, building up what Boianovsky (2015) rightly designates as Furtado's historical-structural method in Latin American political economy. The book presents an historical study which had decisive importance for the acknowledgment that Brazil inherited from its history an economic structure characterized – as is CEPAL's view of the nature of Latin American underdevelopment, according to Rodriguez (1981) – by low product and export diversification and by structural heterogeneity. It shows the establishment of a vast subsistence economy in the sugarcane and mining economic cycles in colonial times, regarded as having outlived the coffee cycle in the 19th century and the first half of the 20th century. The intrinsic conclusion was that the historical evolution of the countries that remained underdeveloped in the mid-20th century was necessarily different from that of developed countries, and that they called for careful planning and wide state support in order to achieve efficient industrialization.

In 1956, ECLA first raised the idea that surplus labour in agriculture in Latin America was being very slowly absorbed by industry, which Prebisch (1963) interpreted as a consequence of the use of labour-saving techniques in the manufacturing sector (Love, 1990a, p. 151). This idea led Furtado (1965) to his second major contribution to structuralism: an analysis of the relations between growth and income distribution. We shall come back to this later in Section 4 of this chapter.

Furtado's third relevant contribution to structuralism was his analysis of inflation as a basically non-monetary phenomenon. The authorship of the structuralist thesis on inflation is traditionally attributed to Noyola (1956) and Sunkel ([1958] 1960), but, as convincingly argued by Boianovsky (2012), Furtado can be said to have been their predecessor.

According to Noyola, inflation is not an essentially monetary phenomenon, but rather a consequence of tensions and imbalances that stem from the actual structures of the economies. Noyola introduced a new model of analysis based upon two concepts, viz., "basic inflationary pressures" (structural balance of payment disequilibrium, food supply inelasticities) and "propagation mechanisms" (struggle over income distribution originally raised by the inflation that stems from "basic pressures").

Noyola's model was improved upon by Sunkel, who classified the factors underlying inflation in four categories: "basic", "circumstantial", "cumulative" and "propagative". The first and last are of the same nature as in Noyola's analysis. Circumstantial factors are shocks such as world price increases and public expenditure arising from a national calamity or from political measures. And cumulative factors are those which arise from distortions in the price system, such as price controls and investment misallocations.

Noyola and Sunkel were Furtado's close intellectual interlocutors at CEPAL in the 1950s. Boianovsky (2012) points out that three central ideas in their analyses of inflation were already clearly argued some years earlier by Furtado ([1952] 1954): the notion of "passive money", the idea of a structural disequilibrium in the balance of payments as a basic inflationary cause, and the idea of "propagative mechanisms" basically pointing at distributive conflicts that would follow basic price increase factors. Boianovsky argues that as part of the latter, Furtado [1952] 1954, p. 179) promoted a discussion of "inertial inflation" – one that was central to Brazilian debates in the 1980s and early 1990s, as will be seen in the next two chapters – when he noticed that price rises with no real effect on real income distribution correspond to "neutral inflation".

Boianovsky (2012) also points out that in an influential paper by Campos (1961) surveying the different views on inflation in Latin America, the terms of the debate had been coined by Campos himself, who used the words "structuralism" and "monetarism" long before monetarism came to be a term related to orthodox macroeconomic policy.

Interestingly enough, according to Bielschowsky ([1985] 2022, ch. 3) Campos' texts written in the 1950s show that he acknowledged the existence of a structurally inherent tendency to imbalances in underdeveloped economies, which he felt to be somewhat vulnerable to balance-of-payment disequilibrium and other inflationary pressures. But his opinion on the matter gradually changed into one in which bottlenecks and food supply inelasticity were rather seen as a result of wrong policies and not essentially as structural causes of inflation. Campos pointed out that although balanced growth is practically impossible, leads and lags in the development process do not necessarily become cumulative and self-feeding. Thus Latin American monetary authorities should avoid policies that could easily transform a restrained inflationary process into an unchecked one.

In this respect, the distinction between Campos' arguments and traditionally orthodox views is less clear. Unlike the orthodoxy, however, Campos pragmatically supported a gradualist attack against inflation and a combination of monetary and fiscal measures by means of which one might avoid losses in investments that were essential to a structural change in the economy – as in negotiations with the IMF during the Kubitschek administration, in 1958–1959 and again in 1964–1967, when Campos was the Planning minister in Castello Branco's first military government.

Furtado, in his turn, wrote for Goulart's administration a Three-Year Plan (Brazil, 1963) in which anti-inflationary policies leaned toward the same position as that adopted by Campos. Though proposing gradualism, the Plan pointed to the need of severe fiscal and monetary controls. It also included politically progressive propositions, such as basic social reforms in land property and education, as well as a fiscal reform to deal with the structurally low level of taxation inherited from the export-led period. This, however, did not make the Plan more heterodox in terms of anti-inflationary measures.[23]

One last note is worth adding before we move on. At the Superior Institute of Brazilian Studies (ISEB), created in 1955, a number of nationalist social scientists, among them economists like Ewaldo Correia Lima and Rômulo de Almeida, gathered together for a multidisciplinary discussion on Brazilian society and economy in the 1950s. Despite being mostly non-Marxists, they somehow shared the Brazilian Communist Party's interpretation that an alliance between a "national-bourgeois" progressive class and the emerging proletariat had been growing in Brazil since 1930, in support of industrialization and in opposition to both the old agrarian oligarchy and foreign capital. In the classification used in the present chapter, ISEB's intellectual production may be viewed as belonging to the nationalist developmentalist current, as most if its authors discussed the economic, social and political conditions for success in Brazilian progress via industrialization, rather than via prospects of change into a socialist regime and economy – the central issue organizing the socialist current of thought.[24]

3.3. The socialist current

To the left of developmentalism, there was a current of authors whose economic ideas were based on the outlook of the socialist revolution or transition to socialism, such as Caio Prado Jr., Nelson Werneck Sodré, Heitor Ferreira Lima, Aristóteles Moura and Alberto Passos Guimarães.[25] This current, made of intellectuals associated with the Communist Party – and in the 1960s and afterwards also of intellectuals dissenting from the party – has been termed "socialist" in this chapter.

The contrast between economic thinking in the socialist and developmentalist currents is enlightening. Up until 1964, socialists, just like developmentalists, advocated the industrialization strategy involving heavy state intervention – as a way of "developing the forces of production", to use their language – and they also defended state investments in basic sectors of the economy, as well as control over foreign capital. The standpoint from which socialists made their analyses was completely different, however, since all their reflections were based on discussing the prevailing phase of the socialist revolution, as defined by the Brazilian Communist Party. This was so regarding all major economic issues debated at the time: foreign capital versus nationalization; inflation and the balance of payments; agrarian reform, etc.

The socialist current was the group mainly responsible for introducing into the economic debate aspects concerning "production relations". Moreover, through intellectuals like Caio Prado Jr. and Nelson Werneck Sodré, they also had a great deal of influence on the introduction and dissemination of a historical perspective into the debate on Brazilian economy.

The discussion of the revolutionary process had historical materialism as its theoretical matrix, i.e. the idea that the evolution of mankind takes place through a well-defined succession of forms of production, through class struggle. It determined both the socialists' analysis in the political scene and the main lines of their economic analysis, and was particularly based on the argument that came out of the 1919 Moscow episode of the Third International regarding "backward economies". Presided by Lenin, the Conference defined as the political strategy to be followed by such economies and societies an alliance between workers and the nationalist bourgeoisie, for the purpose of defeating the two basic enemies of progress and future revolution, namely, land feudalism and imperialism. This came to be known as the "democratic-bourgeois stage of the revolutionary process".

For the Brazilian Communist Party, and in spite of moments of greater radicalism, the mainstream thinking was that Brazilian society was going through a stage of transition from a conservative agrarian society into a modern industrial economy and a more progressive society. Up to that point, their interpretation would be identical to that of developmentalists, were it not for two basic aspects: first, that this transition was seen as a necessary stage in the struggle for socialism, and second, that in order to guarantee this it was imperative to proceed to a radical elimination of two contradictions inherited from the previous period, namely, monopoly of land ownership (the internal contradiction) and imperialism (the external contradiction). The economic analysis of the socialist current had as its points of reference and stimulus the struggle for agrarian reform and against foreign capital, and all basic problems in Brazilian economy were approached from that point of view. In other words, the intellectual production of members of the party was committed to interpreting and enhancing the "democratic-bourgeois" stage of the Brazilian socialist revolution, as defined in 1919.

Socialists rejected the application of current economic theory to the interpretation of Brazilian economy even more radically than structuralists – who just argued that it should be used in a selective manner, adapted to the case of peripheral countries, and who pointed to the right to formulate and use theories applicable to Latin American backwardness. Socialists themselves had made some analytical efforts towards an adaptation of Marxism to the Brazilian case – as in Prado Jr.'s ([1942] 1967) interpretation of Brazilian colonial history – and later on in the dependency theorist's interpretation, to which we will return in the next section.

Regarding the balance of payments and inflation, their reflections were subject to the relation between liberalism and imperialism, and pointed to the political conclusions that could be drawn from them: inflation was the result of insufficient food supply due to the monopoly of land ownership, and exchange rate devaluation was the result of shortage of foreign exchange caused by remittance of profits abroad.

The best effort at systematization of the treatment of foreign capital was a book by Guimarães (1963) that was also a central reference in the proposition of archaic or feudal agrarian relations of production, in line with the Communist Party's argument. According to Guimarães, inflation resulted first from the concentrated structure of ownership, and secondly from an economic policy that was at the service of big capital (exchange reforms and lack of control over external trade, public expenditure and credit designed to increase profits or socialize losses). This interpretation had an affinity with another concern of socialist intellectuals, especially Heitor Ferreira Lima and Aristóteles Moura, namely, that of proving that there was a huge concentration of ownership, particularly in the sectors of the economy where foreign capital predominated. Moura was also the major Brazilian researcher of foreign capital. His book *Capitais estrangeiros no Brasil* (1959) was the socialist current's major effort to gather and systematize information and arguments opposing the country's absorption of foreign capital.

Caio Prado Jr. was the most important and notable author among Brazilian socialists. From his pen (Prado, [1942] 1967, and [1945] 1969) came one of the two most influential interpretations of Brazilian economic history, the other one being the structuralist interpretation, written nearly two decades later by Furtado ([1959] 1963). Prado Jr. centred his interpretation on the idea that the nature of Brazilian colonization was "commercial", oriented to international markets and based on the production of tropical goods in large plantations. Despite being based on slavery, the large-scale plantations that formed the basis of the economy during colonial times followed a capitalist rationale, and can only be properly understood as an integral part of the world market.

Accordingly, Prado Jr. dissented from the official Communist Party's idea that after the abolition of slavery land became feudal in Brazil, and strongly argued that it was ruled by the capitalist mode of production. Hence he dissented from the idea that the struggle against feudalism was the main political strategy in the so-called "democratic-bourgeois" stage of revolution. He agreed with the Party as to imperialism as a major enemy, but argued that wage and other working conditions under capitalism, and not agrarian reform understood as land redistribution, should be taken as the main domestic struggles in the rural areas by the proletariat and other progressive forces (Prado, 1960 and [1966]2004).

In the 1960s there emerged a new group of socialists who dissented from the ideas of a possibility of development under capitalism and of the creation of an agrarian and urban proletariat that might render a socialist revolution feasible. As will be seen in Section 4, this new group was formed by authors who adopted the "dependency" theory and by others who on similar lines stressed contradictions in the Brazilian capitalist system which confirmed the social "status quo" rather than pointing to any significant economic and social changes that could pave the way to future revolution.

Last, but not least, some words on Ignácio Rangel are in order, as he was a particularly creative intellectual in terms of adapting Marxism to the Brazilian case. Though a socialist and a Marxist from the point of view of "institutional work", he was close to nationalist developmentalists in all institutions where he had an important participation, such as Vargas' Economic Advisory Group, BNDE and ISEB, while being independent in his analysis of the Brazilian economy.

Rangel (1957) built his own analytical framework – the theory of the "basic duality of the Brazilian economy" – and used it to examine a number of central issues in the economic debate of the time. According to Rangel, since the 1808 arrival of the Portuguese royal court in Brazil there had been three "dualities": i) From that date until the 1860s, the duality was slavery in plantations and trade bourgeoisie; ii) With the end of worldwide slave trade, this mode of production was replaced by semi-capitalism in plantations, and the economic and political strength of trade bourgeoisie was reinforced; iii) Finally, as the 1929 crisis weakened trade bourgeoisie, the new duality was formed by industrial bourgeoisie and semi-capitalism in land properties, so that economic and political dominance was shared by landowners and manufacturing sector entrepreneurs.

Unlike most nationalist developmentalists and socialists, Rangel considered that although agrarian reform was a good call in terms of social justice, it was both unnecessary in terms of the needs of developing productive forces, which were adequately securing food supply for the urban markets and for export, and a lost battle in terms of political viability.[26] Following this line of reasoning, when dealing with high inflation in the early 1960s he argued against structuralists that it was not caused by food production inelasticity, and against orthodox economists that it was not caused be excessive demand, but by speculation with food stocks by wholesale merchants who acted as oligopsonistic dealers towards producers and as oligopolistic ones towards the retail market (Rangel, 1963).

4. The four currents of ideas in the heyday of developmentalism (1964–1980)[27]

4.1. Introduction: currents of thought and the trajectory of ideas

As seen in the former sections, developmentalist thought in the Sixties was already fully settled in the central spot formerly occupied by liberalism. That settling had occurred during a long ideological cycle that began between 1930 and 1943, progressively matured from 1944 to 1955, and reached its maturity in the years 1956 through 1964. Its heyday, in the period 1964–1980, showed a clear developmentalist hegemony advocated by those who supported the military regime installed in 1964 and by a large number of intellectuals who criticized it.

In the regime's early years, government priorities consisted of gradual monetary stabilization and institutional reforms (fiscal, financial, labour etc.) viewed as necessary for growth and industrialization. On the basis of severe wage controls under new rules, from 1964 to 1967 the inflation rate was reduced from a yearly level of 100% to 20%. At the same time there was a successful effort to avoid recession, and the annual growth rate averaged 4.2%. Ideological developmentalist hegemony proceeded from 1968 through 1973, when it reached its peak ebullience, nurtured by the GDP's accelerated growth of 11% per year, which may be seen as the Brazilian chapter of world capitalism's "golden age". And it was preserved in the subsequent period, 1974–1980 (6% average GDP growth p.a.), though there were already some signs of a relative developmentalist weakening due to an atmosphere of international instability, a strong increase in inflation rates and harsher opposition to the military regime. That allows the period to be characterized as one of "developmentalism resistance". The decline would come only in the 1980s with the foreign debt crisis and accelerated inflation.

As formerly noted and without denying the classification of authors in three currents of thought, i.e., liberal, socialist and developmentalist, members of the latter, in the period 1964–1980, are here subdivided into "advocates" and "opponents" of the strategy and economic policies of military governments ("supporters" and "critics"). In other words, we have dropped the classification of private sector versus public sector (nationalist and non-nationalist) developmentalists that was used in the previous section of this chapter, as entrepreneurs and economists formerly identified in this text as belonging to the non-nationalist public sector, were likely to support the military regime and its socially conservative developmentalist orientation.

In the field of economic thinking, developmentalism was shared by both government supporters and a large number of economists who criticized military administrations. As mentioned before, disagreements between government advocates and critics were of a different nature, chiefly involving support of or opposition to the "development model" adopted by military governments with regard to income distribution – along, that is, with profound political divergences concerning the lack of democratic liberties.

Developmentalist hegemony's historical background was fostered by high growth rates and a radically developmentalist economic policy up to 1980, with strong state participation in the constitution of a diversified and modern industry. The military administrations clearly favoured expansionist economic policy practices and were able to consolidate optimism among the entrepreneurial classes inherited from successful ventures in the former period.

Two topics are approached in this section. The first one covers issues pertaining to macroeconomic instability, especially inflation. The second and major one refers to ideas concerned with the characteristics and determinants of growth, as well as development strategies and patterns. The latter point covers the issue of social inclusion, which, as we have seen, had emerged with importance in the Brazilian political and intellectual scene only in the years immediately prior to 1964.

As formerly noted, in spite of the dictatorial regime, post-1964 intellectual production concerning the course and destinies of Brazilian economy acquired an unprecedented ebullience largely thanks to an entirely new establishment of educational and research institutions. From that period, as we shall see, there came a whole new set of reflections on the nature and dynamics of capitalism in Brazil.

Summing up, developmentalism, whether "pro-government" or "critical", was hegemonic throughout the period 1964–1980. The socialist current had a more significant presence only in the 1960s, while the liberal current was to re-emerge only in second half of the 1970s.

4.2. Liberalism

Old-style liberalism and monetarist orthodoxy in the conduction of macroeconomic policies, as associated to economists like Eugênio Gudin and Octávio Gouveia de Bulhões, were relatively marginal in Brazilian economic thinking throughout nearly that entire period. Not even when Bulhões became Finance minister in the first military administration did he apply an "orthodox" policy as such, but rather a hybrid of orthodox and heterodox elements (Resende, 1990). He focused on his old and praiseworthy purpose of creating a Central Bank, a goal he successfully achieved by not engaging in polemics over the matter of state intervention in the economy, that is to say, by not going against the vision that prevailed among the military who had invited him to that position.

In the field of economic thinking, liberalism and macroeconomic orthodoxy were to have a brief resurgence only in the second half of the 1970s, following the retraction of Keynesianism and developmentalism all over the world.

Such resurgence was supported by a new and eminent associate, former developmentalist Roberto Campos, and gave more voice to authors like Carlos Langoni, José Afonso Pastore and several young economists fresh out of doctoral programs abroad with a neoclassical orientation. With the support of important media outlets like daily newspaper *O Estado de São Paulo*, as well as of active entrepreneurs like Henry Maksoud, the late 1970s was a period of growing attacks against government intervention in the economy, which blended with a wave of more general opposition to the military regime. This included national entrepreneurs – such as those in the capital goods sector – who, despite their developmentalism, were dissatisfied with economic policy decisions taken autonomously by the government that had a direct impact on their business (Oliveira, 2020).

4.3. Government developmentalism

The books, articles and interviews by the four most important finance and planning ministers in the 1964–1980 period – Roberto Campos, Delfim Netto, Reis Velloso and Mário Henrique Simonsen – show an alignment with the governmental project of deepening the process of integral industrialization through planning and strong state support. All of them were implicitly or explicitly developmentalist, except for Roberto Campos in his adherence to neoliberalism in the second half of the 1970s, after he seemed to have lost his desire or hope of again becoming a minister in the military government.

The ideas can be found in two basic sets of evidence. First, in the six plans elaborated and implemented in the decades of 1960 and 1970 (Brazil, 1964, 1967, 1970, 1972, 1974), which favour state-led industrialization and, as in the 1966 Plan, also favour export promotion; second, in the six books published by ministers Roberto Campos and Mário Henrique Simonsen between the mid-Sixties and mid-Seventies. Delfim Netto and Reis Velloso were also relevant participants in the economic debate of the period, but they conveyed their thoughts mostly through newspaper interviews and articles and in the government plans supervised by them.[28]

The books by Campos and Simonsen – one by Campos (1968), three by Simonsen (1969, 1970, 1972), and two compiling individual texts by both authors (1974 e 1975) include a defence of the military government's economic policies, i.e., and gradualism in fighting inflation, so as to reconcile monetary stability and policies to stimulate economic growth and investment. Regardless of the undeniable analytic quality of some of those works, their texts come from ideologues of military governments in the field of economics. They stray from macroeconomic orthodoxy and from the liberal agenda in guiding production and foreign trade, and they favour the public sector's planning and investments in close cooperation with national and foreign private companies. The institutional changes carried out in the period 1964–1966 had produced healthy public finances and made possible the subsequent rapid expansion.

Here and there we find an occasional criticism of the conduction of economic policies, as when the authors criticize excessive customs tariffs in equipment imports, or demand improvements in the management of state-owned companies, and especially when they formulate the idea that gradualism in combatting inflation in the Sixties might have been excessive and run against what had been foreseen in the Strategic Action Plan (PAEG). But those critical comments are marginal to the texts, always carefully written. The authors avoided making them sound like criticisms of military administrations and minimized their opposition to the form of developmentalism practiced by the government. In the case of Simonsen, that attitude was awarded in 1974 with his nomination as Finance minister by (nationalist) president-general Ernesto Geisel. And, despite his leanings toward anti-inflationary caution – in line with Campos – Simonsen agreed to subject himself to Geisel and to minister Velloso regarding the continuation of growth and heavy state investments in infrastructure and basic industry, which were forwarded in the "Second Development Plan" (PNDII), and carried out in spite of the inflationary acceleration that followed the first oil crisis (Carneiro, 1990; Castro and Souza, 1985).

Campos' and Simonsen's confrontation with developmentalists who criticized the military government, on the contrary, was most assertive, although it did not concern the question of state-led industrialization, as there was perfect convergence between them on this issue. Alternating in their criticisms, the two of them employed arguments that were loaded with irony and caricatures, as when attacking oppositionists with the idea that, under the influence of the structuralist school of thought, they were irresponsible in the matter of anti-inflationary policies, or with the idea that they wished to practice an unfruitful nationalism by rejecting multinational companies' access to mineral production. On the same line, they accused oppositionists of advocating a populist income distribution that clashed with the benefit of taking advantage of productivity increases to enhance savings and investment. Incidentally, on a heated debate on income distribution in the early 1970s Simonsen (1972, p. 64), acknowledged that there were excesses in income concentration, but went as far as to say that concentration was a "natural" and necessary condition in stages of accelerated growth, such as the one experienced at the time. The idea was somehow shared by other government officials, as Delfim Netto, as pointed out by Andrada and Boianovsky (2019, p. 8). And in an implicit allusion to a Celso Furtado thesis published in 1965 – to which we shall return further on – they stated that the empirical error of premature redistributivism was proven by the factual refutation, given the ongoing accelerated growth, of the idea that owing to poor income distribution the economic system was bound to stagnate, for lack of demand at the scale required for profitable investment.

4.4. *The permanent dominance of the growth target over the goal of macroeconomic stability in military administrations*

The military regime successfully curbed inflation from about 100% p.a. to 20% p.a. in the initial years of government, thanks to wage squeezing and to the attraction of foreign finance. Price increase remained at approximately the annual 20% level from 1968 through 1973, thanks to generalized indexation, then jumped to around 40% p.a. after the first oil shock, "inertially" sticking to that level until 1979, when it jumped again to approximately 100% p.a., in view of foreign restrictions following the second oil shock.[29]

Government thinking on inflation after 1964 was initially marked by the idea of "gradualism" and had Mário Henrique Simonsen as its major formulator, first in partnership with Roberto Campos, whom he assisted in designing the PAEG, then in his book *Inflação: Gradualismo X Tratamento de Choque* [Inflation: Gradualism vs shock treatment] (Simonsen, 1970).

The PAEG was a gradualistic plan, defined by stages of inflation reduction between 1964 and 1966 that aimed at avoiding the strong depressive effects of shock treatments on the economy, hence at avoiding a confrontation with the avidity for growth shown by the military who had taken over the government. It was a hybrid of orthodox and heterodox components in both its formulation and its implementation (Resende, 1990; Bastian, 2013).

A fiscal reform abbreviated the stage of expenditure curtailment, and the stage of credit restraint was limited to the last trimester of 1964 and the second half of 1966. The innovative element in the anti-inflationary policies of the first military government was the strict application, especially as of 1965, of the formula created by Simonsen to face the wage-price spiral, promulgated by Law 4725 in 1964. Instead of oscillating between frequently readjusted values and contributing to a potentially hyperinflationary tendency that, according to pro-government arguments, would quickly erode their real value, wages began to be annually adjusted on the basis of the average real value of salaries in the two preceding years, added to a factor of productivity increase and a compensation for the inflationary residue forecast for the coming 12 months. Along with that formula there came the establishment of "as peaceful a relation as possible between the economic system and inflation through a wide adoption of the institution of monetary correction" – a reference to the correction of wages, taxes, securities, rentals, utilities, etc. – save for the fact that "the field that is most politically tempting for indexation, that of salaries, has been duly avoided by a readjustment formula based on the average and not the peak value" (pp. 183–184).

Simonsen himself (1970) admits that said formula helped curb inflation, but as of 1965 it represented a fall in real salaries owing to underestimated inflationary residues (pp. 39 and 46–47), and he also refers to complaints by unionists and government opponents. In fact, notwithstanding the military regime's repression of labour unions, resentment against the wage squeeze circulated far and wide in those years. The wage decrease and the income concentration that the formula helped create gave way to a heated debate on the Brazilian development "model", to which we shall return further ahead.

According to Simonsen, the preservation of that formula was part of Delfim Netto's orientation when, upon becoming Finance minister in 1967, he gave some flexibility to credit and public expenditure in relation to policies put in practice by Bulhões and Campos, in a way that was compatible with the idea of "displacing the emphasis on fighting inflation from the demand side to the cost side" (ibid., p. 47). Perhaps due to caution with sensitive government feelings, Simonsen avoided directly stating that Delfim Netto had adopted what some passages of his book called a "dynamics of immediatism"; yet he nevertheless risked stating that there were "more than enough reasons for us to feel apprehensive with an inflationary residue in the order of 20% per year" (ibid., p. 22).

Simonsen's book became the major analytical reference for the wide debate that took place in Brazil on the inflationary process during the next 25 years between its publication in 1970 and the Plano Real, in 1994 – a debate intensified in the 1980s and early 1990s, as analysed in the following two chapters of this book.

Simonsen's thinking on inflation was attractive for its theoretical eclecticism. The author opened an interpretive umbrella covering three analytical approaches, by viewing inflation as the result of the potential effects of three different components: excessive demand; an autonomous component (supply shocks) deriving from "arbitrary" wage readjustments, from the exchange rate and indirect taxes, as well as from effects of an incidental nature, such as poor harvests; and "inflationary feedback", described essentially as a price rise "caused by the economic agents' attempt to recover a share of the national product that had been lost to former inflation" (pp. 127–128).

The latter component, which came to be known as "inertial" in the Brazilian and Argentinian debate of the Eighties, represents the acknowledgement of a distributive conflict during the inflationary process, following the interpretation of "propagative effects" made years before by structuralists Noyola (1956) and Sunkel ([1958] 1960), as well as an independent interpretation made by Felipe Pazos (1972, p. 89, apud Bastos, 2001, p. 215) simultaneously to Simonsen.

Regarding macroeconomic policy, the fundamental point reached by Simonsen's theorization concerned the high real cost of an orthodox shock treatment, given the resistance to a fall in inflation motivated by distributive conflict. In Chapter VI of his book, Simonsen does a regression exercise to the period 1948–1968 using an equation that contains all three components. In assessing the general results, he attributes little merit to them, owing to the precariousness of the data used, but stresses that the equation's utility lies in giving support to the notion of an "inflationary feedback".

In the orthodox field, Contador (1977) and Lemgruber (1978) presented regressions with Phillips curve estimates, concluding on their validity in the Brazilian case, and proposed a monetarist approach in fighting inflation, viewed as an essentially demand phenomenon. Contador advocated the application of a gradualistic treatment, while Lemgruber argued in favour of a shock treatment.[30]

Next, this topic was approached by PUC-RJ professors who were to have an outstanding intellectual and executive participation, years later, in the most relevant moments of the stage when deindexation policies were applied in the decades of 1980 and 1990. Lopes and Resende (1979) carried out an empirical exercise that reinforced opposition to the conventional monetarist approach based on the Phillips curve, and concluded on the irrelevance of demand pressure on inflation, as well as on the relevance of the institutional system of wage indexation.

The intensity of the academic debate on the causes of inflation in the 1970s seems to have fallen short of the importance of that issue, as well as of the tensions publicly expressed by families and economic agents – including labour unions in the second half of the 1970s. After all, inflation was progressively jumping to higher levels from an approximate average 20% p.a. in the period 1970 through 1973 to roughly 40% from 1974 to 1978 and about 100% in 1979 and 1980. The debate on the trinomial pointed out by Simonsen concerning the causes of inflation would truly heat up only in the 1980s, its major references being the interpretations and proposals of heterodox policies for the containment of accelerated inflation elaborated mainly by professors Francisco Lopes, Lara Resende and Persio Arida, from PUC-RJ, and Bresser Pereira and Yoshiashi Nakano, from FGV-São Paulo. This topic is dealt with in Chapters 2 and 9 of this book.

4.5. Critical developmentalists and socialists: determinants of growth, patterns and limits of development

Economists who opposed the military governments developed an intense intellectual activity, often as political exiles abroad. Sometimes in passionate tones, they produced many analytically powerful texts on Brazilian development.

In the "critical" developmentalist line, we may include authors like Celso Furtado, Maria da Conceição Tavares, Antônio Barros de Castro, Carlos Lessa, José Serra, Luiz Carlos Bresser Pereira, Albert Fishlow, Edmar Bacha and Pedro Malan, amongst others. We may also include authors like João Manuel Cardoso de Mello and Luiz Gonzaga Belluzzo, and among sociologists, Fernando Henrique Cardoso – who, regardless of the Marxist leanings of some of their works, were actually in harmony with other critical developmentalists in their writings and had a developmentalist social-democratic political-ideological orientation.

The socialist current was formed by three groups. First there were those intellectuals associated to the Brazilian Communist Party who already stood out before 1964, as the aforementioned Caio Prado Jr., Nelson Werneck Sodré, Alberto Passos Guimarães, Jacob Gorender and Aristóteles Moura, who followed the project of a democratic-bourgeois transition stage into socialism. Second, there were "independents" like Ignácio Rangel, Paul Singer and Francisco de Oliveira. And third, there were the Brazilian authors of the

Latin-American theory of "dependency", above all Rui Mauro Marini and Theotonio dos Santos, whose analyses of Brazilian capitalism pointed to the conclusion that it would be impossible to attain any effective socioeconomic transformation within the bounds of the domestic capitalist relations of production and of imperialism.

Critical developmentalists' and Marxists' reflections on the nature of capitalism in Brazil and on its dynamics were abundant and creative, corresponding to an exceptional phase of interpretations of Brazilian economy. Resorting to a "poetic license" to give approximate titles to their classical works and/or to rename them so as to capture the essence of their interpretations, we provide a list selecting those that had a large impact on the economic thinking of the time: capitalism in transition: heyday and decline of the process of import substitution (Tavares, 1964); capitalism with a tendency to stagnation (Furtado, 1965); dependent capitalism (Santos, 1967, 1970; Marini, 1973); associated capitalism (Cardoso and Faletto, [1969] 1979); unfair but expansive capitalism (Castro, [1969] 1971); dynamic and perverse capitalism (Tavares and Serra, [1970] 1973); capitalism marked by "structural heterogeneity", by Chilean Anibal Pinto (1970) but widely influential on Brazilian structuralist thinking, as in Tavares and Serra, [1970] 1973); capitalism with a political regime that concentrates income (Fishlow, 1972a, 1972b); non-dual capitalism in the exploitation of labour (Oliveira, 1972); capitalism promoting income concentration (Tolipan and Tinelli, 1975); capitalism combining modernity and poverty, or Belindia – Belgium and India in Brazil, (Bacha, 1976); state capitalism (Martins, 1977); mature and cyclic capitalism (Tavares, [1974] 1998a, [1978] 1998b); late capitalism as to the existence of endogenous cyclic fluctuations (Mello, [1974] 1978); and "non-cyclic" capitalism (Castro, 1979). Behind the large majority of those interpretations were two central topics: mechanisms for the expansion of Brazilian economy and a socially unfair growth pattern.

In particular, alongside Simonsen's reflection on inflationary feedback, three other original Brazilian analytical contributions were epoch-making in the 1960s and 1970s. Two of those came from critical developmentalists: the inclusion of the social dimension in structuralist thought, thereby integrating the production structure and the social structure; and, through UNICAMP professors, the theorization about the existence of cyclic dynamics in Brazilian economy, thus overcoming the Cepalian reading of external strangulation as mover of the growth process in Brazil. And in the sphere of socialist thinkers, albeit not only with them, there was extensive theorization on "dependency". In the presentation that follows, those three contributions are given some prominence.

4.5.1. Critical developmentalists

Among opponents of the military regime the predominant current was that of "critical developmentalists". Their main motivation was diagnosing the characteristics and determinants of economic evolution, and particularly the relations between growth, on the one hand, and income distribution and demand profiles, on the other, as well as supply composition considering sectors, technology, investment agents and the finance equation. The main concern was understanding the "style" or "pattern" of Brazilian growth and development. It is interesting to note, by the way, that market orientation on investments, whether domestic or export-oriented, was a relatively minor topic throughout that period, in which the consensus was that growth was bound to take place through the domestic market, being merely seconded by an export effort required by the demand of foreign currency to render import expansion feasible.

A description of the path followed by the most relevant contributions of critical developmentalism to an understanding of the workings of Brazilian economy between 1964 and 1980 is given hereunder. Further on, we shall examine the contributions made by socialists.

Critical developmentalists were mostly centre-left intellectuals who were either sceptical about the chances of success of a socialist revolution in Brazil or simply disagreed with it. They strongly supported state intervention in fostering industrial development.[31] But they opposed the government's developmentalist strategy in the social sphere, just as they opposed dictatorship, the overcoming of which was viewed as a necessary condition for the adoption of a more socially equitable development pattern.

By the mid-1960s, this current of ideas embarked in a trajectory of analyses concerning the patterns of Brazilian growth and economic development, with two essays that became classics: "The growth and decline of import substitution in Brazil" (Tavares, 1964) and "Development and Stagnation in Latin America" (Furtado, 1965).[32]

The former is the major Cepalian essay analysing the dynamics of import substitution, which Tavares interprets as an already outdated engine of growth in the Sixties. In the closing section of the essay, she argues that "in the short run" decreasing returns might occur in sectors with high capital–labour ratios, due to high income concentration and the resulting small size of the market. Such would be the cases of basic inputs, durable goods and capital goods, regarded in principle as next in the timeline of the import substitution process.[33] Given that limitation, the strategy for transitioning into a new growth dynamics would no longer be associated to import substitution, which answered to restrictions in the availability of foreign currency, but would lie in the volume and composition of public sector expenditures and exports, as well as in tackling social imbalances. In the author's eyes, this represented a move to an altogether different model of socioeconomic development.

Furtado's interpretation (1965) was an offshoot of his previously expressed view (Furtado, 1961) that capital intensity per worker in Latin American industrialization grew uninterruptedly and led to the persistence of underemployment and poor income distribution. Furtado generalized the notion of a tendency toward a lowering of scale economies as industrialization advanced in Latin America – a notion that Tavares, without reaching a stagnationist conclusion, applied to the Brazilian case in order to assess the decline of the import substitution dynamics in the early 1960s.

Furtado argued that the increase in the capital–labour coefficient had as a basic consequence an increase in in capital/product coefficient. This corresponded to structuring a production apparatus set up in response to a demand structure led by high income families, and to a tendency toward a drop in profitability and therefore a tendency to stagnation. As duly pointed out by Coutinho (2019), the theoretical basis was the Harrod-Domar model, according to which, given a certain savings and investment rate, the tendency to a raise in the capital/product relation represented, according to Furtado, a tendency towards a reduction in growth rates.[34]

The corollary of that interpretation was that undoing such tendency would require deconcentrating income and rebuilding the supply structure in order to produce popular consumer goods, which were supposedly labour-intensive. An alternative project to the one in course, therefore, would be a transition into a new pattern of development in which the domestic market would be associated to an increase in job positions and a rise in wages, thus allowing for increasing economies of scale, higher productivity and higher capital profitability.

Back in the mid-1960s, Tavares and Furtado inaugurated in Latin America a discussion that is still up-to-date about the relation between growth and income distribution – i.e., about development "patterns", or development "models" or "styles", all of them labels used with the same meaning. However, the accelerated economic expansion of the period 1968–1973 would not only empirically discredit Furtado's stagnationist diagnosis, but also dim the brilliance of his theorization, which lay in integrating into one and the same analytical scheme the structures of production and distribution, or, in other words, the profiles of supply and demand of goods and services.

In fact, it was in the very field of critical developmentalists, where Furtado was the leader, that the first critical comments about the stagnationist hypothesis came up. According to Bresser-Pereira (1970, p. 214), already in 1968, at a conference in São Paulo, Castro had exposed the idea that, unfortunately, one could see a resumption of growth due to income concentration. In his book *Sete Ensaios sobre a Economia Brasileira*, whose first edition was dated 1969, Castro (1971, vol. I, p. 142) went as far as to state – though not develop – the notion that industry

> gains momentum by thoroughly exploring the opportunities created by a minority's purchasing power; . . . as far as possible, it should seek in a permanent diversification of its products the market it cannot find in the purchasing power of the masses.
>
> (1971, vol. I, p. 142)

Bresser Pereira, in his aforementioned book of 1970, also views in income concentration and demand for durable goods a major cause of the resumption of growth started in 1968.

However, it was "Além da estagnação" [Beyond stagnation], an essay by Tavares and Serra ([1970] 1973) whose circulation in mimeo form dates from 1970, that became a reference as the most incisive analysis of the relation between growth and income concentration, the latter interpreted as functional in the growth pattern then in course: by adapting demand composition to the supply profile that was being established, the socially unjust model of growth showed great dynamism. This essay may have been the one in the field of Brazilian economy with the strongest impact during the entire period of the military regime, both for its interpretation of current history and from a political-ideological point of view: the "miracle" of accelerated growth was "perverse".

The essay's title holds a double meaning: on the one hand, the idea that recession had been overcome, and, on the other, that of a refutation of Furtado's stagnationist thesis, i.e., a refutation that there might be a tendency towards a fall in returns owing to a continuous increase of the aggregated capital–product ratio during the establishment of production chains associated to industrial goods for the upper classes. According to the authors, the modern equipment then being installed led to a rise in productivity that compensated for an increase in the capital–labour ratio; investment decisions would seem to be motivated by the high returns expected regardless of capital intensity per worker.

The authors argued that, far from the alleged tendency toward stagnation, deceleration in the period 1963–1967 had sprung from the decreased investment rate that followed the implementation of the Target Plan, resulting from problems related to a conjunctural insufficiency of demand and from problems with funding. The financial and fiscal reforms and growing profits/wages coefficient, together with the emergence of consumer credit, appeared to have been the main determinants of the recovery of private and public investment and of a marked expansion in the demand of durable goods by upper classes.[35]

With Furtado's classical texts and the one by Tavares & Serra on economic growth and income concentration,[36] there began, as formerly noted, a long sequence of reflections, still in course to this date, on development patterns.[37] From an empirical perspective, their starting point was the 1971 publication, by a group headed by Albert Fishlow at IPEA, of a comparison between data from the 1960 and 1970 censuses on personal income distribution, which concluded that there had been a strong concentration between those two dates.[38] Shortly afterwards, Fishlow (1974) published an influential essay against the income-concentrating wage policy of the post-1964 military administrations.

The prevailing tendency at the time was to see "wage-squeeze" as the main element in the anti-inflationary policy of 1964 through 1967. A study required from Langoni (1973) by minister Delfim Netto confirmed income concentration, but interpreted it as a result of the growing demand for skilled labour owing to the scarcity of "human capital", which led to a widening of the wage range. According to this line of reasoning, the definitive solution to poor income distribution would lie in educational policies and labour training.

In a compilation that became a classic, Tolipan and Tinelli (1975) assembled a number of texts dedicated to the Brazilian distributive controversy from a critical perspective. In that book, Fishlow (1975) challenged the empirical validity of Langoni's work, arguing that labour qualification had not been employed as a variable in the author's regressions with sufficient weight to justify his arguments, and Malan and Wells (1975) and Hofmann (1975) made several critical remarks from the methodological point of view. Bacha (1975) likewise argued that far from labour qualification, concentration resulted from the role played by managers in the corporations' chain of command; unlike workers in general, those executives operated as partners in the generation of corporate profitability. Bacha presented evidence of far higher salary raises among managers than among regular workers between 1966 and 1972, and concluded that such tendency originated in functional hierarchy rather than in labour qualification. And Singer (1975), aside from stressing that income concentration came from the wage squeeze and from a regressive tax structure, argued that the educational system strengthened concentration by giving superior professional training to the children of wealthy families.[39]

Another issue in the same debate was the relation between economic growth, income distribution and investment and savings generation. By all accounts, a common acknowledgment was made among economists of different tendencies to the effect that the high profit rate, partially due to salary contention, contributed to the acceleration of investment. However, while a pro-government economist like Amrio Simonsen understood the tendency toward income concentration as a "natural" sacrifice in stages such as the one Brazilian development was going through, critics considered it feasible to combine growth and a better distribution, which might direct investment to sectors with a lower capital density per worker, as advocated by Lopes (1972).

Tavares – who had already stood out as the main interpreter of economic growth after 1930, in the aforementioned works about the "heyday and decline of import substitution" and "beyond stagnation" – continued to contribute in the discussion on growth pattern with two academic dissertations, in 1974 and 1978, both inspired by Kalecki (Tavares [1974] 1998, [1978] 1998).[40] According to her, Brazilian economy featured cyclical dynamics since the 1950s, owing to the fact that from then on a large enough capital goods industry had been established in the country. That analytical construction was conceived of in the context of a theoretical effort, among UNICAMP professors, that included a book called *Capitalismo tardio* [Late capitalism], by Mello ([1974] 1978). According to them, regardless of its merits, the Cepalian approach was limited in view of centring around foreign restriction – as in Tavares's own 1964 text – and therefore losing sight of endogenous investment determinants, i.e., the processes of profit generation, realization and allocation.

Their assessment was that, once the phase in which the accumulation process was fostered by the coffee complex had come to an end, back in 1930, the two and a half following decades had been a period of "restricted industrialization", meaning a period during which the restriction consisted in the inexistence of a sufficiently large national production of capital goods, as compared to the economy as a whole, hence preventing the introduction of cycles into the Brazilian economic dynamics. This would have come to occur only in a "belated" way starting in the 1950s, when the local production of capital goods reached a large enough size to determine a cyclic behaviour in the country's economy. Additionally, the argument was that the expansive investment stages would have come to be temporally concentrated, not only in response to current demand but also anticipating a future demand by large oligopolistic corporations, which would therefore lead the economy at large to strong cyclic fluctuations.

In her 1974 text, Tavares analyses deceleration during 1963–1967 as due to a fall in capital goods purchases owing to the idle capacity generated by a significant capital formation in the preceding years. And in her 1978 text, she points out that a similar process seemed to be taking place since 1974, following accelerated capital formation in the industry during the period 1968–1973. The reason the deceleration then in course wasn't even bigger was that, as an anticyclical mitigating factor, there were strong autonomous investments commanded by the public sector.[41] Larger enterprises, especially foreign-owned ones, led the way in the private sector in this cyclic movement.

The scheme adapting Kalecki to the Brazilian case is ingenious and has two additional components. First, cyclic peaks are intense, but short and bound to decline quickly, because in Brazilian "late capitalism" the size of the segments producing capital goods and of capitalist consumption is small in proportion to the economy as a whole. And secondly, the industrial sector and particularly the sectors of capital goods and capitalist consumption are, at the same time, those that grow most in the economy and that have the highest profit margins. This implies an increased profit share in income and therefore (given the expansion limits of capitalist consumption), if savings from profits are to be invested, it means that investments should be ceaselessly accelerated, something which cannot happen indefinitely.

Foreign capital participation in Brazilian economy was also included in analyses concerning the nature of the capitalist system operating in the nation, especially those by dependency theorists, to the left of critical developmentalists.

For economists attuned to the government, foreign capital made a contribution in savings, technology and company management. Critical developmentalists' view of foreign capital is a topic still awaiting further study. By all accounts, criticism regarding this issue was rather less harsh than concerning income distribution and was made in a relatively more moderate tone.

An in-depth look at this topic may no doubt find, in the production of critical developmentalists, allusions to the idea that though contributing to industrialization foreign companies employed technology that was not quite adequate to production factors available in Brazil, scarcely invested in innovation, and were potentially able to magnify the insufficiency of foreign currency that was typical of periods of crises, due to the remittance of profits and to capital evasion. None of those, however, seem to have had as much relevance as discussions about the "model" that concentrated income, which was the main dividing line between government supporters and opponents, especially until the mid-1970s.

From that point on, economic thinking would concentrate its attention mostly on issues concerning the sustainability of economic growth, which, despite its continuity, suffered a deceleration after the 1973 oil shock. That shock also impacted the economy through inflationary acceleration, which brought to economists a renewed interest in macroeconomic evolution, after a relative "lull" caused by a combination of accelerated growth and inflation containment at the level of approximately 20% from 1968 through 1973.

The second Industrial Development Plan [Plano de Desenvolvimento Industrial] (Brazil, 1974) expressed president Geisel's political decision not to interrupt the rapid formation of the Brazilian industrial structure, despite the oil shock and inflationary acceleration. The government narrative confirmed that decision in the years that followed. The severe macroeconomic instability introduced by the second oil shock and the explosion of interest rates in the USA in 1979 led minister Simonsen to decide for a recessive readjustment already in president Figueiredo's administration, in 1979. That, however, resulted in his replacement in the same year by Delfim Netto, who maintained the government's expansionist policy until the second half of 1980.

The discussion carried out during those years on the possibilities of sustaining economic expansion would require a thorough detailing that is beyond the scope of this text. Only a few brief remarks are offered in what follows.

In 1973, hence at the height of accelerated growth, Singer (1973), an economist of the socialist tradition, but one whose eclecticism and moderation made him close to critical developmentalists, surprisingly argued that there would be a deceleration of investment owing to a profit squeeze, in view of salary raises motivated by the economy's over-acceleration. Given progressive intellectuals' conviction that the Brazilian growth model concentrated income, Singer's reflection was that of an outlier in the economic thinking of the time.

Malan and Bonelli (1976) offered an influential interpretation of the growth deceleration that followed the oil shock, i.e., the view that slower growth became inescapable due to insufficient supply capacity of oil and capital goods in face of the new world economic trends – the "*utmost possible limits*", as evidenced by the large foreign deficit in 1974–1975.

Several other texts covered the weakening of Brazilian economy owing to foreign debt expansion as of 1974. The government's position prior to the 1973 oil shock was that foreign debt did not compromise the health of Brazil's external accounts (Lira, 1970, Simonsen, 1972). Pereira (1974) disagreed and pointed to the unavoidable occurrence of "growing levels of indebtedness"; along the same lines, Doellinger (1976) warned against transferring to the future a serious external problem to the country's economy.[42]

4.5.2. Socialists

Following the 1964 military coup, the most important issue within the Marxist tradition was the dispute between Brazilian Communist Party [PCB] member and dissenters over the idea that the country remained in the "anti-feudal" and "anti-imperialistic" historical stage, in which according to PCB the political strategy should be an alliance between national capital and the proletariat.

Dissenters argued that agricultural social relations were not feudal and that there was no local bourgeois class in conflict with foreign capital, as on the contrary their interests converged.

On the topic of agriculture, the most important work was *A Revolução Brasileira* (Prado Jr., [1966] 2004). In it, the author – who, oddly enough, never had a political rupture with PCB, despite divergences in the field of ideas – repeated his longstanding view that regardless of holding some "archaic" elements, social relations in the countryside were subject to a logic that was eminently oriented to the capitalist market. In that interpretation, he was being consistent with his own masterpiece, *Formação do Brasil Contemporâneo* [The formation of contemporary Brazil] (Prado Jr., [1942] 1967), in which he sees the "meaning of colonization" in "mercantile exploitation". In the 1960s, he opposed the thesis of feudalism and reaffirmed the idea that the Brazilian countryside was attuned to the capitalist mode of production, and he also reasserted his earlier statement Prado Jr. (1962) that the rural workers' major demand concerned labour conditions – salary, social protection, etc. – and not property, as stated by advocates of land reform based on land redistribution.

In an influential work, Oliveira (1972) added that the prevailing capital–labour relations and the general backwardness were a result of exploitation and capital accumulation in Brazil. He argued that the underdeveloped segment of the rural area and urban underemployment were a guarantee of the low wages and high profits incorporated in the operating logic of Brazilian economy, which was essentially capitalist.[43]

On the other major issue, that of foreign capital, the intensive presence of multinational companies in Brazilian industrialization since the former decade had weakened the idea that imperialism was a barrier against the development of the country's production forces. Pre-1960 texts analysing the internationalization of Brazilian industry can be found even among intellectuals from the Brazilian Communist Party (for instance, Moura, 1959, formerly quoted). The most relevant texts in the post-1964 period analysed here, however, are the ones following the dependency theory. There were essentially two versions of those, namely, that of the "associated capitalist model" and that of "overexploitation" by imperialism.

Prebisch's inaugural texts at CEPAL (Prebisch, 1962, ECLAC, 1951, 1952) on centre–periphery relations are obvious non-Marxist predecessors of dependentist theorization. So is Furtado's analysis ([1961] 1964) after the beginning of the massive incorporation of multinational companies in Latin American industry. According to him, underdevelopment is one of the forms of manifestation of the worldwide industrial capitalism practiced by those modern companies in juxtaposition to backward structures, thus creating strongly heterogeneous economic systems.[44]

Fernando Henrique Cardoso (1964) opposed the view that there was a national bourgeoisie in conflict with foreign capital. A few years later, when working in CEPAL, and in partnership with Chilean Enzo Faletto he wrote *Dependency and Development in Latin America* (Cardoso and Faletto, [1969]

1979). The major contribution made by that classical work is methodological and lies in the argument that Latin American history can only be understood when analysed from the perspective of the relationship between social classes and power structures on the basis of two determinants, namely, each country's domestic processes and their historical interaction with groups of economic and political power in the nations with which they have had close relations throughout history. The authors point out that in the 1960s an association was already widely established between national bourgeoisie, transnational corporations and civil and military techno-bureaucracies. In abstract terms, they argue that depending on how national interests harmonize with foreign ones, they may either lead to the continuation of poverty or to an "associated development". In their book, however, the authors opt for not indicating which of those two possibilities they think might prevail in Latin American countries.

The dependentist current of analysis, further to the left, was preceded in their publications by the Latin American dissemination of books by Sweezy, Baran and the German dependentist Gunder Frank. Brazilian leaders in this current were, among economists, Santos (1967, 1970) and Marini (1973), and among sociologists, Florestan Fernandes (1973), authors for whom the capitalist regime and imperialism are the fundamental determinants of continuous underdevelopment and poverty, simultaneously with an advance of modernizing capital accumulation. The industrialization process is just the most recent form of the exploitation to which underdeveloped nations have been subjected for centuries in their relations to dominant economies, and in which workers are subordinated to local owners of the means of production, be they foreign or native. Far from eventual doubts as to whether or not this would be a process of associated development, the affinities of this dependentist current pointed to the Trotskyist idea of "unequal and combined development" (Guimarães and Lopes, 2016, p. 401).

Marini (1973) argues that overexploitation and subimperialism are the basic common features of dependency. Santos (1967, 1970) argues that the industry established as of 1950 produces technological domination by multinational companies and profound inequalities resulting from the overexploitation of workers, whose surplus value is doubly appropriated, either directly by companies in operation in Latin America or indirectly through income transfers to imperialist nations. Fernandes (1973) considers that the combination of domestic structures of ownership and power with foreign domination inhibits socioeconomic development.

Capitalism in Latin America, even when it showed eventual signs of dynamism, implied permanent poverty in the long run, which would justify a transition to socialism. Such dependentist analyses, regardless of what their authors might think of a "correlation of political forces" that could enable an immediate transition to socialism – and it was certainly most unfavourable back in the late 1960s and the 1970s – may have somehow contributed to radicalize opposition to the dictatorship by some small groups of dissidents of the Communist Party, especially during the period of clandestineness to which they were forced when the military regime increased political repression in the late 1960s.

5. By way of conclusion

This chapter has dealt with the currents of economic thought and the trajectory of ideas in the developmentalist era during which Brazilian industrial capitalism was implemented (1930–1980). Two final remarks are added here.

First, the chapter shows that the history of Brazilian thinking in that period is dense and rich, and that it corresponds to a fascinating angle of observation of the actual Brazilian history reflected in the trajectory of that thinking.

Second, developmentalist thinking gradually declined in the 1980s, a decade of crisis in the balance of payments, high inflation and gradual expansion of the neoliberal ideology, which settled in Brazil in the 1990s. The following chapter analyses another equally dense and rich phase of Brazilian economic thought, that of the period 1980–2010.

Notes

1. Bielschowsky is Professor at the Economics Institute of the Federal University of Rio de Janeiro [Instituto de Economia, Universidade Federal do Rio de Janeiro], and Mussi is director of the Brazilian office of the United Nations Economic Commission for Latin America and the Caribbean (CEPAL). The authors heartedly thank Vera Ribeiro for her work in the translation from Portuguese into English of large parts of this text.
2. Starting with an early recovery from the 1930s world recession already in 1932, and excepting a few isolated years of merely moderate growth, continuous fast growth had only two intermissions, namely 1939 through 1942, due to the war, and 1963 through 1967, due to strong macroeconomic instability.
3. See Bielschowsky (1995) for the Portuguese language version of the 1985 publication and Bielschowsky (2022) for the e-book English version of the same text. The authors wish to thank CEPAL for the formal authorization of total or partial republication of the article by Bielschowsky (1991) dealing with the period 1930–1964, published by *CEPAL Review* in December 1991, which is a synthesis of Bielschowsky ([1985] 2022).
4. Regarding authors, see, among other publications: on Caio Prado Jr., Iglesias (1982) and Ricupero (2000); on Roberto Simonsen, Fallangiello (1972) and Curi and Cunha (2015); on Eugênio Gudin, Borges (1996) and Cavalieri and Silva (2021); on Romulo de Almeida, Barbosa (2021), on Ignácio Rangel, Cruz (1980) and Castro et al. (2014); on Celso Furtado, Oliveira (1983), Bresser-Pereira and Rego (2001), Saboia and Carvalho (2007), Boianovsky (2010, 2012, 2015), Bielschowsky (2010), Coutinho (2019) and Quintela et al. (2020); on Octavio Gouveia de Bulhões, Saretta (2001) and Curado (2021), on Delfim Netto, Lisboa (2020) and Hespanhol and Saes (2021), on Roberto Campos, Almeida (2017) and Campos (1994, autobiography); on Mario Henrique Simonsen, Cysne (2001) Boianovsky (2007) and Cabello (2021); on João Paulo dos Reis Velloso, D'Araujo and Castro (2004) on Maria da Conceição Tavares, Boianovsky (2000), Guimarães (2010), Possas (2001), Santos (2013), Robilloti (2016), Tavares (2017), and Pereira (2019); on Antonio Barros de Castro, Prado and Bastian (2011) and Bielschowsky (2011); on Carlos Lessa, Earp (2010), on Edmar Bacha and Pedro Malan, Dacanal (2019). For a collection of articles on Finance ministers from 1889 to 1985, see Salomão (org, 2021).
5. For instance, on Liberalism, Paim (2018); on Marxism, Coutinho (2001); on developmentalism, Fonseca (2004, 2015) and Mollo and Amado (2015); on structuralism and dependency, Love (1990a), and Saad Filho (2005), on structuralism Rodriguez (1981) and Bielschowsky (2009); on stagnationism, Coutinho (2019); on the debate on development within the heterodox tradition, Bastos and d'Avila (2009); on Unicamp's economic thought, Santos (2013) and Oliveira (2020)

6. For instance, on income distribution, see Tolipan and Tinelli (1975), Malta (2011b) and Andrada and Boianovsky (2019); on inflation, see Bastos (2001), Araújo (2017), Bastos and Mello Neto (2014), and Nascimento et al. (2017); on specific periodicals, see Feldhues (2014) in *Desenvolvimento e Conjuntura* on the Brazilian Northeast; and see Andrada et al. (2016) on *Revista Econômica Brasileira.*
7. For instance, see Bielschowsky (2015) regarding the period 1945–1955.
8. Two other warnings are worth adding: first, though some reference is made to the bibliography produced during that period on Brazilian long-term economic history, this chapter does not include a survey of that bibliography; and second, by dealing only with economic thought, a fundamental dimension of the understanding of Brazilian intellectual history in social areas is left out of our account, namely the contributions made by sociologists.
9. For details on the period 1930–1964, see Bielschowsky ([1985] 2022).
10. Amaral (1938) is acknowledged as the main author of the nationalist and corporatist defence under an authoritarian state that advocated planning and intervention in favor of industrialization, in close association with leaders of private interests. In 1938, according to Gomes (2012, p. 4), Amaral translated into Portuguese *Le siècle du corporatisme* (The Century of Corporatism), by Romanian author Manoilescu (1934). Some years before, Manoilescu's book (1929) on unequal exchange and protectionism had been translated at the request of entrepreneurs in CIESP (Centre for the Industries of the State of São Paulo), *apud* Love, 1990b, pp. 87–88. On corporatism in Brazil, see Gomes (2007); on Amaral, see Marco (2020). On a comparison between Romanian Manoilescu, Brazilian authors and CEPAL's structuralism, see Love (1990b and 1996).
11. Austrian-born economist Richard Lewinsohn returned to Europe in 1952. See Boianovsky (2021) for a recollection of non-Brazilian economists and social scientists who came to Brazil mostly to escape Nazism. Among them were Mortara, the father of Brazilian modern demography, and Alexandre Kafka, who after a short period working closely with Gudin at the FGV and in the new Faculty of Economics at Universidade do Brasil (established in 1946) became for 32 years the Brazilian representative on the Board of Executive Directors of the IMF.
12. Due credit is here necessary to an influential yearly Program of courses on development starting back in the late 1950s under the intellectual leadership of CEPAL (the "CEPAL-BNDES" courses).
13. See Baer (1965) for an influential pioneering book on Brazilian economic development.
14. Entrepreneurs from the capital goods sector who opposed the government policy of increasing access to foreign currency through "supplier credits", thus reducing domestic demand for their products.
15. It should be noticed that Gudin was not a theorist and that his leaning towards economic policies is evidenced even in his academic textbook, although he also deals with theory in that work Gudin, E. [1947] 1970. See Bielschowsky ([1985] 2022) for references to Gudin's main texts in the period 1930–1964. And see footnote 4 for bibliographical references on Gudin's and Bulhões' economic thought.
16. The bibliography included in the book summarized in the present section (Bielschowsky [1985] 2022) lists some of Campos's main books and articles from the 1950s and early 1960s.
17. The main document published by CEPAL (ECLAC, 1955) on planning techniques for Latin America was coordinated by Furtado, who as a member of CEPAL worked in BNDES in 1954–1955 on planning in a joint CEPAL-BNDES Commission created to help planning the Brazilian economy.
18. On the journal's content, see Andrada et al. (2016).
19. On the creation of SUDENE, see GTDN ([1959] 1997), a text basically written by Furtado.
20. In the bibliography of the book summarized in the present chapter (Bielschowsky, [1985] 2022) see a list of Furtado's main books and articles in the 1950s and early 1960s.

21. On Prebisch's and CEPAL's thinking, see Rodriguez (1981) and, among others, CEPAL (1969), Gurrieri (1982), Bielschowsky (2000, 2009) and Bielschowsky and Torres (2018).
22. Except for the structuralist thesis on inflation, written by Noyola (1956) and Sunkel ([1958] 1960) – and not supported by Prebisch – the other elements were somehow or other elaborated or advanced by Prebisch during CEPAL's inaugural years, in the late Forties and early Fifties; see ECLAC (1951) and ECLAC (1952).
23. An international meeting on inflation took place in Rio de Janeiro in 1963, gathering influential economists with different points of view on that issue. For its proceedings, see Baer and Kerstenetzky (1964).
24. Regarding ISEB, see Toledo (1997) and Bresser-Pereira (2004).
25. See in the bibliography of the book summarized in this section (Bielschowsky, [1985] 2022) a list of the socialists' main books and articles in the period 1930–1964.
26. An account of other of Rangel's creative ideas, such as investment planning by matching infrastructure shortages and import substitution needs with sectors where idle capacity prevails, can be found in Benjamin et al., 2014.
27. The subtitle of Bielschowsky's book ([1985] 2022) on Brazilian economic thought during the period 1930–1964 calls for a correction: instead of "the ideological cycle of developmentalism" it should read "the first ideological cycle of developmentalism", given that the period 1964–1980 was the heyday of developmentalist strategy. The author wishes to thank José Luis Fiori for having drawn his attention to that mistake during a conversation.
28. See footnote 4 for bibliographical references on the economic thought of the four ministers.
29. See Chapter 9 for the discussions on indexation and inertial inflation.
30. For an overview of a set of regression studies made by monetarists and inertialists in the 1970s and early 1980s, see Bastos and Mello Neto (2014) and Nascimento et al. (2017).
31. Though the general approach was supportive of state-led industrialization, criticisms on superfluous protectionism and lack of selective procedures can be found, as for instance in Suzigan et al. (1974).
32. Among studies published in the 1960s that are considered classics in this current of ideas we find a book with an introduction to economics by Castro and Lessa (1967), the latter's *Quinze Anos de Política Econômica* [Fifteen years of economic policy] (Lessa [1967] 1975), and *Sete Ensaios sobre a Economia Brasileira* [Seven essays on Brazilian economy], by Castro (1971), especially devoted to agricultural changes and regional issues.
33. That statement is qualified by the mitigating argument that decreasing returns might be offset by the use of idle capacity and by the possibility of expanding autonomous state investments substantially and thereby raising the economy's rate of capital accumulation.
34. In a detailed discussion of Furtado's stagnationist interpretation, Coutinho (2019) argued that the author had remained faithful to that view in texts published years after his inaugural 1965 essay, namely, *Análise do modelo brasileiro* and *O mito do desenvolvimento econômico* (respectively, Furtado, 1972, 1974).
35. In *Análise do modelo brasileiro*, Furtado (1972) was to revise his former analysis in the following sense: income and credit policies that favoured the purchase of durable consumer goods by the upper classes had been favouring a perverse offsetting of the tendency toward stagnation.
36. As pointed out by Boianovsky (2000, p. 418), the interactions among income distribution, investment demand and production structure pointed out by Tavares & Serra were formalized by Bacha and Taylor (1976) in a three-sector model with elastic supply of low-skilled workers, leading to an expansion spiral with growing inequality.
37. A post-1980 moment of those reflections is worth mentioning, in view of its effect on the Lula administration's adoption of a growth project with income redistribution through the domestic mass consumption market (Brazil, 2003), namely a paper by Antonio Castro ([1989] 2011, pp. 365–385).

38. The trailblazing articles assessing income concentration on the basis of the 1960 and 1970 censuses were written by Fishlow (1972) and by Hofman and Duarte (1972).
39. See Andrada and Boianovsky (2019) on the income distribution debate and on its political context under the authoritarian regime.
40. Regarding the principle of effective demand in Tavares' and UNICAMP's texts, see Serrano (2001) and Oliveira (2020, p. 31–32), in which the authors argue that the "great advance" in the work by Tavares and Serra (1973) lay in the adoption of Keynes's and Kalecki's effective demand principle in the analysis of Brazilian economy.
41. The most important criticism to this line of argumentation can be found in Castro (1979) in an article titled "Por que não Kalecki" [Why not Kalecki], in his book with the equally suggestive title *O capitalismo ainda é aquele* [Capitalism is still the same].
42. Another developmentalist who was a government opponent and strongly criticized the PND II was Carlos Lessa ([1978] 1998), in whose view the state's action was tantamount to a megalomanic stance of the authoritarian regime guided by the purpose of building Brazil as a power.
43. His book is titled *Crítica à razão dualista* and opposes the "dualist" Cepalian analysis, which Oliveira (known as Chico de Oliveira, for Francisco de Oliveira) considered unsuitable to explain Brazilian capitalist accumulation – without prejudice to his acknowledgment of the virtues and relevance of Cepalian thought and particularly of Celso Furtado, for whom he had been the "right-hand man" in Sudene's board of directors.
44. See Love (1990a) for a comprehensive analysis of the influences of both CEPAL's structuralism and Marxism in dependency analysis.

Bibliography

Almeida, P.R. 2017. *O Homem que pensou o Brasil, trajetória intelectual de Roberto Campos*, Curitiba: Editora Appris.

Almeida, R. 1950. "A experiência brasileira de planejamento, orientação e controle da economia", *Estudos econômicos*, Rio de Janeiro: Confederação Nacional da Indústria, 2 June.

Amaral, A.A. 1938. *O Estado autoritário e a realidade nacional*, Rio de Janeiro: José Olympio Editor.

Andrada, A. and Boianovsky, M. 2019. Economic Debates under Authoritarian Regimes: The Case of the Income Distribution Controversy in Brazil in the 1970s. Center for the History of Political Economy at Duke University, Working Paper Series 2019-12.

Andrada A., Boianovsky, M. and Cabello, A. 2016. "O Clube de Economistas e a *Revista Econômica Brasileira* (1955–1962): Um episódio na história do desenvolvimentismo nacionalista no Brasil", Anais do XLIII Encontro Nacional de Economia.

Araújo, P.F.R. 2017. *Pensamento Brasileiro sobre Inflação: Evolução e Análise Crítica (1939–1964).* PhD dissertation, IE/UFRJ.

Bacha, E. 1975. "Hierarquia e remuneração gerencial". In: Tolipan, Ricardo and Tinelli, Arthur (eds), *A controvérsia sobre distribuição de renda e desenvolvimento*, Rio de Janeiro: Zahar Editores.

Bacha, E. 1976. "O rei da Belíndia: uma fábula para tecnocratas". In: *Os Mitos de uma Década*, Rio de Janeiro: Paz e Terra.

Bacha, E. and Taylor, L. 1976. "The Unequalizing Spiral: A First Growth Model for Belindia", *Quarterly Journal of Economics*, 90(2), 197–218.

Baer, W. 1965. *Industrialization and Economic Development in Brazil*, Homewood, IL: Richard D. Irwin.

Baer, W. and Kerstenetzky, I. (eds). 1964. *Inflation and growth in Latin America*, Homewood: Richard D. Irwin.

Barbosa, A.F. 2021. *O Brasil Desenvolvimentista e a Trajetória de Rômulo de Almeida*, São Paulo: Alameda.

Bastian, E.F. 2013. "O PAEG e o Plano Trienal: uma análise comparativa de suas políticas de estabilização de curto prazo", *Estudos Econômicos*, 43(1), 139–166.

Bastos, C.P. 2001. "Inflação e estabilização". In: Fiori, J.L. and Medeiros, C. (eds), *Polarização mundial e crescimento*, Petrópolis: Editora Vozes, 201–241.

Bastos, C.P. and D'avila, J.G. 2009. "O debate do desenvolvimento na tradição heterodoxa brasileira", *Revista de Economia Contemporânea*, 13(2), 173–199.

Bastos, C.P. e Mello Neto, M.R. 2014. "Moeda, Inércia, Conflito, o Fisco e a Inflação: Teoria e Retórica dos economistas da PUC-RJ", Niterói: UFF, *Revista Econômica*, 16, 1.

Benjamin, C., Bielschowsky, R. and Castro, M.H.M. 2014. "Notas sobre o pensamento de Ignácio Rangel no centenário de seu nascimento", *Revista de Economia Política*, 34(4).

Biderman, C., Cozac, L.F.L. and Rego, J.M. (eds). 1996. *Conversas com economistas*, São Paulo: Editora 34.

Bielschowsky, P. 2015. "A prematura alvorada do pensamento econômico brasileiro: frações da grande burguesia e sua expressão ideológica no período 1945–1955". Doctoral degree dissertation, Niterói: UFF.

Bielschowsky, R. 1991. "Ideology and Development", *CEPAL Review*, 45, 155–179.

Bielschowsky, R. 1995. *Pensamento Econômico Brasileiro, 1930–1964 – O ciclo ideológico do desenvolvimentismo*, Rio de Janeiro: Contraponto.

Bielschowsky, R. 2000. "Cinquenta anos de pensamento na CEPAL: uma resenha". In: Bielschowsky, R. (ed.), *Cinquenta anos de pensamento na CEPAL: textos selecionados*, Rio de Janeiro: Record.

Bielschowsky, R. 2009. "Sixty Years of ECLAC: Structuralism and Neo-structuralism", *CEPAL Review*, 97, 71–192.

Bielschowsky, R. 2010. "Vigência das contribuições de Celso Furtado ao estruturalismo", *Revista CEPAL*, No TCEX03, 7–15, Santiago de Chile: CEPAL, Nações Unidas.

Bielschowsky, R. 2011. "Emerência do Professor Antônio Barros de Castro", *Revista de economia Contemporânea*, 15(2), mai./ago.

Bielschowsky, R. [1985] 2022. *Brazilian Economic Thought; the Ideological Cycle of Developmentalism (English Edition)*, eBook, Rio de Janeiro: Contraponto.

Bielschowsky, R. and Torres, M. (eds). 2018. "Desarrollo e igualdad: el pensamiento de la CEPAL en su séptimo decenio. Textos seleccionados del período 2008–2018", *Colección 70 años*, 1.

Boianovsky, M. 2000. "Maria da Conceição Tavares". In: Dimand, R., Dimand, M.A. and Forget, E. (eds), *Biographical Dictionary of Women Economists*, 1st ed., Aldershot: Elgar, 415–422.

Boianovsky, M. 2007. "Simonsen, Mario Henrique (1935–1997)". In: Durlauf, S. and Blume, L. (eds), *The New Palgrave Dictionay of Economics*, 2nd ed., v. 4, London: Macmillan, 1552–1553.

Boianovsky, M. 2010. "A View from the Tropics: Celso Furtado and the Theory of Economic Development in the 1950s", *History of Political Economy*, 42(2), 221–266.

Boianovsky, M. 2012. "Furtado and the Structuralist-Monetarist Debate on Economic Stabilization in Latin America", *History of Political Economy*, 44(2), 277–330.

Boianovsky, M. 2015. "Between Lévi-Strauss and Braudel: Furtado and the Historical-structural Method in Latin American Political Economy", *Journal of Economic Methodology*, 22(1), 1–26.

Boianovsky, M. 2021. "Economists, Scientific Communities, and Pandemics: An Exploratory Study of Brazil (1918–2020)", *EconomiA*, 22(1), 1–18.

Borges, M.A. 1996. *Eugênio Gudin, Capitalismo e Neoliberalismo*, São Paulo: EDUC.

Brazil. 1963. *Plano Trienal de Desenvolvimento Econômico e Social, 1963–1965*, Brasilia: Presidência da República.

Brazil. 1964. *Plano de Ação Estratégica do Governo*, Brasilia: Secretaria de Planejamento da Presidência da República.

Brazil. 1966. *Plano Decenal*, Brasilia: Secretaria de Planejamento da Presidência da República.

Brazil. 1967. *Plano Estratégico de Desenvolvimento*, Brasilia: Secretaria de Planejamento da Presidência da República.

Brazil. 1970. *Metas e Bases*, Brasilia: Secretaria de Planejamento da Presidência da República.

Brazil. 1972. *Plano Nacional de Desenvolvimento I*, Brasilia: Secretaria de Planejamento da Presidência da República.

Brazil. 1974. *Plano Nacional de Desenvolvimento II*, Brasília: Secretaria de Planejamento da Presidência da República.

Brazil. 2003. *Plano Plurianual 2004–2007*, Brasília: Ministério do Planejamento, Orçamento e Gestão.

Bresser-Pereira, L.C. 1970. *Desenvolvimento e Crise no Brasil*, São Paulo: Editora Brasiliense.

Bresser-Pereira, L.C. 1997. "Interpretações sobre o Brasil". In: Loureiro, M.R. (ed.), *50 anos de ciência econômica no Brasil (1946–1996)*, ch. 1, Petrópolis: Vozes.

Bresser-Pereira, L.C. 2004. "O conceito de desenvolvimento do ISEB rediscutido", *Dados*, 47(1).

Bresser-Pereira, L.C. and Rego, J.M. (eds.). 2001. *A grande esperança em Celso Furtado*, São Paulo: Editora 34.

Cabello, A.F. 2021. Mario Henrique Simonsen-simbiose entre política econômica e academia. In: Salomão, I.C. (org), *Os Homens do Cofre*, São Paulo: UNESP.

Campos, R. 1968. *Do outro lado da cerca*, Rio de Janeiro: Editora APEC.

Campos, R. 1994. *A lanterna na popa*, Rio de Janeiro: Topbooks.

Campos, R. and Simonsen, M.H. 1974. *A nova economia brasileira*, Rio de Janeiro: Editora APEC.

Campos, R. and Simonsen, M.H. 1975. *Formas criativas de desenvolvimento econômico*, Rio de Janeiro: Editora APEC.

Campos, R.O. 1961. "Two Views on Inflation in Latin America". In: Hirschman, A. (ed.), *Latin American Issues*, New York: Twentieth Century Fund.

Cardoso, F.H. 1964. *Empresário Industrial e desenvolvimento econômico*, São Paulo: Difusão Europeia do Livro.

Cardoso, F.H. and Faletto, E. [1969] 1979. *Dependency and Development in Latin America*, Los Angeles, CA: University of California Press.

Carneiro, D. 1990. "Crise e Esperança: 1974–1980". In: Abreu, M.P. (ed.), *A Ordem do Progresso*, Rio de Janeiro: Editora Campus.

Carone, E. 1976. *O pensamento industrial no Brasil (1880–1945)*, São Paulo: Difel.

Castro, A.B. [1989] 2011. "Consumo de massas e retomada do crescimento". In Castro, A.B. (ed.), *O desenvolvimento brasileiro: da era Geisel ao nosso tempo*, Rio de Janeiro: INAE/Reis Velloso org, 373–385.

Castro, A.B. [1969] 1971. *Sete Ensaios sobre a Economia Brasileira*, Rio de Janeiro: Forense.

Castro, A.B. 1979. *O capitalismo ainda é aquele*, Rio de Janeiro: Forense Universitária.

Castro, A.B. 1993. Renegade Development: Rise and Demise of State-Led Development in Brazil". In: Smith, W., Acuña, C.H., and Gamarra, A.E. (eds), *Democracy, Markets and Structural Reform in Latin America*, 1st ed. Miami: Transaction Publishers.

Castro, A.B and Lessa, C. 1967. *Introdução à economia, uma abordagem estruturalista*, Rio de Janeiro: Forense.

Castro, A.B e Souza, F.E.P. 1985. *A economia brasileira em marcha forçada*, Rio de Janeiro: Editora Paz e Terra.

Castro, M.H.M., Bielschowsky, R. e Benjamin, C. 2014. "Notas sobre o pensamento de Ignácio Rangel no centenário de seu nascimento", *Revista de Economia Política*, 34(4).

Cavalieri, M.R. and Silva, V.C. 2021. "Eugenio Gudin, -Uma ilha neoliberal em mar desenvolvimentista". In Salomão, I.C. (org), *Os Homens do Cofre*, São Paulo: UNESP.

CEPAL. 1969. *El pensamiento de la CEPAL*, Santiago: Editorial Universitaria.

Contador, C.R. 1977. "Crescimento Econômico e o Combate à Inflação". *Revista Brasileira de Economia*, 31(1), 132–167.

Cosentino, D.V.e Gambi, T.F.R. 2019. *História do Pensamento Econômico, Pensamento econômico brasileiro*, São Paulo: Eduff e Hucitec Editora.

Coutinho, M.C. 2001. "Incursões marxistas", *Estudos Avançados*, 15(41), 35–48.

Coutinho, M.C. 2019. "Furtado e seus críticos: da estagnação à retomada do crescimento econômico," *Economia e Sociedade, Campinas*, 28(3), 741–759.

Cruz, P.R.D.C. 1980. Ignácio Rangel, um pioneiro: o debate econômico do inicio dos anos sessenta. MsC dissertation presented at the Universidade Estadual de Campinas, Instituto de Economia.

Curado, M. and Cavalieri, M. 2015. "Uma crítica à interpretação inflacionista do desenvolvimentismo". *Economia e Sociedade, Campinas*, 24(1), 57–86.

Curado, M.L. 2021. "Octávio Gouveia de Bulhões – para além do neoliberalismo". In Salomão, I.C. (org), *Os Homens do Cofre*, São Paulo: UNESP.

Curi, L.F.B. and Cunha, A.M. 2015. "Redimensionando a contribuição de Roberto Simonsen à controvérsia do planejamento (1944–1945)", *América Latina en la Historia Económica*, 22(3), 76–107.

Cysne, R.P. 2001. "Mario Henrique Simonsen", *Estudos Avançados*, 15(41).

Dacanal, P.H. 2019. "Edmar Bacha e Pedro Malan: visões de uma alta modernidade periférica – ciência econômica, intelectualidade e política no Brasil (1960–1980)", Master degree dissertation, FFLCH/USP.

D'Araujo, M.C. and Castro, C. 2004. *Tempos Modernos, João Paulo dos Reis Velloso, memórias do desenvolvimento*, Rio de Janeiro: FGV.

Dean, W. 1969. *The industrialization of Sao Paulo, (1880–1945)*, Austin, TX: The University of Texas Press.

De Oliveira, F. (ed.). 1983. *Celso Furtado*, São Paulo: Ática.

Doellinger, C. 1976. *Endividamento e Desenvolvimento: Algumas Lições da História, in PPE*, vol. 6, no. 2, Rio de Janeiro: IPEA.

Earp, F.S. 2010. "Carlos Lessa", *Revista de Economia Contemporânea*, 14(2), 423–432.

ECLAC. 1951. *Economic Survey of Latin America 1949 (E/CN.12/164/Rev.1)*, New York: United Nations.

ECLAC. 1952. *Theoretical and Practical Problems of Economic Growth (E/CN.12/217)*, New York: United Nations.

ECLAC. 1955. *Introduction to the Technique of Programming (E/CN.12/363)*, Mexico City: United Nations.

Fallangiello, H. 1972. *Roberto Simonsen e o desenvolvimento econômico*, M.Sc. thesis submitted to FEA/USP, mimeo, Sâo Paulo.

Feldhues, P.R.P. 2014. *A Confederação Nacional da Indústria e o Nordeste brasileiro: o desenvolvimentismo nas páginas de Desenvolvimento & Conjuntura (1957–1964), 2014.311 f., il.* Doctoral degree thesis, Brasilia: Universidade de Brasilia.

Fernandes, F. 1973. *Capitalismo de pendente e classes sociais no Brasil*, Rio de Janeiro: Zahar Editores.

Fernandez, R.G. and Supriniak, C.E. 2015. *Creating Academic Economics in Brazil: The Ford Foundation and the beginnings of ANPEC*, Belo Horizonte: CEDEPLAR, Textos para Discussão, 514.

Fernandez, R.G. and Suprinyak, C.E. 2019. "Manufacturing Pluralism in Brazilian Economics," *Journal of Economic Issues*, 53(3), 748–773.

Fiori, J.L.C. 2014. *História, Estratégia e Desenvolvimento: Para uma Geopolítica do Capitalismo*, Rio de Janeiro: Boitempo.

Fishlow, A. 1972a. "Brazilian Size Income Distribution", *American Economic Review*, 62, 391–402.

Fishlow, A. 1972b. Some reflections on post-1964 economic policy. In Authoritarian Brazil (ed.), *A. Stepan*, New Haven, CT: Yale University Press.

Fishlow, A. 1974. "Algumas reflexões sobre a Política econômica do governo", *Estudos CEBRAP*, 7.

Fishlow, A. 1975. A distribuição de renda no Brasil, in "Distribuição da renda e desenvolvimento econômico no Brasil". In Tolipan, Ricardo e Tinelli, Arthur (eds), *A controvérsia sobre distribuição de renda e desenvolvimento*, Rio de Janeiro, Zahar Editores, 159–189.

Fonseca, P.C.D. 2004. "Gênese e precursores do desenvolvimentismo no Brasil", *Revista Pesquisa e Debate*, 15(2), 26.

Fonseca, P.C.D. 2015. *Desenvolvimentismo: A construção do conceito, IPEA, texto para discussão 2103*, Brasilia: IPEA.

Furtado, C. [1952] 1954. "Capital Formation and Economic Development", *International Economic Papers*, 4, 124–144.

Furtado, C. [1959] 1963. *The Economic Growth of Brazil – A Survey from Colonial to Modern Times*, Berkeley, CA: University of California Press.

Furtado, C. [1961] 1964. *Development and Underdevelopment*, Berkeley, CA: University of California Press.

Furtado, C. 1965. *Development and Stagnation in Latin America: A Structuralist Approach*, v. 1, n. 11, Yale: Yale University Economic Growth Center.

Furtado, C. 1972. *Análise do modelo brasileiro*, Rio de Janeiro: Editora Civilização Brasileira.

Furtado, C. 1974. *O mito do desenvolvimento econômico*, Rio de Janeiro: Paz e Terra.

Gomes, A.C. 2007. "Autoritarismo e corporativismo no Brasil: intelectuais e construção do mito Vargas". In: Pinto, Antônio Costa and Martinho, Francisco C. Palomanes (orgs), *O corporativismo em português: Estado, política e sociedade no salazarismo e no varguismo*, Rio de Janeiro: Civilização Brasileira.

Gomes, A.C. 2012. "O século do Corporativismo, de Michael Manoilescu, no Brasil de Vargas", *Revista de Sociologia & Antropologia*, 2(4), 185–209.

GTDN. [1959] 1997. "Uma Política de Desenvolvimento Econômico para o Nordeste", *Revista Econômica do Nordeste, Fortaleza*, 28(4), 387–432.

Gudin, E. [1947] 1970. *Princípios de economia monetária*, Rio de Janeiro: Agir.

Guimarães, A.P. 1963. *Inflação e monopólio no Brasil*, Rio de Janeiro: Civilização Brasileira.

Guimarães Jr, M.C.P. and Lopes, T.C. 2016. "O Desenvolvimento Desigual e Combinado: paralelos entre as obras 'História da Revolução Russa' de Trotsky e 'Dialética da Dependência' de Ruy Mauro Marini", *Rebela*, 6(2), 396–410.

Guimarães, J. (org). 2010. *Leituras Criticas Sobre Maria Da Conceição Tavares*, Belo Horizonte: Editora UFMG.

Gurrieri, Adolfo. (comp.). 1982. *La obra de Prebisch en la CEPAL*, México: Fondo de Cultura Económica.

Hespanhol, G.C.M.G. and Saes, A.M. 2021. "Antonio Delfim Netto-a moderna retórica económica". In: Salomão, I.C. (org.) *Os Homens do Cofre*, São Paulo: UNESP.

Hirschman, A.O. 1958. *The Strategy of Economic Development* (Yale Studies in Economics: 10), New Haven, CT: Yale University Press.

Hofmann, R. 1975. "Tendencias da distribuição de renda no Brasil e suas relações com o desenvolvimento econômico". In: Tolipan, R. and Tinelli, A. (eds), *A controvérsia sobre distribuição de renda e desenvolvimento*, Rio de Janeiro: Zahar Editores.

Hofmann, R. and Duarte, J.C. 1972. "A distribuição de renda no Brasil", *Revista de Administração de Empresas*, 12(2), 46–66.

Ianni, O. 1971. *Estado e planejamento econômico no Brasil (1930–1970)*, Rio de Janeiro: Civilização Brasileira.

Iglesias, F. (ed.). 1982. *Caio Prado Jr.*, São Paulo: Brasiliense.

IPEA. 1977. *A controvérsia do planejamento na economia brasileira*, Rio de Janeiro: Ipea/Inpes (Coleção Pensamento Econômico Brasileiro, vol. 3).

Langoni, C.G. 1973. *Distribuição de renda e desenvolvimento econômico no Brasil*, Rio de Janeiro: Expressão e Cultura.

Leme, M.S. 1978. *A ideologia dos industriais brasileiros (1919–1945)*, Petrópolis: Vozes.

Lemgruber, A.C. 1973. "A inflação brasileira e a controvérsia sobre a aceleração inflacionária", *Revista Brasileira de Economia*, 27, 31–50.

Lemgruber, A.C. 1978. *Inflação, moeda e modelos macroeconômicos*. 1ª edição, Rio de Janeiro: Editora FGV.

Lessa, C. [1967] 1975. *Quinze Anos de Política Econômica*, São Paulo: Brasiliense.

Lessa, C. [1978] 1998. *A estratégia de desenvolvimento 1974–1976: sonho e fracasso*, Campinas: Unicamp, Instituto de Economia.

Lima, H.F. 1975. *História do pensamento econômico no Brasil*, São Paulo: Cia. Editora Nacional.

Lira, P. 1970. *Endividamento Externo – Problema e Política, in Segurança e Desenvolvimento, Ano XIX, número 141*, Rio de Janeiro: ADESG.

Lisboa, M. 2020. "A oportunidade perdida em meio à revolução inesperada: a contribuição de Antonio Delfim Netto para a economia brasileira", *Estudos Econômicos*, 50(2).

Lopes, F. 1972. "Desigualdade e Crescimento,: um modelo de programação aplicado ao Brasil", *Pesquisa e Planejamento Econômico*, 2(2), 189–226.

Lopes, F. and Resende, A.L. 1979. *Sobre as causas da recente aceleração inflacionária*. Texto para discussão n. 06, Rio de Janeiro: Departamento de economia da PUC-RJ.

Loureiro, M.R. (org.). 1997. *50 anos de ciência econômica no Brasil (1946–1996)*, Petrópolis: Vozes.

Love, J. 1990a. "The Origins of Dependency Analysis", *Journal of Latin American Studies*, 22(1).

Love, J. 1990b. "Theorizing Underdevelopment: Latin America and Romania, 1860–1950", *Estudos avançados*, 4(8).

Love, J. 1996. *Crafting the Thirld World: Theorizing Underdevelopment in Rumania and Brazil*, Stanford, CA: Stanford University Press.

Luz, N.V. 1961. *A luta pela industrialização no Brasil: 1808–1930*, São Paulo: Difel.

Magalhães, J.P.A. 1964. *A controvérsia brasileira sobre o desenvolvimento econômico – Uma reformulação*, Rio de Janeiro: Record.

Malan, P. and Bonelli, R. 1976. "Os limites do possivel: notas sobre balanço de pagamentos e industria nos anos 70", *Pesquisa e Planejamento Economico*, 6(2).

Malan, P. e Wells, J. 1975. "Distribuição da renda e desenvolvimento econômico no Brasil". In Tolipan, R. e Tinelli, A. (eds), *A controvérsia sobre distribuição de renda e desenvolvimento*, Rio de Janeiro: Zahar Editores.

Malta, M. (coord.). 2011a. *Ecos do desenvolvimento, uma história do pensamento econômico brasileiro*, Rio de Janeiro: IPEA/Centro Internacional Celso Furtado.

Malta, M. 2011b. "Sensos do contraste: o debate distributivo do Milagre". In *Ecos do desenvolvimento, uma história do pensamento econômico brasileiro*, Rio de Janeiro: IPEA/Centro Internacional Celso Furtado.
Manoilescu, M. 1929. *Théorie du protectionnisme et de l'échange international*, Paris: Marcel Giard.
Manoilescu, M. 1934. *Le siècle du corporatisme, Doctrine du corporatisme integral et pur*, Paris: Félix Alcan.
Mantega, G. 1984. *A Economia Política Brasileira*, Petrópolis: Vozes.
Mantega, G. 1997. "O pensamento Econômico Brasileiro de 1960 a 1980: os anos rebeldes". In: Loureiro, M.R. (org.), *50 anos de ciência econômica no Brasil (1946–1996)*, ch. 3, Petrópolis: Vozes.
Mantega, G. and Rego, J.M. (orgs). 1999. *Conversas com Economistas II*, São Paulo: Editora 34.
Marco, T.R.A. 2020. *Origens do desenvolvimentismo no pensamento político brasileiro – Azevedo Amaral um desenvolvimentista das origens, tese de doutorado*, Rio de Janeiro: UERJ.
Marini, R.M. 1973. *Dialéctica de la dependencia*, México City: Ediciones Era.
Martins, C.E. (org). 1977. *Estado e Capitalismo no Brasil*, São Paulo: Hucitec.
Mello, J.M.C. [1974] 1978. *O capitalismo tardio*, São Paulo: Brasiliense.
Mollo, M.L.R. and Amado, A.A. 2015. "O debate desenvolvimentista no Brasil: tomando partido Economia e Sociedade," *Campinas*, 24(1), 1–28.
Mollo, M.L.R. and Fonseca, P.C.D. 2013. "Desenvolvimentismo e novo-desenvolvimentismo: raízes teóricas e precisões conceituais", *Revista de Economia Política*, 33(2), 222–239.
Moura, A. 1959. *Capitais estrangeiros no Brasil*, São Paulo: Editora Brasiliense.
Nascimento, J.G., Silva, D.F.R. and Fernandez, R.G. 2017. "The Dispute between the Phillips Curve and the Inertialist Analisys in the Formulation of Brazilian Inflation Theories During the 1970s–1980s". www.anpec.org.br/encontro/2017/submissao/files_I/i1-551c31a0a1076e9ce2f8ec5d35a69824.pdf
Noyola, J. 1956. "El desarrollo economico y la inflacion en Mexico y otros países Latinoamericanos", *Investigacion Economica*, 16, 603–648.
Oliveira, B.R. 2020. *Três Ensaios sobre Economia Brasileira no Período 1967–1988: Inter-relacão entre Aspectos de Economia Política e Política Econômica e o Surgimento e Consolidação do Pensamento da Unicamp*. Doctoral degree Thesis, IE/UFRJ.
Oliveira, F. 1972. *A Economia brasileira: crítica à razão dualista*, São Paulo: Estudos Cebrap.
Oliveira, F. (org.). 1983. *Celso Furtado*, São Paulo: Editora Ática.
Paim, A. 2018. *Historia do liberalismo Brasileiro*, São Paulo: LVM Editora.
Pazos, F. 1972. *Chronic Inflation in Latin America*, Nova York: Praeger Publishers.
Pereira, H (org.). 2019. *Maria da Conceição Tavares: vida, ideias, teorias e política*, São Paulo and Rio de Janeiro: Fundação Perseu Abramo/Expressão Popular/Centro Celso Furtado.
Pereira, J.E. 1974. *Financiamento Externo e Crescimento Econômico no Brasil*, Rio de Janeiro: IPEA/INPES.
Pinto, A. 1970. "Naturaleza e implicaciones de la 'heterogeneidad estructural' de la América Latina", *El Trimestre Económico*, 37(145).
Possas, M.S. 2001. "Maria da Conceição Tavares", *Estudos Avançados*, 15(43), 389–400.
Prado Jr., C. 1962. "Nova Contribuição à análise da questão agrária no Brasil", *Revista Brasiliense*, 43, 11–52.
Prado Jr, C. [1942] 1967. *The Colonial Background of Modern Brazil*, Berkeley, CA and Los Angeles, CA: University of California Press.
Prado Jr., C. [1945] 1969. *História econômica do Brasil*, São Paulo: Brasiliense.
Prado Jr., C. [1966] 2004. *A Revolução Brasileira*, São Paulo: Brasiliense.

Prado, L.C. and Bastian, E.F. 2011. "Um Economista no labirinto: um obituário de Antônio Barros de Castro", *Dados*, 54(3), 243–258.

Prebisch, R. [1949] 1962. "Economic Development of Latin America and Its Principal Problems", *Economic Bulletin for Latin America*, 7(1), 1–22.

Prebisch, R. 1963. *Towards a dynamic development policy for Latin America*, New York: United Nations, E/CN.12/680/Rev.l

Quintela, A., Galvão, C.F.G., Bolaño, C., Patricio, I., Manzano, M., Macedo, M.M. and Le Coqc, Nelson (orgs). 2020. *Celso Furtado: os combates de um economista*, São Paulo: Fundação Perseu Abramo: Expressão Popular.

Rangel, I. 1957. *Dualidade básica na economia brasileira*, Rio de Janeiro: ISEB.

Rangel, I. 1963. *A inflação brasileira*, Rio de Janeiro: Tempo Brasileiro.

Resende, A.L. 1990. "Estabilização e Reforma: 1964–1967". In: Abreu, M.P. (ed.), *A ordem do Progresso*, Rio de Janeiro: Editora Campus.

Ricupero, B. 2000. *Caio Prado Jr. e a Nacionalização do Marxismo no Brasil*, São Paulo: Editora 34.

Robilloti, P.C.N.S. 2016. *O desenvolvimento capitalista na obra de Maria da Conceição Tavares: Influências Teóricas, Economia Política e Pensamento Econômico. Dissertação de Mestrado*, Campinas: IE-Unicamp.

Rodriguez, O. 1981. *La teoría del subdesarrollo de la Cepal*, Mexico City: Siglo Veintiuno.

Saad Filho, A. 2005. "The Rise and Decline of Latin American Structuralism and Dependency Theory". In: Jomo, K.S. and Reinert, E.S. (eds), *The Origins of Development Economics: How Schools of Economic Thought Have Addressed Development*, London: Zed Books and New Delhi: Tulika Books, 128–145.

Saboia, J. and Carvalho, F.J.C. (orgs). 2007. *Celso Furtado e o século XXI*, São Paulo: Manole.

Salomão, I.C. (org.). 2021. *Os Homens do Cofre*, São Paulo: UNESP.

Santos, F.P. 2013. "A economia política da "Escola de Campinas": contexto e modo de pensamento Cadernos do Desenvolvimento", *Rio de Janeiro*, 8(12), 17–42.

Santos, T. 1967. *El Nuevo carácter de la dependencia*, Santiago: Centro de estudios Socio-Economicos, Universidad de Chile.

Santos, T. 1970. "The Structure of Dependence", *The American Eco nomic Review*, 60(2), 231–236.

Saretta, F. 2001. "Octávio Gouveia de Bulhões, in Pensamento Econômico no Brasil Contemporâneo", *Estud.av*, 15(41).

Schumpeter, J.A. 1954. *History of Economic Analysis*, New York: Oxford University Press.

Serrano, F. 2001. "Acumulação e gasto improdutivo na economia do desenvolvimento". In: Fiori, J.L. e Medeiros, C.A. (eds), *Polarização mundial e crescimento*, Rio de Janeiro: Vozes.

Simonsen, M.H. 1969. *Brasil 2001*, Rio de Janeiro: Editora APEC.

Simonsen, M.H. 1970. *Inflação: gradualismo e tratamento de choque*, Rio de Janeiro: Editora APEC.

Simonsen, M.H. 1972. *Brasil 2002*, Rio de Janeiro: Editora APEC.

Simonsen, R. [1937] 2005. *História econômica do Brasil (1500–1820)*, v. 34, Brasilia: Edições do Senado Federal.

Singer, H. 1950. "The Distribution of Gains between Investing and Borrowing Countries", *American Economic Review*, 40(2), 473–485.

Singer, P. 1973. *As contradições do Milagre*, n. 6, Sao Paulo, Estudos Cebrap, 59–77.

Singer, P. 1975. "Desenvolvimento e repartição da renda no Brasil". In: Tolipan, R. and Tinelli, A. (eds), *A controvérsia sobre distribuição de renda e desenvolvimento*, Rio de Janeiro: Zahar Editores, 73–104.

Sunkel, O. [1958] 1960. "Inflation in Chile: An Unorthodox Approach", *International Economic Papers*, 10, 107–131.

Suzigan, W., Bonelli, R., Horta, M.H.T.T. and Lodder, C.A. 1974. *Crescimento industrial no Brasil – incentivos e desempenho recente*, Rio de Janeiro: INPES/IPEA.

Szmrecsányi, T. and Coelho, F.S. (orgs.). 2007. *Ensaios de história do pensamento econômico no Brasil contemporâneo*, São Paulo: Atlas.

Tavares, J.M.H. 2017. *A Economia Política da Internacionalização Financeira e Tecnológica: uma análise das contribuições de François Chesnais e Maria da Conceição Tavares*. tese de doutorado, IE-UFRJ.

Tavares, M.C. 1964. "The Growth and Decline of Import Substitution in Brazil", *Economic Bulletin for Latin America*, 9(1), 1–59.

Tavares, M.C. [1974] 1998. *Acumulação de Capital e Industrialização no Brasil*, Campinas: Unicamp.

Tavares, M.C. [1978] 1998. *Ciclo e Crise: o Movimento Recente da Industrialização Brasileira*, Campinas: Unicamp.

Tavares, M.C. e Belluzzo, L.G. 1982. "Notas sobre o processo de industrialização recente no Brasil". In: Belluzzo, L.G. e Coutinho, R. (eds), *Desenvolvimento Capitalista no Brasil*, São Paulo: Brasiliense.

Tavares, M.C. and Serra, J. [1970] 1973. "Beyond Stagnation: A Discussion on the Nature of Recent Developments in Brazil". In: Petras, J. (ed.), *Latin America: From Dependence to Revolution*, New York: John Wiley & Sons.

Toledo, C.N. 1997. *ISEB, Fábrica de ideologias*, Campinas: Unicamp.

Tolipan, R. and Tinelli, A. 1975. *A controvérsia sobre distribuição de renda e desenvolvimento*, Rio de Janeiro: Zahar Editores.

Wells, J. 1975. "Distribuição de rendimentos, crescimento e a estrutura de demanda no Brasil na década de 60". In Tolipan, Ricardo e Tinelli, Arthur (eds), *A controvérsia sobre distribuição de renda e desenvolvimento*, Rio de Janeiro: Zahar Editores.

9 The end of developmentalism, the globalization era and the concern with income distribution (1981–2010)

Eduardo F. Bastian and Carlos Pinkusfeld Bastos

1. Introduction

Owing to the debt crisis, the 1980s were a turbulent period of transition for the Brazilian economy, marked by a low rate of growth, much lower than the "historical" post-Second World War average, and very high inflation. It was also a transitional period in terms of the dominant economic thinking and policymaking. Following the international trend, the traditional developmentalist ideology and policymaking (in developing countries) and the conventional *Keynesian consensus* (in developed countries) were both progressively substituted by a neoliberal orientation. This new consensus became dominant in the first half of the 1990s, but its inability to foster economic growth and promote social justice – or at least improve income distribution and substantially lower poverty rates – spurred growing theoretical and political criticism. Accordingly, that criticism stressed the importance of social policies and, to some extent, the return of policy interventions favoring economic development, namely industrial policies.

This chapter addresses the foregoing ideological trajectory in the Brazilian case, highlighting its particularities, its timing and, in the dawn of the 21st century, some attempts to modify the economic model and include some redistributive policies.

Following this Introduction, Section 2 covers the negative impact of the external crisis on Brazilian economy, a crisis that also had a strong impact on schools of thought and policymaking. We show that the inability of existing conventional policy proposals to deal with high inflation in the first half of the 1980s made room for the appearance of a new economic research center: the Graduate School of the Pontifical Catholic University of Rio de Janeiro (PUC/RJ). The economists in that research program came up with the so-called Inertial Inflation model and with stabilization plans that were close to the traditional Keynesian school (or the traditional Keynesian synthesis) wherein cost-push equations are the basic theoretical tenets. Their models and policy proposals came to life with the first heterodox shock, the Cruzado Plan, in 1986. Its disastrous results had several implications not only for future stabilization plans, but also for a reorientation of PUC's economic analysis up to the 1994 *Real Plan*, a stabilization program that finally brought inflation rates down after a succession of failed plans in the late

DOI: 10.4324/9781003185871-13

1980s and early 1990s, starting with the Cruzado Plan. Given the leading role of the PUC/RJ research group, Section 2 follows its intellectual evolution from the 1980s to the 1990s. Alongside this analysis, it presents the controversies aroused with other schools of thought, such as the orthodox school, which gathered especially around the Getúlio Vargas Foundation in Rio de Janeiro (FGV/RJ), and the heterodox school of the Institute of Economics of the State University of Campinas (UNICAMP). It also mentions the research group of the Getúlio Vargas Foundation in São Paulo (FGV/SP), which independently developed ideas similar to those espoused by PUC/RJ regarding inertial inflation.

Section 3 deals with the change in Brazil's development model in the 1990s during the governments of Fernando Collor de Mello (1990–1992), Itamar Franco (1992–1994) and Fernando Henrique Cardoso (1995–2002). During that period, there was a debate polarizing supporters of the new *neoliberal* development model – for instance, most of PUC/RJ economists of the 1980s – and the *developmentalist* position, which found support especially at UNICAMP and at the Institute of Industrial Economics (later Institute of Economics) of the Federal University of Rio de Janeiro (UFRJ). Finally, Section 4 describes the debates surrounding the two terms of Luís Inácio Lula da Silva's administration (2003–2010), which advanced an agenda of income redistribution and tried to increase state activism in certain areas, in contrast to the neoliberal era of the 1990s. The section covers the *social developmentalist* position – which to a large extent corresponds to the core policies of Lula's governments – and its major critics, namely the *new developmentalists*, whose main concern was the ongoing deindustrialization process, and the *neoliberals*, who favored a continuation of the development agenda of the 1990s and insisted on the need for additional institutional reforms.[1]

The first economics graduate centers were created in the 1960s, and from the mid-1970s on several new centers emerged, leading to a boom in economics research in Brazil. This was also due to growing research activities in already existing research centers, such as the Institute of Applied Economics Research (IPEA), and in other institutions like the National Development Bank (BNDES), all of which lead to the emergence of academic journals. As a result, there was an outburst in the production of academic materials in Brazil as compared to previous decades, which makes it impossible for the present chapter to cover all those publications and contributions and to provide a fully comprehensive picture of them. The chapter merely picks the major authors and most important debates of the period 1980–2010, highlighting the leading Brazilian schools of thought and the main controversies.

2. The debate on inflation and stabilization policies in the 1980s and 1990s

2.1. Origins of the debate in the 1970s and in the first half of the 1980s

Brazil's economy was severely hit by the sequence of crises initiated in 1979. There was a huge fall in the terms of trade, and access to international capital markets became increasingly harder.

A particular feature of Brazilian economy prior to the 1979 shock, one that in considerable measure set the tone for the theoretical and policy discussions to come, was the high level of inflation. Before the 1979 shock, it stood around 40% per year, an average monthly rate of 2.9%, and then jumped to almost twice that annual level and close to an average 5% per month.

After the 1982 Mexican default, there was a halt in voluntary financial flows to the periphery. Unable to finance its external deficit, with its international reserves nearly depleted and in virtual default in terms of external solvency, Brazil had to turn to the IMF for financial help. As is always the case with IMF interventions, Brazil had to implement an austerity program including a strong exchange rate devaluation that had the collateral effect of accelerating inflation.

Regarding the challenge of high inflation and economic growth deceleration, it soon became clear that the traditional schools of thought or institutions that had vied for dominance over policymaking through the 1970s had no useful policy guidance to offer.

On the one hand, the so-called UNICAMP school[2] had always been devoted to questions of economic development, capital accumulation and industrialization, with scarce contributions regarding topics like fiscal policy or inflation. Given the high inflation of the 1980s, UNICAMP economists developed their own ideas on the subject. Tavares and Belluzzo (1986) produced their seminal work around that period, but in that paper we cannot identify any breakthroughs in either theoretical or empirical terms.[3] On the other hand, the orthodox/marginalist school of Fundação Getúlio Vargas in Rio de Janeiro (FGV/RJ) had serious shortcomings regarding their traditional explanation, as:

a) inflation acceleration in the early 1980s happened in a scenario of substantial reduction of growth. Therefore, the conventional narrative concerning excess demand lost much of its explanatory power.[4]
b) the high levels of inflation and its associated inertia put in check traditional demand restriction policies.[5]

This theoretical and policy void was filled by a body of research developed by a new economics graduate program pertaining to a traditional undergraduate program at the Catholic University of Rio de Janeiro (PUC/RJ). The two aforementioned weaknesses in explaining inflation through the conventional approach were, so to speak, the starting point of the theoretical contribution made by this new approach, which also brought PUC/RJ economists to the forefront of the policy discussion.

The "crucial" step taken by PUC authors was basically to criticize the empirical results of the then-existing Phillips curve estimates. In two seminal papers that questioned the traditional interpretation of inflation which provides theoretical grounds for the recommendation of austerity policies, Lara-Resende and Lopes (1981) and Lopes (1982) criticized the traditional estimates of the Phillips curve in the Brazilian case. They argued, for example, regarding Contador's 1977 estimation (Contador 1977), that it had low values for R^2

and Durbin-Watson statistics. Lara-Resende and Lopes then showed that these flawed specifications tended do overestimate the income/employment elasticity coefficient, which lead to a rather crucial policy implication, i.e. a certain degree of optimism with respect to austerity measures. If elasticity was high, then a recession would have a strong effect on reducing inflation.[6]

Lara-Resende and Lopes (1981) show that this wrong empirical specification would lead to a totally inadequate policy. If a new specification is applied, taking into consideration nominal wages indexation, the coefficient of the GDP gap becomes statistically nonsignificant and rejects the existence of a connection between excess demand and inflation.

A further specification of the Phillips curve by Lopes (1982) found a significant coefficient for the GDP gap; however, in terms of stabilization policies, the simulation showed it would make almost no difference:

> The 7% reduction of the inflation rate in 1982 [from 99% in 1981 to 92% in 1982] was the worst single result of the major depression in the level of activity in Brazil's recent economic history.
>
> (Lopes, 1982, p. 38)

Another author from the same graduate school, Eduardo Modiano (1988a), reached a similar conclusion: stabilization policies would be extremely inefficient without the elimination of the extensive formal and informal price indexation mechanisms used to deal with inflation in the Brazilian economy, which lead to a certain "inertia" within high inflation levels.

The empirical results had an important consequence both in theoretical and policy terms. Given that the traditional treatment of inflation was largely discredited by some shaky econometric estimations of the Phillips curve, it was necessary to establish a new approach and, consequently, a new policy proposal to deal with the pressing inflation problem.

The logical consequence of demonstrating the crucial role played by the inertial component was that any successful stabilization plan had to deal primarily with this element. The answer to this challenge came in the form of the so-called Inertial Theory of Inflation and the "innovative"[7] stabilization policy proposals.

Some of those ideas were arguably already present, at least in *embryonic* form, in the work of authors like Pazos (1972) and Simonsen (1970) (see details in Bastos 2002, pp. 74–87). However, as previously noted, the group of economists working at PUC/RJ advanced those crude ideas to a new level of development and policy proposals.

In basic theoretical terms, the models developed by this school could be characterized as typical cost-push inflation equations. These models (see for example Lopes and Lara-Resende [1981], Lopes [1982] and Modiano [1988a, 1988b]) depart from a basic cost-(i.e. wages and industrial inputs)-plus-markup price equation. Inputs were divided into two types as either imported or locally produced.[8]

A central element in the inflationary mechanism proposed by "inertialist" authors is the process of nominal wage formation. It assumes that at each round of wage negotiations workers will try to obtain the former peak value, since combined with the expected future inflation it will provide the intended real wage. The inertial character of inflation depends on an important variable, namely adjustment intervals: a constant interval characterizes an inertial inflation while, *ceteris paribus*, a shortening of the interval between adjustments means a higher real wage. Therefore, the inertial or accelerating nature of inflation in the model depends on a combination of variables, i.e. the interval between adjustments and compatibility between demanded real wages and the distributive balance. One might say that if workers demand the past nominal wage peak and expect future inflation to repeat past values, and provided the adjustment interval does not change, there will be no distributive conflict but rather a process of rendering inflation *inertial*.

There is a problem here, of course, in identifying an inertial process. The ex-post nominal wage increase cannot be viewed as the value workers truly desire. It depends on their bargaining power, but also on institutional and political arrangements.

Therefore, a period when inflation reaches a "*plateau*" – with nominal wages increasing according to inflation past values – does not necessarily show that there is no relevant distributive conflict, or that workers are satisfied with their previous real wage. This assumption is crucial for the success of a stabilization policy that may have as an essential feature its neutrality in terms of income distribution. If workers are satisfied with their real wages, a stabilization plan that eliminates inertia and sets a nominal wage that is consistent with the previous real wage will do the job. In this case, there will be no pressure from the wage side on costs, hence no upward pressure on prices.

Of course, the very existence of the idea that workers are satisfied with their real wages and only demand nominal wage increases that equal past inflation, which is also the expected future inflation,[9] needs explaining: why should inflation be perpetuated by nominal cost increases, specifically nominal wage increases, if this behavior is not "entirely" rational?

The explanation of this phenomenon has to do with lack of coordination. It may be illustrated by the "sports audience" metaphor: if a group of people stand up during a game, the whole audience is also forced to stand up, otherwise they won't be able to watch the game. It would be much more sensible for all spectators to coordinate their collective action, so that the whole crowd might sit down and comfortably watch the game (Bacha, 1985). This metaphor applies to wage indexation in the sense that not all wage contracts have the same length and/or anniversary. Therefore, if several wage categories with different adjustment dates agree to bring their nominal wages to a certain value that guarantees their desired real wages, it is possible that a category might demand full indexation with past inflation (even though future inflation has no reason to rise), and the impact of just one or two categories' full wage indexation on aggregate inflation would be negligible for the entire economy. Nevertheless, this creates a free rider problem. And according to the inertial approach to inflation, it explains the need to design coordinating schemes that are crucial for the success of any stabilization plan.

Luiz Carlos Bresser Pereira also made a contribution to the inertial inflation literature, which he developed during the same period but independently from the PUC/RJ research group. As he himself reminds us in Bresser-Pereira (2010), paternities in economic theory are hard to determine. Bresser Pereira – who was a professor at FGV/SP before becoming Finance Minister in 1987 – raised a few hypotheses as to why PUC economists' inertial inflation models had become more renowned than his own, which he claimed to have been developed before PUC/RJ's contributions (see Bresser-Pereira, 2010, p. 169). We do not wish to dwell on this *paternity debate*, but just highlight a few interesting original points in Bresser Pereira's work, which was jointly developed with Yoshiaki Nakano, another FGV/SP professor (see, for example, Bresser-Pereira and Nakano, 1984). Initially, they got their inspiration from Ignácio Rangel, a Brazilian economist with very singular and original ideas, who emphasized in his inflation theory the role of market structures and the ability of firms to protect their profit margins during economic downturns, and thus freed his theory from the need to connect inflation acceleration to excess demand. A second point that is strongly present in Bresser Pereira and Nakano's inertial model is the idea that, in a production process with several stages and given increased input costs, producers will attempt to maintain their profitability by adding a markup to these higher costs and will thus make price evolution independent of demand conditions. Finally, Bresser Pereira has a peculiar way of presenting the concept of distributive conflict. We mentioned earlier that a neutral plan is successful only if economic agents have their income demands satisfied, or at least accept their remunerations. Bresser Perreira calls this situation a "defensive conflict" (p. 176) wherein agents merely defend their previous real averages. What we called a conflict situation is renamed by him as an "aggressive conflict".

Before going into further details on that discussion in Brazil, it is important to draw attention to other conditions that were supposedly important for the implementation of a neutral stabilization plan for the country.

The first significant point was the fact that in 1984 and 1985 the economy presented a roughly balanced current account.[10] Among PUC's economists, it was Franco (1986) who stressed the importance of the external balance or the existence of an equilibrium *exchange* rate that clears the external constraint. Although Franco's work was published after the first contributions made by the inertial inflation approach, it seems clear – also from the importance attributed to it by the explanation of inflation acceleration through external shocks (external prices plus exchange rate devaluation) – that the external balance was mandatory for a successful neutral stabilization program.

A second relevant element in the discussion of the inflation process in the first half of the 1980s was public deficit. As previously mentioned, the idea of excess demand inflation was rejected by these authors, as inflation acceleration occurred simultaneously with a steep deceleration in the rate of economic growth, which became much lower than the then-believed potential historical rate of 7%. The idea that acceleration of inflation was the result of exogenous shocks and indexation was dominant among these authors. However, apart from this, Arida and

Lara-Resende (1986) recognized that the fiscal adjustment implemented under the IMF's adjustment program had been quite severe, with a reduction of PSBR from 8% to 3.5% from 1982 to 1983.[11] In any case, an official document provides a telling statement which clearly presents a traditional Keynesian analysis of the macroeconomic impact of the fiscal situation at the time:[12]

> The current government deficit does not impose any risk of inflationary pressure on an economy that intends to follow a path of accelerated development. Economic growth demands proportional increases of the amount of public both monetary and non-monetary. Given the natural increase of the demand for public debt, the government needs to supply financial assets that may at the same time finance its own deficit. We estimate that this potential normal growth of debt demand is compatible with the present deficits between 2% and 3% of GDP. There is no question that Brazilian deficit is decidedly under control and presents no risk as an inflationary source.
>
> (SEPLAN, 1986, p. 136)

Having laid down the basic theoretical elements of the inertial theory, we need to discuss two main policy proposals for dealing with alternative de-indexation schemes that are necessary to stabilize an economy.

Economist Francisco Lopes (1986), of PUC/RJ, argued for a "shock" to bring prices or, more specifically, wages to their previous real value, i.e. their average between nominal adjustment dates, and then impose a price freeze. This measure would be required to somehow "erase" the inflationary memory. Once wages were brought to their real value and, according to the theory, there was no distributive tension, the coordination problem would eliminate inflation and the price freeze would be necessary to abolish pricing behaviors based on past inflationary experience, or the inflationary memory. Once agents perceived the new situation, with the same distributive structure but no inflation, previous pricing behaviors would be given up, and the economy would be ready to follow a non-inflationary path.

The other policy proposal, the so-called *Larida Model*[13] (1984), follows an important historical precedent, namely the monetary reform that stabilized the German hyperinflation in 1924.[14] The idea is actually rooted in an even older origin, based as it is on the Gresham Law. In short, it proposes the coexistence of a new indexed money with an old currency, private agents migrating to the new one and gradually abandoning the old one. We shall revert to the subject later in this chapter.

The theoretical and policy proposal briefly presented earlier had its political opportunity to become the official anti-inflationary policy on February 28, 1986, the date when the Cruzado Plan was launched. It followed almost one year of the newly elected government's failed attempts to use more conventional stabilization policies. The plan answered a pressing political demand, as inflation was considered the major economic and therefore political problem.

Its failure can be viewed as a watershed in Brazilian economic thought and policy proposals.

It should have become clear from the foregoing presentation (and from the previous chapter) that a new player had entered the traditional structuralist/developmentalist *versus* "monetarist" debate over the interpretation of Brazil's economic policies. In fact, the economists in PUC/RJ's research group were sometimes referred to as neo-structuralists, though the definition of what neo-structuralism might mean was rather vague. In a 1978 paper, Francisco Lopes explicitly calls Simonsen's inflation model (Simonsen, 1970, 1974) a neo-structuralist one because "it incorporates the core elements of CEPAL's inflation theory – namely structural inflationary pressures (stemming from relative price adjustments) and propagation mechanisms – into a structuralist specification (compatible with a non-vertical long-term Phillips curve)" (Lopes, 1979, p. 19). In the Introduction to a book with a collection of his own papers, Edmar Bacha (1986) – also from PUC/RJ – writes that his papers consist of an attempt to combine the contribution of Latin American structuralist authors – like Prebisch, Furtado, Noyola and Pinto – with modern analytical techniques (Bacha, 1986, p. 7). Presser (2001) is one of several economists who called the PUC/RJ school a neo-structuralist one. He argued that neo-structuralism included other departments and economists around Latin America in the 1980s.

In this regard, it is worth stressing that this new player in Brazil's public debate centered on stabilization policies instead of development strategies or capital accumulation. Moreover, it followed, loosely speaking, a conventional Keynesian approach.[15] It is also true that over the 1980s the post-war Keynesian mainstream was already changing into a much more orthodox marginalist approach, and from the 1990s on the so-called *New Keynesian consensus* clearly became the dominant theory informing policymaking. In the Brazilian case, however, there is a particular aspect one should not underestimate: the impact of the Cruzado Plan's failure on its intellectual creators, which led them to progressively shift from a fully heterodox perspective into a less heterodox one. In the 1990s, many of them soon became strong supporters of the orthodox/neoliberal approach that became prevalent in Brazil and worldwide. It is important to stress that in spite of this transition from a more heterodox into a more orthodox approach, both in theoretical terms and in the policy stance taken by the economists who were behind several stabilization attempts during that period, some specific policies to deal with very high inflation were part of the original thinking and proposals of those authors. Therefore, there is a continuum or a persistence of policy proposals from the first failed stabilization Cruzado Plan up to the successful Real Plan.

2.2. The debate on failed heterodox stabilization plans and the successful Real Plan (1994)

The failure of the Cruzado Plan in 1986 raised distinct interpretations, each of them emphasizing the effects of specific factors. A brief list of such factors is required here to allow for a proper illustration of the different positions at stake and suggest references where this debate can be found.

The main elements pointed as culprits for the Cruzado Plan's failure are relative price misalignments, some prices being caught at their peak and some at their trough on the day of price freezing, in terms of their real past value, with intermediate cases of prices above and below their previous average value. This problem was amplified by a longer than initially planned period of price freeze. Another limitation was the impossibility of controlling prices in the informal sector. Moreover, the rates of growth of both demand and costs were accelerating, the latter in part due to an agricultural shock in the second half of 1985 and to a shortening of wage adjustment intervals in specific unionized sectors. The economy's heated growth trend was reinforced by the wage adjustment at the beginning of the plan, which established a real growth of 8% in general wages and 16% in the minimum wage. Another element explaining a strong demand pressure on prices was the end of the credit repression that is characteristic of high inflation regimes. In this case, economic agents were able to either finance the purchase of durable goods or use savings that had been accumulated for that purpose, thus taking advantage of the price freeze period. Trade balance deterioration in a situation of near lack of voluntary external capital flows was another weak spot during the Cruzado experience. This trend pressed for devaluating the exchange rate, which in turn triggered a cost-wages-prices spiral, a situation that showed an inability to control the exchange rate in such a way as to accommodate conflicting distributive claims. This very fact is at odds with the inertial/distributional neutrality hypothesis that buttressed the plan's foundations.[16]

Lack of demand control after adoption of the price freeze was a generally accepted argument and led to a policy prescription emphasizing control of the public deficit. That view was commonplace among critics of the Cruzado Plan, such as, for instance, Barbosa et al. (1989) from FGV/RJ. Barbosa's 1999 recollection of his 1989 criticism on the Cruzado Plan's approach to fight inflation said:

> I think the Cruzado had conceptual problems . . . because [the plan] had ideas like "demand is not relevant", disdained fiscal issues, fiscal deficit issues, money issues. . . . [it said] indexation is just a propagation mechanism, but not the cause of the problem . . . hence if one eliminates indexation, but not the causes of inflation, then inflation will return. That's what happened in the case of the Cruzado.
>
> (Barbosa, 1999, pp. 318–319)

Excess demand is also connected to growing external imbalance in a situation of lack of external financing. This was stressed by authors like Lopes (1989), who stated that:

> The Cruzado Plan failed because it caused a domestic excess demand pressure that affected exports. The exchange rate crisis that followed and

> virtually depleted the country's foreign currency reserves was what effectively pronounced the plan's death sentence.
>
> (Lopes, 1989, p. 63)[17]

The foregoing analysis emphasizes that the consumption bubble became Brazilian economists' favorite explanation for the Cruzado Plan's failure, and that included its own creators. The reasons for this have already been presented, but to be more specific, one important author from that school (Franco, 1987) stresses that the discussion about the "consumption bubble" is related to the plan's management, not to the origin of inflation:

> regardless of conventional wisdom, the evidence of the relevance of a monetary and fiscal origin is not convincing. . . . Therefore, it is not easy to justify the necessity of contractionary policies in a "heterodox" program. Yet, an important point that requires stressing is that the need of "orthodoxy" is in fact a demand management problem, which varies from case to case after each "heterodox shock".
>
> (p. 13)

The same author also stresses that the effects previously described are related to the drastic deflation of the stock of public assets by the private sector and do not necessarily result in relevant expansionary pressures, nor are they related to the very nature of heterodox shocks (Franco, 1987, p. 14).[18] Nonetheless, in 1988, Bacha (1988) argued that this view – dominant up to that point among members of the inertial school – began to change. Bacha initially assumes that for authors following this tradition, the inflation tax would be a "blessing" and that, once the heterodox stabilization plan was put in place, the loss of that revenue wouldn't be of great importance since a "benevolent government" (*sic*) would be able to obtain the same amount through other taxes, or even during the first steps of the plan, through the process of re-monetization (Bacha, 1988, p. 12).

However, Bacha (1988) partially disagrees with the first empirical criticism raised by his peers at PUC/RJ when he argues that there might be an asymmetry in the Brazilian Phillips curve: "the inertial specification is valid for decelerations, . . . but for accelerations the Phillips curve should be taken into consideration along with expectations" (p. 10). Therefore, once the economy is no longer indexed, long-term inflation is caused by the "monetary expansion necessary to finance the government's operational deficit" (p. 10).

It is a rather important argument that while empirical criticism on existing Philips curves is valid in specific cases, it is no longer valid after stabilization, i.e. inflation after stabilization is explained by the traditional monetarist argument, notably by monetary expansion to finance public deficits.

However, Bacha (1988) takes one step further to detach himself from the original inertial model. According to him, the inflationary regime had changed since the model's first contributions in the early 1980s, and recent "accumulated evidence" would suggest that Brazil had entered a regime of "repressed hyperinflation" (p. 13) and no longer of inertial inflation. More importantly,

> Hyperinflation seems to result from the fact that the government's requirement of revenues from the inflation tax shows a tendency to be higher than the feasible upper bound, and from the fact that wages and administered prices indexation tends to perfection.
>
> (p. 13)

This is an interesting quotation because, even though it is "eclectic", it clearly points to a rather monetarist diagnosis whereby the government needs to *increase inflation*. This is so because higher inflation rates shrink the monetary base, so that financing the deficit requires generating more inflation.

Lara-Resende (1989) exerts some caution when he says that the public deficit "is not always the primary cause of inflation, or there is a bi-univocal relation between the level of public deficit and the rate of inflation" (p. 11). According to this author, public deficit [is not] necessarily the primary source of inflationary pressure in chronic processes, but its reduction to an amount compatible with a non-inflationary domestic credit expansion is a *sine qua non* to eliminate this unbalance (pp. 12–13).[19] We may say that this theoretical tendency came full circle with Bacha (1994), while in policy terms, as formerly mentioned, the fiscal balance or fiscal adjustments were already central elements in stabilization policies. However, before addressing the way these elements were introduced at least at a rhetorical level within the Real Plan – very much in line with the neoliberal order that became dominant in the first half of the 1990s – we should mention two events that were not mainstream in terms of economic thought and policy.

The first one concerns the secondary role played by other schools, such as traditional developmentalist or structuralist economists, but also by orthodox mainstream economists. As stated earlier, the debt crises put a *de facto* end to the developmentalist period, as severe external constraints imposed a harsh limitation to any policy that had fast economic growth as its central tenet. The policy discussion that drew everyone's attention at the time was "how to control inflation", and it was dominated by the theories and economists we presented earlier.

The UNICAMP school – which could in some measure be considered heir to the traditional Latin American structuralist school of thought – also shifted its analytical views. Following Serrano (2001), we may identify that change in the focus of their theoretical and policy concerns during the 1980s, switching from an emphasis on the dynamic process of Kaleckian effective demand to the importance of adequate schemes for funding long-term investment.[20]

Another distinguishing feature of this school at the time was their identification of the public sector's fiscal and financial crises of the 1980s that could undermine the state's ability to preserve the developmentalist pact. Those crises didn't seem to refer to the size of the public deficit but to some "difficulties in financing the public sector, especially its funding" (Baer, 1993, p. 41). This interpretation relates the alleged financing difficulties of the public sector to a shorter length of the stock of public debt, which hindered the creation of a long-term financial market for private firms (see Carvalho and Pimentel, 2019). Therefore, though in no traditional way, UNICAMP's analysis of the Central Bank's alleged operational problems somehow coincided with the more conventional analysis that the public sector or its financing were among the most pressing problems of the second half of the 1980s and the early 1990s. That argument can be found in different forms in several contributions by authors related to this approach: Almeida (1994), Biasoto (1995), Coutinho and Belluzzo (1996), Belluzzo and Almeida (2002), and Carneiro (2002).

An outlier in terms of structure and theoretical foundation when compared to other stabilization plans of the period under exam, namely the 1990 Collor Plan, reflects in some measure this type of non-traditional approach to public finance. The Collor Plan had serious shortcomings and severe consequences, causing one of the greatest recessions in Brazil's history – a GDP fall of 4.35%.

This plan had some features in common with all the others, i.e. conversion of wages and price freezing. However, on top of these measures, the Collor Plan established a compulsory, temporary *confiscation* of financial assets owned by the private sector.[21] The rationale behind this highly unusual measure was the perception that there was an anomaly in Brazil's monetary policy, a concentration of a very short-term public debt structure and repos. Accordingly, it would be utterly difficult to control either monetary expansion or the growth of M1, something that would endanger a stabilization process with price freezing, given the risk that agents might withdraw from financial accounts, as had been the case in the Cruzado experience.

Regarding the intellectual origins of that plan, there is no clear-cut line connecting theory and stabilization proposals. On the one hand, Affonso Pastore, a prestigious Brazilian orthodox economist, argued that the plan was not monetarist because it focused on monetary stocks instead of monetary flows (Pastore, 1991). On the other hand, UNICAMP's "outlier" in terms of the theoretical foundation of inflation policies seems to have somehow inspired the Collor Plan.[22]

As pointed out by Carvalho (1996), there were official and extra-official leaks that allowed the stock of private assets to be "replenished" faster than had been designed in the original plan. As a matter of fact, this event might be seen as proof that credit money is endogenous and demand-driven. The plan pushed the economy into a deep recession without having any positive effect on price stabilization, reinforcing the point that Brazil's high inflation rates were not a demand-pull phenomenon. The plan was a complete flop but left some useful lessons for the future regarding what policymakers should avoid at all costs.[23]

There was no change in the neoliberal agenda set from the start of the Collor government, neither after the failure of the anti-inflationary plan nor after the impeachment of the president in 1992. In fact, new liberalization measures were implemented at the financial front and, together with the restructuring of the external debt under the Brady Plan, brought Brazil back into the then quickly changing international financial markets. As argued by a good number of authors (for instance, Castro, 2011; Bastos, 2002; Carneiro, 2002), this new context was extremely important for the implementation of the Real Plan.

Although the Real Plan was just one among several successful stabilization plans on the continent from the late 1980s and early 1990s, it has some interesting particularities that stemmed from the learning process related to previous failed plans.

The first of them was the now-avoided "mistake" of imposing a price freeze on a given date. This time the "heterodox shock" – as a tool to erase inflationary memory – was substituted by a "shock" new currency. Wages were converted to their previous average and then indexed to a "currency of account" that would vary daily according to a series of price indexes, called URV. From then onwards, wages, costs and prices were fully and daily indexed and quoted in a new currency that had a daily conversion rate with legal tender. This possibility of price conversion to the new account currency gave plenty of time for producers to negotiate within production chains, with exact knowledge of their real costs in terms of wages, inputs and the exchange rate. Therefore, the misalignment of relative prices was solved and when the old currency (legal tender) was substituted by a new one, producers just needed to convert their prices in the account currency to the new legal tender. In other words, the new currency had again all of its basic properties. In any case, it is worth noting that the idea of avoiding price freezing was not new. In fact, the Real Plan was a direct heir to the Arida and Lara-Resende (1984) proposal – the "Larida" formula – but it introduced an indexed unit of account (URV) instead of a parallel currency, as would be the case in the Larida original plan.

A second aspect of the Real Plan that made it extremely different from previous experiences was the use of the exchange rate as an anchor for stabilization. Of course, this option was not available for policymakers before the return of the economy to the voluntary international capital market. This return allowed not only an important accumulation of international reserves but also the continuous motion of fresh capital flows.

Finally, it pays to mention the fiscal aspect related to the policy development of the Real Plan, given the increasing relevance acquired by this macroeconomic aspect among Brazilian economists. In theoretical terms, fiscal adjustment policies were somehow justified in a paper written by Bacha (1994). This paper's basic equation is a Laffer curve where each level of public deficit is financed by money (given a limit for public debt demand) representing the traditional inflation tax mechanism. Government prints money to finance its deficit, and according to a quantitative equation a level of inflation results. The Laffer curve has two sides, each with a low and a high inflation equilibrium. This type of reasoning would explain why the same value of public deficit can generate two different levels of inflation. Bacha's (1994) contribution to this traditional and extensive literature[24] is to add a public deficit function with a negative relation with respect to inflation. The literature usually assumes that there is a negative effect of inflation on public deficit due to its impact on tax revenue. The so-called Tanzi effect relates to the loss of real revenue due to the time gap between the economic event that generates the tax receipt and the deposit in government coffers. According to Bacha (1994), the opposite was true: revenues during high inflation in Brazil were efficiently indexed while expenses were not. Hence, as soon as inflation had a sharp fall, this "positive" effect on the deficit by reducing expenditures would cease to exist, and a higher deficit could endanger the stabilization.

2.3. Macroeconomic policies under Fernando Henrique Cardoso's government (1995–2002)

Stabilization of the economy and financial and trade liberalization did not bring about an acceleration of economic growth – as was expected by some economists. In fact, the post-stabilization average rates of growth during the two Fernando Henrique Cardoso (FHC) terms were quite similar, something around 2.5%. This left a bitter feeling among economists who advocated liberalization as the way to put the country back on the track to high economic growth, as well as among those who pointed to inflation as the main cause of the dismal record of the 1980s.

Government officials argued that the difficulties were due to the instability of the international financial capital market. After the Mexican crisis, Asian countries were hit in 1997 by a balance of payment crisis with ripple effects felt by all developing countries. In 1998, it was Russia's turn to experience its balance of payment crisis. At that point, Brazil was facing a growing deterioration of its current account, and in order to keep the exchange rate as the anchor of its anti-inflationary policy, increasing interest rates was almost inevitable, with negative effects on aggregate demand and output. The latter deteriorated fiscal indexes, which was the opposite of what was supposed to happen for them to be a necessary condition of price stabilization.

What did the academy have to say about this period in terms of critical interpretations?

From the orthodox front, we basically find criticisms on the lack of fiscal commitment to the conventional or orthodox intertemporal balance. Pastore and Pinotti (1999) are a case in point. They stress the inability of the FHC government, during its first term, to control the fiscal deficit. In fact, as mentioned earlier, there was a deterioration of fiscal indexes in the period, with the government disrespecting the "intertemporal budget constraint". Therefore, in the absence of a fiscal "anchor" for inflation, the combination of a nominal exchange rate stabilization anchor with a lack of fiscal discipline generated an external deficit and the need to raise interest rates, which then arrested the GDP rate of growth. These authors stress the role of the late 1994 Mexican Crisis, which caught the economy in a credit expansion cycle,[25] and the strong increase of interest rates (basic interest rates grew from 9% to 35% per year in two months) that was responsible for an increase of non-performing loans.

According to the authors, the instability of the international financial market had an impact on Brazil's economy, forcing the Central Bank to raise interest in order to avoid capital flight and a balance of payment crisis, but the lax fiscal policy played a detrimental role, amplifying the external shock in terms of the domestic output's negative effect:

> If the fiscal policy had been austere, the domestic absorption would have decreased, and if the exchange rate had not appreciated the way it did, the difference between imports and exports would have been smaller. . . . A smaller current account deficit would also have required a smaller inflow of capital, which would have allowed for lower domestic interest rates and a less severe social cost of the adjustment.
>
> (p. 36/37)

In short, this kind of criticism doesn't show any theoretical break from the general understanding of which economic policy should be adopted, but rather from its execution.

On the other hand, the heterodox criticism of the period, specifically in the first FHC term, stresses similar points of weakness, but with different causes.

One initial point made by Tavares (1998b)[26] is, as in the previous criticism, the overvaluation of the exchange rate. According to this author, it results from a tendency stemming from the liberalization of capital regulations that renders an international financial market inherently speculative. Examples of this trend are the successive balance of payment crises that occurred in different countries all around the world. In the Brazilian case, the combination of a financial deregulation and an imprudent commercial one led to a dramatic change in the current account, from a surplus of US$ 13.3 billion to a deficit of US$ 5 billion in 1996. A large current account deficit leads not only to increasing external debt but also to the need of a high domestic interest rate to finance it. Tavares (1998b) recognizes – as do Pastore and Pinotti (1999) – the negative influence of the high interest rate on economic activity and stresses its impact on the increase of public deficit and debt:[27]

> The substantial growth of the federal public debt during the three years following the stabilization plan – a 219% increase, compared to the June 1994 outstanding value – is not the result of the fiscal deficit, as stated by several economists inside and outside the government, but of the monetary-exchange rate arrangement put in place to sustain the Real (the domestic currency).
>
> (p. 112)

With regard to public finances, Tavares (1998b) follows the aforementioned ideas espoused by several UNICAMP authors, notably the existence of a "structural tendency" towards a "state fiscal crisis". The argument is that the trap set by the external deficit forced the Central Bank to increase interest rates, thereby entailing an "explosive fiscal crisis and the devaluation of public debt" (p. 125).

Another main aspect of the forementioned UNICAMP approach which had been a major policy issue was the funding problem. Tavares (1998b) identified no more than a thousand firms that could resist the new economic environment of fierce external competition, but even those companies lacked "an internal source of long-term financial resources", in areas like construction, utilities, agricultural production of domestic foodstuffs, and other assorted small and medium businesses. At this point, Tavares (1998b) established a connection between a more macro-critical appraisal of neoliberal microelements.

In the following section, we describe and detail criticisms of the neoliberal policies that affected the industrial structure. In any case, it is worth noting that Tavares (1998b) extends and connects them to macroeconomic aspects. Restructuring negatively affected a number of economic activities and their formal jobs, which by itself had a negative macroeconomic effect in terms of induced consumption and even credit expansion, because access to it depends heavily on the worker having a formal labor post. As shown by Tavares (1998b), reduction of formal labor positions was severe in various economic sectors, such as financial services, the manufacturing industry, industrial services, and utilities. The most dramatic case happened in the manufacturing industry, which accounted for more than half of the total loss of formal employment. In connection with this phenomenon, Tavares (1998b) also criticizes productivity gains as somewhat spurious. What really happened was the destruction of a whole series of industrial components of production chains, whereby inputs, parts and components were imported rather than domestically produced. Therefore, productivity gains by worker (in terms of production in the manufacturing industry sector) did not reflect actual technological gains, and hence it could not be expected to spur a healthy economic growth.

Supporters of FHC policies admitted that the first FHC administration had performed poorly regarding high unemployment levels and low creation of formal jobs. They also recognized the role played by low demand growth, and strongly recommended labor market flexibility as a mandatory tool to foster higher employment growth (as in Pinheiro et al., 1999, pp. 31–34).

We should add two final notes before the next section. First, in policy terms, after surviving two contagious crises (Mexico and the Asian BP crisis), the macroeconomic policy mix adopted since the Real Plan did not resist the Russian crisis of 1998. The Real had been facing a speculative attack since the second semester of 1998, so at the beginning of 1999 the government was almost forced to let the currency float, which initially led to a maxidevaluation that was only partially reversed with an interest rate increase. This abandonment of the exchange rate policy, which had anchored stabilization since the start of the Real Plan, paved the way for the adoption of a macroeconomic regime that could be called a "*state-of-the-art*" new macroeconomic consensus. In a nutshell, it consisted of a so-called *tripod* formed by: 1) an inflation-targeting policy based on a Taylor rule; 2) a dirty floating exchange rate policy; 3) a primary surplus that should be able to counterbalance the impact of interest on the aggregate fiscal deficit (avoiding public debt to follow an unstable path). By means of raising taxes, the government was able to generate primary surpluses that answered in large measure the main orthodox criticism of FHC's first term's economic policy (see Giambiagi, 2002).

Second, whilst inflation was kept under control, higher growth and low employment rates didn't happen. Given that the macroeconomic regime was now following the dominant orthodoxy by the book – including a large fiscal primary surplus – the neoliberal (or orthodox) explanation for such economic behavior concentrated on institutional factors, whereas the general heterodox criticism just followed the same critical arguments it had been raising since 1995.

3. The new development model of the 1990s

We now move to the Brazilian economic debate on the development model installed in the 1990s. In order to do so, a brief historical background is necessary.

Brazil's state-led development model – based on protectionist legislation and state-owned enterprises – came under growing stress in the 1980s. In a context of macroeconomic instability and indebted public enterprises, arguments that the model was over became increasingly widespread. International trends reinforced these arguments, due to the advance of the *neoliberal agenda* in the North during the 1980s. This agenda would not take too long to find its way into Latin America. Mexico was among the first to embrace its principles in the late 1980s.[28] Brazil and Argentina followed Mexico's steps in the early 1990s. In Latin America, this agenda became popularly known as the *Washington Consensus*. The name came from Williamson (1990), who suggested a set of policies and reforms that was a consensus among the US Department of State and multilateral institutions located in Washington, DC as the correct strategy for Latin American countries to solve their macroeconomic problems and resume high economic growth rates.

Despite some minor relaxations in the protectionist regime in 1988 and 1989, it was Fernando Collor de Mello's government (1990–1992) that introduced the neoliberal agenda in Brazil. Although the state-led development of the previous decades had helped build a rather complete industrial structure in the country, Collor policymakers argued that the resulting structure was inefficient, uncompetitive and technologically obsolete. The new development model was therefore supposed to expose Brazil's productive structure to foreign competition and spur the private sector to invest, thereby inducing a process of rationalization and technological upgrading. In this respect, Collor's policymakers regarded foreign direct investment as a key source of *state-of-the-art* technology, hence a crucial factor for technological upgrading. Accordingly, they started a program of privatization of state-owned enterprises and a program to dismantle the protectionist regime.[29]

After Collor's impeachment in 1992 and with his replacement by vice-president Itamar Franco, government policies were kept in place, especially the removal of trade barriers, financial liberalization, and privatization, as in the case of a key public enterprise of the state-led development period, namely the steel company *Companhia Siderúrgica Nacional*.[30]

In the 1994 presidential election, Senator Fernando Henrique Cardoso – who had served as Itamar Franco's Finance Minister from 1993 to early 1994 – became Brazil´s new president, later re-elected in 1998. During his two terms, economic liberalization and attraction of foreign capital continued to be key elements of the development strategy. Moreover, the privatization process gained momentum in the telecommunications system and in some privatizations in the electrical sector. Another key enterprise from the state-led years was privatized, namely the mining company *Companhia Vale do Rio Doce*. Furthermore, Brazil's giant state-owned enterprise Petrobras lost its monopoly in the oil sector. Cardoso's government created several regulatory agencies, thus marking a switch of state activities from the direct provision of goods and services to the regulation of the private sector's provision of goods and services.

The new development model of the 1990s and its consequences led to sundry controversies during the 1990s and early 2000s between two opposing groups. Whilst one of them – the *neoliberals* – defended the new model; the other – the *developmentalists* – was critical of it.

Mendonça de Barros and Goldenstein (1997) and Franco (1998) provided a good summary of the neoliberal position. All three of them were part of Fernando Henrique Cardoso's economic team: Gustavo Franco was director and later president of Brazil's Central Bank during Cardoso's first term (1995–1998), whereas José Roberto Mendonça de Barros was Deputy Finance Minister and Lídia Goldenstein was Advisor to the President of Brazil's National Development Bank in the same period. As there was no official document stating the government's development strategy, the forementioned two articles provided a *semiofficial* view of Cardoso's development model (Erber, 2002, p. 21). In any case, the new development model also found support from outside the government. For example, Moreira and Correa (1996), Bonelli (1999) and Giambiagi and Moreira (1999) agreed with most of the arguments offered by Mendonça de Barros and Goldenstein (1997) and Franco (1998) regarding the potential *virtuous cycle* stemming from globalization and an economic strategy based on economic openness and privatization.

In the late 1980s, Gustavo Franco – then a professor at PUC/RJ – was one of the first advocates of a shift in Brazil's development strategy. In a 1989 paper jointly written with Winston Fritsch,[31] his colleague at PUC/RJ, he argued that old strategies based on import substitution were both obsolete and unfeasible, and that fostering productivity growth through widespread liberalization should be the main target of a development strategy in the late 1980s[32] (Fritsch and Franco, 1989, pp. 5–6). From the 1970s on, thanks to the diffusion of information technology, there had been an ongoing process of dispersion of multinational activities around the globe, including not only manufacturing but also design and R&D activities, which culminated in the 21st century with the formation of global value chains. This change in the industrial structure opened new opportunities for developing countries by means of attracting direct foreign investment.[33] Accordingly, Brazil introduced policies to catch those companies' interest, including for instance trade openness[34] (Fritsch and Franco, 1989, pp. 10–20).

In a 1998 paper, Franco reproduced most of these arguments.[35] In a context of globalization, he stated that *transnational* companies played a major role in economic development.[36] For instance, transnational companies were responsible – directly or indirectly – for two thirds of world trade. Furthermore, in the 1980s there was an international process of vertical disintegration, outsourcing and relocation of production, resulting in a direct foreign investment boom. Brazil did not benefit from that process. Due to its macroeconomic instability and protectionist legislation in the 1980s, Brazil's share in global direct investment fell in this decade. Moreover, thanks to the former development model's dynamic – wherein serving the domestic market was the main target – transnational companies in Brazil had a comparatively low propensity to export. Hence, a new model based on an open and stable economy was mandatory for the country to profit from globalization opportunities, notably by attracting FDI.

In this new developmental model, the engine for economic growth was productivity growth stemming from the private sector. In this regard, growing competition due to economic openness was regarded as a crucial way to increase productivity levels. In suchlike models, the role of the state needs to be reduced: investment depends on a stable and reliable macroeconomic framework rather than on public sector investment plans. Furthermore, increasing productivity levels makes room for growing real wages, thus guaranteeing income distribution improvements in line with productivity growth. In sum, this model would help build a more efficient and less unequal economy.

Mendonça de Barros and Goldenstein (1997) provided a complementary view with regard to Franco's arguments. They maintained that in the 1990s Brazil was facing and undergoing sundry transformations. Besides the international phenomenon of globalization, there were important internal changes, namely economic openness, privatization of state-owned enterprises, and macroeconomic stabilization. As a result, the *tripod* that had been the core of Brazil's capitalism up to the 1980s – notably state-owned enterprises, national family-owned enterprises, and multinational companies – was being restructured in a move towards productivity increase. This new context of macroeconomic stability and economic openness, privatizations of state-owned enterprises, and denationalization of national family-owned enterprises meant attracting a huge amount of foreign direct investment, which was more diversified than former FDI flows. In spite of coming mostly in the form of the purchase of domestic assets instead of *greenfield* investment, according to Mendonça de Barros and Goldenstein (1997), this was good news.[37] Although the short-term impact of denationalization was an increase in imports, they expected these *denationalized* companies to expand investments, reduce imports and increase exports in the mid-term. Moreover, due to the new macro conditions (price stability and economic openness), the remaining national private companies and the foreign companies that had been operating in Brazil before these transformations were thus deemed to increase their productivity and competitiveness[38] (Mendonça de Barros and Goldenstein, 1997, pp. 27–30).

A dissenting perspective regarding the new policy model came from the so-called *developmentalists*. They gathered especially around UNICAMP, but also in the Institute of Economics at the Federal University of Rio de Janeiro (UFRJ). As previously noted, both departments had a historical record of research on Brazil's productive structure, including for instance broad surveys on Brazil's industry at the time of trade opening in the 1990s, such as Coutinho and Ferraz (1993) and Ferraz et al. (1995).

Developmentalists were critical of neoliberal policies. They were very skeptical about the potential benefits of globalization, thus rejecting a passive adaptation to it. In this context, they believed that the state still had a crucial role to play by means of a *national project of development* (Tavares, 1999, p. 23). This would come in the form of industrial policies,[39] something that was disregarded by neoliberals, at least as a strategy of *picking the winners* (Erber, 2002, pp. 27–28).

It is important to stress that the term *industrial policy* usually means state interventionism in the sense of choosing specific sectors (picking winners). This is the reason why neoliberals were so firmly against it. Franco (1998) observes that any kind of policy for the industrial sector should be horizontal, meaning policies that would not help any specific sector or company. Mendonça de Barros and Goldenstein (1997) recommended some public policies regarding the industrial restructuring process, but they tried to highlight that their proposals did not mean a return to old-style industrial policies. In any case, according to developmentalist economists Laplane et al. (2003a), "for the policymakers of the 1990s, a greater exposure to international competition would replace – with advantages – industrial policies in the job of advancing Brazil's industrial development process" (Laplane et al., 2003a, p. 8).

As for the new development model, developmentalists argued that it was leading Brazil's industrial structure to a *regressive specialization* (Coutinho, 1998, p. 245), which meant a loss of competitiveness of the value chains in sectors of high-added value or high technological worth, so that the country was keeping its competitiveness only in low value-added commodity producing sectors (Coutinho [1998] and Erber [2002]). Whilst the share of the resource-intensive industrial sector's output grew from 27% in 1989 to 38% in 1998, the science-based sector's share remained stable, and the share of other sectors, namely those that were labor-intensive, scale-intensive, and specialized suppliers, underwent a fall in the same period (Coutinho, 1998, pp. 244–245; Erber, 2002, pp. 28–29).

The new model was causing a combination of deindustrialization and denationalization, resulting in the shrinking of Brazil's national value chains (Coutinho, 1998). As a consequence, to paraphrase Joseph Schumpeter, leading Brazilian developmentalist economist Maria da Conceição Tavares called Brazil's 1990s' experience under neoliberal policies a *non-creative destruction process*.[40] In sum, neoliberal policies were destroying the basis of the former development model without providing a true road map to sustained growth.

There were several studies along these lines, including for instance Coutinho (1998), Laplane and Sarti (1997), Gonçalves (1994, 1999), Carneiro (2002) and Erber (2002). A 2003 book organized by UNICAMP professors Mariano Laplane, Luciano Coutinho and Célio Hiratuka (Laplane et al., 2003b) provides a summary of the critical arguments of developmentalists against the regressive specialization of the Brazilian economy due to the neoliberal policies of the 1990s and early 2000s.

In their chapter in that book, Fernando Sarti and Mariano Laplane offered what is perhaps the most acute criticism of the new development model, by contesting the link between foreign direct investment and both GDP and exports growth. They showed that most of the FDI that came to Brazil in the 1990s was not greenfield investment, meaning that the FDI surge of the decade was to a large extent just for the denationalization and privatization of existing domestic firms. Moreover, this change in property control did not induce investments (in the macroeconomic sense): FDI as a share of investment increased, but investment as a share of GDP remained relatively stable in the same period[41] (Sarti and Laplane, 2003, pp. 11–28).

The process also had some serious consequences in the foreign trade and current balances. Many of the firms that were denationalized in the period belonged to non-tradable sectors. Therefore, the change in property control had a modest impact on exports. However, their acquisition by foreign firms impacted the imports share, since some of these foreign companies replaced domestic suppliers by foreign ones after denationalization. The contribution of multinational branches to the country's trade balance during the second half of the 1990s was much lower than the one made by national firms of the same size. Moreover, multinational branches did not have a higher propensity to export than the latter, but they had a higher propensity to import than national firms (Sarti and Laplane, 2003, pp. 29–32). Although Sarti and Laplane (2003) recognized that increases in the imported content of the domestic industry helped boost productivity growth, they highlighted their poor impact on export levels. In short, they concluded that "internationalization targeted the domestic market", so that "the process could be regarded as an internationalization of the domestic market" (Sarti and Laplane, 2003, p. 50).

Antonio Barros de Castro, another leading developmentalist economist from the Federal University of Rio de Janeiro, had a somewhat particular view concerning the industrial restructuring of the 1990s. Castro (2001, 2003) divided the Brazilian experience of the 1990s into two periods, namely before and after the 1994 macroeconomic stabilization under the Real Plan. Whilst in the first phase there were modernizing efforts by domestic firms through production rationalization, incorporation of modern management techniques, and market repositioning, the second phase was marked by new investments, production internationalization and the relocation of manufacturing plants to the hinterlands. More importantly, his conclusions regarding the overall impacts of this process are in between the virtuous cycle defended by neoliberals and the pessimistic regressive specialization emphasized by developmentalists.

4. The economic debate under President Lula (2003–2010)

4.1. Social developmentalism

As previously noted, a sizable heterodox/developmentalist academic group developed around the graduate centers of UNICAMP and UFRJ, though it was also present in different levels of representation in various graduate centers all over the country. This group continued to thrive, even after the *neoliberal wave* shifted the orientation of the developmental model during the 1990s. In the meantime, the Workers Party (PT) consolidated its position as Brazil's most important leftist party. PT's president, Luis Inácio Lula da Silva, was the party's candidate in the presidential elections of 1989, 1994, 1998, before finally winning in 2002. This trajectory naturally positioned the party at the opposite end of the neoliberal agenda that had dominated the Brazilian economic and political scene since the end of the 1980s. Therefore, these two trends (academic and political) naturally converged in terms of policy proposals by means of a "cross fertilization" process.

Even before winning the 2002 election, Lula was under fierce pressure not to change the ongoing orthodox/neoliberal policies, under the argument that changes could "upset" financial market interests, thus triggering a process of capital flight and/or a balance of payments crisis. In a movement viewed by some of his followers as a form of "*capitulation*", Lula signed a letter to the population wherein he promised not to break contracts and not to radically change economic policies. In practice, the new government let the basic macroeconomic regime upheld by the *tripod* remain largely *untouched*. Furthermore, confronted with accelerating inflation (which in the last quarter of 2002 alone reached an accumulated rate of 6.6%), it sharply increased interest rates and the primary surplus in 2003.

Lula's first years as president reflected a dispute over economic policymaking. For example, he picked Marcos Lisboa – a supporter of the neoliberal agenda – as Deputy Finance Minister. Considering that Antônio Pallocci, the Finance Minister, was a politician, it was Lisboa who designed the technical guidelines of the Ministry. Moreover, Lula picked Henrique Meirelles, a former banker, as his new president of the Central Bank. In addition to keeping the core policies, he also advanced some reforms like the Pension Reform in 2003.[42]

Some of the orthodox measures at the beginning of the Lula era were later partially relaxed. Interest rates were brought down, even though their level was still one of the highest among developing countries. Government expenditure started to grow at a solid rate, but without changing the target for primary surplus, a combination that was possible given the increase of revenue due to the acceleration of growth. The restrictive fiscal stance was relaxed in 2008 and 2009, and then the government adopted a successful anti-cyclical policy, which allowed Brazil to overcome the recession quite rapidly in the face of the North-Atlantic Subprime Crisis.

However, though this overview suggests perhaps more continuity than rupture, there were some specific policies that were able to deliver a combination of higher growth and improvement in terms of income distribution. A turning-point was Palocci's resignation in early 2006 and his replacement by Guido Mantega, making room for more heterodox/developmentalist guidelines.

As pointed out by Barbosa Filho and Souza (2010), there was an intense dispute in 2006 between neoliberals and developmentalists over the economic policy strategy. On the one hand, neoliberals defended an *expansionary fiscal contraction*, i.e. an increase in the government's primary surplus that would create space for lower interest rates and induce positive expectations, thus increasing investments. They also advocated the reduction of inflation targets to lower levels. On the other hand, developmentalists favored expansionary macroeconomic policies as a tool to foster higher economic growth rates, and also defended a key role for the state in long-term planning (Barbosa Filho and Souza, 2010, pp. 67–74). In 2006, the developmentalist view prevailed.

The most important among the new measures was certainly the continuity of the minimum wage policy, which since 2004 allowed persistent and strong real minimum wage gains. There are several effects of the minimum wage increase on wages in general and income distribution (see Medeiros, 2015). However, there are also indirect impacts via social security payments that are indexed to the minimum wage and have it as a floor. Another successful social transfer program was the *Bolsa Família*, and there were other programs like *Minha Casa Minha Vida* (a housing program for low-income borrowers) and grants for private universities to assist low-income students. Financial innovations also helped increase credit growth and, as a consequence, autonomous consumption. In fact, the combination of income redistribution and credit growth paved the way for a consumption boom, creating an opportunity for the diffusion of durable goods and services in poor segments of the population that had been unable to afford them earlier on.

The process of income redistribution during this period led to academic controversies. Neri (2011) observed an increase in the share of Class C among Brazilian economic classes (from A to E) from 37.56% in 2003 to 55.05% in 2011 and concluded that this quantitative ascent by Class C meant the emergence of a *New Middle Class*. Pochmann (2014) disputed Neri's conclusions. He accordingly observed that many of the members of this so-called new middle class lacked access to basic public services and education, whence it made no sense to consider them part of a middle class simply because quantitative measures based on income distribution suggested it was so.

These very social pro-growth measures were the ones that sometimes became known as a "*social developmentalist*" model, a label that, according to Paulo Zaluth Bastos – apparently the first author to give the term "social developmentalism" an effective use in the Brazilian economic debate – describes a developmentalist state-led policy wherein income distribution is an explicit objective. Bastos (2012) acknowledges that this set of policies is not "a full academically organized body of ideas" (p. 793), but it had a strong influence on PT's governments. In opposition to other approaches that stress the importance of exports to determine the output of growth, social developmentalism emphasizes the "role of the domestic market and the role of the state influencing both income distribution and investment allocation" (Bastos, 2012, p. 794).

The social policies adopted by Lula's government were the subject of an intellectual debate that began in the 1990s and evolved around the dichotomy between targeted social policies and broad social economic policies, under a "universalist" approach. The former policies basically used to provide a residual compensation for individuals who were unable to become part of market activities. Some authors like Barros and Foguel (2000) were pioneers in the targeted policies approach in Brazil. Several others opposed it and defended the universalist approach, as was the case of Kerstenetzky (2006), who argued that "targeted policies . . . are a minor component of the broad rationale of the economic system and its global efficiency" (p. 568). For this second group of participants in the debate, only broad social policies or universalist policies – rooted in Brazil's new 1988 Constitution – would comprehensively tackle social and economic inequalities and injustices, which are seen almost as a natural consequence of the market system. Those measures would make up a modern welfare state and a macro set of policies, as in the cases of progressive taxation and public outlays, thereby characterizing ample state intervention in a market economy.[43]

Equally important as part of social developmentalism was the idea of growth *cum* income redistribution via domestic mass production and consumption as the new engine of growth, in opposition to the historically established pattern of growth with income concentration. As argued by Bielschowsky (2012, p. 738), the idea was present in Lula's 2002 presidential campaign and in his 2004–2007 Pluriannual Plan. On analytical grounds, the plan was the outcome of a long sequence of discussions over the Brazilian "growth model", starting with Celso Furtado (1965) – as argued in the previous chapter, the first author in Brazil to integrate production and income distribution in a single model – and having a powerful more recent formulation with Castro (1989). Castro relied on household sample surveys to argue that, contrary to what economists used to think, rising incomes in poor families lead to an expansion of the market for goods produced in the country's existing modern segments of the economy. Therefore, the strategy for building Brazil's future should be based on the possibility of expanding these modern segments, with strong productivity gains associated to economies of scale made possible by the size of the Brazilian domestic market.

The "developmentalist" part of such an approach also appears in another "engine of growth" that is held dear by the developmentalist tradition: public investment. Even though the absolute value never reached a level consistent with a fast-growing economy, Lula's government substantially increased public investment.[44] Another important tradition cherished by developmentalists and resumed in Lula's government was the adoption of industrial policies – the object of three plans[45] and a policy executed by Petrobras and based on purchases of inputs from domestic producers. Industrial policy was supposed to be the answer to the loss of density in the metal mechanics production chains, a problem that had led to strong criticism of previous administrations.[46]

In short, the so-called social developmentalist school was an approach that inherited several elements from the classical development theory but added to them a strong concern for social issues. It partly reflected President Lula's (real or presumed) policymaking limitations, which put the spotlight not so much on radical macro changes as on economic growth and specific policies aimed at increasing social justice. The recent literature by social developmentalists seems to have incorporated this characteristic in order to set this approach within the heterodox literature, as clearly put by Biancarelli and Rossi (2013): "Lula's government is a clear example of gradual and important changes in the developmental strategy which occurred despite the continuities in the macroeconomic regime" (p. 147). This line of argument is well documented in books by authors like Fagnani and Fonseca (2013), Rossi et al. (2018), and Carneiro et al. (2018).

In the next section, we discuss the New Developmentalist agenda. Whilst social developmentalists argue for a wage-led growth model based on the expansion of domestic consumption, new developmentalists advocate an export-led growth strategy in the same vein as the historical experiences of Asian countries like South Korea. Carneiro (2012), Ferrari Filho and Fonseca (2015), and Mollo and Amado (2015) are basic references for a discussion of the two different developmentalist currents of thought.

4.2. New developmentalists

A group of economists proposed an alternative development agenda in the early 2000s. Their main concern was deindustrialization and the process of real exchange rate appreciation initiated in 2003. The leading figure in this group was former Finance Minister Luiz Carlos Bresser Pereira, but there were followers within his department – the Department of Economics at FGV/SP – plus other economists from different economics departments all over Brazil. They called themselves *New Developmentalists*.

In a newspaper article, Bresser-Pereira (2004) announced the principles of *New Developmentalism*. He observed that the need for a new type of developmentalism stemmed from the fact that Brazil was in a different developmental stage than in the classical developmentalism period of import substitution industrialization. Therefore, new developmentalism was not a rejection of classical developmentalism, but an update of its guidelines. Accordingly, though it advocates that the state still has a major role to play in the form of strategic planning, heavy trade protection and direct public sector investment in specific segments are no longer needed. Moreover, a core principle of new developmentalism that was absent in classical developmentalism is the advocacy of sound fiscal policies.

Bresser Pereira argued that new developmentalism is different from orthodoxy because its concept of macroeconomic stability is broader than the one embraced by orthodox economists, including balance of payments equilibrium and full employment besides price stability and fiscal sustainability. Regarding

BP equilibrium, new developmentalists strongly recommended the adoption of devalued real exchange rates as a means to avoid deindustrialization and current account deficits. They further defended an economic growth strategy based on *domestic savings* instead of *foreign savings* (current account deficits).

After the 2004 article, Bresser-Pereira and his followers wrote several policy and academic papers in which they further developed and defended the principles of New Developmentalism. In 2006, for instance, Bresser came up with four principles. Firstly, he defended the need for a new *national development strategy*. New developmentalism was this new national development strategy itself. Despite stressing the importance of the state, he argued that it should have a merely supporting role when it comes to fostering private investment. That way, though the state might invest in specific sectors through industrial policies, the private sector would be able to do most of the job. Secondly, he argued against trade protectionism but stressed the need for a pro-export strategy. Thirdly, he emphasized the crucial role of fiscal discipline, and accordingly argued that "new developmentalism rejects the wrong idea that economic growth should be demand-led and based on public deficits" (Bresser-Pereira, 2006, p. 15). Finally, he advocated strict inflation control. In any case, he reaffirmed the idea that macroeconomic stability was more than price stability because it should also include full-employment and balance of payments equilibrium.

The four principles paved the way to more concrete macroeconomic policy proposals, notably: 1) Obtaining positive public savings; 2) Giving the Central Bank a double mandate (price stability and BP equilibrium) and two instruments (the interest rate and the exchange rate); 3) Operating a *managed floating* exchange rate policy with the possible adoption of capital controls (Bresser-Pereira, 2006, pp. 14–21).[47]

During the first decade of the 2000s, the boom in commodity prices and the continuous appreciation of Brazil's nominal and real exchange rates caused new developmentalists to be increasingly concerned with Brazil's loss of industrial competitiveness and the risks of deindustrialization. In this context, Bresser argued that Brazil was facing the so-called *Dutch disease* or *curse of natural resources*, i.e.

> the chronic overvaluation of a country's exchange rate caused by its exploitation of abundant and cheap resources, whose commercial production is consistent with an exchange rate clearly below the average exchange rate that paves the way for tradable economic sectors using state-of-the-art technology.
>
> (Bresser-Pereira, 2008, pp. 51–52)

The problem with Dutch disease is that it is consistent with the intertemporal equilibrium of foreign accounts, so it can last for a long time. As a result, it can cause severe losses in the domestic industrial structure. Therefore, Bresser concluded that developing countries suffering from Dutch disease face two possible equilibrium exchange rates. The first is the *current* equilibrium exchange rate, which corresponds to the exchange rate that guarantees the intertemporal balance of the country's current account. The second is what he called the *industrial equilibrium exchange rate*, meaning the rate that "enables the production of *tradable goods* in the country without the need of duties and subsidies"[48] (Bresser-Pereira, 2008, p. 53). Neutralizing the Dutch disease – by means of converging the values of the two exchange rates – thus becomes a major task for policymakers. One way of achieving it is taxing the goods that cause the disease plus creating an international fund (sovereign fund) with the resources earned from the tax.[49]

4.3. Neoliberals

Neoliberals' claims in the 2000s were very much the same as those of the 1990s. They kept arguing against state activism and in favor of economic openness. At the beginning of Lula's government, they advocated, for instance: 1) the increase of domestic savings by means of fiscal control;[50] 2) the continuation of state reforms; 3) the increase of trade openness; 4) the redefinition of property rights (Reis and Urani, 2004, pp. 17–20). Another key proposition was financial openness. Arida (2003) argued, for example, for the full convertibility of Brazil's national currency, in the sense of eliminating all constraints in the foreign exchange market. According to him, there was a *convertibility risk* that tended to raise domestic rates, so that allowing free foreign exchange would eliminate this risk and open room for lower domestic interest rates. Arida, Bacha and Lara-Resende (2005) would later claim that the absence of a large long-term domestic credit market in Brazil was due to the country's *jurisdictional uncertainties*, namely "uncertainties associated to the settlement of contracts in the Brazilian jurisdiction" (Arida et al., 2005, pp. 268–269). In this context, they recommended the elimination of *distortions* by means, for instance, of lifting convertibility restrictions and abandoning bad policy interventions, like the artificial lengthening of public debt maturities and the imposition of compulsory saving funds.

In a nutshell, neoliberals defended the continuation and deepening of FHC's government policies and reforms, but paid increased attention to *institutions*, as is clear in the case of the *jurisdictional uncertainty* claims. The set of institutional reforms they recommended included, for instance, a pension and labor market reform (see Giambiagi et al., 2004).

Throughout Lula's government and beyond, neoliberals questioned the developmentalists' concerns regarding Brazil's deindustrialization. For example, Bacha (2013) argued that some degree of deindustrialization was a natural outcome for a country like Brazil in the context of a period of high commodity prices and abundant international liquidity, as was the case from 2005 to 2011. Accordingly, the benign external scenario opens room for increasing domestic expenses, thus raising the demand for both tradable and non-tradable goods. On the one hand, there is a reduction in exports and an increase in imports in the tradable sectors. On the other hand, there is an increase in the prices of non-tradable goods, since it is not possible to increase their supply by importing more. The growing demand for non-tradable goods also increases employment levels, thus raising wages. Due to increasing wages, the profitability of tradable sectors decreases. Hence, in a context of full employment, as seemed to be the case in Brazil in the late 2000s, the result was a decline in the domestic production of tradable goods (Bacha, 2013, pp. 97–98).

Bonelli et al. (2013) provided a complementary perspective by minimizing Brazil's deindustrialization process. Firstly, they argued that the degree of deindustrialization was largely overestimated due to methodological changes in the national accounts of the 1990s. After controlling these methodological changes and using the revised series at constant prices, they concluded that the industry's share in total value added fell from (approximately) 22% in 1985 to 17% in 2010, instead of a fall from 36% to 15% in the same period, as had been widely diffused by different economists in previous years. Moreover, they argued – based on a *cross-section* analysis of 88 countries in different time periods – that the industry's share in Brazil (in current prices) up to the mid-1980s was higher than one would expect on the basis of the country's characteristics. They called this phenomenon the *Soviet disease*. Hence, the fall in Brazil's industry share of GDP in the following decades simply made it converge to the expected levels, according to Brazil's characteristics.

5. Concluding remarks

This chapter describes a process of transition and deepening of a theoretical and policymaking pattern. Brazil's economy in the 1980s started abandoning the developmentalist orientation that had been its main economic policy since the 1930s, tentatively at first, before the Second World War, and explicitly after that. The severe balance of payments crisis of the 1980s made it difficult to continue to pursue policies that would concentrate on economic growth, industrialization, and structural change. The transition to a more neoliberal policymaking stance was in line with the international trend.

In spite of this overall context, the failure of conventional austerity measures and the empirical academic works proposed by both orthodox economists and the IMF during the 1980s paved the way to a more heterodox approach in macroeconomic terms.

That is why the heterodox ideas proposed by PUC/RJ economists of the inertial inflation current received growing support among scholars and authorities. As we showed along the chapter, those ideas and models had a cost-push flavor, with their models comprised of traditional Kaleckian cost-plus-markup equations.

However, the failure of the first stabilization experience following these guidelines led to a widespread interpretation that its flop was due to the lack of demand control policies, which was the starting point of the increasing conversion of those economists to a less heterodox orientation, in accordance with an international environment of growing dominance of the neoliberal paradigm in policy terms, and the neo-Keynesian consensus in theoretical terms.

Economic thought in Brazil evolved in the 1990s following that international trend, as well as policy proposals and implementation of trade and financial liberalization, deregulation, reduction of state size and the pursuit of fiscal balance. With regard to macroeconomic policies, the only successful stabilization plan, i.e. the Real Plan (1994), used several elements of the original heterodox shock proposals of the 1980s plus some lessons derived from their shortcomings. Structural conditions were quite different, of course, and in the mid-1990s Brazil and in fact the whole of Latin America had already returned to the voluntary financial market that allowed those countries to utilize the exchange rate as their inflation stabilization anchor.

In spite of its smaller influence, the heterodox/developmentalist tradition kept producing academic analyses and policy proposals that would continue throughout the 1990s and early 2000s as a dissent voice against the dominant view.

The successful Real Plan (1994) was a watershed in terms of price stabilization in Brazil's history. Nevertheless, it was unable to bring back robust and sustained growth, a failure that was tackled by both heterodox and orthodox economists.

More than just macroeconomic issues, in the opinion of developmentalist authors, the structural changes that followed the liberalization policies since the beginning of the 1990s imposed obstacles to economic growth that would only be eliminated once those policies were partly or totally abandoned. The interpretation of a *regressive specialization* contrasted with the optimism of supporters of neoliberal policies and reforms, who foresaw a *virtuous cycle* thanks to these policies.

In 2002, the traditional center-left candidate, Luis Inácio Lula da Silva, won the presidential election, and four years later he won a second term. During his eight years' government, Lula implemented policies that were not a complete break from conventional macro policies, but at the same time included some important social and welfare elements. This new mix of policies, called social developmentalism, was also reflected in economic literature and gave rise to discussions that developed a life of their own, in spite of the change in the political scenario. The debate on president Lula's two terms had a particularly critical view, provided by the so-called new developmentalism – which claimed policies of devalued exchange rates and fiscal *responsibility* were the means to prevent Brazil's deindustrialization – as well as by *neoliberals*, the group that supported the first wave of neoliberal reforms in the 1990s and later demanded a second one.

Notes

1. The insistence of neoliberals on institutional reforms reflects the growing influence of *new institutionalism* on mainstream economics in the 2000s. New institutionalists argued that institutions are the key elements to explain economic development and economic backwardness.
2. The foundations of this school can be seen in the works of Maria da Conceição Tavares (1998a [1978]) and J. M. C. Mello (1982), as argued in the previous chapter of the present book. Possas (1983) surveys and organizes the main theoretical thrusts of this school. For a brief description of UNICAMP's major influences, see Presser (2001, p. 50). For a review of the contribution and characteristics of the UNICAMP economics school, see Serrano (2001).

3. On the heterodox field, it is also worth noting CEPAL's [or ECLAC's in English. Editor's decision] attempt to renew the traditional structuralist approach with an emphasis on income distribution and a more socially balanced development model. See CEPAL ([1990] 2016).
4. For instance, in 1981 and 1982, while inflation hovered around 100% a year, the economy accumulated a GDP decrease of 3.5%, whereas in 1983 inflation doubled and GDP fell by approximately 3%. Bacha (1983) says, for example, that it is "impossible to swallow [macroeconomic policies] in the name of a doctrine that associates inflation with an alleged and inexistent 'excess demand' in Brazilian economy" (p. 174).
5. Bresser Pereira (1996, p. 166) recollects a 1984 meeting with the then–Central Bank president Affonso Pastore, one of Brazil's leading orthodox economists. According to Bresser, Pastore was puzzled by the fact that the recession didn't bring inflation rates down.
6. Besides Contador (1977), other estimations followed the same faulty specification such as Lemgruber (1978).
7. As we shall see, these are some of the proposals that either had an historical background or had been used to fight the 1920s hyperinflation. But the study of such historical events and the utilization of old policies and ideas to deal with contemporary problems should be credited to these authors.
8. Lopes and Lara-Resende consider imported and non-imported inputs, while Lopes (1982) and Modiano (1988b) also consider agricultural costs, which together with industrial prices would compose the aggregate price index. Agricultural prices would also be divided between imported and non-imported inputs, the former following the international commodity plus exchange rate variation tendency and the latter being influenced by domestic demand conditions. Although a demand element is thus introduced, Modiano shows that reducing demand for domestic agricultural goods is almost irrelevant in a high-inflation environment.
9. Serrano (1986) questioned the assumption of inexistence of a distributive conflict in the Brazilian case and the idea that the ex-post inflation behavior reflects distributive claims.
10. Thanks to investments made through the II National Development Plan, Brazil reduced its dependence on oil and capital goods imports in the first half of the 1980s, while also increasing its exports of manufacturing goods, which helped the country turn its trade deficits of the early 1980s into trade surpluses in the mid-1980s (see Castro and Souza, 1985). The recession of 1981–1983 and the 1983 exchange rate maxi-devaluation also helped in this regard.
11. In fact, Brazil's public deficit was smaller than that of countries with high inflation and similar income *per capita* in that period, like Israel, Argentina and Peru, and it was also lower than the average for the period 1983–1985 in OECD countries (see SEPLAN, 1986, p. 135).
12. It pays to note that this was not an academic paper; therefore, it might have a policy bias that should be taken into consideration. However, the source of this document – the Planning Ministry – was precisely the "stronghold" of economists originally belonging to PUC.
13. The name *Larida* resulted from combining parts of the names of the model's proponents, André Lara-Resende and Pérsio Arida.
14. For a description of the so-called "miracle of the *Rentenmark*", see Franco (1986).
15. Even without going deeper into the history of economic thought in the second half of the 20th century, we refer here to the conventional neoclassical synthesis as Keynesianism, which was the dominant school of thought in various graduate centers up to the 1970s. It should be noted that several of PUC's economists had studied in those graduate centers (like Harvard, MIT, Princeton). Given the nature of their cost-plus-markup models, these authors might even be called *Kaleckians*. Edmar Bacha explicitly admitted in his textbook that in the short run he would adopt a Kaleckian interpretation.
16. Two additional stabilization attempts followed in broad lines the Cruzado model, namely converting wages to the previous average and freezing prices, though in both

cases the fiscal policy was present as a necessary element for the plan's success. There were differences between them. The first attempt, the Bresser Plan, in 1987, was initially thought to be more of a "superindexation" plan that would, after an initial heterodox shock, synchronize all prices through a coordination scheme. The second attempt, the Summer Plan [Plano Verão], in 1989, added a tight monetary policy to the traditional "recipe", and its originality lay in establishing extremely high nominal interest rates. However, both attempts failed a few months after being launched.

17. An alternative interpretation of the external problem is based on the distributive conflict approach. If the origin of inflation acceleration is deterioration of the terms of trade with a negative impact on wages, it is reasonable to expect that this distributive conflict would be solved by some degree of real exchange rate accommodation in the opposite direction of the initial negative shock. The inability to keep a stable nominal exchange rate that might result in some degree of real appreciation was, as mentioned before, at the center of the nominal exchange rate devaluation that was the first element from the cost side to trigger the return of inflation. For this interpretation of the Brazilian case, see Bastos (2001), and for a more general model of distributive conflict and high inflation, see Franco (1986).
18. Ortega (1989) adopts an eclectic position with respect to the inflation tax: "the existence of the inflation tax deteriorates the real value of monetary stocks by transferring resources to the government and partially financing its deficits. In this context, the inflation tax also operates in other models than the monetarist one" (p. 63).
19. One might say that this type of argument in purely theoretical terms is not altogether different from the foregoing one stating that Brazilian public deficit prior to 1986 was compatible with the potential GDP growth rate, and then somehow, according to Lara-Resende (1989), the public and private credit creation was no longer compatible with the growth rate of the potential GDP. Leaving aside the consideration that this statement was made without any empirical evidence or even a rough estimate, what we are rather interested in is the policy stance behind the rhetoric of this group of authors at different points in time: the public deficit goes from a non-factor to a crucial element in a stabilization policy.
20. This question relates to the scale and organization of firms. Brazilian capitalism, according to this interpretation, should have created large business enterprises, by bringing together financial and non-financial companies that might end up creating "true financial capitalism, a characteristic of the modern monopolistic capitalism" (Miranda and Tavares, 1999, p. 327). This new form of capitalism would simultaneously solve the financing/funding problems liable to hinder a company's investing capability and generate endogenous technical progress. The long-term economic drive would be autonomous investments stemming from technical innovation. The absence of this endogenous nucleus of technical progress in Brazilian productive structure – which was present in developed countries like Japan and Germany and later in developing countries like South Korea – was therefore a key element to understand Brazil's low rate of growth (specifically industrial growth) in the second half of the 1980s and early 1990s.
21. There was a threshold for each financial asset. For details, see Bastos and Ferraz (2021).
22. The idea that the debt structure and financing of the public sector have certain peculiarities during periods of high inflation is highly debatable. As with private debt, it would be unlikely for public debt in a high inflation environment to have a long-term profile, or for banks not to concentrate their operations on repos. Central Banks use the purchase and sale of treasury securities as a main policy instrument to keep the interest rate at the desired level. In more abstract theoretical terms, this discussion boils down to the acceptance of the endogenous money theory. This idea was first proposed by heterodox authors like Moore (1988), but has been recently embraced by the mainstream (see McLeay et al., 2014a, 2014b). In policy terms the new consensus determines an interest rate that follows Taylor's rule, rather than any quantitative target. After the initial sequestration measure in March 1990, the government implemented other operational rules in

May to limit the Central Bank's ability to accommodate normal clearance operations. As was to be expected, the rules didn't work and were first circumvented and then abandoned. For a review of the Collor Plan, see Bastos and Ferraz (2021).

23. Besides the stabilization plan, the Collor government also introduced the neoliberal agenda in Brazil in the form of open economic measures and a privatization program. We address these issues in detail in the next section.
24. See Bruno (1993).
25. One should remember that high inflation has a negative impact on credit expansion. Therefore, even if after the Real Plan interest rates were set at a high positive level, this was not enough to avoid a cycle of credit expansion.
26. This is an article written for a book published by UNICAMP and edited by Aloisio 1997), an academic/politician who made several contributions following the same line of argumentation developed by Tavares, one of the most influential economists who supported this approach. Her article provides a good summary of it.
27. Tavares also acknowledges that the growth of the stock of public debt was influenced by the substitution of state debt by Central Bank debt, as well as by the program to rescue private banks with solvency problems (PROER).
28. In fact, Chile under Pinochet was the first Latin American country to adopt the neoliberal agenda. However, Chile's experience under neoliberalism was rather particular because it started in the 1970s, before Reagan and Thatcher`s governments in the developed world.
29. See Fritsch (1991) and Suzigan (1991) for different perspectives on the new development model during the Collor government.
30. For a summary of Collor´s microeconomic agenda, see Bastos and Ferraz (2021).
31. Winston Fritsch later became Deputy Finance Minister (1993–1994) during Itamar Franco's government.
32. Due to the vertical integration of Brazil's industry at that point, new projects of import substitution were unlikely to generate big inter-sectoral impacts, meaning that this strategy lost appeal as a way of triggering higher economic growth rates. Moreover, there was a fiscal crisis, which meant that the public sector could not sustain the same levels of subsidies and investment that it used to spend in the past. Finally, rich industrial countries were likely to pressure Brazil to dismantle its protectionist regime in the coming years (Fritsch and Franco, 1989, pp. 5–6).
33. Fritsch and Franco (1989) argued that access to developed countries' markets would become increasingly difficult. Therefore, multinational branches in developing countries were likely to have more access to these markets than national companies from developing countries (Fritsch and Franco, 1989, p. 20).
34. Fritsch and Franco (1989, p. 21) also argued that freedom to import is something crucial to multinationals.
35. Franco originally wrote the paper in June 1996 when he was a director of Brazil's Central Bank.
36. According to Franco (1998), the term *transnational companies* comes from the idea that multinational companies' activities became so global that they "lost their original nationality" (Franco, 1998, pp. 122–123), while the term *globalization* describes a process wherein both trade and services flows and international investment grow at a higher rate than production. Moreover, it encompasses an international process of vertical disintegration, outsourcing and relocation of production.
37. Franco (1998) also recognized that a great deal of the foreign direct investment boom was likely to come in the form of acquisitions of existing firms rather than greenfield investment (Franco, 1998, p. 126).
38. They observed, however, that there were sectoral differences regarding the impacts of the new international and national conditions of the 1990s. For instance, the automotive industry was undergoing a successful restructuring process, whereas the clothing

industry was facing difficulties to modernize (Mendonça de Barros and Goldenstein, 1997, pp. 27–30).

39. There was no consensus among developmentalists when it came to the best form of industrial policy to adopt in the 1990s and early 2000s. See Coutinho and Sarti (2003) and Castro (2001) for examples.
40. This was the title of Tavares' 1999 book, which was a compilation of the texts she had written during Fernando Henrique Cardoso's first term (1994–98) when she was a congresswoman in Brasília.
41. For an analysis of sectoral investment in Brazil in the 1990s, see Bielschowsky (2002).
42. Lula appointed developmentalists to other positions within the government, like Planning Minister Guido Mantega and the National Development Bank's (BNDES) president Carlos Lessa, a professor from UFRJ and one of Brazil's leading developmentalist economists. Although this group opposed the economic strategy of the Finance Ministry and the Central Bank, neoliberal views prevailed during Lula's first years in office. Some progressive economists criticized Lula's economic policies from a heterodox perspective. See Paulani (2008) for a summary of such arguments.
43. See Kerstenetzky (2006) for a more nuanced and complex analysis of the nature of social policies.
44. Barbosa Filho and Souza (2010) show that public investment as a share of GDP grew from an average 0.4% in 2003–2005 to 0.7% in the period 2006–2008. Furthermore, there was an 11.7% accumulated minimum wage growth from 2003–2005, whereas this value was 24.7% for the 2006–2008 period.
45. The three Plans were named Política Industrial Teconológica e de Comérico PITCE, Política de Desenvolvimento produtivo, PDP, and Plano Brasil Maior, PBM.
46. However, its rather disappointing results regarding investments in the manufacturing sector gave way in the 2010s to a second wave of criticisms.
47. Bresser argued that the exchange rate is the "most strategic macroeconomic price in an open economy" (Bresser-Pereira, 2006, p. 8). In a 2008 paper, he argued that "the exchange rate is actually the main variable to be studied by development macroeconomics, since it plays a strategic role in economic growth" (Bresser-Pereira, 2008, p. 49).
48. In a paper named "The Industrial Equilibrium Exchange Rate: an Estimation", Nelson Marconi (2012), another new developmentalist economist from FGV-SP, tried to estimate the industrial equilibrium exchange rate.
49. In a very recent paper, Bresser-Pereira (2020) suggested the economic policy agenda of New Developmentalism to be:

    > 1) keeping the government's fiscal balance stable or balanced; 2) keeping the current account balance or showing a surplus if and when the country has the Dutch disease; 3) maintaining a satisfactory rate of profit in the more sophisticated sectors of the economy (namely the industrial sector); 4) keeping the basic interest rate around the level of the international interest rate adjusted by the country's risk; 4) maintaining a competitive exchange rate; 5) keeping the rate of wage rising in line with productivity increases; 6) maintaining a low inflation rate by rejecting all types of price indexation.
    >
    > (Bresser-Pereira, 2020, pp. 191–192)

    He also acknowledges that exchange rate appreciation has two possible origins: a trade surplus effect as the result of an increase in commodity prices, and a financial effect due to capital inflow to take advantage of a high domestic interest rate, or a high differential between domestic and international rates of interest. However, he correctly associates the first effect with the well-known term "Dutch disease".
50. Neoliberals strongly supported the macroeconomic regime adopted in Fernando Henrique Cardoso's second term, notably the so-called *tripod* based on an inflation-targeting regime, primary fiscal surplus targets, and floating exchange rates.

References

Almeida, J. S. G. D. (1994). *Crise econômica e reestruturação de empresas e bancos nos anos 80*. Unpublished PhD dissertation. Campinas: Instituto de Filosofia e Ciências Humanas da UNICAMP.

Arida, P. (2003). Por uma moeda plenamente conversível. *Revista de Economia Política*, 23(3): 497–501.

Arida, P., Bacha, E. L., & Lara-Resende, A. (2005). Credit, interest and jurisdictional uncertainty: Conjectures on the case of Brazil. In: Giavazzi, F., Goldfajn, I., & Herrera, S. (eds.), *Inflation Target, Debt and the Brazilian Experience: 1999 to 2003*. Cambridge, MA: MIT Press, pp. 265–293.

Arida, P., & Lara-Resende, A. (1985). Inertial inflation and monetary reform in Brazil. In: Williamson, J. (ed.), *Inflation and Indexation: Argentina, Brazil and Israel*. Washington, DC: Institute for International Economics, pp. 27–56.

Bacha, E. (1983). Por uma política econômica positiva. In: Arida, P. (ed.), *Dívida externa, recessão e ajuste estrutural: O Brasil diante da crise*. Rio de Janeiro: Paz e Terra, pp. 71–80.

Bacha, E. (1985). *Inflaflução: os preços em alta no país do futebol. Nova imagem*. Rio de Janeiro: IBGE.

Bacha, E. (1986). *El Milagro y la Crisis: Economia Brasileña y Latinoamericana – Ensayos de Edmar L. Bacha*. Ciudad de Mexico: Fondo de Cultura Económica.

Bacha, E. (1988). Moeda, inércia e conflito: reflexões sobre políticas de estabilização no Brasil. *Pesquisa e Planejamento Econômico*, 18(1): 1–16.

Bacha, E. (1994). O fisco e a inflação: uma interpretação do caso brasileiro. *Revista de Economia Política*, 14(1): 5–17.

Bacha, E. (2013). Bonança externa e desindustrialização: Uma análise do período 2005–2011. In: Bacha, E., & De Bolle, M. B. (eds.), *O futuro da indústria no Brasil: desindustrialização em debate*. Rio de Janeiro: Editora Civilização Brasileira.

Baer, M. (1993). *O rumo perdido: a crise fiscal e financeira do Estado brasileiro*. Rio de Janeiro: Paz e Terra.

Barbosa, F. H. (1999). Fernando de Holanda Barbosa. In: Rego, J. M., & Mantega, G. (eds.), *Conversas com Economistas Brasileiros II*. São Paulo: Editora 34, pp. 305–331.

Barbosa, F. H., Brandão, A. S. P., & Faro, C. (1989). O reino mágico do choque heterodoxo. In: Barbosa, F. H., & Simonsen, M. H. (eds.), *Plano Cruzado: inércia x inépcia*. Rio de Janeiro: Globo.

Barbosa Filho, N., & Souza, J. A. P. (2010). A inflexão do governo Lula: política econômica, crescimento e distribuição de renda. In: Sader, E., & Garcia, M. A. (orgs.), *Brasil entre o futuro e o passado*. São Paulo: Boitempo, pp. 60–90.

Barros, R. P., & Foguel, M. (2000). Focalização dos gastos públicos sociais e erradicação da pobreza no Brasil. In: Henriques, R. (ed.), *Desigualdade e pobreza no Brasil*. Rio de Janeiro: IPEA.

Bastos, C. P. M. (2002). *Price stabilization in Brazil: a classical interpretation for an indexed nominal interest rate economy*. Unpublished PhD dissertation. New York: New School for Social Research.

Bastos, C. P. M., & Ferraz, F. (2021). A economia brasileira na primeira metade dos anos 1990: inflação, mudança estrutural e estabilização. In: Araújo, V. L., & Mattos, F. A. M. (eds.), *A Economia Brasileira de Getúlio a Dilma – novas interpretações*. São Paulo: HUCITEC, pp. 388–423.

Bastos, P. P. Z. (2012). A economia política do novo-desenvolvimentismo e do social desenvolvimentismo. *Economia e sociedade*, 21: 779–810.

Belluzzo, L. G. M., & Almeida, J. S. G. (2002). *Depois da queda: a economia brasileira da crise da dívida aos impasses do Real*. Rio de Janeiro: Editora Record.

Biancarelli, A., & Rossi, P. (2013). A política macroeconômica em uma estratégia social-desenvolvimentista. In: Fagnani, E., & Fonseca, A. (eds.), *Políticas sociais, desenvolvimento e cidadania*. São Paulo: Fundação Perseu Abramo, pp. 147–166.

Biasoto, G., Jr. (1995). *A questão fiscal no contexto da crise do pacto desenvolvimentista*. Unpublished PhD dissertation. Campinas: Instituto de Filosofia e Ciências Humanas da UNICAMP.

Bielschowsky, R. (Coord.). (2002). *Investimento e reformas no Brasil. Indústria e infra-estrutura nos anos 1990*. Brasília: CEPAL/IPEA.

Bielschowsky, R. (2012). Estratégia de desenvolvimento e as três frentes de expansão no Brasil: um desenho conceitual. In: *Economia e Sociedade* 21, Número Especial, pp. 729–747, dez.2012.

Bonelli, R. (1999). A note on foreign direct investment and industrial competitiveness in Brazil. *Oxford Development Studies*, 27(3): 305–327.

Bonelli, R., Pessoa, S., & Matos, S. (2013). Desindustrialização no Brasil: fatos e interpretação. In: Bacha, E., & De Bolle, M. B. (eds.), *O futuro da indústria no Brasil: desindustrialização em debate*. Rio de Janeiro: Editora Civilização Brasileira.

Bresser Pereira, L. C. (1996). Luiz Carlos Bresser Pereira (1934). In: Biderman, C., Cozac, L. F., & Rego, J. M. (eds.), *Conversas com Economistas Brasileiros*. São Paulo: Editora 34, pp. 152–187.

Bresser-Pereira, L. C. (2004). O novo desenvolvimentismo. *Folha de São Paulo*, September 19. Available online: www1.folha.uol.com.br/fsp/dinheiro/fi19 09200411.htm. Last access: July 29, 2021.

Bresser-Pereira, L. C. (2006). O novo desenvolvimentismo e a ortodoxia convencional. *São Paulo em Perspectiva*, 20(3): 5–24.

Bresser-Pereira, L. C. (2008). The Dutch disease and its neutralization: A Ricardian approach. *Brazilian Journal of Political Economy*, 28(1): 47–71.

Bresser-Pereira, L. C. (2010). A descoberta da inflação inercial. *Revista de Economia Contemporânea*, 14(1): 167–192.

Bresser-Pereira, L. C. (2020). Principles of new developmentalism. *Brazilian Journal of Political Economy*, 40(2): 189–192.

Bresser-Pereira, L. C., & Nakano, Y. (1984). Fatores aceleradores, mantenedores e sancionadores da inflação. *Brazilian Journal of Political Economy*, 4(1): 5–21.

Bruno, M. (1993). *Crisis, Stabilization, and Economic Reform – Theory by Consensus*. Oxford: Clarendon Press.

Carneiro, R. (2002). *Desenvolvimento em crise: a economia brasileira no último quarto do século XX*. São Paulo: UNESP, IE/UNICAMP.

Carneiro, R. (2012). Velhos e novos desenvolvimentismos. *Economia e Sociedade* 21: 749–778.

Carneiro, R., Baltar, P., & Sarti, F. (2018). *Para além da política econômica*. São Paulo: Editora Unesp Digital.

Carvalho, C. E. F. (1996). *Bloqueio da liquidez e estabilização. O fracasso do Plano Collor*. Unpublished PhD dissertation. Campinas: Instituto de Economia, Universidade Estadual de Campinas.

Carvalho, M. H., & Pimentel, L. K. (2019). *Visões alternativas sobre as possibilidades e limites da política econômica em países de moeda soberana*. Campinas: Annals of XIX Encontro Internacional da Associação Keynesiana Brasileira.

Castro, A. B. (1989). *Consumo de Massas e Retomada do Crescimento – Sugestões para uma estratégia*. Brasília: Seminar to prepare Brazil´s Bank Strategic Plan.

Castro, A. B. (2001). Reestruturação industrial brasileira nos anos 90: Uma interpretação. *Brazilian Journal of Political Economy*, 21: 369–392.

Castro, A. B. (2003). El segundo catch-up brasileño. Características y limitaciones. *Revista de la CEPAL* 80: 73–83.

Castro, A. B., & Souza, E. P. (1985). *A economia brasileira em marcha forçada*. São Paulo: Paz e Terra.

Castro, L. V. (2011). Privatização, abertura e desindexação: A primeira metade dos anos 90. In: Giambiagi, F., Villela, A., Castro, L. B., & Hermann, J. (eds.), *Economia brasileira contemporânea*. Rio de Janeiro: Elsevier.

CEPAL. (2016 [1990]). Changing production patterns with social equity: The prime task of Latin American and Caribbean development in the 1990s. *ECLAC Thinking, Selected Texts (1948–1998)*. Santiago: CEPAL, pp. 473–485.

Contador, C. R. (1977). *Ciclos econômicos e indicadores de atividade no Brasil*. Rio de Janeiro: IPEA.

Coutinho, L. (1998). O desempenho da indústria sob o real. In: Mercadante, A. (ed.), *O Brasil pós-Real: uma política econômica em debate*. Campinas: UNICAMP.

Coutinho, L. G., & Belluzzo, L. G. M. (1996). Desenvolvimento e estabilização sob finanças globalizadas. *Economia e Sociedade*, 5(2): 129–154.

Coutinho, L. G., & Ferraz, J. C. (1993). *Estudo da competitividade da indústria brasileira*. Campinas: Papirus.

Coutinho, L., & Sarti, F. (2003). A política industrial e a retomada do desenvolvimento. In: Laplane, M., et al. (eds.), *Internacionalização e desenvolvimento da indústria no Brasil*. São Paulo: Editora da UNESP/Instituto de Economia da UNICAMP, pp. 333–347.

Erber, F. (2002). The Brazilian development in the nineties – Myths, circles, and structures. *Nova Economia*, 12(1).

Fagnani, E., & Fonseca, A. (2013). *Políticas sociais, desenvolvimento e cidadania*. São Paulo: Fundação Perseu Abramo.

Ferrari Filho, F., & Fonseca, P. C. D. (2015). Which developmentalism? A Keynesian-Institutionalist proposal. *Review of Keynesian Economics*, 3(1): 90–107.

Ferraz, J. C., Kupfer, D., & Haguenauer, L. (1995). *Made in Brazil: desafios competitivos para a indústria*. Rio de Janeiro: Campus, p. 386.

Franco, G. H. B. (1986). *Aspects of the economics of hyperinflation: Theoretical issues and historical studies of four European hyperinflations*. Unpublished PhD dissertation, Harvard University.

Franco, G. H. B. (1987). *Política de estabilização no Brasil: algumas lições do Plano Cruzado*. Texto para discussão n. 155. Rio de Janeiro: Departamento de Economia, PUC.

Franco, G. H. B. (1998). A inserção externa e o desenvolvimento. *Revista de economia política*, 18(3): 71.

Fritsch, W. (1991). A política industrial do novo governo: um passo à frente, dois para trás? *Revista Brasileira de Economia*, 45: 344–348.

Fritsch, W., & Franco, G. H. B. (1989). O investimento direto estrangeiro em uma nova estratégia industrial. *Brazilian Journal of Political Economy*, 9(2): 5–25.

Furtado, C. (1965). Development and stagnation in Latin America: a structuralist approach (v. 1, n. 11). Yale: Yale University Economic Growth Center.

Giambiagi, F. (2002). Do déficit de metas às metas de déficit: a política fiscal do período 1995–2002. *Pesquisa e Planejamento Econômico*, 32(1): 1–48.

Giambiagi, F., & Moreira, M. M. (1999). *A economia brasileira nos anos 90*. Rio de Janeiro: BNDES.

Giambiagi, F., et al. (2004). *Reformas no Brasil: balanço e agenda*. Rio de Janeiro: Editora Nova Fronteira.

Gonçalves, R. (1994). *Ô abre-alas: a nova inserção do Brasil na economia mundial*. Rio de Janeiro: Relume-Dumará.

Gonçalves, R. (1999). *Globalização e desnacionalização*. Rio de Janeiro: Paz e Terra.

Kerstenetzky, C. L. (2006). Políticas Sociais: focalização ou universalização? *Brazilian Journal of Political Economy*, 26: 564–574.

Laplane, M. F., Coutinho, L. G., & Hiratuka, C. (2003a). Introdução. In: Laplane, M. F., Coutinho, L. G., & Hiratuka, C. (orgs.), *Internacionalização e desenvolvimento da indústria no Brasil*. São Paulo: Ed. UNESP.

Laplane, M. F., Coutinho, L. G., & Hiratuka, C. (2003b). *Internacionalização e desenvolvimento da indústria no Brasil*. São Paulo: Ed. UNESP, pp. 11–58.

Laplane, M., & Sarti, F. (1997). Investimento Direto Estrangeiro e a retomada do crescimento sustentado nos anos 90. *Economia e Sociedade*, 8: 143–181.

Lara-Resende, A. (1989). *Da inflação crônica à hiperinflação, observações sobre a crise atual*. São paulo: Revista Brasileira de Economia Política, 9, No 1, Jan–March, 7–20.

Lara-Resende, A., & Lopes, F. L. (1981). Sobre as causas da recente aceleração inflacionária. *Pesquisa e Planejamento Econômico*, 11(3): 599–616.

Lemgruber, A. C. (1978). *Inflação, moeda e modelos macroeconômicos: o caso do Brasil*. Rio de Janeiro: FGV.

Lopes, F. L. (1979). Teoria e política da inflação: uma revisão crítica da literatura. In: Sayad, J. (ed.), *Resenhas da Economia Brasileira*. São Paulo: Saraiva, pp. 10–19.

Lopes, F. L. (1982). Inflação e nível de atividade no Brasil: um estudo econométrico. *Pesquisa e Planejamento Econômico*, 12(3): 639–670.

Lopes, F. L. (1986). *O Choque Heterodoxo*. Rio de Janeiro: Campus.

Lopes, F. L. (1989). *O desafio da hiperinflação*. Rio de Janeiro: Campus.

Marconi, N. (2012). The industrial equilibrium exchange rate in Brazil: An estimation. *Brazilian Journal of Political Economy*, 32(4): 656–669.

Medeiros, C. (2015). *Inserção externa, crescimento e padrões de consumo na economia brasileira*. Rio de Janeiro: IPEA.

McLeay, M., Radia, A., & Thomas, R. (2014a). *Money in the modern economy: An introduction*, v. Q1. London: Bank of England Quarterly Bulletin.

McLeay, M., Radia, A., & Thomas, R. (2014b). *Money creation in the modern economy*, v. Q1. London: Bank of England Quarterly Bulletin.

Mello, J. M. C. (1982). *O capitalismo tardio: contribuição à revisão da formação e do desenvolvimento da economia brasileira*. São Paulo: Editora Brasiliense.

Mendonça de Barros, J. D., & Goldenstein, L. (1997). Avaliação do processo de reestruturação industrial brasileiro. *Revista de economia política*, 17(2): 66.

Mercadante, A. (1998). *O Brasil pós-Real: a política econômica em debate*. Campinas: UNICAMP.

Miranda, J. C., & Tavares, M. D. C. (1999). Brasil: estratégias de conglomeração. In: Fiori, J. L. (ed.), *Estados e moedas no desenvolvimento das nações*, 2nd ed. Petrópolis: Vozes, pp. 327–350.

Modiano, E. (1988a). A dinâmica de salários e preços na economia brasileira: 1966/81. In: Modiano, E. (ed.), *Inflação, inércia e conflito*. Rio de Janeiro: Editora Campus.

Modiano, E. (1988b). Salários, preços e câmbio: os multiplicadores dos choques numa economia indexada. In: Modiano, E. (ed.), *Inflação, inércia e conflito*. Rio de Janeiro: Editora Campus.

Mollo, M. L. R., & Amado, A. M. (2015). O debate desenvolvimentista no Brasil: tomando partido. *Economia e Sociedade*, 24(1): 1–28.

Moore, B. J. (1988). *Horizontalists and verticalists: The macroeconomics of credit money*. Cambridge: Cambridge University Press.

Moreira, M. M., & Correa, P. G. (1996). *Abertura comercial e indústria: o que se pode esperar e o que se vem obtendo*. Texto para Discussão n. 49. Rio de Janeiro: Banco Nacional de Desenvolvimento Econômico e Social (BNDES).

Neri, M. C. (2011). *A nova classe média: o lado brilhante da base da pirâmide*. São Paulo: Editora Saraiva.

Ortega, A. E. (1989). *O Plano de Estabilização Heterodoxo: a experiência comparada de Argentina, Brasil e Peru.* Rio de Janeiro. BNDES.

Pastore, A. C. (1991). A Reforma Monetária do Plano Collor. *Revista Brasileira de Economia,* 45(ed. espec.): 157–174.

Pastore, A. C., & Pinotti, M. C. (1999). Inflação e estabilização: algumas lições da I Experiência Brasileira. *Revista Brasileira de Economia,* 53(1): 3–40.

Paulani, L. (2008). *Brasil delivery: servidão financeira e estado de emergência econômico.* Rio de Janeiro: Boitempo.

Pazos, F. (1972). *Chronic Inflation in Latin America.* New York: Praeger Publishers.

Pinheiro, A. C., Giambiagi, F., & Gostkorzewicz, J. (1999). O desempenho macroeconômico do Brasil nos anos 90. In: Giambiagi, F., & Moreira, M. M. (eds.), *A economia brasileira nos anos 90.* Rio de Janeiro: BNDES.

Pochmann, M. (2014). *O mito da grande classe media: capitalism e estrutura social.* São Paulo: Boitempo Editorial.

Possas, M. L. (1983). *Dinâmica e ciclo econômico em oligopólio.* Unpublished PhD dissertation. Campinas: Instituto de Filosofia e Ciências Humanas da UNICAMP.

Presser, M. F. (2001). Ecletismos em dissenso. *Estudos Avançados,* 15: 49–66.

Reis, J. G., & Urani, A. (2004). Uma visão abrangente das transformações no Brasil. In: Giambiagi, F., et al. (eds.), *Reformas no Brasil: balanço e agenda.* Rio de Janeiro: Editora Nova Fronteira.

Rossi, P., Dweck, E., & de Oliveira, A. L. M. (2018). *Economia para poucos: impactos sociais da austeridade e alternativas para o Brasil.* São Paulo: Autonomia Literária.

Sarti, F., & Laplane, M. F. (2003). O investimento direto estrangeiro e a internacionalização da economia brasileira nos anos 90. In: Laplane, M. F., Coutinho, L. G., & Hiratuka, C. (eds.), *Internacionalização e desenvolvimento da indústria no Brasil.* São Paulo: Ed. UNESP.

SEPLAN. (1986). Livro Branco do Déficit Público. *Revista de Economia Política,* 6(4).

Serrano, F. (1986). Inflação inercial e desindexação neutra. In: Rego, J. M. (ed.), *Inflação inercial, teorias sobre inflação e o Plano Cruzado.* Rio de Janeiro: Paz e Terra.

Serrano, F. (2001). Acumulação e Gasto Improdutivo na Economia do Desenvolvimento. In: Fiori, J. L., & Medeiros, C. (orgs.), *Polarização mundial e crescimento.* Petrópolis: Editora Vozes, pp. 135–164.

Simonsen, M. H. (1970). *Inflação: gradualismo x tratamento de choque.* Rio de Janeiro: APEC.

Simonsen, M. H. (1974). *Política antinflacionária: a contribuição brasileira. Ensaios Econômicos da EPGE.* Rio de Janeiro: Ed. Expressão e Cultura.

Suzigan, W. (1991). O plano de estabilização e a política industrial. *Revista Brasileira de Economia,* 45: 339–343.

Tavares M. C (1998a [1978]). *Ciclo e crise: o movimento recente da industrialização brasileira.* Campinas: UNICAMP.

Tavares, M. C. (1998b). A economia política do real. In: Mercadante, A. (ed.), *O Brasil pós-Real: a política econômica em debate.* Campinas: UNICAMP.

Tavares, M. C. (1999). *Destruição não criadora: memórias de um mandato popular contra a recessão, o desemprego e a globalização subordinada.* Rio de Janeiro: Editora Record.

Tavares, M. C., & Belluzzo, L. G. (1986). Uma reflexão sobre a natureza da inflação contemporânea. In: Rego, J. M. (ed.), *Inflação inercial, teorias sobre inflação e o plano cruzado.* Rio de Janeiro: Paz e Terra, pp. 47–71.

Williamson, J. (1990). What Washington means by policy reform. In: Williamson, J. (ed.), *Latin american adjustment: how much has happened?* Washington, DC: Institute for International Economics, pp. 7–35.

Index